Liberalism:
Fatal Consequences

by W. A. Borst, Ph.D

HUNTINGTON HOUSE PUBLISHERS

Huntington House Publishers
P.O. Box 53788
Lafayette, Louisiana 70505

Library of Congress Card Catalog Number 98-75318
ISBN 1-56384-153-3

Dedication

For the women in my life,
from my saintly mother, my loving wife,
my ebullient daughter and my
adorable granddaughter.

Contents

PART IV—Society's Shaken Pillars

PART V—The New World Order

Acknowledgments

Besides the emotional support of my immediate family, especially my wife of thirty-two years, Judy, my two sons, Mark and Matt, and daughter-in-law, Patty, I would like to thank all those who helped make this book a reality. It would not have been possible without the professional editorial and content critique of my ever-so-smart daughter, Michelle, who spent an entire summer red-lining my manuscript. I also profited from my sessions with good friend Randy Ehret, the deep friendship of all at the pro-life office, especially Molly and Al Kertz, Katie Gardner and Lucy Jochens; my wonderful friends at Birthright, especially Mary Kay Wynne; the stimulation provided by the engineers and my fellow talk show hosts at WGNU; the staff and faculty of Maryville University; and the editors at the *Suburban Journal*. In addition, I would like to thank Dr. Mike Suden, Dick and Pat Schnarr, Nancy Valko, Howard Phillips, Don Griffin, Kathleen Niemeyer, Professor Jim Hitchcock, of St. Louis University, Dr. George Roche, and Dr. John Willson, both of Hillsdale College. I would be remiss if I left out the special people at *Huntington House Publishers,* especially Mark Anthony, Kathy Doyle, and Jaynell Trosclair.

PART I

ON THE AIR

1 / The Culture War
The Storm of Civilization

The first rumbles of a new storm . . . fast approaching the American political arena (a storm) which will quickly replace the old battles over the conduct of the cold war.

—William Rusher in Houston in 1992

Civil War General William Sherman remarked that "war is hell!" I believe this thought can be generalized to include all kinds of war, not just those fought with armies on some god-forsaken field or in some distant town or hamlet. The Culture War or new American Civil War is one of the most complex and profound wars that the United States has ever witnessed, with consequences even more pronounced than the wars of 1865 or 1945. This Culture War, at its most primitive level, is about power—the unadulterated power of those who determine the norms by which we live and by which we define and govern ourselves—the basic questions of what is good, true, beautiful, right, wrong, moral, and immoral. The Culture War also revolves around who should be responsible for the moral teaching of the next generation. In a nutshell, this war is about the content and control of the American culture. The Culture War ostensibly grew out of the cultural revolution of the sixties, whose leaders attempted to overturn the basic moral, religious and legal pillars of our society. During the sixties, the country bought the promise of sexual liberation, abandoning its morals for the social chaos which followed. For the past thirty years, liberals have subordinated the transcendent truths of the Judeo-Christian ethic to their personal desires and the resulting "liberation" from reality has proven catastrophic according to any index. Conservative philosopher Russell Kirk has concisely described the Culture War as a tug-of-war between permanence and progress. On the one hand is belief in the eternal verities of religion and tradition. On the other hand is belief in the evolutionary process of eternal change and progress.

American culture is deeply conflicted. It seems stuck on a dunghill of vices and maladies that signal not merely the decline of Western Civilization but its disintegration. Secular humanism, moral relativism, tolerance of crime, 1.6 million abortions annually, pederasty, pornography, government debt, inflation, public pandering to minorities, an the inability to cope with and fully assimilate all our immigrants, especially our illegal ones, have all eaten away the moral fabric of the American people. What we have is a theology of self, a *me-first* mindset, promoted in seminars for self-actualization and culminating in a national fascination with muscles and body shapes. This notion dates back to Protagoras and the Greeks who gave the humanists their credo: man is the measure of all things. As columnist Joseph Sobran so sagely suggests:

> It's a sort of cultural version of AIDS: the whole immune system of the West has broken down. It has no convictions, no comprehension of hostile alien cultures, no resistance to assault on its tradition. Some would say fatally conflicted. It should come as no surprise that the twofold law of our land is that "everybody knows it is wrong but no one can say it is wrong." The country seems to have lost its spiritual moorings—its very foundations within the context of the Judeo-Christian code. Pope John Paul II has called it a "Culture of Death."

There are several historical parallels for this historical struggle. The American Civil War was really a *kulturkampf,* an intramural battle between what had by 1861 become two distinctive ways of living. The South, with its peculiar institution, of slavery, had grown apart from the society of its Northern brethren. The South resented the economic favoritism that the Congress had afforded the Northeast. They were not fooled by arguments for national unity, such as those found in Henry Clay's "American System," a seminal vision that divided the nation into interdependent regions, with each one performing specific economic function. The linchpin of Clay's system was the protective tariff which would have provided the revenue for the internal improvements, canals, rivers, highways and later, the railroad that would unite the individual sections of the country into a viable economic unit. It was a nice dream, but in reality, the tariff limited the economic progress of the South, which in turn, inevitably led to the war. While slavery was not the actual cause of the war, it served as a useful symbol for the deep rift in the nation's social and political fabric.

Adolf Hitler's rise to power in Nazi Germany during the 1930s is another example of cultural division. Hitler codified national socialism within the German culture that became the real *kulturkampf,* literally tearing Germany asunder. Similar to slavery, the Holocaust, or what was euphemistically known as the "Final Solution," did not so much ignite World War II as serve as a useful metaphor to illustrate the depth and intensity of change within Germany. The German rift was as deep and as harmful as that of America during its Civil War. In 1990, ABC anchor Peter Jennings hosted a two-hour discussion group that was aptly titled, *Abortion: The New Civil War.* Abortion did not cause the new civil war in this country, but like slavery and the Holocaust, it serves as a valid example that can illustrate the depth and intensity that culture humanism has taken.

To understand the Culture War, it is necessary to go back to the Enlightenment which radically changed the philosophical underpinnings of Western Civilization. Prior to the age of great thinkers, Medieval philosophy held that God was the center of the universe and man was relatively unimportant in the final scope of things. The Enlightenment demarcated the discovery of pure reason with all of its man-centered corollaries. At first, philosophers did not eliminate God but merely shifted Him to outside the universe. This view maintained God's historic role as Creator and Prime Mover but neglected his active providential role. He became more a disinterested observer than an active participant. With man and reason at the center of the universe, the prime questions for the philosophers concerned man's nature, the problems of good and evil, the idea of freedom, and the relationship of people to their governments. Dichotomies and crass distinctions filled the public discourse. Was man innately good, basically evil or somewhere in-between? Though the conventional wisdom of the times leaned toward the latter, given the doctrine of original sin, no conclusions were established until history intervened with the idea of freedom. This idea unleashed a fire that warmed and, in some cases incinerated, the minds of those who felt its flame.

Beginning with the American Revolution, man's freedom became the central theme in this debate. In truth, the American Revolution was to preserve the status quo. Under England's pragmatic policy of salutary neglect from 1607-1763, the colonies had been virtually left to themselves to form their own ideas and traditions and to establish their own local government and economic and civil alliances. Great Britain was preoccupied with the affairs, duties and pressing responsibilities of maintaining its world empire. Concerns for the thirteen American colonies were independent in comparison with India, Ireland and the wars on the European Continent. With their victory in the Seven Years' War, or the French and Indian War, as it was known in the American colonies, Parliament attempted to reinstitute imperial control with its strict and arbitrary tax and trade policies. This undermined the colonists' notion of freedom and their obligations of British citizenship. These ill-conceived imperial policies were met with severe opposition, eventually leading to the American Revolution. After the Peace of Paris in 1783, the colonists had, in effect, secured the blessings of liberty that they had enjoyed prior to 1763. The tripartite goals of life, liberty and the pursuit of happiness, seemed much more realistic and possible than what was to transpire in France.

The French Revolution followed with a more distinctive bang. Its more ambitious goals included the complete destruction of the status quo. French society was founded on three pillars: the crown with its royal nobility, the Catholic Church with its strict moral codes, and the bourgeoisie, or middle class. The French revolutionaries proposed a radical change in the way the

French people acted, worshipped and lived their daily lives. The French Revolution fostered an anarchic situation that led to violence, bloodshed and wholesale murder. The final result was that France yearned for a dictator who would save them from the chaos inspired by Daulton, Ropspierre and Marat. Bonaparte, a military officer from the island seedbed of revolution, Corsica, answered the call and redirected the utopian fantasy of liberty, equality and fraternity, into an imperialism that nearly conquered the world. At the basis of this real revolution was the writing of the French Philosophers: Voltaire, Dedirot and most importantly, Jean Jacques Rousseau who established the notion of the perfection of mankind. Unlike Thomas Hobbes, who believed that man was evil and could only exist within the context of a strict dictatorship, Rousseau believed that man was innately good and that evil existed as a result of social institutions like the monarchy, the Catholic Church and the middle class. The annihilation of these faulty pillars would allow man to return to his natural state of perfection. Rousseau's revolutionary ideas were best reflected in his novel, *Emile,* which established the concept of the "noble savage." It was this concept that helped lay the foundation for what became the reign of terror that sent thousands to the guillotine. His philosophical insights also inspired the thinking of Georg Wilhelm Friedrich Hegel, who influenced Karl Marx, John Dewey, Charles Darwin, Nicolai Lenin, Friedrich Nietzsche, Adolf Hitler, and Josepf Stalin. His philosophy also unduly influenced the presidencies of Woodrow Wilson, Franklin Roosevelt, Lyndon Johnson, Jimmy Carter and Bill Clinton.

At the heart of the Culture War in America, is the idea of liberalism that has fueled the revolutionary fire that still burns in the minds of millions of men and women today. Gnosticism is an ancient Christian heresy that has animated liberalism for several decades. The Gnostics were an ancient religious cult that promised deliverance from the evil of the world through a type of special knowledge: the Greek "gnosis." Its rationale centered around the belief that it was possible to stamp out evil in the world and create an earthly paradise by remaking man according to a formula for moral perfection. Gnosticism is sometimes called "millenarianism" or "chiliasm" because of its tenet that it is possible to create conditions comparable to those of the millennium, as described in *Revelations XX.* In this Biblical millennium, the devil is confined to a bottomless pit and there is no evil in the world. Gnosticism is the heresy which substitutes a dream of a perfect, mundane society for the "City of God" and lies at the root of the clamorous ideologies which compete for the support of the modern crowd. In the gnostic dream world, non-recognition of reality is the first principle. Modern gnosticism promises salvation from earthly evil through knowledge. That is why the United States has so many experts and social engineers. Eric Voegelin saw the Gnostics as spiritually diseased. He believed that they try to do what only God can do and, as a result of this internal conflict, they rebelled against Him. At the heart of this idea is utopianism, the gnostic delusion which in Voegelin's opinion, voiced in his book *The New Science of Politics,* are various social idealisms, such as the abolition of war, unequal distribution of property, fear and want. The result will then be the active mysticism of a state of perfection, to be achieved through a revolutionary transfiguration of the nature of man, as in Marxism of national socialism.

Irving Kristol believes the Culture War to be an eternal debate about the nature of reality. Gnosticism is a passionate reaction to the existential reality in which we all have to live. What makes gnosticism relevant to the Culture War is the fact that gnostic movements are antinomian in that they tend to be hostile to all existing laws and all existing institutions. Many of the reforms in the Catholic Church since Vatican II are as gnostic, as are those of the *Social Gospel* movement of 19th century Protestantism. All the important-*isms* of our culture are gnostic in origin and intent—feminism, multiculturalism, homosexual liberation, socialism, nihilism, egalitarianism, progressivism, idealism, scientism, secular humanism, and Freudianism. As Americans become more uncertain about the future, they can be expected to look further to these anti-cultural groups to see where history is headed and what they can do to bring about a utopia. Each of these movements has a millenarian temper that presents an unfair world in which we all live; though it's a veritable hell on earth, it can be radically corrected. This notion differs from the function of orthodoxy in all religions, which encourages people to assume a stoical temper toward all the evils in the world. In essence, orthodoxy concerns itself with the spiritual governance of human beings who have to live in the real world where one's religious faith is being tested every day.

One of Gnosticism's essential elements is the absence of any notion of original sin. The modern notion of progress is incompatible with the idea of original sin. The doctrine of original innocence, by contrast, suggests that the potential for human transformation here on earth is infinite—this is the basic gnostic hope. When this potential is joined with man's eventual mastery over nature and over human nature through the social sciences, a *novus ordo seclorum*, a new world order, will prevail. According to Irving Kristol, we have become so utopian that we do not even know when we are utopian or to what degree we are utopian. We utter utopian cliches in politics as if they were really cliches. There are many examples of establishing a new order of men, a new way of human behavior, unprecedented in the annals of the nation's heritage, from Woodrow Wilson, to Bill Clinton. We have envisioned the world safe for democracy, peace in our time, a world without war, safe, legal and rare abortion. This utopian strain of thought, in effect, dooms liberalism to failure because the quixotic reconstruction its advocates envision can never occur. History has demonstrated this with socialism, communism, and Nazism. Gnosticism by its very nature always degenerates into something else, usually much worse than what preceded it.

The first great gnostic thinker was Machiavelli who proposed that new modes and orders for a great leader would save Italy from foreign domination. The modern secular world as it has emerged after the Renaissance and the Reformation is permeated with gnostic influences. All the anti-cleric leaders of the French Revolution and its communistic heirs were all gnostics. Prior to the 18th century, anyone who enunciated that politics, and not religion, were concerned with the expectation of a universal regeneration of humanity, of the world, would have been regarded as mad. The true liberals in the 18th and early 19th century, including Voltaire, Auguste Comte, Saint-Simon, Comte, Fourier to Marx, had a strong sense of gnosticism, as did the totalitarians of the late 19th and 20th century such as Friedrich Nietzsche, Adolf Hitler and Joseph Stalin.

St. Thomas More wrote *Utopia* in 1516. The title refers to an imaginary island that literary means "nowhere" and to a notion that has served children and heirs of the enlightenment for centuries as they have tirelessly attempted to create a perfect world on earth. There is such a thing as the "utopian paradox." Utopians believe in unrestrained human freedom, yet at the same time they devise ways to completely organize and control freedom, so much that they chain people into slavery. They intrude upon and usurp the prerogatives and attributes more properly belonging to God. They make their collective will a new idol that must be worshipped. Thinkers, such as Machiavelli, Feuerbach and Marx, have fostered the assumption that God was merely a projection of man's aspiration or more precisely, that man was a god himself.

Utopianism was the driving force behind the ill-fated League of Nations, the United Nations and those who for years have worked for a new world order. If history is any guide, like all pipe dreams, these efforts at reinventing mankind and establishing world order, are doomed to failure and will most likely result in an inevitable reign of terror.

There is a blatant contradiction between utopian and conservative thinking. Utopians believe that it is enough simply to demand the world become virtuous since our original moral purity has never been stained only obscured by unfavorable circumstances. The utopian assumes that perfection is easily achieved in this life since he has no reason to believe that man's own fallen nature is responsible for most of the world's miseries. As Professor Thomas Molnar wrote in his perceptive study, *Utopia: The Perennial Heresy,* the utopian assumes with an almost naive faith that communication techniques and ease in travel forge a new mankind, a global melting pot in to which each man adds his own unique contribution. Utopians often betray an underlying gnostic tenet, the *deus absconditus,* which suggests that the transcendent God is known by just a few, the so-called "elect," through supernatural revelation. Since the world is imperfect and evil, the real God could not have created it. He is above it and it is His elite whose mission it is to bring it to perfection. Molnar has demonstrated that there exists throughout history an invisible thread that has linked utopian thought, with its philosophical theories about God, man, nature and community, to religious heresies, various gnostic doctrines, Marxism, spiritual evolutionism and even modern liberalism. This proves that utopianism is a perennial type of thinking, as irreducible as realistic philosophy itself.

Simply stated, the philosophical motivation behind utopianism lies in the natural temptation of the mind to consider the universe as one entity, diversified in space and time by various immanent forces—evolution for example—but still just one substance, universal, self-creating and self-suffi-cient. The existence of God is only acceptable if He functions as part of the whole. The history of utopianism is the story of the Tower of Babel which all mankind built to reach as high as heaven. Utopians fall prey to the temptation of pride. Pride is as permanent as our imperfect condition and the root of original sin. One can say that utopianism is the first temptation: to be godlike and create a heaven on earth without the stain of sin and the rigors of salvation.

In his book, *Crossing the Threshold of Hope*, Pope John Paul II reminds us that the French philosophies were able to accept a God outside of the world primarily because He was an unverifiable hypothesis. It was crucial that the idea of a personal God be expelled from the world. What the Left has done in this country is anathema to what the Pope calls the moral patrimony of Christianity. The Left maintains all the trappings of a religion, a true Church, from infallible doctrines to venerable saints. Its true believers can be as rabid as any Christian and its followers as naive as a medieval serf. Its chief strength is its lack of any moral patrimony which makes anything and everything possible. While Christians believe that history's greatest event happened 2000 years ago, the Left maintains that utopia awaits them just over the horizon. With its inherent strain of utopian reasoning, it is now clear that the American Culture War revolves around what we commonly refer to as liberalism. While the term did not have opprobrium until the 1972 Presidential election when George McGovern exposed the philosophy's true meanings, Woodrow Wilson, with his notion of the world citizen, changed the course of American thinking and inevitably led to a drastically weakened nation that now fears for the survival of its very civilization. Liberalism is the end result of the philosophy that shook the world in 1789, 1917, and 1939.

James Burnham aptly described liberalism as the ideology of Western suicide. This geopolitical analyst meant that liberalism rationalized every setback for Western interest as a triumph of Western ideals. It disguises the shoddiest and most morbid appeals to people's base instincts. No presidency has exhibited this tendency more than that of Bill Clinton. Joseph Sobran calls Bill and Hillary Clinton "the Jim and Tammy Baker of liberalism," both milking specious sympathies to the last drop until their fraudulence is completely exposed. Their compassion is reserved for the suffering of large and well-organized constituencies like the National Education Association and the trial lawyers and they aren't adverse to inflicting acute pain on isolated people who get in their way, like the much-maligned Billy Dale and his colleagues in the White House Travel Office. In the liberal lexicon, compassion means not specific acts of charity, but a more generalized sense of feeling sorrow for the plight of mankind. In many ways liberalism echoes the belief of Lucy Van Pelt in the cartoon, "Peanuts": she loved mankind! It was just individual people she disliked. This species of utopianism, personified by Rousseau, notoriously loves humanity but not humans. Rousseau preached that man was naturally good while he abandoned his own five children. Sex education, abortion, multiculturalism, political correctness, reverse discrimination, the loss of permanent standards in religion, education and history, apocalyptic environmentalism, are all end results of this insidious philosophy. The legacy of liberalism has left a societal pathology of broken families, crime, gangs and illegitimacy. Liberals have seemingly made a Faustian pact with the devil to sell out the country for power and prestige. Liberal thinkers and leaders are like Dr. Frankenstein who experimented in the human laboratory and created a new man actually more monstrous than anything Mary Shelley could have dreamed. By falling prey to the oldest and most formidable temptation—that alternate faith of mankind—*Ye shall be like gods*, liberals share a metaphysical kinship with Adam in the Garden of Eden. Just as philosophers have explained the world, liberals feel they must change it. While their vision is powerful and compelling, it is an empty fiction of man without God.

Liberalism is, by definition, concerned with freedom (personal autonomy). In the case of abortion, personal freedom has become a license to kill the unwanted members of our species before birth. It is ostensibly about caring, using the federal government to coerce people to do social work whether they like it or not. The liberal only pays lip service to these moral platitudes for his first concern is maintaining his power base and making his electorate dependent on him. Fear and the tactical use of fear are very important weapons in the liberal arsenal. William Kristol, Republican strategist, has observed that modern liberalism grew out of classical liberalism by expanding its central ideas, liberty and equality while jettisoning the restraints of religion, morality and law, even as technology lowered the constraint of hard work imposed by economic necessity. Liberalism is really about power and control. To insure freedom for the most people, power has to be diffused among a number of different sources. This was the genius of the United States Constitution. Liberalism has taken us away from this idea and we are paying the consequences of that drift every day. Liberals have used the elastic clause and the notion of implied powers, coupled with the interstate commerce clause to continually and systematically dismantle the tenth Amendment and any hope of curtailing and limiting the expansion of coercive and intrusive federal power.

Liberalism received an important contribution in its American development from an unlikely source. Charles Darwin's book, the *Origin of the Species* and its evolutionary tenet of natural selection provided the missing link in eliminating a personal God from the universal norm of creation. While God had been relegated to the periphery in the seventeenth century,

His Being, His Church and His divine strictures severely limited mankind's moral behavior. The divine Commandments forbidding one to kill, steal, commit adultery or covet another's goods were limitations on the progressive notion of freedom that permeated the Enlightenment. Somehow God had to go. Darwin provided the rationale for creation without a Godhead, a Divine perfect Being, or a Prime Mover. Liberals raised the Darwinian idea of social Darwinism—that life was a jungle and it was every man for himself, above the social gospel which envisioned the progressive improvement of mankind, culminating in an earthy paradise in the future. Freedom, evolutionary progress and ultimate perfection were the ideas that gave mankind the impetus to recreate the world in its own likeness. Without God, liberals believed, in the words of Fyodor Dostoyevsky in *The Brothers Karamazov:* everything is possible. Liberalism has echoed the first sin committed in the Garden of Eden. Ye shall be like gods!

Neo-conservative Irving Kristol was on target when he wrote that liberals were wrong because they are liberals. What is wrong with liberals is *liberalism*—a metaphysics and mythology that is woefully blind to human and political reality. Modern liberalism is particularly a disease of our cultural elites, the people who control the institutions that manufacture or disseminate ideas, attitudes and symbols—universities, some churches, the national media, much of the Congressional Democratic Party and some Republicans. Liberals constantly clamor for unadulterated change. In Congress, they don't care what is in the bills they pass, as long as they are perceived to be working for change. In doing so Congress is often in violation of what C. K. Chesterton called "the democracy of the dead" the voices of the wise men of the past whose prescriptive wisdom could help the nation avoid its inevitable progress toward decline and even dissolution. Roger Rosenblatt boldly proclaimed in a February issue of the *New York Times* magazine: the Triumph of Liberalism. Critic Herbert London provided a keen look at the pathology that has resulted in the liberalism's sad triumph. America under liberalism has seen illegitimacy become a national scourge, crime increase, drugs invade neighborhoods across the land, popular entertainment become coarse and degrading, the jury system become a mockery dependency on government handouts increase, inflation erode personal savings, and, perhaps most significantly, optimism about the future—an article of faith in American life—decline. London also says that it is fair to contend that much of contemporary conservatism is based on a nineteenth century liberalism. The Enlightenment ideas of Adam Smith and John Locke inspired *laissez-faire* capitalism and constitutional government. But contemporary liberalism has nothing in common with its nineteenth century forbearers. It is utopian. It does not recognize the need to limit governmental authority and it has adopted its theory of man from a sanitized version of the fringe groups of the Enlightenment: the Marxists and the Freudians.

It would be impossible to fully comprehend the nature of the Culture War, without contemplating the nature of evil. Dennis Prager has a brilliant chapter on psychology and the denial of evil in his book, *Think A Second Time*. It is evil that lays at the heart of the Culture War. Evil is the third party that the liberals will not recognize. In their minds, Rousseau, Hegel, Marx, Nietizche, Darwin and Freud eliminated the idea of evil. All they needed to do was contemplate progressive goodness. Those who recognized evil in society could not believe that it had anything to do with individual human beings. Socioeconomic forces or social institutions, such as churches, big business and groups such as the Nazis in Germany, the KKK in the United States, and some Democrats, and some Republicans were the reincarnation of evil. But individual men and women, especially the new humans of the liberal faith were immune to evil. The concept of original sin was just some vague superstition that celibate men had dreamed up centuries ago to frighten their followers into blind obedience. Black comedian Flip Wilson was right in the middle of the *Zeitgeist* of the seventies, with his high-pitched outcry of his character Geradine: *the devil made me do it!*

There has been a two-pronged attack on the very notion of evil. The first is moral relativism, which forms the core of what is known as secular humanism today. As historian Paul Johnson has stressed, the West has erroneously applied Einstein's theory of relativity in physics to good and evil, creating moral relativism. *Everything is relative* has come to envelope morality, which is a sad irony given that Einstein firmly believed in objective standards. Psychology provides the second attack on good and evil. Good has been replaced by the morally indifferent "healthy" while evil is merely diagnosed as "sick," a disavowal of any responsibility for one's behavior. It is this latter view that has led the United States to become what Charles Sykes so prophetically calls, *A Nation of Victims*. We are at a stage in our history where too many people feel that those who rob, kill, rape and molest children are merely sick. We have become a sick society. What the well-meaning but morally obtuse general public fails to grasp is that much of this negative social behavior is committed by people who are not sick but merely bad people, people who have chosen to do bad things to other people because of who they are, what they have, or because they are bored by the nihilism of mundane living. In his book, *The Politics of Experience*, psychiatrist, R.D. Laing wrote that normal men have killed perhaps 100 million of their fellow normal men in the last fifty years. America has lost its sense of virtue, having replaced it with a system of weak or nonexistent moral values that have blinded its soul and national conscience to the existence of evil. C. S. Lewis was not the first to realize it, but he was well aware of the fact that the best thing that the devil can do is make people believe that he does not exist.

In a comprehensive, yet not exhaustive cover article, that bastion of Judeo-Christian morality, the *New York Times Sunday* magazine devoted its 4 June 1995, issue to *Evil's Back*. Editors hyped the issue as a theological journey into the dark heart of America, with such modern theologians as former New York Governor Mario Cuomo, the doctor of moral equivocation, actor/director Quentin Trantino, and television talk show host Maury Povich. The Susan Smith murders were the focal point of the provocative issue. Smith murdered her two small sons by strapping them into their car seats and then driving the car into a lake. People could not believe that a woman could do that to her own flesh and blood. Yet 4000 abortions happen every day in this country. Though the method of extinction was different, Susan Smith really had not done anything different than what she might have done at an abortion clinic. Her children were unwanted. Their existence got in her way. She wanted to marry another man, but he did not want children. The children were an obstacle to her happiness, her peace of mind, her quality of life. They had to go! Did that make her sick? Was it society that made her that way? Was it the system? Or was Susan Smith merely an heir to the enlightened thinking that told her to indulge her wants, to do it her way and go for the gusto because she came around only one time. The abortion ethic, which is really at the basis of her act, implied that her children were her sole property and she should be able to dispose of that property with impunity. Susan Smith was exercising her moral autonomy free from any objective standard of right and wrong. While the social ethos of the liberalism of the sixties and seventies might have created the moral climate for her action, this no more excuses her actions than the climate of "Blut und Land" excused the Nazis from the moral responsibility of what they did in Germany during World War II.

Rosenblatt's article on liberalism makes the point that evil exists because we have freedom—that is, we wouldn't be free if we were not free to choose evil as well as good. I believe that it is a truism that people will never choose what they think is bad for them. Susan Smith viewed the death of her children as a good in that it would lead her to the happiness she desired. Society may have seduced her into believing that she could have what she wanted by any means necessary, even to murdering her two children. An action, such as the killing of two children, might be bad for others, but the end result of this behavior might be good for some. Twenty-five hundred years ago, Aristotle wrote in his *Protagoras* that no one can know good and evil and then choose evil. This was probably what led to the fall of Adam and Eve. People do evil when they mistakenly think either by deception or their own fault, that they are doing themselves good. While there is some truth to this, some people seek their ultimate good without any consideration for the good of others, as illustrated by many of Ayn Rand's self-possessed literary characters. Rand singularly championed reason, egotism and capitalism, viewing man as an heroic figure who should not submit his will to that of the mob, as the socialists demanded, or to any god. For her, every human relationship took on the character of a market transaction. She had no sense of moral obligation to anyone but herself. Christianity was a violation of her personal ethic. While Voltaire believed that if God did not exist, man would have to invent him, Rand seemed to agree with Bukharin that if God did exist, it would be necessary to destroy him. Howard Roark in *The Fountainhead* represented Rand's idea of a man-god of the human ideal. Her ideology is distinct from true conservatism. Rand ordered her life down to the smallest detail without any regard for divine absolutes or revealed religion.

Another aspect of evil is that some people confuse the notion of disaster with evil. Floods, earthquakes, hurricanes, and tornadoes are natural acts. They are not evil because no human is doing them to another human. Evil is only harm done by men to other human beings. People who ask the question why God allows evil to exist have misunderstood the nature of the world and its relationship to God. In the first place, evil has to exist, by definition, if there is to be good. One definition of evil is the absence of good. The word *good* implies that it must have an opposite to exist. If God is all good, there must be a force that is all bad. God has to allow evil to exist because, without it, there could be no good. Nor would people have free will. Men and women would be automatons without the human ability to do good and love one another. There is an existential choice here and what people choose to do involves this choice. Any discussion of evil would be incomplete without the mention of Adolf Hitler. Even the most hardcore denial of the existence of evil is refuted because Hitler personified the evil among us. Historian Hugh Trevor-Roper takes exception to this view. He says that while Hitler's deeds were evil, *Der Fuhrer* was convinced of his own rectitude. Others have said that Hitler was a prisoner of his pathological unconscious drives. While it may be no more than splitting hairs, there is no definitive consensus of Hitler's personal guilt among academics.

A more provocative example involves the sordid case of Erik and Lyle Menendez, a pair of young men who brutally murdered their parents in order to get their inheritance in order to maintain their lavish lifestyles. The jury could not believe that these sweet young men could have committed such a heinous act. They must have been suffering from low self-esteem. Their case rested on the accusation that their late father, unable to defend himself, had sexually abused them. The Menendez brothers personified the typical Jewish definition of *chutzpah*, which means having outrageous courage or defiance in the face of cold reality. Consider that they literally threw themselves on the mercy of the court by saying that they were poor little orphans; murdering their parents had caused their pathetic state of being without parents.

Andrew Delbanco has proposed a compelling theory in his book, *The Death of Satan: How Americans Have Lost Their Sense of Evil.* He has noted an important shift in how Americans view evil. Before the Puritan sects that founded New England left Europe, they had a pronounced Augustinian attitude toward evil. While St. Augustine sometimes spoke of Satin as the source of evil, his work, which became the Christian theology and the defining Christian belief about evil, defined it in terms of non-being. Evil was absence, emptiness, privation of the Good without a positive embodiment. There was no satanic incarnation.

To allay the terror and the uncertainty of the New World, the Puritans had to embody evil so they would have a human image on which to focus their disgust and revulsion. This led to the witch hunts and trials of the late seventeenth century. Delbanco traced the *caesura* in the evolution of evil, what he calls "the death of Satan" in the 1830s, to a period of great social reform in American history. This era saw the rise of the cult of individualism, the cult of the self-made man in the self-made land, a despiritualized postapocalyptic religious faith. Belief in Satan's literal presence faded like the ectoplasmic emanation of a spiritual medium. Without the prince of darkness to focus on, Americans started to demonize groups such as the immigrants during a period of nativism and leading to the purges of the McCarthy days (in the 1950s). The reaction against xenophobia, racism and ethnic prejudice caused many people to eliminate the use of the word *evil.*

There is a ghoulish quality to daily reporting of the incidents of blood and gore that dominates the urban scene today. The horrific crimes involving celebrities, such as O. J. Simpson and the serial killers, Jefferey Dahmer and John Wayne Gacy, attract, excite, and hold the rapt attention of millions of people who have a vicarious attraction for the evil deeds of others. Some have gone on television hawking trading cards depicting Jefferey Dahmer and other killers. The merchandising of abject evil demonstrates how low American culture has sunk. The successful film, *The Silence of the Lambs,* produced another example of personified evil, in the cannibalistic Hannibal Lecter. President Bill Clinton joined the debate when he called the men who had blown up the Oklahoma federal building "evil cowards." Is there a bridge back to a belief in the existence of evil? Rosenblatt says that this desire to recognize evil explains the popularity of the film, *Pulp Fiction.* The protagonists, Vincent and Jules, engage in mindless chitchat about the relative merits of Big Macs and Quarter Pounders and the relativity of value systems. What they say is that the different names are just a different way of saying the same thing, different ways of expressing the weight, for the same greasy slab of meat. This suggests that all systems of value, religious and otherwise, merely categorize behavior according to different linguistic and cultural frameworks of whomever is categorizing. This is a multicultural relativistic version of burgers.

Life is hard. Life is a vale of tears because of man's sin. When people refuse to recognize evil, it is really sin they want to ignore or deny. Sin is evil that individuals have committed and bear a responsibility for. God never promised us a rose garden. He only promised the Cross that He Himself had to carry. He will help us carry our daily crosses, some of which may be very heavy, as in the case of violence, torture and death. These evils have to be borne, often by innocent people, because it is through our acquiescence to God's Divine Will that we attain eternal happiness, not some impossible human utopia on this planet.

It is within the scope of all these historical and ideological abstractions, in their mutual conflict and interdependence that the Culture War has come to the surface. The literature attempting to explain the Culture War is already rich and varied. Among these many monographs is James Davison Hunter's *Culture Wars: The Struggle to Define America,* the seminal study on this issue. Hunter properly identifies that the great fault lines lie not between ethnic or racial groups but between differing world views or *Weltanschauung,* cosmologies and visions of human origins and destinies. Bob Rosio's *The Culture War In America: A Society in Chaos* stresses a return to the basic underpinnings of America's constitutional heritage to thwart the decline of our Judeo-Christian culture. E. Michael Jones and his *Culture Wars Magazine,* has provided a regular intellectual antidote to the cultural struggle. It is an impressive periodical with a host of scholarly articles on the Culture War in each issue. Of all the sources on this subject, the best to date is Robert Bork's comprehensive book, *Slouching Towards Gomorrah: Modern Liberalism and America's Decline.* Judge Bork correctly identifies modern liberalism as the enemy within, a way of thinking that is intellectually bankrupt. Bork emphasizes the twin pillars of this corrosive agent as radical egalitarianism—the equality of outcomes as opposed to equal opportunities, and radical individualism—the drastic reduction of limitations to personal gratification. His profound understanding of the issues points out that opposition to the culture inspired by modern liberalism is what the Culture War is all about. According to Bork, what liberalism has constantly moved away from are the restraints on personal liberty imposed by religion, morality, family and community. With this statement he properly frames the issue as it relates to American civilization. Liberals have traditionally heralded the importance of enlightened thought in the country's history. American society was founded with enlightened philosophy as part of its root culture. Americans looked at mankind through this starry-eyed lens, only to have two world wars, the Holocaust, the Gulag, Cambodia, the Cultural Revolution and Bosnia cloud its vision. Many liberals have recognized and lamented the dismal failure and decline of enlightened thought. The sixties' counter-culturalist Todd Gitlin reveals his frustration with the Balkanization of identity politics in his book, *The Twilight of Common Dreams: Why America is Wracked by Culture Wars.*

Another book on the subject reflects the problems cultural warriors can get into. Tom Sine's *Cease Fire: Searching for Sanity in America's Culture Wars* is a self-proclaimed example of intellectual appeasement. On all levels of this fight, cultural warriors are being urged to surrender the fight to compromise with the other side as if they were only engaged in a friendly game of touch football. I do not believe Sine realizes the consequences of the common ground approach he proposes. Like so many people who are fatigued by the stresses, strains and enmities of important fights, whether for or against abortion, the budget, or even the culture itself, all talk of compromising with the enemy in hope of some vague accommodation is pure, unadulterated folly. He reminds me of Neville Chamberlain without the umbrella in 1938. Tired of all the bickering, name-calling and shouting, not to mention the violence, Sine proposes an accommodation with the forces of enlightened secularity he so thoroughly decries in his book. There is virtually no mention of the debilitating effects of Big Government. His book only repeats the same banal platitudes that denounce all the cynicism and complaints of the talk show hosts on the radio who poison patriotism with all their criticism and venom. Sine is akin to the pacifist who is weary of war and feels that winning is not justified by the means required to achieve victory. He hopes for an elusive third way, cutting through the animosities of the religious right-wing, whom he seems to fear much more than anyone on the Left. Unfortunately, his hope of Jesus returning to earth through the Shalom, resembles the gnosticism that has plagued past movements of peace and brotherhood. He chides those conservative Christians who are convinced there is a conspiracy afoot to impose abortion rights on poorer countries and redefine the family unit to include homosexual couples. Ideologues on the Right apparently believe that the only way to communicate their concerns is through unholy mayhem. This is a grossly inaccurate charge that misses the thrust of the liberal agenda.

Like so many in the Catholic Church, Sine has an Old Testament view of this struggle. The Jewish people's hope for a Messiah centered on this world. Their Messiah was going to come and set up a kingdom, a perfect world on this earth. Christ's kingdom was not of this world but the next. His book, while exuding an enviable spirituality, makes no mention of the Cross, of the necessary willingness to join Christ in his suffering and death on the Cross. This is the essence of Christianity. Anything else is mere wishful thinking. His implicit acceptance of the environmental forewarnings of the burgeoning world population reveals a deep-seated approval of much of the agenda that is fostering the liberal side of the Cultural War. For someone supposedly in the middle, Sine seems to have chosen sides. Sine attacks New Jersey Congressman Chris Smith for his lack of understanding of the urgent global problems precipitated by out-of-control population growth, has little compassion for the world's poor and shows little willingness to join others in reasoned discussion of these complex issues. This is straight out of the liberals' handbook.

As *Culture Wars Magazine* points out in its December 1995 review of Sine's book, "to call what the World Bank and its allies proposed at Cairo 'constructive conversation and cooperation' is a bit like calling the smokestack at Auschwitz a vehicle for Jewish upward mobility." Sine misses or is uninterested in the darker side of the liberal agenda. Otherwise he would realize that both sides are not equally at fault here. The call for a cease-fire in the face of such unmitigated evil is the same as genuflecting before an icon of *Playboy's* Hugh Hefner. Sine runs up a white flag in a gesture of surrender, not a cease fire, without even understanding the consequences of his actions. Sine appears oblivious to origins of the eugenics state and its message of sustainable development or population control, which could easily lead to genocide. His intention could conceivably lead to the end of Western Civilization as we now know it.

Another viewpoint on the existing cultural situation comes from the Washington Post's Robert Samuelson, whose book, *The Good life and Its Discontents: The American Dream In an Age of Entitlement, 1945-1995,* says that most Americans have bought the empty promises of a utopian fantasy land. An economist by training, Samuelson notes that the economy is a mirror of the culture. To get out of this funk, as President Clinton once said, Americans must reassert their spirit of individualism. The regulatory regime which presided over a union between corporations and the federal government has allowed us to function on the premise that we live in a representative democracy not a socialist democracy. Ever since Franklin Roosevelt, Americans have acted as if their government were not socialistic. This has, in effect, created a time bomb that is ticking in the welfare state. The defining issue, according to Samuelson, is not Vietnam, not Watergate, but the government's role of mediating among interest groups. The problem lays in the fact that to equalize opportunities, the government had to polarize its citizens through policies such as affirmative action, welfare, regulation, and high taxes. One segment of the population, the taxpayers, are coerced, not only to subsidize the other half, the beneficiaries, but are also demonized as the villain responsible for the plight of the underachievers. This has led to a highly cynical and extremely frustrated middle class.

Probably the most perceptive writer on this subject is columnist, Don Feder. In his book, *A Jewish Conservative Looks at Pagan America,* Feder defines the Culture War as a battle over fundamental issues and values, a battle between moral relativism and the traditional values of the Judeo-Christian heritage. A war between those who want to maintain traditional family values and those who want to break down as many barriers as possible. Ideas do have consequences. The consequences of liberalism fill our jails, drug rehab centers, divorce courts, shelters for the battered and abused, mental hospitals, singles bars, abortion clinics, and provide a roster of guests for the *Phil Donahue* or *Oprey Winfrey* shows.

In his book, *A House Divided,* author Mark Gerzon sees the Culture War as more fractional in scope. He views it not as a Manchian struggle of cosmic proportions, but as a more ordinary and natural conflict between six different states which include: *Patria,* or the Religious State; *Corporatia,* the Capitalist State; *Dsia,* the Disempowered State or the state of victimhood; the Superstate of Media; *Gaia* the Transformational state; and *Officia,* the governing state. Gerzon has the notion that someday these six states will be able to find a common ground that will unify them in the form an imposed solution from the *Officia.* There can never be any common ground. To paraphrase Gresham's Law, bad culture drives out good culture! When one side is dominated by a philosophy of evil, there can be no common ground, as with the Biblical idea of the "house divided." Eventually one side must prevail. Pope Pius XII said that peaceful coexistence with Communists was immoral. The same can be said of peaceful co-existence with the forces of cultural semantics, hedonism and secular humanism. It is what the farmer says to the turkey until Thanksgiving.

The relativist is really saying, *we'll compromise, provided I dictate the terms of the compromise.* Moral relativism is an incoherent philosophical system but it has great propaganda value and gives naive people the illusion of understanding. How can someone compromise on the volatile issue of abortion? Can there ever be any real common ground on an evil such as the dismemberment of a human being? Abortion is and has always been on the cutting edge of the Culture War. It has become the Culture War's defining issue and, as a result, will play a dominant role in explaining all the vistas that this book will encompass. Its pernicious influence extends into many other aspects of our culture. The media protects it as if a holy rite. Educators encourage the kind of promiscuous behavior that will by necessity lead to a greater incidence of abortion. Politicians, actors and actresses, and anyone who subscribes to the sexual revolution promote its spread and acceptance. They viciously dispute and malign anyone who attempts to put a finger in the cultural dike before the flood that will suffocate the vitality of American civilization.

The Culture War betrays a growing chasm in this country's moral and social thinking. We often hear that American pluralism is an unambiguously good thing and public orthodoxy a bad thing. But pluralism itself is public orthodoxy. It demands, in effect, that we regard our deepest convictions— truths of natural law and divine revelation—as purely subjective preferences. In effect, we are expected to behave as if we believed the most crucial truth were able to change. Pluralism has become a synonym for moral relativism as public orthodoxy. You have your morality and I have mine. I won't impose my morality on you and you must not impose yours on me. I must never force you to get an abortion and you must never prevent me from getting one. This battle is being fought on many levels in this country—in the courts, the university lecture halls, movie studios and newsrooms. Relativism is not the same as respecting the differences between Yankee and Mets fans. Both agree the game is good but only differ in personal allegiances or geographic loyalties. Relativism has as its *raison d'etre,* the accommodation and eventual enshrinement of the enlightened view of mankind, extirpating the Christian view, especially with regard to sexual mores.

The Sardinian Communist Antonio Gramsci provides an insight to the abject threat that traditional American culture faces from the left. He foresaw the connection between his ideas and the capturing of a culture, which is the central thesis of the Culture War. He theorized that it would take a long march through the institutions, the media, the universities, public interest groups and other religious and cultural institutions before socialism and relativism would be victorious. By capturing these institutions and using their power, cultural values would be changed, morals broken down and the stage would be set for the political and economic power of the West to literally fall into the hands of the radical left. Given the current climate in the United States, it is clear that Gramsci had a flare for prophesy. Liberal groups have made a concerted effort to chip away at the belief that there are a set of divinely inspired moral absolutes. Someone once said that today's extremism is tomorrow's conventional wisdom! Modern socialism says it will create a good society which will then create good people. There is no political doctrine more contemptuous of the Judeo-Christian tradition which says that there cannot be a good society unless there are first good people. The notion that a handful of true believers can create a good society inhabited by good people by manipulating the masses is pernicious nonsense! Socialism says that we do not need self-interest, that we can rely on the notions of altruism and the pure spirit of fraternity. In his 1995 encyclical *The Gospel of Life,* the Pope boldly explained the issue without equivocation: "We are facing an enormous and dramatic clash between good and evil, death and life, the 'culture of death and the 'culture of life.' We find ourselves necessarily 'in the midst of this conflict.' " We are all involved and we all share in it with the inescapable responsibility of choosing to be unconditionally pro-life.

Society cannot exist without a shared conscience, a national apprehension of right and wrong. We are fast losing this way of thinking as the cultural relativists twist and obliterate our national moral traditions. It is madness to let each individual determine the moral boundaries of his own universe. We are fast developing an unhealthy chasm between two alien cultures. The prophetic words of St. Ignatius Loyola, the founder of the Society of Jesus, to St. Francis Xavier are applicable to American culture as a whole. With his thinking in mind, I ask what would it profit a nation if it gained the whole globe and suffered the loss of its national soul?

2

Homeric
Commencement
An Intellectual Odyssey

Nobody grows old merely by living a number of years—people grow old by deserting their ideals.

—Samuel Ullman

One pundit asked President John F. Kennedy how he became a war hero. He glibly answered, *They sank my boat.* In the same way, I never intended to be a cultural warrior. It just happened. I had attended a church coffee after Mass one Sunday and I ran into Dr. Mike Suden, an oral surgeon who was very active in the pro-life movement. He was wearing his *fetal feet* pin, considered by many to be the international symbol of the pro-life movement. The tiny pin is a life-size model of unborn feet at ten weeks' gestation. I was amazed at how perfectly formed and how human they looked. At that precise moment in May of 1985, I dove headlong into the choppy waters of the Culture War.

What I did intend was to be a world thinker. My early interest in various ideas led me to a deep curiosity about IQ, especially my own. One of the funniest renditions of IQ and people's attitude's toward it occurred on an episode of the old *Bob Newhart Show. Nick at Night* airs the reruns of my favorite show, the eponymous *Bob Newhart Show.* I was fortunate to see a rerun of the show where Emily (Suzanne Pleschette) gives Bob an IQ test. At first, he is reluctant to take it, and this was many years before the publication of *The Bell Curve,* but he finally complies. When he begs her to tell him his score, a 129, he is elated, until she admits to him that hers was a superlative 151. From that point on, the show details his puerile reaction to having an intellectually superior wife. This humor, in the form of social satire and the historic war between the sexes, is extremely funny. This particular show often leads me to thinking about my own IQ. Unlike Bob, I don't want to know what my wife's is. Husbands and wives should know virtually everything about each other but their relative IQ. To this date, and I am well into my fifties, I still do not know my own IQ. I do remember the last IQ test I took. I was a senior at Xavier High School, a highly competitive Jesuit prep school in Manhattan. There was a question about some Dickens character I believe, perhaps exposing an English literature bias, but I was never informed of my score. The only hint of my intelligence quotient dates back to the eighth grade at Our Lady Queen of Martyrs in Forest Hills, New York. Four of us wanted to take the entrance test of Brooklyn Tech, a difficult school that catered to young men with strong mathematics skills. Only one of us wanted to go there but our principal stressed that the exam would be good practice for the more important Catholic high school entrance tests. I remember she mentioned IQ to us, and when I asked her what mine was, she told me that it was over 100, which is the average.

This self-examination began when I was a junior at Xavier, the same school that Justice of the Supreme Court Antonin Scalia attended seven years before me. The idea to write a book, my memoirs so to speak, first occurred to me while riding the subway to and from school. I was a member of the track team and I thought that my experiences would provide a sufficient number of anecdotes to make a hilarious book. The only memorable thing about those years was losing my underwear at East River Park—but that is another story. My senior year was an important one in my intellectual development. Our study of religion was heavily laden with theological evaluations, such as proving the existence of God. Eschatology has always fascinated me. I remember discussing, debating, and analyzing many of these theories with most of the twenty-two young ladies who consented to go out with me that senior year (seldom more than once I might add). Social acceptance, personal importance, and the like, have never meant that much to me. I just want to be right in what I think and what I do. I believe my life should depend on being in the right. The fear of not having friends has driven many adolescents to despair, even suicide. As I reflect on my youth, I realize that I had few, if any, close friends. I was not what is commonly known as "popular." As an only child, I learned to cope with the incessant loneliness that comes with chronic boredom. On the positive side, being alone allowed me to develop an individuality that has left me beholden to no one. Solitude helped foster the spirit of independent thought that has served me as an adult. Consequently, my thoughts and ideas have had a more reasonable foundation than those of people who seem easily governed by emotions.

While I enjoy being in groups, I do not fear being outvoted or overruled on issues that I strongly believe in. I am not threatened by group dynamics so important to social intercourse. My self-esteem in not dependent on anybody's approval. Yet most people think I am a fun person. I have an innate ability to entertain a group with witty repartee and high-minded enthusiasm. Some might even deem me popular, yet not at the loss of any independence of thought. As I watch the people around me, I see so many of my contemporaries afraid of being alone that they seek out group activities for fear of losing their reason for being. Many have to have a television or radio on for company as if the impersonal sound of someone else's voice will validate their existence, providing the approval they need.

I also became interested in a TV commentator, Dr. Albert Burke. Dr. Burke had his own half-hour television show, called *A Way of Thinking*. The show's name revealed much about its attraction for me. Burke held a Ph.D. in chemistry, not one of your standard opinion-shaping curricula like history, political science or even philosophy. In many ways, Burke was a man years ahead of his time. He did a show on the environment and another segment I'll never forget. It began with Burke describing a silhouetted figure in the background who had suffered years of second class citizenship and discrimination. Of course, I, and probably 95% of the TV audience, thought he was talking about blacks. The year was 1961 and we were at the dawn of a great Civil Rights movement in this country. But when the spotlight shone brightly on the figure, it revealed a woman sitting on the floor dressed in black. He fooled us! He had prefaced his comments with something about their bodies being different. I do not believe that his oration on women and their role in American society would have surfaced in the present cauldron of abortion rights and excesses of the gender feminists of today, but in his own way, Dr. Burke was well in advance of the intellectual and social currents of thought of the late twentieth century. My dad, a medical doctor and a very intelligent man, was skeptical of this program, implying that Burke might even be a Communist. In those post-McCarthy days, my dad thought that anyone who was not overtly in agreement with him was a Communist. I think it was at that precise moment in my life that I decided what I wanted to do with my life. I wanted to be an intellectual, plain and simple. I have not looked lately, but, at that time, there was not much of a market for intellectuals. There were, however, many ways I could express my own way of thinking, whatever that might have been in 1961. I knew then that I wanted to be like Dr. Burke, to have my own television or radio show where I might write, teach, and speak on anything that was working in my mind.

The times were ripe for this idea. John F. Kennedy brought an entire intellectual class into his administration. He, more than any other president before or since, with the possible exception of Franklin Roosevelt, deified the force of brain power in solving national and global problems. David Halberstram's seminal study of the Vietnam War, *The Best and the Brightest*, totally squashed the myth that intellectuals can do it better. The intellectual class has not yet recovered from its debacle of Vietnam. Consider the success of the highly acclaimed *Forrest Gump*, which underscores the idea that sometimes it is the simple-minded who have really been blessed with the wisdom of social understanding. I continued to pursue my dream at the College of the Holy Cross in Worcester, Massachusetts, another school run by the intellectually-driven, Society of Jesus. I might add that another Justice on the Supreme Court, Clarence Thomas, graduated from Holy Cross six years after I did. Holy Cross proved to me that my IQ was not as high as I had hoped. It was not a life and death struggle, but I really did have to work hard to get B's. I finished with a cumulative 2.978967 grade point average (out of 4), including some summer work at another Jesuit school, Fordham University in the Bronx. In my freshman class of 512, just 12 made the Dean's list in our first semester. The last semester of junior year, 78 made the Dean's list and that did not include those who matriculated in Paris and Vienna. At Holy Cross, I took mostly liberal arts. We had a small education program run by Joseph Maguire, a good man with a heart to match his girth. I felt that I would be better off teaching in a Catholic environment since all of my previous scholastic experience had taken place within this setting. I did not have to waste my time taking worthless education courses. The University of Massachusetts had a course on *How to Write on the Black Board*. Practical? Yes! But devoid of all intellectual content. It was my belief that these education courses were heavy on method but lacked substance, direction and elevated learning. I had something to teach. My enthusiasm for and love of my discipline would show me the way to teach. Just to be safe, I took a methods course from Maguire. At that time, the Catholic schools did not require you to be board certified.

After graduation, in the true spirit of John Kennedy's inaugural address, I joined the *Catholic Lay Extension Volunteers*. This organization can be best described as a Catholic version of the government's *Volunteers in Service to America (Vista)*. They sent me to Charleston, Missouri, in the Cape/Springfield Diocese, sometimes referred to as "the pagan diocese." I suffered an immediate culture shock. I was an Easterner from the largest metropolitan area in the country. Charleston, which is located in the middle of Missouri's bootheel in the southeast corner of the state, had a population of 5,911 (1960 census). *Extension* was designed to serve parishes that had a number of Catholics but few priests and nuns. My job, for which I received a net stipend of $47.50 a month, plus lodging and $10 a week for food, was threefold. I taught history as well as physical education at St. Henry's High School. I was the varsity and junior varsity basketball coach and I was to offer spiritual guidance and moral education to my 80 students. In a word, I was there to save souls. This was quite a challenge for someone who had forgotten to dry behind his ears.

The people of Charleston were friendly and genuinely happy to have us there. My roommate was Ernie Marquart, an accredited teacher from New Jersey. His seven years of experience in the public school system were a godsend to me. I quickly learned that teaching was tougher than it looked. I knew my subject but discipline was another story. I had been trained by nuns and at a Jesuit military school, which is a tautology. I tried to be tough and hard. Joe Maguire had told us the cardinal rule of new teachers: *Don't smile before Christmas*. That was impossible for me. My combination of risible outlook and genuine love of learning did not mesh well with a stern, humorless sense of discipline. The harder I tried to be tough, the more the students rebelled. I was also a hard grader. No curve for these sons and daughters of farmers. During one quarter, 60% of the class flunked my freshman civics class. A bright, skinny youth, by the name of Michael

O'Rourke, was the exception, along with a gaggle of girls. O'Rourke's average was close to perfect, confirming my belief that it was them and not me. My 1965 Mustang got a weekly baptism of eggs. One young man threw my overcoat out the second floor window. Fortunately, I was not wearing it at the time. The basketball team nearly quit in November because I had suspended one of my starters for missing a game because it was deer season. I was referred to by such terms as "Shinto," because I had taught my sophomores a good deal about Asia that was not in the *World Civilization* text book. They were telling me that I was acting like a god. Maybe it was a bitter self-irony.

Not long after I arrived, I met the love of my life, Mike O'Rourke's sister, a beautiful young nurse named Judy O'Rourke. By February, I had started seeing her full time. In some ways, I quit on the students as they had quit on me. I played out the string. We got married that following August and I, unwittingly, moved this insecure woman, who had spent nearly all of her life on a farm on the outskirts of Charleston in a colorful area they called Big Lake, to a burgeoning metropolis of nearly 15 million. Judy suffered her own culture shock in the Big Apple. In many ways, living in New York was much harder for her than living in Charleston had been for me. My next teaching job was in Brooklyn, where I taught eighth grade history to 169 students at the Sts. Simon and Jude Elementary School, on Avenue T. The hardest part of this job was learning to pronounce some of the students' surnames. I thanked God for Pulaski, the only remotely pronounceable name in the class. Names like Petorino, Bruno, and Iorizzo gave me some initial qualms, but they were really great students and I will remember them forever. Discipline was hard but these students were younger than those in Charleston. There were stricter nuns to back me up when I sounded too tough. For my brighter students, I held a discussion group on international affairs after school. I totally rejected the egalitarianism that has permeated education today. When it comes to education, I am an elitist. I had a lot to say and a lot to give and I always aimed high. I could not tolerate the pedestrian and passive attitude too many young people had when it came to school and old fashioned book-learning. Television had turned too many of them into mindless robots whose attention span approximated the life span of an ice cube in hell.

My next teaching position was at Chaminade High School. I earned nearly $6,000 that year, a high jump from the $3,500 I had made in Brooklyn. My attempt to impose discipline failed me at this prestigious high school on Long Island that produced Robert Wright, the President of NBC, and a classmate at Holy Cross. They were the brightest students I had encountered but also the most devious. My scowl and stern demeanor were like a red flag to my homeroom of wild bulls. This particular group of young hellions had already tasted the blood of my predecessor who had shown them a weakness they despised. They made it a class project to get him fired and eventually succeeded in driving him from Chaminade and probably from teaching altogether. The class ringleader was a very bright but emotionless young man. I called him *Kingfish,* after Huey Long, because he was a natural leader with great oratorical skills. But there was a sense of abject hostility beneath his cool exterior that made me think he was capable of anything. He targeted me and slowly unified the class behind him. They did everything in their adolescent power to divert, annoy and distract me from my goal of teaching American History. Their animus spread to most of my other sections. The harder I tried to fight back, the worse it got. My tires were flattened. We had prank phone calls at all hours of the night. I tried to work through the system and informed the administration of my problems. It was the worst thing I could have done. I had showed them a weakness that educational bureaucracy dreads worse than the plague itself. In March of 1968, a month after the Tet Offensive, an irony that was not lost on me, the administration finally stepped and mercifully relived me of my duties with pay. I was willing to see it through but they thought it best I leave quickly and quietly during the Easter recess.

The beauty of teaching in all of these places was that I learned a great deal about people, and most importantly, myself. I had learned it is always wise to be yourself and not attempt to discipline young people with the threat of force unless you were willing to pay the price. Because of those combined experiences, I learned that I had to be firm but more diplomatic. Losing the Chaminade job was a very traumatic experience for me. My wife was wonderful in her support and kindness through what I considered a personal humiliation.

During this early period, while teaching in the daytime, I attended St. John's University at night. I took my Masters Degree in Asian History, thinking that this would be an area of great interest, what with Vietnam and the so-called Sino-Soviet rift. I thought it would be interesting and economically fruitful for a young would-be intellectual. It took me three years to obtain the degree and Judy encouraged me to go further with my studies.

Despite Albert Burke and all my other teachers, I never really had considered it possible for me to get a Ph.D. Perhaps it was fear of what that dreaded IQ score might have been. After my failure at Chaminade, the prospect of teaching in college, where students were not a captive audience, readily appealed to me. Judy was miserable in New York. My parents made every effort to make her feel welcome but the general impersonalism of the frightening city and its strange surroundings were just too much for her. We decided that I would apply to the two major universities in St. Louis, about 170 miles north of Charleston. I was struck by the friendly and personal consideration I received from Father Francis Bannon, the legendary chairman of St. Louis University History Department.

My most memorable professor at St. Louis University when I began my doctoral studies in 1969 was John Willson, now a professor at Hillsdale College in Michigan. Willson personified the bombastic, enthusiastic intellect so in love with his scholarly discipline that his students could not help but be infected with that reverence. He had an air about him that hovered between arrogance and self-confidence. Willson was the academic equivalent of Dizzy Dean's statement: *If you can do it, it ain't bragging!* I took two courses from Willson that first semester. To maintain my position in the Ph.D. program I needed a *B+* average. Since the University did not give *B+*s, I needed one *A* for every *B*. For his course in *US Intellectual History,* Willson required us to write stylistic essays on different topics in Hemingwayesque economy of verbiage. I worked extremely hard on those papers but could get no better than high *B*'s. As much as I liked Dr. Willson, I got two *B*'s that first semester.

Having a Ph.D. did not immediately bring the satisfaction and economic prosperity I had hoped it would. Judy and our two children, Mark, five and Michelle, two, were willing to go anywhere so I could begin my quest as a deep thinker. During my dissertation year, I went to all the history conventions, wrote 350 letters, had twenty-five interviews and learned the subtle art of begging. I saved over a hundred of these rejection letters. I interviewed with some schools which were located in towns I would not even care to visit. There was Columbia College in Columbus, Georgia. Two years before, it had been a Community College. Had I been offered that job, I would have had to teach a midnight course to laborers as they came out of the rice fields. In retrospect, it would probably have been an improvement on midnight basketball. In addition, I would have had to take a weekly 120 mile round trips to the army base at Fort Bragg to teach military students there. I was not thrilled by this prospect and should have thanked these men for not hiring me. I did have a promising interview with representatives from the University of South Florida at Tampa. The thought of teaching all morning and then basking in the Florida sunshine was very tempting to me. They were interested in me because of my Asian History background but cautioned me that I had to have a facility in either Chinese or Japanese. I did study Chinese one summer and had taken a Japanese reading program as partial fulfillment of the Ph.D. language requirements but it is accepted that to be facile in Chinese, which does not have its own alphabet, takes about ten years, and Japanese, which does have an alphabet, takes about five years. You needed to be more of an artist with a calligraphy pen than a linguist for Japanese. The only thing that I remember how to say is *Wa i nee,* which means "I love you!" To this day, I have never had the opportunity of using those words.

There were some better prospects at a pair of Tennessee community colleges. My favorite one was Shelby State. It was a new school and was hiring its first faculty. Judy and I really liked Memphis. We had spent a few of our wedding anniversaries there. I wanted that position! The dean of faculty had a bright smile and a head to match. He told me what I wanted to hear, implying that I would be joining his new faculty in the fall. In the following months, however, he never returned my phone calls and sent me impersonal letters, vaguely dismissing me. I also traveled to *Volunteer State*

Community College in Galletin County, just north of Nashville, Tennessee. Their history chairman was pleasant, and honest about my teaching prospects. He told me he had received 100 applications for their only opening, and twenty-seven of them had Ph.Ds. He also told me that a liberal at his school was someone who thought Earl Warren should be impeached. (I wondered if any of their students did or would ever make it to the Supreme Court.) He said my application was good, but at the moment, I ranked behind two aspiring professors with Ph.Ds. from the University of Tennessee. Just as well, I thought, because I really do not like Country and Western music.

Frustrated by the glut of young men and women in the job market, I decided to resort to the best way of securing employment in any industry: using people I knew. My father-in-law, Al O'Rourke, was a highly respected farmer whose late father, the irrepressible *Daddy Elmo,* was a near-legend in Southeast Missouri for his wit, good business sense and generous heart. One of the family's friends acted on the request of Daddy Al and tried to get me a job at Cape State College, now known as Southeast Missouri State University, in Cape Girardeau, the boyhood home of Rush Limbaugh. This friend had a contact with the history department, but to no avail. He also highly recommended me to Rollins College in Florida. I did manage to get an interview there but the chairman informed me that there were two ahead of me, both with Ph.Ds., one from Duke and the other from North Carolina. The ironic thing was that I was at another history convention and in talking to a woman, she mentioned having an interview with Rollins that afternoon. I immediately called him and asked if there were another job I could apply for. He said in polite but dismissive tones that he was sorry but he was only looking at women. I was too disappointed to contemplate the humor of his ambiguous phraseology. Rumors with a strong foundation in reality told of a black woman, with a Ph.D., or near Ph.D., coming to the convention and before she could unpack her bags, she had four job offers. That was my welcome to the wonderful world of affirmative action.

By graduation, I still had no job. I have always been a realist but it was frustrating to go into the summer with a brand new degree and no job. My closest call with gainful employment happened at Lindenwood College in St. Charles, Missouri, two weeks after graduation. It was the only interview I had where I got a free lunch. I was elated about the prospect of teaching only a half an hour away from St. Louis. After my interview, we went to Williamsburg, Virginia for a much-needed vacation. Of course, they would not inform me of their decision until I got back so it was not really a relaxing vacation. When we did return, after driving nonstop to catch the last half-hour of our baby Michelle's second birthday, I learned that I had finished second, this time to a Ph.D. from Harvard whose family had once lived in Charleston. Many years later, I met the Harvard man's sister at my nephew's wedding and politely asked her to tell her brother how he ruined my vacation twenty-two years previously. Ironically, he spent just that one year at

Lindenwood, before leaving the teaching profession for good. Maybe I was the lucky one?

After that interview, I returned to baseball, one of my great boyhood loves, as a refuge during my summer of discontent. From all of the above, it probably appears that I had gone over the deep edge and had some sort of mental breakdown. As depression started to take hold, I decided to do something I had always wanted to do: write a book about the Brooklyn Dodgers. We had money in the bank and I thought this might be the only time I would ever have the opportunity to explore this inner desire. I had been a fan since 1952 and the Brooklyn Dodgers had always been my favorite team. At the time I did not realize how the little 115-page book would shape my life, invariably leading me to the Cultural War with its many personal and intellectual ramifications. I have always believed in God's Divine Providence—His special plan for me. The absence of any serious job offerings, combined with my love of the Brooklyn Dodgers, eventually sent me in the direction of the most serious undertaking of my life, writing this book.

I spent the summer researching the last five years the Dodgers spent in Brooklyn (1953-1957) before their move to Los Angeles. In July of 1972, on my wife's birthday, I drove to Louisville, Kentucky to interview Dodger captain Pee Wee Reese, the first real hero I had as a child. I spent a delightful hour-and-a-half with Reese in the same room Roger Kahn had interviewed him in for the *Boys of Summer*, the most successful baseball monograph in history. I did not finish the book that summer. Maryville College called and told me they had a part-time job for an American historian. I jumped at the chance. Later I found out what university politics had an ugly hand in this situation. I spent two years at Maryville. I was not satisfied teaching just one course a semester. I wanted them to let me teach an Asian History course at night. Barcey Fox, their public relations director asked me what would make my course different from the ones at St. Louis or Washington Universities. I did not have a convincing answer for her. Finally, I decided to propose teaching an accredited course in baseball history. They were intrigued by this original idea, which of course I had adapted from Dr. Harold Seymour, the dean of American baseball scholars, who had offered such a course at Finch College in New York City. I had read Seymour's book, *Baseball: The Early Years*, during the summer of 1972. This book had served as his doctoral dissertation. I wished I had thought of that!

The course attracted eighteen students and two walk-ons, who audited the course. One of the latter became a good friend and the other my plumber. My guest speaker was James "Cool Papa" Bell, a debonair black man who starred in the Negro Leagues for nearly thirty years. Bell later made it to the National Baseball Hall of Fame at Cooperstown, New York. He mesmerized the students with his stories about base hits and racial prejudice. The course had attracted a great deal of local publicity. I appeared on the Channel Four 5 o'clock *News* with *Bob Buck*, the youngest brother of

Hall-of-Fame broadcaster, Jack Buck. If self-publicity is an addiction, I had my first fix that night. There was something magical about the lights, the cameras and the effort required to keep my composure when asked a basic question like what my name was. I had not disavowed my thinking about personal popularity but there was something very attractive in public exposure and the status of a media "luminary." Radio spots on KMOX followed and, all of a sudden, I was a local celebrity.

Maryville let me teach the course during their special May program in 1974. By that time, I knew I was being phased out because of budget restrictions so I went big time. I sent a letter to Gene Shalit of the *NBC Today Show*. A month later one of his producers called and we set up my debut on national television for 9 May 1974. I spent three-and-half minutes discussing Moses Fleetwood Walker, who was the last black baseball player to play in major leagues before Jackie Robinson re-integrated baseball in 1947, and St. Louis Browns owner, Bill Veeck's midget, Eddie Gaedel, in front of ten million people. If I could not break into academia through the front door, I would try to sneak in one of the windows.

I spent the next dozen years reading, studying and writing about baseball. I self-published several short books beginning with *Baseball In a Nutshell*, which served as a history text for my baseball class when I got the opportunity to teach such a class. My most successful book was *Last In the American League*, a short history of the St. Louis Browns who last played in St. Louis in 1953. I had inherited the idea from a member of the *Society of American Baseball Researchers* (SABR), a group of baseball junkies who since then have reached international acclaim and respect. Bob Broeg, the prolific author of several baseball books including the definitive biography of Stan Musial, dubbed me the "Baseball Professor." I later used this term as the name of the baseball variety show I did on local cable television from 1982-1983. Most of my books failed to make any money, but writing and self-publishing were a good experience.

In 1984, I founded the *St. Louis Browns Historical Society*, popularly known as the *Browns Fan Club*. For more than 14 years, I have used my historical skills to resurrect and foster the historical memory of a team that was most likely the worst team in baseball history. I was able to get a pair of small publishers to publish a rewrite of *Last In the American League*, which I greatly expanded to *Still Last In the American League* (Northmont Publishing, 1992) and *The Best of Seasons: The 1944 St. Louis Cardinals and Browns* (McFarland, 1994). A May 1987 issue of *Sports Illustrated* featured an article and photo, about my interest in the Browns. In October of 1987, I ran into Joe Garagiola on the field prior to the second game of the Championship Series between the San Francisco Giants and the Cardinals at Busch Stadium. I had interviewed him in 1974 for an article that never was published. So I thought I would go over to him and reintroduce myself. As I nervously approached him and introduced myself, he paused, looked at me with big Italian eyes and said, "Oh yeah, St. Louis Browns, St. Louis Browns!" He calmly walked away, leaving me with an open jaw and a surprised look on my face. I could see my tombstone now: he brought the Browns back to life and then he died!

I finally published my Dodger book ten years after I started it, under my own label, *Krank Press*. There is probably nothing more difficult than trying to sell a book on the Brooklyn Dodgers in a community that loathes the very mention of the name and detests the color blue. I did manage to get an interview on an Illinois station, WGNU, which broadcast on both sides of the Mississippi River. Mike McEvoy was the host and though he was a high school guidance counselor, he had his own sports talk show which aired twice a week. Appearing on these shows was easy and a lot of fun. A month later, Jack Herman, a sportswriter for over thirty years with the *St. Louis Globe-Democrat* and the Cardinals official scorer, gave up his position doing a sports talk show three weekday nights. McEvoy tried to do five shows a week but could not continue once school was in session. He recommended me for the vacancy and I assumed two of Herman's nights. This led to an association with WGNU that has run through 1998. I did a sports call-in show for three years.

After the first years, Chuck Norman, the station's owner asked me to audition for the *Partyline*, his regular talk show that ran throughout most of the day. I had a natural proclivity for talking and dealing with all sorts of people. In many ways, my education has broadened since I began my tenure as a weekly host on *Partyline*. My experiences on WGNU radio have provided me with tests of another kind. Being a teacher and one who sees the educational value of talk radio, I have an ax to grind with the *National Education Association*. The NEA has hurt the art of teaching and robbed the profession of its dignity and character. It has instituted a dull, insipid curriculum, replete with a panoply of touchy-feely courses lacking any intellectual substance. I wonder if many of today's students will have the same respect and affection for some of their teachers, as I did. I believe when you stop learning, when things of the mind cease to mean anything to you, you have lost a great deal of the richness of life and a good deal of your humanity. We have discussed many issues on my show some that have to do with American culture. What began in the subways of New York City, came back to life once I was behind that WGNU mike.

It was during my tenure as a talk show host that I became a cultural warrior. At first, I had no idea what a Culture War was all about. After years of study and hundreds of hours of arguing and talking on the radio, I learned that the concept of the Culture War was not new. The battle for America's moral soul can be seen in contrast to the *Kulturkampf* that plagued Bismark's Germany prior to the turn of the century. At the time, the term was used to describe the political fallout of Bismark's unification of the German principalities into a nation state. There was more to this than met the naked eye. It also pitted Catholics against Protestants with their dissimilar outlooks on morality and education. The Culture War in the United States is fundamentally different than Bismarkian Germany's. It is a broader concept and its main currents runs deeper with many more streams flooding every aspect of the American way of life. Education, as discussed in a subsequent chapter, is just one synchronous tide.

The Culture War has arisen over a fundamental difference in the way in which individuals define moral authority, the truth, the good, and our obligations to one another—ultimately over the definition of the meaning of America. This definition includes the freedom to do whatever one desires without restriction. We are, however, beings with a weak basic nature, seemingly bent on self-destruction. The Culture War is an attempt to re-define America by attacking traditional values (or family values) substituting newly constructed rights, such as abortion rights, and gay rights, that attack the structure of the traditional family. As a result of the Culture War, we are in danger of becoming a totally divided nation, not unlike the Balkans in the early twentieth century. We are becoming two nations: one concentrated on rights and laws, the other on rights and wrongs. One is radically individualistic and dedicated to the actualized self; the other is communal and dedicated to invoking the common good.

We have come to the situation in which liberals say, *you have your values and I have my values*. I hear this on the radio all the time. It is a Pilatian refrain, a discussion stopper. What is truth? Each person is free to decide his truth. My truth is as valid as your truth. Freedom, unfettered by truth, or consequence or responsibility is license which is ultimately the undoing of authentic freedom. This is the basic thrust of Pope John Paul II's landmark encyclical, *Veritatis Splendor*. The Pope also excoriates post-modernist thought which believes morality is created by culture.

If there is one central issue that serves as the nexus for the country's cultural divide, it is abortion. It was those little fetal feet that hooked me into the forefront of the battle before I even knew there was a battle raging. Much of what I say and do on the air revolves around abortion, which can function as a metaphor for so many of the conflicting opinions in this country, from family values to the welfare state. Abortion bleeds into many other issues that dominate the cultural scene, including education, women's rights, multiculturalism, racism the environment and even the New World Order. It is about euthanasia, eugenic engineering and the protection of the radically handicapped. There are many people today who believe that abortion is wrong. They recognize that medical science has long since proven conclusively that human life begins at fertilization. They accordingly can not and do not deny that abortion is killing. Most people agree that abortion is against God's will but many feel that the need to protect a woman's right to choose is compelling enough to override the legally unsupported right of her baby to live. If abortion is wrong, then both mother and baby should be protected unless it can be shown that one's life (the mother's) might be lost if the pregnancy were allowed to continue. Only the act of preserving one life is grave enough to justify taking another. But there is no logic in the liberal standpoint because the basic underpinnings of the liberal, who supports abortion, is rooted not in logic but in feelings and emotion. The liberal wants to encase himself or herself in a cocoon of protective feelings so that one never has to deal intellectually with such contradictory positions.

Another issue that dominates my weekly radio agenda is politics. To participate fully as a cultural warrior, I had to learn just what the terms liberal and conservative really meant. Most of the great conservatives, dating back to Edmund Burke, were insistent that conservatism was not an ideology or a doctrine. It was not conservative wisdom but human arrogance, disguised as the dogma of liberalism that prompted Vaclav Havel to create a universal theory of the world. The real conservative realizes that the human condition proves such utopian theories wrong, sometimes at the great cost of human life.

Much of my initial forays into conservatism emanate from my Holy Cross roommate of three years, Peter Lawrence. He had a subscription to William F. Buckley's publication, *The National Review* and had read Russell Kirk's seminal work, *The Conservative Mind.* What's more, Peter was one of the most verbally proficient men I have ever known.

According to Kirk, conservatism is not an ideology but a prescriptive disposition, a preference for tested tradition and tested ways. It is an affection for what human beings have created so far and a mistrust of efforts to tear those things down in the name of quixotic and untested ends. The word *vision* is not often applied to a conservative unless it is in terms of an historic vision of the past that Ronald Reagan so effectively described. Abstractions are for visionaries who deal in what they hope the world can be, not what it has been or can never be. Conservatives believe in government but only that government where powers and responsibilities are plainly spelled out and diffused amid an intricate but enforceable system of checks and balances.

A dogma of liberal thought contends that the races are identical except for skin color—an absurdly superficial view. To ignore culture is to ignore the soul. The liberal society has been a society of the soulless, a sub-nation alienated from its historical roots and spiritual underpinnings. Liberals have wrongly assumed that inside every poor black was a member of the white middle class that was screaming to get out. Liberals campaign mostly against the white race but they have done more harm than good for blacks. As evidenced by an illegitimacy rate rapidly approaching 70%, the full effects of the sexual revolution, another liberal brainstorm, have been most visible in the black community where family and church have lost their power. The new morality was supposed to allow responsible consenting adults to fornicate with contraceptives, affecting no one outside the privacy of their bedroom walls. It has turned out to mean twenty-five year old black men preying on fifteen year old girls with impunity. The 1996 movie, *When We Were Colored* demonstrated in an honest and realistic way just how much the black community has lost in terms of family solidarity and joy of living due to the social pathologies of crime, illegitimacy and underemployment. The freedom of the sixties was a two-edged sword that resulted in family crisis from which blacks may never recover.

The Culture War has taken its toll on me. For the last 14 years, I have been involved in this Culture War by debating and discussing the nature, causes and instances of this cosmic battle. I have become a counter-revolutionary in an institution run by the inmates. To paraphrase radical author, Ken Kesey, I am Randle P. McMurphy, the one who flew over the Clinton nest. My situation can be characterized as a sense of impending alienation, though not in the Marxist definition of the word, that has left me constantly on guard against statements coming from my Catholic Bishops and my government. I have always had a sense of healthy skepticism about what I read in the left-wing press, yet now I have had to read the conservative press with a greater scrutiny. Since the death of Russell Kirk, the current dean and high priest of conservative thought, William F. Buckley has often made comments that I thought smacked of intellectual inconsistency and appeasement. The *Weekly Standard*, reputed to be a new and vibrant vessel of conservative principles and thought, has disappointed me and occasionally made me doubt the basic intellectual honesty and integrity of its editors. Even my idol and mentor in many ways, Rush Limbaugh, with his special emphasis on a Republican victory in November of 1996 without any regard for his conservative principles, has given me cause for concern.

My sense of dread has spread even to my favorite advocation, namely sports. It has always been my contention that the world of sports, especially baseball, is reflective of the culture. Baseball, football, basketball, and even hockey, are all undergoing their own type of Culture Wars. The use of the "Designated Hitter" (DH) in the American League, the strike zones, football's constant tampering with the rules, sports' unfettered expansionism, and many other changes designed to exploit the general public at the risk of ruining the games' integrity, have caused much of my interest to wane. While professional sports are primarily for entertainment, they tell us something about the nature and depth of our society's descent. Ever since I can remember, I have been a sports fan. Sports were not only a temporary escape from the pressures of mundane life, they took on a life of their own. Sports provided a realm of the mind where right was right and wrong was wrong. Sports taught much about character, self-sacrifice, discipline, manly values and the virtues of fair play. But the more I immerse myself in the Culture War, the more I think that sports have become turgid, not only have sports degenerated to nothing more than cotton candy for the mind or time spent in the sandbox. Yet in many ways, sports reflect the depth and extent of the Culture War. The radio has offered me an opportunity to make my voice heard and fight the battles that need to be fought. Since it has served as my bloody pulpit, I hate to take even a vacation to give up the opportunity of advancing the values and ideas of my side of the Culture War.

3 / WGNU Radio
My Bloody Pulpit

Radio is all you need!

—Commercial jingle played on WGNU

The doctor is in and the disease we will treat today with medicated verbiage is that of "liberalism." Another name for social disease has infected too many of us with an insatiable need to look to the federal government for everything we need and desire. It manifests itself with symptoms like talking about feelings; a fear that without the Great White Father we can do nothing. We owe everything to Uncle Sam. For our freedom, he's willing to care for our every need until we become a burden on him. Then we have the responsibility of terminating our lives when they no longer have any social utility. If you have any of these symptoms, call us. The doctor is in and I intend to make you well today!

So began one of my shows on WGNU-Radio, 920 on the AM dial, with the muted tones of Carley Simon's *Haven't Got Time for the Pain* playing in the background. Since the 1920s, the radio has played an enormous role in American life. For millions of people, especially shut-ins, the sick, and the elderly, radio has provided not only a great deal of enjoyment but a solace as well. Despite the incursions of video and, more dramatically, cable TV, radio is still something special. With just a turn of the dial, one can bring in the outside world; into the kitchen, the bathroom, the car and even the bedroom, radio is there. People wake up to the radio, fall asleep to it, eat with it, work with it and even make love to it. When asked about her attire during the shoot for her notorious nude calendar in the late 1940s, Marilyn Monroe quipped, "The only thing I had on was the radio!"

Talk radio has changed a great deal since the nonpareil of St. Louis radio, Jack Carney, died in 1985. Thomas Pauken in his book, *The Thirty Years War,* states that talk shows have been a boon to conservatives for years. It is an effective means of getting the conservative message out daily. Talk shows are a natural for conservatives in an era in which the dominant culture is leftist. It is a vital and powerful weapon in the Cultural War arsenal, thanks mainly to the bombastic and brash approach of Rush Limbaugh, a college dropout from Missouri. Part of the appeal of talk radio is that, unlike the predictable liberalism of the major networks and newspaper chains, it offers almost every shade and hue of opinion. Though calls are screened, radio does not suffer from the overt sanitation and verbal ecology of the other media where the liberal elite have to interpret, cushion and fine tune the news before it ever gets to the audience. It is one forum where the average man or woman can actually be heard. It is real democracy on the air. Talk radio is raw meat for the mind. It is the unwashed and uncooked news that might be hard to digest, but will readily increase one's appetite for the real thing. As black conservative host and columnist Ken Hamblin has called it, talk radio is "the last neighborhood, or a giant backyard."

Ron Rosenblatt quoted TV talk show host, Maury Povich in his article *Evil's Back* in the Sunday *New York Times* magazine as saying that we can trace all our problems to past abuse of one kind or another, and that once explained, we are absolved. Talk show culture has been the last refuge of the enlightenment belief that to understand all is to forgive all. The talk show has, in essence, become the twentieth century equivalent of public confession, though with a satanic twist. What is really sought is not forgiveness but public approval, of their dysfunctional or perverse behavior. Rosenblatt says that shows like Povich's have become the American equivalent of the Athenian Agora, where citizens, sophists and philosophers batted around questions of behavior. These shows can be barometers of public feeling on good and evil. How many Americans form their opinions based on the sordid lives they see on these shows is the real problem. We have lost our moral ability to discern what is right and wrong. We even use public opinion polls to explain this. In the words of conservative theorist, Russell Kirk, we have become a nation of philodoxers, or lovers of opinions. Povich feels that he can tell at the precise moment when the dial of national consciousness shifted from permissive green, or liberalism, to angry, conservative red: the moment Lyle Menendez reloaded and literally blew off his bleeding mother's face. In doing so, Povich believes that Lyle Menendez blew away the delicate fabric of empathy that talk-show confessionals had woven around those who excused their crimes with tales of childhood abuse. Although Rosenblatt and Povich were talking about television talk shows, their comments can be universalized to include radio talk shows because they all revolve around the dissemination of personal opinions. While most people think they are entitled to their own opinions, there is a false assumption about the sovereignty of the personal opinion. Over the past thirty years, the virus of relativity has infected much of which used to pass for intellectual exchange. Now the saying goes, *my opinion is as good as yours!* With such an empty-headed, anti-intellectual mindset, growth, maturity and real education are virtually impossible. On WGNU, I have never accepted the false logic of the statement, *my opinion is as good as yours!* People used to believe that the world was flat or that the woman determined the sex of her children.

Science has laid these blatant falsehoods to rest. Not all opinions are equally valid. They must be supported by reality—what has actually happened, not the perception of reality.

I have always been amazed by the science of radio. In my senior year of high school, I flunked the one test we had on radio. Knowing nothing about tubes and filaments, I could do little more than turn it on. I still don't know how it works but I have learned to understand the real power involved behind the mike: thousands of people I have never met, and may never meet, can listen to what I have to say and maybe agree with or learn from my words and ideas. For two hours each week, I am free to say virtually anything I think appropriate. Doing talk radio is really not that hard. You have to be able, first of all, to talk. You have to be informed, conversational and opinionated. Having a good sense of humor, as I do, can only enhance your performance. While I would gladly have paid for the opportunity to shoot my mouth off, I actually got fifteen dollars an hour for doing what the late sports commentator Howard Cosell used to call "telling it like it is."

When we first moved to St. Louis in 1969, Jack Carney had just returned from a hiatus in San Francisco to host a morning show. Over the years, I smiled a lot more because of his wry wit, his pleasant demeanor, and the delightful way he bantered with the diverse likes of Rex Davis, Bobby Costas and the unforgettable Miss Blue. In 1973, I was teaching an accredited baseball history course at Maryville College. I sent Carney a copy of my final exam. He and hockey announcer, Dan Kelly, spent nearly an hour "playing" with it on the air. Right then, I made it a life's ambition to appear on his show. In August of 1982, I got my chance. I had self-published a book on the Brooklyn Dodgers and Jack had a long friendship with Los Angeles Dodger Manager Tommy Lasorda. It still reigns as one of the most enjoyable hours of my life. On the last day of 1992, I made it into my second generation of Carneys by guesting on a show with Jack's only son, John Carney. Blessed with an infectiously warm smile not unlike his dad's, John Carney started filling my plastic cup with champagne at 10:30 in the morning. After discussing my history of the old St. Louis Browns with Carney, and sipping an ample supply of bubbly, I attempted to navigate my way back to my car. Feeling a little bit too celebratory, I went to the newsstand and thumbed through magazines for a half hour before the wooziness dissipated.

The radio bug really bit me and I was soon asked to host a sports show for Chuck Norman on WGNU. Over the next two years, I impressed a few people with my encyclopedic knowledge of baseball history, legend, and lore. It was at about this time that Bob Broeg of the St. Louis Post-Dispatch started calling me the "Baseball Professor." After two years of talking to such habitual callers "Backdoor Benny," "Sunshine," and "Diamond Lil," Chuck asked me to switch to the *Partyline*. In 1986, I became a regular *Partyline* host. I usually treated most subjects with a degree of irreverence unparalleled by other host. Over the years, I have gone from being an "airhead," with "Mr. Happy Talk" as my theme to the thoroughly pretentious "Nobody

Does it Better." As a history professor without a regular teaching position, WGNU has become my university. I often include W-G-N-U as one of my advanced degrees.

WGNU is a special place, but hard to describe. In 1986, we broadcast from what I affectionately called the "twin trailers." Our combination office and broadcast studio located in Granite City, Illinois were precisely that— a pair of old trailers, connected by a short concrete walkaway. The interior of the studio had the visual impact of a housing project in need of repair. The walls were gritty, the floors yellowing, and the only window had at least one broken pane where the summer wasps buzzed menacingly around the torn screen. But to me, it was a home and, more importantly, a real radio station that projected 500 watts of my voice once a week. The surroundings improved vastly when we moved to a high-rise building on Union and Lindell in St. Louis. The atmosphere was more conducive to exploring controversial ideas on the air.

Chuck Norman, the station's owner is an interesting man, who has spent most of his life in radio. While his station has undergone several changes in format through the years, which is true of most radio stations, it has been talk radio where his force and influence, as well as his profits, have been consistently found. Chuck believes fervently that controversy sells. He likes his hosts to make waves on the air, to create controversy, ostensibly in the pursuit of truth.

While the station has endured a plethora of hosts over the years, by far the most successful has been Richard "Onion" Horton, an irate black man with a strong attraction for the separatist philosophy of Louis Farrakhan. Onion started on WGNU about the same time I moved to the *Partyline*. In the beginning, he had ten hours a week of air time, the lifeblood of any talk show host. As his success and his following increased, his air time doubled to twenty hours every week. Onion parlayed his brand of ghetto populism into a highly successful career in berating the white-oriented politics of the St. Louis area with a vehemence and illogic that served to further divide the races within the city. Onion has also been able to increase the pride and aggressiveness of his black people with alarming frequency, underscoring his personal power. For all his anger and postal system mentality, his 67 sponsors insured that he has been handsomely rewarded. The irony of Onion Horton's spleen is that the greatest critic of the man and his system became the biggest capitalist on the station. Chuck Norman and his station profited greatly from Onion's verbal hostility, until Horton ran afoul of station sponsorship policies, vanishing as quickly as he had appeared in 1985.

Horton's inflammatory rhetoric made life much more difficult for most of the white hosts. Without the money he brought in, the station would not have been able to afford hosts such as me, who provided the other side of many of the issues Onion addressed. In many ways, Onion Horton was the station and most of us knew and accepted that. Onion was an enigma. He could be warm and friendly at times, while on other occasions, the cultural pigmentation that divided us in his mind transformed his demeanor. Jesse Jackson and his entourage of hard-looking, well-dressed black men invaded the station for an interview. Onion and Jackson totally ignored my presence, as well as that of all the other whites in the studio. It was as if we did not exist. Onion cast his eyes down without a word as Jesse and he vacated the broadcast booth. I said that it was just as well, since I would probably have slipped and referred to Reverend Jackson in the mocking tones of Rush Limbaugh.

Onion did an interview for one of the local black papers and virtually excoriated his fellow hosts by saying that he believed that 99 of every 100 white talk show hosts were racists. It made me angry and the best way I could think of to get even with him was to mention on the air that Onion was just doing "shtick," entertaining, as they constantly say about Limbaugh, and that what he said on the air was not what he really believed. He actually went out for a few beers after the show with the white hosts. On his next show, Onion went ballistic and spent the better part of two days denying what I had said. Onion played the race card more than anyone I have ever met in my radio experience. He seemed poisoned by the harm and abuse he suffered as a young black man growing up in an insensitive Southern city forty years ago. He seemed unable to reconcile himself with that past, living with a blanket denunciation of most whites with whom he came in contact. He is adamantly opposed to interracial marriage and many other social advances his race has made over the last thirty years. While he denounced white racists, meaning all those who oppose his ideas, especially the "police," he failed to see or understand that he makes many of his judgments on the basis of race. According to his intellectual construct, only the people in power can be racists and since blacks are not in power, no matter what they say or do based on their race, they can not be considered racist. After being denounced as a racist on my show by one of Onion's compatriots, I quipped that I can not be a racist at WGNU because, by definition, I have no power on the station. I had 67 fewer sponsors than Onion. Therefore, only Onion Horton can be a racist because his 67 sponsors gave him almost all the power on WGNU.

The most irresponsible and potentially dangerous problem I ever had with Onion involved the highly contentious Rodney King beating in 1991. Until the O.J. trial, no event better illustrated the cultural divide between many blacks and whites in the Culture War. The news of King's beating was announced just as I was signing off on that Wednesday at noon. By the time I returned to the air, I had pretty much calculated what conciliatory words I would use to discuss the issue without aggravating the racial climate. Onion had a field day with the volatile situation. On the Friday morning following the incident, I was driving on Highway 40 and I happened to tune in to Onion. He was in the midst of a debate with some white caller who suggested some sympathy or defense for the white policemen, only to have his call terminated with Onion yelling, "Take that up with the white boy on

Wednesday!" *White boy on Wednesday!* Whom could he mean? Certainly not me! Onion has this thing about calling whites, "boy." What we know to be a sign of great disrespect if uttered to a black man, to Onion is unimportant. I can only respond with: *Do unto others as you would have them do unto you!*

In retrospect, I believe his rhetoric did a grave disservice to the St. Louis community. Before his departure in 1995, I had always thought that the station would have been better off, from a social responsibility standpoint, without his racist invective. Horton later surfaced at KATZ radio in St. Louis, a black-owned station, where he continued his black perspective on local and national events. In May of 1996, a black group, called the *Coalition for Free Speech* accused him and colleague, Mark Kasen of promoting racism on the station. Kasen is Jewish and, like Onion, an alumnus of WGNU. I found him as distasteful and inflammatory as Onion Horton. It is Kasen's view that white people don't like black people. The real problem is white people. Kasen takes a decidedly opposite view of Minister Louis Farrakhan than do most Jews. The worst thing I ever heard him say on the air was in relation to the pro-life issue. As I was putting my car in the garage one evening, I heard him say, while complaining about the activities of Randall Terry and his militant *Operation Rescue,* "I want my daughter to do natural things, such as have sex and get an abortion." He also has no love for conservatives.

Another controversial host is septuagenarian Virginia McCarthy, who has been with the station for over twenty years. Despite her limited grasp of world events and inability to handle difficult calls, she has a loyal and devoted following. Unfortunately, in the Culture War, she became an instant casualty for liberals who wished to direct their barbs toward an easy conservative target.

One of my favorite hosts on WGNU has had her own special theatre in the Culture War. In fact, Sally Miller Purdue, a tall, vivacious woman in her fifties was on the frontlines. She had a story to tell about President Bill Clinton. I would hardly call her a bimbo—she was a stately, elegant woman, who had been Miss Arkansas in 1959—but erupt she did on the *Sally Jessy Raphael Show* in July of 1992. In 1983, after a second painful divorce, she took up with then Governor Bill Clinton, whose youth and charm revived her feelings as a woman. She admitted to a four-month affair that ended abruptly when Sally hinted that she might want to go into politics by running as a Republican in the mayoralty election of her hometown Pine Bluff. Clinton balked, telling her that she didn't have a chance against the big boys. When she persisted, he left her and looked elsewhere for fun and diversion. Sally ran, but lost in 1984.

Sally joined WGNU just before the 1992 election. She had a good voice and a pleasing personality. She had had her own three-hour radio talk show in Pine Bluff and, later, was a chanteuse, not unlike Gennifer Flowers. Sally recorded her own theme before her show. She was good at dealing with the public. Her show was light and airy. If Sally had one fault, it was that she talked too much about herself. I don't mean that she had an ego problem, but she gave too much personal information that many of her detractors used against her. In December, she promised to tell all the sordid details about her affair with Governor Clinton. I had never seen the station more eager to promote anything in my life. For weeks they previewed what they believed would be a dynamite revelation. When the appointed day arrived, right after Clinton's inauguration had come and gone, the station had egg on its face. Not only did Sally not tell any of the details, she did not even show up for her turn at the mike. It was a big letdown and the station executives rightfully muttered "phony" "unprofessional" etc. Later she explained that her attorney advised her not to discuss the issue at all, especially not on the air. Some of the callers, especially those who were still enamored with Bill Clinton, attacked her as a whore and worse. The callers' savagery did not approach the type that Virginia McCarthy received, because Sally was a fighter. She had weathered the storms of two broken marriages, an abortion, and years of sexual harassment. She stoically fought back, dismissing one critic as a whining whoredog, and she did it in a tone that almost made it sound complimentary. Sally's stay at the station was less than two years. She had been studying at Lindenwood College and, after receiving her diploma, she left for China to teach English.

No mainstream liberal American paper even acknowledged she had ever existed. The British *Sunday Telegraph,* dated 23 January 1994, printed the whole story, under the banner headline, "I was threatened after the Clinton affair." The article, by Ambrose Evans-Pritchard, quoted Sally as saying that she was threatened with dire consequences if she refused to behave like a good girl during Clinton's successful bid for the White House. This interview occurred after the *American Spectator* broke the story of Clinton's highway patrol officers covering up his frequent trysts, including the one with Sally Purdue. She said that state troopers brought the Governor to her condominium at Andover Square about a dozen times, usually in nondescript police vehicles. They routinely stopped at a wooded area about 30 feet from her door. When he was ready to come out, he would signal by flicking her patio lights on and off. One time, he pulled up in the Governor's official Lincoln, an act Sally deemed to be careless and irresponsible. I believe this was just part of Clinton's in-your-face attitude, his moral arrogance, spitting in the eye of traditional morality. Does this all sound too familiar?

After she went to work at WGNU, there were at least two incidents of damage done to her jeep. Although there is no direct link to President Clinton or those close to him, she told of meeting with Democratic politico, Ron Tucker from Marion, Illinois, who said he was speaking on behalf of Democrats in high places. During their meeting at the Cheshire Inn, on August 19, 1992, Tucker promised her a job Sally estimated paying $60,000 a year. She was told that if she did not take the offer, then they knew that she went jogging by myself and couldn't guarantee what would happen to her pretty little legs. The "offer" really frightened her.

These words were overheard by her friend and Lindenwood co-worker, Denison Diel, whom Sally had stationed at the bar near her table. Diel later signed and filed an affidavit with the FBI, stating that he heard everything Sally claimed Tucker had said. Tucker later denied everything about his meeting with Sally. According to the British newspaper article, he shouted into his phone: *the woman is childish. You people are foolish. I don't know a thing about the Clinton thing.* His former employer at Marion Mining, John Newcomb, says he overheard Tucker talking about the subject in September of 1992 and confronted him about his call. Ron Tucker told him that somebody from the Democratic Party in St. Louis had asked him through a friend to get to this woman and get her to shut up. As a result of Sally's refusal of Tucker's offer, she lost her job at the admissions office at Lindenwood College. This was followed by threatening mail and phone calls. One particularly twisted letter stated, "I'll pray you have a head-on collision and end up in a coma; Marylyn Monroe got snuffed." Her name has been popping up in some major news articles, books and the tabloids as the Whitewater scandal threatens to dissolve the Clinton presidency. My entire relationship with her consisted of a weekly three-minute chat about Bill Clinton, Hillary and their Arkansas cronies like Web Hubbell.

Sally's slot was eventually filled by Betty Tannenbaum, who would never be mistaken for a beauty queen. Bright, energetic and highly aggressive, she made up in persistence what she might have lacked in physical charm. One of the things I miss most about Sally was that near the end of a show, when I was down to an empty board, I would usually have a minute or two to fill, I would describe what Sally was wearing. Sally had class and style and brought a sophisticated sense of color to the otherwise drab station. I would try my best to recreate the ambience from an episode of Lorreta Young, who used to enter her TV show like a whirling dervish. In contrast to Sally's style, Betty was a real warrior, belonging to one of the Missouri militias. She often dressed as if she were on maneuvers. I still attempted to capture the same kind of playful entry. Betty often played along, even unbuttoning three top buttons of her blouse before the engineer begged her to stop.

Another popular host, is Ray Yztania, a sixty-something veteran of twenty years in the United States Army, including four terms of service in Vietnam. Ray, known as "the babbling Basque" because of his Spanish Pyrenean heritage, brought a humorous, yet conservative perspective to the Culture War. Policemen, little old ladies in tennis shoes and veterans of any war, immediately took a shine to his folksy demeanor. A teacher at Meramec Community College, his background in history served him well during his tenure at the "GNU" and in the Cultural War trenches. It was Ray who coined the term "WGNU Ph.D." in reference to some of the know-it-alls who patronized his show.

Alan Anderson was on the station just over a year. He was probably the brightest of our contentious conservative talk show hosts. Alan would say and do some very intellectually challenging things. One day he told his listeners that he had seen the light and was switching to the liberal philosophy. This really upset me and Ray. He was merely attacking the absurdity of some of President Clinton's ideas and actions by being absurd himself. A brilliant stratagem! The next time I was on, I severely tongue-lashed him for his breech of faith. I waxed Shakespearean, lamenting how we three had been "a happy band of brothers."

Another conservative host is Dory Potts, a vivacious grandmother whose high pitched voice reminds me of Aunt Bea on the old *Andy Griffith Show.* Dory has been at the station as long as I have been and, uses her master's degree in History with great aplomb in fighting the good fight against the twin evils of ignorance and liberalism. She has a theatrical talent and has performed on the stage as such unique characters as Lillian Handlan Lemp, the Lavender Lady, Madame Louise Bourgeois Choteau, and Hetty Howland Robinson Green, known as "the Witch of Wall Street." Dory was a charter member of the *Exchange,* a discussion group I christened at our meeting place Blueberry Hill, in the University City loop, in the shadows of ultra-liberal, Washington University. Actually the *Exchange* was little more than a glorified coffee klatsch. We met there monthly to go over our shows and give each other aid and comfort amidst the Culture War that raged in American society. We also exchanged ideas and information on our callers. Some callers thought we were plotting some sort of pro-life conspiracy amid the stack of hamburgers and fries.

Another Christian soldier, who enlisted in the Culture War was Dr. Pat Coughlin, formerly a part-time college professor. She achieved a certain celebrity status by showing a seven-minute videotape of several aborted fetuses to her social work class at Washington University in 1993. This so piqued the consciences and sensibilities of some of her students that they complained to the administration and Dr. Coughlin's tenuous position at the university was eliminated shortly after. In answer to the protests from the left-leaning students that dominate this institution, Coughlin said, "if it's hard to watch, then maybe abortion shouldn't be allowed." In my book, Dr. Pat is a bonafide profile in courage in the Culture War with the battle scars to prove it.

On the other side of the ideological spectrum is Liz Brown. Another attorney, she got the break of her life when Onion Horton left the station. A weekly host, like me, she was summoned by Chuck Norman to fill the black liberal void created by Horton's departure. Far more intelligent and articulate than Onion, Liz jumped in with her mouth blazing, attacking conservatives and the Republicans Party with the full venom of her liberal bias. Describing herself as "living the life of a liberal and loving it," the corpulent daughter of an army soldier, foists her "I-dare-ya" attitude on her listening audience five mornings a week. By her own admission, she is liberal and powerless. In the true spirit of the liberal, she attacks black conservatives as doing a disservice to themselves by supporting the Republican philosophy. She says they should ask themselves, *Why am I affiliated with a party that is so hateful, so divisive, so elitist, so religiously wrong?* She also opines that black conservatives don't have any respect for themselves, any true concern for what they are saying and the impact of this kind of talk. Liz is very good at browbeating her people into staying down on the liberal plantation and perpetuating another generation of illegitimates, dependents, and illiterates. One of our sales people, knowing my support of the pro-life cause, solicited a series of ads from *Birthright,* the international helper of women in crisis pregnancies. Not to be outdone, Liz went out and got an ad from *Planned Parenthood.* Her brand of educated ignorance and prejudicial logic has created a strong following that got her voted the most popular talk show host in St. Louis by the left-wing *Riverfront Times* only a few months since she assumed full-time hours. It makes me wonder.

During my first few years on the air, I usually kept my show light and airy. However, around 1988 the nature of my calls changed more to the relevant issues of the day: abortion, racism, education, politics, multiculturalism, and other economic and social trends. During my tenure on the station, my callers and I have discussed an amazing variety of subjects. Less predictable subjects have included the cannibalistic tendencies of the Aztec Indians, America's bimodal crisis, the Tuskegee Institute syphilis experiments of the 1930s, Egyptology, as well as Tomas De Rorquemada of the Spanish Inquisition, Australian aborigines and Bo Derrick's anatomy. There is not one personal belief that I subscribe to that has not been challenged or vilified on the show. I spend at least three days a week preparing for all the possible avenues our callers can take. I have learned more doing this show than I did in six years of graduate study.

I have always had quick analytical skills and a glib wit but now I have an arsenal of different arguments and tactics to use on the radio. The mike has empowered me with a sense of social awareness and activism I would never have dreamed. In many ways, the *Partyline* has become my bloody pulpit. The debate over a woman's right to choose and those of her baby's right to life has been at the center of some of my most strident exchanges on the air. It is not something I relish doing but some subjects are not debatable. I don't think anyone can honestly argue the relative merits of forcible rape, drunk driving or mass murder. Sometimes the battle becomes very heated as emotions run high in this bitter debate.

Though some of my calls can get a little contentious, there have been few if any threats. One of my colleagues was accosted outside the station on a couple of occasions. The only known case of a talk show host being murdered was the assassination of talk-jock, Alan Berg in Denver, Colorado in 1986. There was a play, followed by a movie, entitled *Talk Radio,* loosely based on his life. My favorite scene revolves around a soliloquy from the protagonist that I believe should be required reading for all radio talk show hosts. I opened a show with a taped copy of his narration but nobody seemed to get or understand it:

> I don't give a damn about you or the world! That's the truth.
> Who the hell are you? You, the audience are on me like a pack
> of wolves because you can't stand facing what you are and what
> you've made. Yes, the world is a terrible place! Yes, cancer and
> garbage disposals will get you! Yes, a war is coming! Yes, the
> world is shot to hell and everything is screwed up and you like
> it that way. You're fascinated by gory details. You're mesmerized
> by your own fear. You revel in floods, car accidents. . . .
> unstoppable diseases. You're happiest when others are in pain.
> That's where I come in isn't it? I'm here to lead you by the hand
> through the dark forests of your hatred, anger and humiliation.
> I'm providing a public service . . . You're so scared . . . like a little
> child under the covers, afraid of the bogey man. But you can't
> live without him—your fears. Your lives have become your en-
> tertainment.
>
> Next month millions of people will be listening to this show and
> you will have nothing to talk about. Marvelous technology is at
> our disposal and instead of reaching up to new heights, you are
> trying to see how far down we can go. . . . How deep in the muck
> we can immerse ourselves. What do you want to talk about?
> Baseball scores, your pet, orgasms? You're pathetic! I despise
> each and everyone of you! You have nothing! Absolutely noth-
> ing. No brains, no power, no future, no hope, no God! The only
> thing you believe in is me! Where are you if you don't have me?
> I'm not afraid! See! I come in here every night. I make my case!
> I make my point! I say what I believe in! I tell you what you are.
> I have to I have no choice. You frighten me! I come in here every
> night. I tear into you! I abuse you! I insult you! What's wrong
> with you? You just keep talking. You just keep coming back for
> more. Why do you keep calling? I don't want to hear any more!
> Stop calling! Go away! You're a bunch of yellow-bellied, spine-
> less, bigoted, quivering, drunken, insomniac, paranoid, disgust-
> ing, perverted, voyeuristic, little obscene phone callers. Well, to
> hell with you! I don't need your fear and stupidity! You don't get
> it. It's wasted on you. Pearls before swine. If one person out there
> has any idea what I'm talking about . . . (Exhausted, Barry takes
> more calls).

I have never fantasized that I was at all like Barry Champlain but his
commentary was an indictment of human nature and the people who used
his medium to mitigate and escape their petty lives. Champlain, more than
any nonfiction interpreter, realized how powerful talk radio could be, yet at
the same time, how frustrating it was when his listeners did not understand

the depth and the intended wisdom of his ideas and his social critiques. Like so many talk show hosts, myself included, Barry recognized the vital importance of his message and falsely assumed that the listening audience and his callers would quickly adopt his way of thinking. I often feel the same way on WGNU. I have good and sometimes very deep insights on the forces threatening the soul and spirit of the country. I complain about the perverse effects of unfettered liberalism, the scandals of the Clinton administration and how they seem to be taking us down the road to perdition, if not eventual destruction.

Watching *Talk Radio* for the third time, I realized how much Barry's callers remind me of my own on WGNU. Although I like to think I am the star of the show, our callers are often the main attraction. The raw combination of zanies and characters who call us are hard to fathom. Whether they are aware of it or not, in their own small way they are foot soldiers, battling in the cultural war of ideas as we all, left and right, struggle to define what is right and proper for the American people. Talk shows, such as mine on WGNU, are the populist forum of the late twentieth century. We do not screen callers, so you really never know who is on the other side of the mike. I have had to respond to barking dogs, flushing toilets and dead air. It does not bother me to be taunted, as it is par for the course. You develop a resiliency and an attitude of levity toward that type of harassment, which I believe adds to the entertainment value of the show. I have a sense of humor that I wear like a bullet-proof vest!

Most, but not all, of our callers identify themselves by their "handles" as they used to call people's pseudonyms when CB radios were in vogue. I love the idea of a pseudonym because it personalizes what is mostly an impersonal medium. It also emboldens the callers to speak their minds more acutely. I did have a hand in naming one of the regulars on the station. He had an arrogant, whiny sort of air. He called me regularly for years always on the attack for what I or some of my good callers had to say. Someone called him "Mr. Negativity." I never thought that fit his attitude. He was highly intelligent and very articulate, though not the kind of guy I would like to have a beer or two with after the show. We debated on abortion many mornings. He said that my callers and I were stupid. He implied that my IQ was lower than most inanimate objects. So when I threw the idea back into his court, he said that his IQ was better than average, which is 100. So I started calling him "Mr. 101," which is better than average but also signifies the basic instructional college course. It fit him perfectly because even though he was bright, his ideas often betrayed a superficial knowledge of a subject. He has not called me in a long time and I miss the heated banter.

We had the token white racist in a caller named *Dutch* from the South side. Dutch was irascible. He did not like black people presumably because all he did was read from the *Post-Dispatch* about the high incidence of crime in the black neighborhoods. Many of our black callers hated him. There were few tears from them when he died, reportedly a suicide victim.

Someone who could really sing was one of my favorite callers, "Diamond Lil." Lil has been calling the station for many years and feels a certain proprietary right over the station and its many hosts, which she exercises on occasion. She has a marvelous singing voice, evidence of her profession many years ago in the Missouri Bootheel. I let her sing on my show, partly as a divergence from the verbal heat of the hour and partly because she expects it. Many listeners enjoy her singing, though the engineer often starts howling like a dog. I guess she has sung about 75 songs total for me, most of them about a moon over some place. I once said that she was singing *acappella,* which I said meant that she did not have any clothes on. That made her day!

Another favorite of mine, is "Veronica," whom I call "Ronnie," because that's what she likes. She is a modest, devoutly religious Catholic, with a nasal twang to her voice that makes it appear as if she has trouble breathing. She has a good heart and is not afraid to speak out, though the verbal cruelty of some of the other callers often hurts her feelings. She has sent me and my family several prayer cards and yearly devotions to the Sacred Heart. She is always a joy to talk to.

Then there is a sweet-sounding woman from West County, a devoutly pro-life nurse, who takes a lot of heat from the left-wing busybodies. She calls herself, "Nurse Ratched," after the Ken Kesey character in *One Flew Over the Cuckoos' Nest.*

"The Great Carbudah" nearly defies description. He is an eccentric black man in his sixties, who quotes the Bible the way Bill Clinton quotes the latest polls. He says angels speak to him and interprets all the natural and man-made disasters we have been having as part of God's divine reparations for the sins of mankind. I think he has been married a few times, holds a steady job and is despised by many of our black callers. I find him very intelligent and perceptive, though he does not have a very good command of the English language. He is, however, a great storyteller. I met the *Great One* at the annual Christmas Party years ago. He is a cultural warrior who really wears his own uniform. He cuts a dashing figure in his dark beret, blue Eisenhower jacket with gold epaulets. With his shaven head, he looked just like Lou Gossett in the movie *An Officer and a Gentleman.*

Probably no caller has made my day, more often than "Minister Mike." He was just Mike, an unemployed Mike who often reminded me of Clark Griswold's luckless cousin, Eddie, until a few years ago when he got religion. Like the feckless Eddie, Mike has been holding out for a managerial position. Mike was upset with the economic system that did not have a high-paying job for a man of his talents with a tenth grade education. Though his knowledge of economics is not enough to fill a thimble, he is ardently pro-life and can wax poetic with a simple wisdom on the subject. He also reminds me of an unsuccessful Forrest Gump. Mike was a Democrat but was willing to dump his party in favor of the unborn. He believed in the minimum wage and believed government should guarantee everyone $50,000 a year. Nice work if you can get it. People would call up to criticize his religious fervor, implying he got his degree from one of the mail-order catalogues. He once called back to try to prove he was not stupid as a previous caller had stated. He argued that some people had gotten their degrees in ministry from colleges and such, but they were not real ministers because they were not close to Jesus Christ. He said that God had spoken to him and that his ministry was between God and himself. I said that was all well and good except I thought there were probably thousands of available young women who had heard a similar refrain: *in the eyes of God we are really married,* at some sleazy motel.

"The White Devil" is a caller who has aptly christened himself. His philosophy lies somewhere between that of Mark Furhman and Randy Weaver. He is a patriot of the kind who would join a militia. He is ready for war with any angry blacks who attempt to limit his freedom or invade his neighborhood. He is my worst nightmare of where the racial animus could lead before too long. I agree with the honesty of much of what he says yet I am uncomfortable in that agreement. I am on a quest to find the truth of what these major issues are all about and it disturbs me when a man so quick to proclaim his right to violent retaliation holds some of the same truths I hold. I get along with him but wince every time he says something inflammatory that might indict me by association from some of my more moderate black callers. He is a work of art who has sent me letters, newspapers, and pamphlets, detailing many of his ideas. I find myself in agreement with him in opposition to certain issues, such as abortion, affirmative action and gay advocacy. But our mutual agreement leaves with me with an uncanny discomfort, analogous to the United States' alliance with the Soviet Union during World War II.

"The Pilgrim Lady," is a seventy-something intelligent women, who spends most days immersed in studying and reading world and local news, not to mention calling our station every day. Her ideas and beliefs are pretty much mainstream and I always get a kick out of her keen sense of fairness and extreme good humor. All senior citizens should be as sharp and as dignified as she is.

"Bob the Economist" is one of the brightest callers we have ever had as a regular on our station. He has been on as long as I have been working at WGNU. He has quizzed me and nailed me on a couple baseball trivia questions. Well read, with a tendency to lean to the liberal point of view, Bob presses his arguments with statistics gleaned from *Fortune Magazine* and several trips to the local library. I have learned much about economics from my interviews with him.

I have had some of my greatest philosophical and ideological battles with the caller known as "the Roosevelt Man." Though some of our debates have been heated, argumentative, and nearly hostile, I have always enjoyed the man and respect his devotion to the *Great White Father,* Franklin

Roosevelt. A pro-choice Catholic, I believe he has made it a point, if not an obsession, to demonstrate that I am just one of those cold-hearted, uncaring, right-wing conservative Catholics whose personal life is a sham and needs to be saved by the social gospel proponents he recognizes in the modern church. He is easy to tweak and many of other callers often complain about his several calls each day to the station. He is one of those special people who make WGNU what it really is.

One of the strangest, and sometimes, scariest callers is the man who calls himself presumptively, the "Prophet." He's an indignant black man with a messianic complex who begins each caller sermon by proclaiming from 1 John 4:4 "Greater is He who is in me than he who is in the world." He often condemned President Reagan as the anti-Christ not only because of his policies but because his name numerically represents the devil—666. Each word in Reagan's name does contain six letters: Ronald Wilson Reagan. He also felt that his people were the authentic Jews, the lost tribe of Israel because in the Bible the descendants of Ham were described as dark. Jews in this country and in Israel are all impostors and should be eliminated.

"The Red Man," was one of my most enjoyable callers. I doubt if he were a real Indian. He seemed to parody the multicultural movement and had a good time doing it. He provided me with my greatest unrehearsed moment in radio. Sometimes I walk the fine line between the risque and good taste, usually to get a laugh. I had been talking about the 1990 census which disappeared from my mail after our annual spring trip to spring training to see the St. Louis Cardinals in St. Petersburg. I was lamenting about not getting a replacement. He called in to concur, stating that they would send a young lady out to my house to interview me, as they had done to him. Married a couple times and keeping time with a woman, he called himself "the Red Man," and had always considered himself a sort of Lothario, a modern day lady's man. He said the young woman had asked him several personal questions, such as how many sexual experiences he'd had. His answer to this unbelievable question was, "Of course I have had many!" I countered with my own question, "Were you alone at the time?"

"Christian Conservative Bob from Clayton," an overly-long name to say, is an astute and knowledgeable caller who seem to have a deeply embedded prejudice against his own Catholic Church. I also like "Gertie," the German lady who survived the horrible Dresden bombing in 1945, in which 125,000 German men, women and children were incinerated. It is believed that she had a couple of brothers who were in the SS. To say the least, she has taken some profound heat over the years she has been calling. I have spent some fascinating moments with the likes of *Darth Vader*, the *Babysitter*, *Florence Nightingale*, and the *Insurance Lady*. As the Bible should have said, many call but few are chosen!

I have had some other great regulars. Some of them were so good at fighting the Culture War and stirring up interest in current topics that Chuck hired them to be hosts just like me. One such fellow was a man who aptly calls himself the "Couch Potato." He sent us an impressive resume, including the plays he had written. Since being on the air, he has become one of the more controversial hosts. There was a fellow named "Mike Square," a black Realtor who coaxed me to put up or shut up about possible bloodshed in South Africa after the fall of the white government there a few years ago. I bet him lunch there would be bloodshed within a year and that was one bet I was more than glad to pay off.

Not all my callers have been as enjoyable as these. Cultural War issues do stir the emotions and some of our verbal skirmishes have gotten nasty. Some of the most dispirited and cantankerous callers include "Aunt Jemamiah," the "St. Charles Lady," and the "Prisoner of Love," an odd black man, obsessed with pedophilia and the Catholic priesthood. Probably the most formidable caller I have ever had to battle with was a very bright, though hostile man who attacked every aspect of my political and spiritual credo. He did not have a self-proclaimed handle. Somebody called him "the liberal," though agnostic or atheist would probably have suited him better. He came up with ingenious defense for free and unlimited abortion that sent me to the book shelves more than once. I enjoyed sparring with him though I do admit our struggles usually turned up the room temperature. At best, I rated a draw with him. He taught me a lot and I wish he would call back. Another caller of similar persuasion provided me with a fascinating conundrum. He stated that according to my pro-life belief, male masturbation would be an abortion activity because the ejaculated sperm was alive and therefore human. Only on WGNU can you get such callers!

It is true that many of our regular callers would not be allowed to say what they say on our station anywhere else in St. Louis. Many, such as "Donna from Afton," have been banned from certain segments on KMOX . She's an intelligent woman whom I have heard on the *Larry King Live* show. We have debated the relative merits of NAFTA and voting for Bob Dole. That makes WGNU a paragon of the First Amendment.

Callers' reasons for calling are as varied as reasons not to vote for Bill Clinton. Some like to hear the sound of their own voices, to test the waters of their own ideas, to inform the public of the truth of their ideas and/or the fallacy of those of others—or to just chew the fat with the host. We have callers who like to vent their spleen, stand up for a principle, tear down those of others, point out the hypocrisy or error of a statement, compliment others for their ideas or their courage or just reach out and touch somebody—that inexorable need for human contact which is especially acute in some of our elderly shut-in listeners. Whatever the reason, I just hope they keep calling.

My sentiments about WGNU are akin to those of Daniel Webster's feelings for Dartmouth College. In the Dartmouth College case he was arguing, Webster reverentially intoned that Dartmouth was a small school but there are those of us who love it. I feel the same about WGNU.

4 / Rush Limbaugh
A Tarnished American Icon

> When a Conservative complains about too much government, it is called hate. When a liberal complains, it is called commentary.
>
> —Neal Boortz, radio talk show host,
> in the *New York Times*, 30 April 1995

My colleague at WGNU, Alan Anderson, was the first person who told me about Rush Limbaugh. Alan had borrowed some of Rush's tactics, such as dealing with the absurd by being absurd, leading me to believe that he was more clever than he really was. It only took a few short weeks of listening to Rush before I realized that Rush Limbaugh was something special in the Culture War. He had a battle front that stretched across the country and an arsenal of verbal weapons that often sent the forces of liberalism scurrying for the cover of illogic and the *ad hominem* defense.

The name *Rush Limbaugh* immediately conjures up an emotive response in most people. This is difficult to imagine that anyone has not formed some opinion of this portly man from Cape Girardeau, Missouri, just 120 miles south of St. Louis. You can not turn on the television, the radio, pick up a news magazine, or read a newspaper without running across something he has said or what others have said about him. The *Letters to the Editor* column often overflows with ardent opinions, both pro and con, of this bombastic man with the deep conviction and the stentorian vocal cords. He is a walking corporation. His business and intellectual pursuits include two best-selling books, a popular newsletter, a syndicated TV show, his daily radio show and now a line of loud and colorful designer ties that blow his conservative cover off.

Radio stands out as the medium through which Rush has made his greatest impact. It is an understatement to say that radio has great power and influence. Many commentators, including a number of presidents, have realized the influence that the medium has held for the articulate and the clever. From the avuncular and warm *Fireside Chats*, of Franklin Roosevelt, to the pessimistic musings of Jimmy Carter, through the pleading of Bill Clinton, our presidents have used the radio in an attempt to convince the American people of the relative importance of their policies. In the critical period prior to America's involvement in World War II, "the Radio Priest," Father Charles Coughlin, tried to use the power of the air waves to prevent Roosevelt's political agenda from leading the country down the road to serfdom. It is into this long history that Rush Limbaugh began introducing his own brand of political and social wisdom.

As the media giants, such as Rupert Murdock, consolidate newspapers with TV stations, leading to an informational oligarchy on the news and information, institutions, talk radio will eventually emerge as the sole arbiter of the rectitude of world and national issues. Rush Limbaugh serves a vital public service because he is the other side. Without his daily monologues and philosophical lectures, the public would be forced to depend on the Dan Rathers, the Connie Chungs, the Tom Brokaws or the Peter Jennings, even Larry King, for their understanding of world events. In eight short years on the national scene, Rush Limbaugh has achieved the status of an American icon.

For two years I refused to listen to him. I watched his TV show and read his books but I would not listen to him. This was not out of disdain for his views, 99% of which I agree with, but because I toiled under the delusion that I was funnier than he. Rush is on during one of my two hours on Wednesdays (10 A.M. to 12:00 P.M.). I wish he'd play golf or go fishing when I'm on the air. When I did start listening, however I quickly became addicted. The man is not only intelligent, articulate and informed, he's much more charitable to those who disagree with him than I am. You will find none of the personal attacks that characterize the leftist airwaves in his program. He deals strictly with the relative merits of the issues. Commentators like Rush Limbaugh, who spent half his life in sterile jobs in radio, provide the balance and fairness that a news oligarchy will ultimately drive away. Limbaugh finally made the big time in 1988 when his show became nationally syndicated. Since then he has gone from a humorous entertainer with some serious view points to a serious commentator who occasionally deviates into comic ribaldry. There is a common misconception that most hosts lean to the conservative side of the political spectrum. In truth, there are more liberals in the field than there are conservatives. The *Times Mirror Center for People and the Press* found that 39% of talk show hosts voted for Bill Clinton in 1992, while only 23% voted for Bush. Ross Perot had 18% of the survey vote. Conservative talk show hosts dominate the air waves because of their inordinate and unusual sense of humor. That is what really gave Rush Limbaugh his early success. Limbaugh is a born satirist, a latter-day Jonathan Swift who often hits the exposed nerve with his humor. I would argue that liberal hosts are not as popular because they have to defend the status quo or are mere apologists for the liberal philosophy which is at ground zero in the new American Culture War. Liberals can't stand this intrusion of biting satire into their cultural hegemony. It shows in their having to resort to personal attacks to engender any response. CNN's Peter

Arnett has called Limbaugh a "cretinous liar." If these conservatives and their dim-witted callers ever got real power, left-wing poet Allen Ginsberg warns, there would be concentration camps and mass death. After many years of listening to Limbaugh, I am convinced that he is also a cultural warrior. I seriously doubt he would concur with this appellation but within the context of the bitter public debate on national politics, abortion, the environment, and economic issues, Rush's perspective and the impact of his thought consistently fits in perfectly with the battle at hand.

Limbaugh was born on 12 January 1951. He was reared in Cape Girardeau, Missouri, a small city on the Mississippi that offers all the best and worst features of a college town. Rush now lives and works in the largest metropolis in the country, New York City, with its millions of hustling and harried citizens, but he is still basically a small town boy at heart. His voice sometimes betrays a sense of disbelief, as if he were saying to himself, *How can this be happening to me, a man from tiny Cape Girardeau?*

Rush's father, Rush Hudson Limbaugh, Jr. was a fighter pilot in World War II and served as a lawyer in Cape for many years until his death in 1990. His grandfather, who was born in 1891, was the oldest practicing attorney in the country until his death in April of 1996 at the age of a 104. To understand Rush's deep-seated conservatism, it is necessary to understand his close intellectual and familial roots with these two men. The male Limbaughs fostered a love of ideas in Rush, especially political ideas. Rush's dad was an ardent Republican in a town that, until the coming of George McGovern in 1972, was historically Democratic. The basis of his political education took place at meal time. They debated political issues incessantly for hours, the way most men talk about sports today. The conversations were lively, inspiring and at times contentious. The dinner table was the university that served Rush more than anything he would learn in his thirteen years of formal education. Here, Rush discovered how to question and, more importantly, how to listen. Politics was a passion that he kept hidden through most of his early years as a deejay in Pittsburgh and Kansas City. Only when he could not keep his ideas bottled up did he get himself into trouble with some local women's group and, eventually, the station management.

At the basis of Rush's personal philosophy is an inspiring belief in what has been trivialized by the term "family values." The give and take of family life, with its internal network of mutual concern, encouragement, and criticism motivated him to achieve success in this life. Rush also has an endearing belief in a personal God, though he seldom reveals any deep or abiding theological views on his shows. A patriot at heart, he believes that America is God's chosen country and consequently it has a moral and social obligation to lead the world by example, not economic or political domination. Rush believes in a rugged individualism, though not the kind of Neo-Darwinist thinking, intent on having the poor and the elderly destroy themselves leaving more of the country's material benefits for the survivors. In reality, Limbaugh exudes more compassion for the truly downtrodden and those who can not honestly help themselves than either Democratic President Bill Clinton or Minority Leader Dick Gephardt. Just check the record.

When it comes to lazy, good-for-nothing whiners who would rather stick their hand out for some government entitlement than do an honest day of work, Limbaugh takes no prisoners. He is literally a self-made man who is extremely proud of his accomplishments. His thoughtful derision of the idle rich who rely on trust funds or clip coupons, rather than scaling the ladder of success, as he had to do, betrays a hint of the class envy argument that he often decries in his political debates. This liberal tendency often clouds his ability to recognize the philanthropic and volunteerism that characterize the lives of many rich people.

Rush has gotten himself into trouble with such gimmicks as "caller abortions." When he was tired of a particular caller he would abort the call, accompanied by a horrible vacuum sound not unlike the suction machine that tears an unborn child literally limb from limb in the abortion procedure. While this is a macabre idea, the horror is that real abortions are immensely more gross and should be the focal point of the listener's real objection. Rush is singled out for being insensitive yet what he really is doing is reminding his listeners where the real horror lies. One of the secrets to his great success and the reason why Rush is often misunderstood is that he treats absurdity by being absurd. It takes a listener a minimum of six to ten weeks of listening to be alert for all the nuances that dominate and highlight his three hours of commentary every day.

Another source of criticism is Limbaugh's use of the term *Feminazi* to refer to the hard corps element in the *Women's Movement* who have taken the term "battle of the sexes" literally. They champion the idea that all men are rapists and marriage is slavery. Many of these women, such as First Lady Hillary Clinton, would stop at nothing to empower themselves so that they could be in control of many of the social institutions. By *Feminazi*, Rush originally had in mind the denizens of the National Organization of Women (Rush prefers calling them the National Association of Gals). In recent years, he has distanced himself from this biting term, limiting his inclusion to about twenty woman who think abortion is the answer to all their problems.

A personal experience will better illustrate what a *Feminazi* really is. I had attended an abortion debate at one of the local colleges a few years ago. After it was over, I stood outside the lecture hall, continuing the discussion with a few friends. One of the women in our group started talking about how men were left-brain and women were right-brain. Though I had no idea what she was talking about, I had to get my two cents in by stopping her in mid-sentence to interject, "Before you go any further, Laurie, you have to prove to me that women have a brain!" Now I did not know Laurie that well, but I felt she knew enough about me and my corny sense of humor through the pro-life movement, and would realize I was kidding her. Before she could even respond, some older woman in the foreground barked: *"That's not funny!"* We were all startled by the interruption. In my quick apologetic mode, I replied sheepishly, "It was just a joke, lady."

"It's still not funny!" she rejoined. Her harsh rejoinder agitated me.

I questioned, "Who invited you into this private conversation? What are you, the P.C. police?" I must have struck one of her feminist nerves. As she strutted by us in a huff, she gave me a broadside of *Feminazi* fire power,

"The trouble with you, is that your brains are in your penis!"

My riposte was, "So are yours!" A good but indelicate comeback that I think ended the skirmish. I think Rush would have been proud of me.

Rush inspired a great deal of rancor, some of it warranted, for saying that he liked the *Women's Movement*, especially when walking behind it. Sexist? Not really! Funny? Yes! Limbaugh proves time and time again that many of these leftist groups are so obsessed with their power that they are incapable of laughing at themselves. These criticisms are just distractions to the real heart and soul of Limbaugh's radio and TV shows which is politics: pure and simple, unadulterated American politics. Rush has made a career of attacking the president's positions. Many of his attacks have centered on the president personally and they have been the nexus of much of the vitriolic attacks Limbaugh has suffered in turn, from the media. In truth, never have we had a president who carried so many scandals into the White House. Certainly other presidents, including Republican Warren G. Harding and Democrat John F. Kennedy had sordid pasts filled with sexual misdeeds. But those were mostly in simpler times, when a president's private life was not subject to open discussion. The presidency of Bill Clinton has brought with it the scandalous baggage of adultery, influence peddling and abuse of government power. If Clinton had been a Republican, he would have been dismissed by the media as quickly as it took to say *John Tower* but the Democratic Party was so desperate to regain the White House after twelve long years without the presidency that their many willing accomplices in the media deemed that Clinton's character (or lack of character) should not be an issue. No idea could be farther from the truth. Character has everything to do with one empowered with life and death authority over 280 million Americans. Clinton's presidency was near dissolution from the very beginning as everything he did, or attempted to do, smacked of petty political cronyism. Yet scandal after scandal was dismissed by the media. Had they done their job properly on Whitewater, the country would not have needed someone like Rush Limbaugh.

While it is the administration of Bill Clinton that has borne the jabs and barbs of Rush's rapier wit contrary to the vast number of his detractors, Rush's main focus is not the bumbling and verbal deceptions of President Bill Clinton. While Limbaugh is at his creative best when parodying the Clintons and their erratic and obtuse minions, such as Joycelyn Elders, Robert Reich and David Bonior, Rush does not hate Clinton. He has backed Clinton when he can, as he did with NAFTA, GATT and, in 1995, his initial reaction to the Oklahoma City bombing. The real focus of Rush's line of fire is liberalism, more accurately, socialism. Like so many conservatives of his generation who fear the ever-increasing encroachment of government into their personal lives, Rush serves as a standard-bearer to dispute liberals, revealing the many lies they tell in the name of openness and diversity.

It is obvious that Rush is a Republican. Many of them have catered to him. After the tremendous and largely unanticipated Republican victory in November of 1994, the freshman class of the 104th Congress, made him an honorary member. George Bush was one of the first guests he had on the air. William Bennett, and Speaker Newt Gingrich have called in often. *B-1 Bomber* Bob Dornan, a conservative representative from California, who suffered defeat in the 1996 election, has even substituted as host. You will not find Dick Gephardt or Ted Kennedy getting any air time on Rush's show. Rightfully so, because they get more media coverage then they really deserve in traditional media outlets.

Limbaugh's one hero, other than his dad and his grandfather is Ronald Reagan. Reagan is at the core of his conservative belief and with that, at the heart of his enlistment in the Culture War. He brims with emotion and respect whenever he mentions the former president's name. One of the constant themes of his program is a defense of the 1980s, which has been unfairly and erroneously characterized by leftist demagogues as the decade of greed and corruption. Rush also has a strong sense of the rural populist in him. During a radio program on 22 November 1996, Rush reiterated much of his philosophy as it relates to the people and his intense belief in their ability to do the right thing. He said:

> It is the power of the people that bring about changes . . . The election in 1994 was not a fluke or a fad. The reason I am optimist is because I think that there are millions of people like you who believe in the right thing. . . . We never see or read what we feel and believe in the media. Go to the movies, read books, listen to trash on TV and radio. People think that nobody speaks for the people. . . . Look what is happening. . . . (Like something out an Ayn Rand novel.) My belief in the people and their good instincts is what energizes me every day. I believe that the people will not be intimidated into silence. It increases the odds that the necessary changes that are necessary. I have high hopes for the kids in the future. Many complain about the lack of self-discipline have. . . . Most people raise their children with discipline and denial. Our government doesn't. It raises us with the notion that there will be a social Utopia but there never will be.

Limbaugh is not without faults. Most people, when they first start listening to him, are turned off by his bombastic approach to the issues of the day. He starts by referring to his talent "on loan from God," and he often thwarts liberals with one half his brain tied behind his back. He usually says this in a deep baritone voice that lets you know he is employing hyperbole. However that does not mean there is not some truth to what he says. When one analyzes the first statement about his talent, it is apparent that it is essentially a very religious idea. Everything we have comes from God, who is merely lending it to us. This is another example of Rush's Bible Belt roots coming to the surface. One of his favorite lines is "If you can do it, it ain't braggin'!" Though he erroneously attributes this Dizzy Dean bit of braggadocio to Babe Ruth or Yogi Berra, he correctly underscores the validity of Dean's wisdom.

In his book *Cease Fire*, evangelical author Tom Sine erroneously attributes agreement and approval that characterize most of Limbaugh's callers (the so-called dittoheads), as their approval of his doing their thinking for them. When most people who like Rush do so because he voices what they have already said or thought in their own homes, or at the office. As Limbaugh modestly puts it, "I validate your thinking."

Rush's persistent attack on liberals and their agenda of programs and cultural changes has provoked a series of retaliatory strikes that have attempted to quell the seriousness and accuracy of his thinking by demonizing the messenger and ignoring the message. In his seminal book, *Not Without Honor*, history professor and my Holy Cross classmate, Richard Gid Powers, explained the historical analogy of the *Brown Scare*, that linked critics of communists in America, like Senator Joseph McCarthy, with the fascist ideas emanating out of Nazi Germany. This is a scurrilous tactic that liberals, such as New York Representative Charles Rangel, have become quite proficient.

Next to Adolf Hitler, I do not know anyone more vilified in my lifetime, except maybe Ollie North or bedeviled Reds owner Marge Schott. William F. Buckley and his brother-in-law, Brent Bozell wrote a book, aptly titled, *McCarthy and His Enemies in 1954*. I believe a similar book could be written about Limbaugh and his gaggle of strident and angry enemies. Rush's detractors seize upon every syllable they can twist against him. In 1994, a group know as FAIR published a report alleging 43 errors he had made over the course of his career. Even if these accusations were correct, that is not a high percentage of error, given the fact that Limbaugh is on the air 15 hours a week on radio, and 2½ hours on television. If FAIR were really fair they would apply the same scrutiny to the talking heads on the network news.

In the fall of 1994, Rush published his own White Paper, which effectively treated and dismissed, each and every charge FAIR had to make with one exception. Rush attributed a quote on the separation of church and state to James Madison in his first book, *The Way Things Ought To Be*. Investigation revealed that this quote, which had been attributed to several sources since

1934 was actually said by a Bishop James Madison. A regrettable error, yes, but certainly not of the magnitude made in the mainstream media each day.

Most of the personal attacks on Rush are of the garden variety *ad hominem*. His weight is a constant source of mockery. Rush is a heavy man and has at times, been obese. He likes to eat, has imbibed in vintage alcoholic beverages and smoked Churchillian-size cigars, personal habits all that make him a constant target of the self-appointed custodians of our personal health. On his television show, when he sometimes moves swiftly from one side of the studio to another, he reminds me of the late Jackie Gleason, requesting a little traveling music.

Other critics assume a more malevolent attitude. Richard Byrne, in his weekly media column in the *St. Louis Riverfront Times*, has called Limbaugh "the demagogue of the nineties," slanderously comparing him with Father Joseph Coughlin, the radical radio priest of the thirties, whose views bordered on Anti-Semitism. In another vitriolic column, Byrne assigned him to a place in hell along with eight other conservatives and Ollie North, whom he despised.

The flaky Molly Ivins, who has had her own problems with the truth, called Rush a "lyin' bully," in an article for the left-wing rag, *Mother Jones*. Her short article merely rehashed the FAIR accusations without any new or analytical input on her part. In the same May/June issue of *Mother Jones*, Stephen Talbot, the producer of a PBS documentary on Limbaugh entitled *Rush Limbaugh's America* also put in his two cents worth about the "Wizard of Ooze." I am truly amazed at the selective sensibilities of liberals who will only direct their innate feelings of compassion and concern for people who agree with them or are in a need of their custodial help.

Talbot, who spent six months working on his special, included the perfunctory comparisons to Coughlin and even the shrill Morton Downey Jr. While it has the standard liberal bias, there are some interesting observations in the article. The article was related to a 1994 *Times-Mirror* survey that divided the right-wing electorate into three main groups: libertarians, moralists and entrepreneurs. Rush Limbaugh appeals to all three of these groups. According to their pollster, Andrew Kohut, the typical Limbaugh listener is a white male, suburbanite, conservative, with a better-than-average job, but not really a great job. Anyone familiar with the writings of Marx, Engels and Lenin, know that the middle class is the intended target of most socialist programs and tax policies. It is the harried middle class which have borne the brunt of fifty years of liberalism. It is not surprising that they should make up the vast identifiable majority of his listeners. Talbot adds that Limbaugh's fans are not country club Republicans. They are K-mart conservatives who consider Rush one of them, even if he did make $25 million over the past two years.

Anne Keefe, a former local radio personality and a liberal in her own right, compared Rush Limbaugh to another local conservative, Phyllis Schlafly.

I think he is very smart and I think he will say things that he will
deny later . . . I think he says not what he believes but what he
thinks you want to hear. I think Rush Limbaugh is dangerous.
I think much of what he says in a very offhand way, his feminazi (sic) remarks, are not only mean-spirited but I think they
give permission to mean-spirited people to follow his path . . .

Keefe is obviously unfamiliar with Rush, even though he broadcasts on
her former station, KMOX, and is blinded by her own left knee-jerk reaction to his popular success.

Because of his outspoken opinion, his extreme financial success and his
antagonism to the left of the political spectrum, it has become a money-
making venture to attack Rush Limbaugh. Bashing Limbaugh has turned
into a highly lucrative cottage industry. At the height of his popularity,
several critics have surfaced to attempt to knock him off his high economic
perch. The most puerile is Brian Keliher who publishes a newsletter named
The Flush Rush Quarterly. The title alone immediately defines the level and
inspiration for most of its commentary. He also has a book out under the
same title which labels Limbaugh as "the most dangerous man in America."
To liberals, that is probably a fair assessment, because anyone proclaiming
the truth exposes the great liberal lie and would be a threat to their dominance and control of America's culture.

Charles Kelly has a book entitled, *The Great Limbaugh Con.* It is the
work of an economic scholar that attempts to dissolve the daily Limbaugh
gasbag with the hard facts about the corporate powerbrokers he is fronting
for and the future direction who a progressive American democracy can
take. The personal vindictiveness of this book clearly indicates that the
author's personal prejudice against Limbaugh in particular and conservative
ideas, in general, swiftly relegates Kelly's book to the trash bin of useless
commentary. Ray Perkins, Jr., another college professor, attempts to demonstrate that Limbaugh is not the most clear-thinking media personality he
pretends to be. Many of Limbaugh's comments are taken out of context.
Added to that, the stress of thinking while speaking on an unlimited number of topics and without writers or a teleprompter, while it does not excuse
a talk show host's irresponsibility, does open a corridor for some slight,
acceptable variance from truth and accuracy. I would like to see Perkins
apply the same high intellectual standards to any liberal media celebrity,
such as Phil Donohue, Larry King, Brian Gumbel, Tom Brokaw and Ted
Koppell. They would all pale by comparison with Limbaugh's ease of deliv-
ery, depth of information and spontaneity of thought. Any public speaker
would.

Criticism of Limbaugh has even found a stage in a theatrical production lampooning Limbaugh. Actor Charlie Varon debuted in March of
1995 at the *Second Stage Theater* off Broadway in a one-man "mockumentary"
entitled *Rush Limbaugh in Night School.* The play, which Varon also wrote,

is more than a spoof. Varon demonizes him as a most-favored villain in many liberal homes. He describes the play as satirical but it borders on the lunatic fringe element that is fast becoming mainstream in the so-called performing arts. I got the feeling that his play was a juvenile attempt to garner some negative publicity for the man he despises so much. The plot is a unique brand of imaginary fantasy that only a liberal could have produced. Rush is taking Spanish classes at the *New School for Social Research* in Greenwich Village, so that he can reach a multicultural audience. (I guess Varon never heard of Berlitz). While there, he falls in love with a feminist, Nina, who had been a member of the sixties' radical group, the Weathermen. To increase his audience, Limbaugh agrees to play Othello in a Shakespeare-in-the-Park production, with Garrison Keillor as Iago, Cokie Roberts as Desdemona and Jackie Mason as Roderigo. From there the plot becomes unfathomable. The FBI move in to arrest Nina; feminists demonstrate against domestic violence; fallout from the end of the OJ trial; a gay performance artist prepares to urinate on Rush. The play aptly demonstrates to what great extremes liberals will go to defeat those Cultural Wars that threaten their political and social hegemony.

Probably most of the consistent criticism comes from the press. There are frequent attacks on Limbaugh in the Gannett newspapers and the *New York Times* is no stranger to Rushphobia, a new disorder that I define as the incessant fear or dread that Rush Limbaugh will expose yet another example of the liberal myth that has dominated American culture for the last fifty years. There is no known cure or control for this psychological malady. Some commentators wanted to blame him for the 1995 Oklahoma City bombing because he got people angry at their government. According to *Time* magazine's Richard Lacayo, Limbaugh should have been named an unindicted co-conspirator in the blast. I am especially attuned to the vitriol that comes from the only major St. Louis paper, the *St. Louis Post-Dispatch*. I could make a career of watching this paper for all the negativity that it prints about Rush, both in its news section and its *Letters from the People*. I have answered a few of these letters and have had a couple letters published on Limbaugh's behalf. Rushphobia has also infected KMOX, the heralded beacon of truth and fairness for generations in St. Louis. One of their talk show hosts, Kevin Horrigan, a former journalist now with a rival radio station, directly preceded Rush five days a week. In an article for the *Post,* Horrigan condemned Limbaugh wannabes, who make people feel good about themselves and their political beliefs without being 'ashamed that people are starving somewhere! It was an egregious and highly offensive sentiment. Horrigan is an anomaly. He's a pro-life commentator with an uncharacteristic liberal bias. In some ways, Horrigan is a scalawag in the Culture War. The arrogance of his 50,000 watts demonstrates how out of touch with reality, liberals such as those who populate the station's daytime hours really are. If anything makes the wannabes angry, it is this kind of dogmatic and extremely predictable anti-intellectual pap that vainly attempts to derail conservative thinking. I consider myself an expert on Rush, or a "Rushologist," not only because I have been listening to him for years but because I have made a conscientious study of the man and the media star. I have been one of just a handful of teachers to offer a Rush Limbaugh college course. It provided me with the basis for this chapter and many of the observations I have included have come from that course preparation.

In objectively analyzing Limbaugh's ideas and life, I find there are three areas where he is most vulnerable to the slings and arrows of his enemies. The first one is the draft. His attacks on President Clinton's apparent cowardice notwithstanding, Rush Limbaugh did not charge out and volunteer for the United States military in 1969 after graduation from Cape Central High. Even though he is always praising the military and has a great deal of respect for what they do, the war and government service did not loom as large in his life as it did for most young Americans growing up more than a quarter century ago. Unlike the President who lied about his intentions and manipulated the system until he got a favorable draft exemption in the lottery, Rush Limbaugh failed his physical. He has a peiodinal cyst and a bad knee. Limbaugh, with no sign of the hero or super-patriot in him, took full and legitimate advantage of a physical condition that virtually exempted him from military service. To compare his ordinary and understandable decision to someone who was a mature graduate student—a leader with serious ambitions of being the Commander-in-chief of the entire United States military establishment—is akin to comparing a flea to an elephant. Rush is for family values, that amorphous notion that has been so used and abused that most thinking people scoff at its very mention. It should be more honestly referred to as family virtues that are nurtured within the context of the traditional family. He has been married three times and according to his unauthorized biographers, cohabited with each woman a few months prior to each marriage. Sexual behavior has never really been a topic on his show. Only in the context of illegitimacy, abstinence and AIDS has he ever lectured on the mores of sexual intercourse. It is a subject that quite properly belongs to the private Rush, a privacy his enemies are only too willing to violate. If the accusations are indeed correct, it does not lessen his stance on family values or any other issue for that matter because Limbaugh is not proclaiming himself as a beacon of honor with regard to premarital chastity for adults.

The abortion issue and *Feminazism* aside, Limbaugh's position on women is laden with poignant irony. His girth and feelings of inferiority have made him shy around women. Paul Colford's unauthorized biography, *The Rush Limbaugh Story,* describes his failed marriages with Roxy McNeeley and Michelle Sixta. Around his wives, Rush Limbaugh has been shy, inward, and cuckold. He is not the loud, brash, egotistical fool that his critics have painted. Colford's Rush is endearing, sad and heartbroken at having failed with his first two wives. Michelle was too young for him; she wanted to party and travel while he was happy working long hours and watching the

Pittsburgh Steelers on the weekend. He could have been the inspiration for the term "couch potato." Rush's failed marriages evokes an Aldaesque reaction from women who have sensed his deep hurt. I think he really is as he described himself to Barbara Walters on her show, "a lovable little fuzzball!" Michelle got him to lose over a 100 pound, so that he would be more presentable with her. The change did not fit or suit him and the weight came right back; Michelle left him in 1989 at the dawn of his great financial and professional success. With the failure of his second marriage, Rush seemed to resign himself to a life as a lonely workaholic. Technology, especially computers, has always fascinated him. Rush is a computer aficionado who can carry on esoteric and highly informative discussions on this subject. At times, he overdoes it. The only subjects that I will turn off are when he is endlessly, pushing the Steelers, computers, and his cigars. Like most of his regular audience, I believe his show is much better when driven by the issues of the day.

It was while cruising the information highway on *Compuserve,* one of his many sponsors, that Rush started "talking" with a twice-divorced woman from Florida, Marta Fitsgerald. Their E-mail correspondence led to romance and they were married in 1994 by Supreme Court Justice Clarence Thomas, one of Rush's new friends in high places, who performed the ceremony at the justice's Virginia home. Limbaugh could do things for her he never was able to do for his previous wives. Rush had taken her to the Super Bowl and several "insiders" spots. A new dimension opened in his life as Limbaugh was now welcome at clubs, owners' boxes, and courtside seats. He had easy access to the corridors of power and the excitement was intoxicating, both for him and his new wife. His success had filled the marital void he had with Roxy and Michelle. Material success was the best thing that ever happened to Rush's self-esteem. Sometimes he sounds like one of those infomercials for self-help and business success that run at three o'clock in the morning. The *Feminazis* and those who despise him, thinking he hates women, should listen to the mushy and saccharine way he refers to his wife. It is obvious who wears the pants in their home.

The final vulnerability is his admission that he tried marijuana at a party, when a young man in Kansas City. Rush is not a drug user today. He does not drink to excess and appears to be faithful to his wives when married. His only vice seems to be the big ugly cigars he proudly smokes at every opportunity. There are very few subjects Rush will not broach and he seems well versed in most anything, which is what a good talk show host must be. One subject he angrily shies away from is the notion of conspiracy theory. I must confess a weakness for ideas of plots and intrigues. Anyone familiar with European history or even the inroads of communism in the United States since 1917, cannot easily dismiss conspiracies as being the paranoid visions of deranged kooks and wackos. Rush makes me angry with his blanket denunciation and blatant mockery of conspiracy theorists. In a

way, I can now gauge why liberals find him so offensive. He is different
when he is goring your ox.

On my WGNU segment, there are no subjects I will not discuss. Of
course, Limbaugh has a lot of sponsors and I don't. He has to be very careful
not to give extra ammunition to his enemies, lest he wind up in the dustbin
of radio history. Molly Ivins' statement in *Mother Jones* about Rush's show,
"I have not seen so much hatred in politics since the heyday of the John
Birch Society in the early sixties," supports this contention. Rush cannot
afford to give even the slightest nod of assent to any group that is not
acceptable in the mainstream of Republican and Democratic thought. This
makes it impossible for Rush to be a true disciple of democracy and can
seriously limit his relentless search for the truth. It is ironic, that in what can
be termed a reactive triangulation of criticism, Rush is targeted not only by
the liberal left, but also the conservative right. The John Birch Society (JBS),
a group he shunned after attending meetings in the seventies when he
worked for the Kansas City Royals baseball team, has especially been critical
of Limbaugh. The 10 July 1995 issue of *The New American,* the provocative
intellectual organ of the JBS, devoted its cover story to *All Talk: The Politically Correct Conservatism of Rush Limbaugh.* John McManus, another Holy
Cross alumnus and now President of the JBS, lambasted Limbaugh in his
article, *Establishment Dittohead.* The liberal establishment would be surprised by this article which is mainly a compilation of damning quotes that
place Limbaugh many miles from the frontlines in the cultural battle for the
soul of America, rather than in its vanguard. The article was fair in its intent
and, despite a cheap shot about his three marriages, it attempted to put
Limbaugh in his proper perspective. McManus' quotes cover the broad
spectrum of his seven years in the public eye and, as a result, fail to distin-
guish the growth and subtle changes that have taken place since 1988. I
believe that when Limbaugh first started, he concentrated more on the
business of radio. He realized that his satirical wit hit a risible cord in the
American people. He was funny and entertaining and often would dismiss
his more serious outbursts as mere entertainment. I do not believe this
assessment to be totally accurate today. With the demise of the Republican
Party under George Bush and Bob Dole, I think Limbaugh heard a calling.
He realized he could have a dramatic impact on the course of political events
in the country's history. Commerce and entertainment slowly evolved into
power and influence. Limbaugh has a strong political gene in his make-up.
His experience has taught him that power is far more seductive, far more
satisfying than money or fame. Forget the dollar signs! Forget the laughter.
As a cultural warrior, Rush Limbaugh is part of the power game that is
changing the internal debate and possibly the course of American history.

John McManus hit upon what I perceive to be the only personal weakness that could end Limbaugh's domination: his undying loyalty to the
Republican Party of his grandfather, his father, and his youth. Rush is in the
enviable position of attempting to keep the politicians honest without being

blindly partisan. Unless he monitors his enthusiasm for their policies with close personal scrutiny, Limbaugh will emerge as nothing more than a Republican propagandist, the right-wing counterpart to Tom Brokaw and Dan Rather. Limbaugh boasts that he is conducting a relentless search for the truth. While the Republican Party in recent years has sought and backed more legitimate truth and reform than anything the Democrats have done in many years, truth is an elusive mistress that does not wear a GOP negligee. The Republicans are involved in power politics, just like the Democrats. If Limbaugh is to maintain his lofty position of being above the fray, he can not afford to join the team, as he declared at a GOPAC dinner in November of 1995, without suffering a commiserate loss of intellectual credibility. I have always contended that Rush Limbaugh would prove his detractors wrong when he attacked the Republicans for doing the same negative and liberal things that the Democrats have been doing for forty years. Rush's near sycophantic support of Bob Dole's presidential candidacy and his constant harping on winning above everything else threatens to prove me wrong. Rush's weakness is that he thrives on popularity. His huge audience and great numbers have let him inside the board rooms of power. He is friends with the likes of George Bush, Jack Kemp, Newt Gingrich, Bill Bennett and Clarence Thomas. A chubby boy from Southeast Missouri is rubbing elbows and trading quips and stories with some of the most influential and powerful people in the country, if not the world. Understandably he does not want to do anything to upset them or risk their censure. Rush knows that just like any great ball player or entertainer, the other half of the ticket can be cashed in tomorrow and he can be on a bus back to the Cape in a moment's notice.

McManus has clearly documented Rush's development as a propaganda accessory of the Republican Party. McManus pinpoints Rush's enlistment at the moment when George Bush invited him to spend the night in the White House before the 1992 election. Rush spent a sleepless night in the Lincoln Bedroom phoning everyone he knew to exclaim: *You'll never guess where I am!* McManus is not the only one to notice this change. In a critical *Atlantic Monthly* book review of Rush's two books, cleverly titled, *Talent on Loan From the GOP,* liberal journalist James Fallows wrote:

> As Limbaugh became more and more a party operative, his subject matter shifted too, from positions he'd develop to those he had obviously been fed. . . . He is clearly working from clips and theories someone else has handed him, very much like the Hollywood liberals he ridicules, who are working from clips about the plight of whales or the rain forest.

While Fallows' cynicism may be overstated, Rush's national program has served as a conduit for much of the Republican agenda. In truth, Rush believes in that agenda and reasons that anything that he can say to advance Republican ideas will ultimately recapture the country for the party's values and traditions. The problem I find is with his equating the Republican agenda with the conservative side in the Cultural War. The Republican Party too often has appeared little different from the liberalism of the Democrats. Republican 1996 presidential candidate Bob Dole's long political career is a perfect example of their accustomed attitude of going along to get along. As promoted by Dole, Republican incrementalism has been characterized by a gradual drift to the left that over time has resulted in the same big government policies of the Democratic Party. Bob Dole, as a senator and majority leader, voted for tax increases, welfare programs including food stamps, and a myriad of extensions of federal power and control. In Phil Grammian terms, the wagon is still going in the same direction, only just a little more slowly. Rush's near-unquestionable acceptance of Bob Dole as a conservative soldier in the Culture War was dispiriting and demoralizing. Dole was a disappointing standard-bearer for the so-called *Republican Revolution* that was supposed to limit government by turning the wagon around. Going more slowly will only keep us on the same course—what F. A. Hayek called, "the road to serfdom, or unrestricted Socialism." On the same point, before the Republican Convention in August of 1996, Rush seemed too quick to defend this traditional conservative principles as the Republicans tried to "draft" stealth candidate Colin Powell. The General frightened me because of his liberal views, which uncharacteristically did not seem to matter too much to Limbaugh. Winning the election at all costs seemed to be too much on his mind. Limbaugh was too quick in his blind acceptance of Republican dictates about Powell and later Dole. To me, this was a definite sign that being a team member was more important to him than the relentless pursuit of the truth.

Another subject that might betray Rush's undying allegiance to the party is *The Republican Contract*. Republican supporters were very enthusiastic about the contract after it energized the Republicans in recapturing both houses of Congress in the 1994 elections. When time came for the passage of the ten proposals, the Republican 104th Congress was able to pass just a small part of the contract, namely the *Shays Bill*, the *Line Item Veto* and the promise of welfare reform. The rest were lost in the Senate or were vetoed by President Clinton. The contract created much debate about Republicans ideas but, in effect, it achieved little. What became Limbaugh's spin and that of the Republican National Committee (RNC), as well as many of its allies in the conservative media, was that the Republicans only promised to bring them to a vote, not pass them! This disingenuous bit of word play embroiled me in a loud and bitter debate on the air with one of my "friendly" callers in the September before the 1996 elections. He said that the contract had been a big success. I questioned his use of the word "success," only to be berated for interrupting him. He pushed the notion that just bringing the ten proposals to a vote was a success because that's all Gingrich had said they would do. The Speaker had never promised that the contract would become law, only that they would try their best. In this strictly limited sense, Rush, the RNC and my caller were absolutely correct! Their spin, however, sounds very much like unadulterated symbolism. Limbaugh is always attacking the liberals for the abject symbolism of their programs and attitudes. He has repeatedly, *ad nauseam,* attacked President Clinton for treating his vainglorious attempts to effect liberal reform as victories. I have always been a realist and the theory of the Republican Contract is no good unless it is enacted into law. To claim victory without the Contract becoming law is deceptive and self-serving.

I have never been formally introduced to Rush. I have talked to his *aid-de-camp,* Kit Carson on the phone and at the TV show I attended in June of 1995, I did get to ask Rush a question in the pre-taping warm-up. I asked him how one can apply for a faculty position at the EIB (what he calls his show—*Excellence in Broadcasting*) University? This was in line with the pose he often assumes as the dean of a prestigious conservative university—his radio university. He seemed taken aback by my purposeful query. I was hoping he would ask me what my qualifications were and then I could tell him about my course at Maryville University. But he never did. The best he could say was, "Send us a resume" and went on to another member of the studio audience.

Rush was constantly on the defensive during the 1996 Republican primaries. Sticking to his premise that he does not take sides in the primary, some of his regular listeners have been ganging up on him. Callers flatly told him that he was out of touch. Limbaugh has always prided himself on the undeniable fact that he has consistently reflected what the people were thinking and that was the reason for his continued popularity. He said that he would not alter his beliefs and principles to suit the whims of the public. It is possible that as Limbaugh's attraction to the members of the Washington elite, such as Kemp and Bennett, has reflected their principles more than his own and those of his millions of dedicated listeners. Maybe Rush Limbaugh no longer accurately reflects the popular will nor validates the thinking of the legion of fans who have suffered through his implicit repudiation of passive disregard for the cultural issues? On one program, I heard him argue that abortion and other cultural issues could all be reduced to pure economics. This was a definition worthy of a neo-Marxist. As the Republican Party regulars shelve the important cultural issues of the day, so too it seems that Rush Limbaugh has lost touch with his millions of fans and the principles that originally set him apart. If so, the Culture War has witnessed one of its leading warriors desert. Limbaugh should get back to the basics that have made him the favorite of millions of Americans, placing principle and his relentless search for the truth ahead of popularity and Republican conformity. There may still be hope. As the Clinton sexual and legal scandals continued to unfold in the early months of 1998, Rush finally joined the chorus of conservatives who have been attacking the Republican leadership of Newt Gingrich and Trent Lott for their compliant inertia.

PART II

THE
SLIPPERY SLOPE

5 / Abortion
A Metaphor for Civil War

Loving mothers have abortions every day.

—Anna Quindlen, 23 June 1992

The level of a society's civilization can best be determined by how it treats the least fortunate, the unwanted, the downtrodden and the unprotected. Because no group is more vulnerable, more unprotected than the unborn, no issue better defines or expresses the broad and complex dimensions of the Culture War better than abortion. Not since the nineteenth century has the United States had to confront an issue that so deeply divides households. Abortion runs as deep as the fratricidal war that tore this country asunder in the 1860s. While abortion has not separated North from South, it has in some cases divided brother against sister and mother against father. Several years ago, NBC saw fit to broadcast a round-table TV show called the *Abortion: The New Civil War*. While it is fairly evident that this civil war will not lead to an all-out military confrontation or even guerrilla hostilities, it is a divisive issue that has set party against party, friend against friend, and, most significantly, man against woman.

While there have been some isolated pockets of violence, isolated protests of the sit-in or an occasional murder of an abortionist, the battles of this war will be fought in Congress, the lecture halls of our colleges and universities, from the pulpit, on national television and radio, and in many homes. Its major weapons will remain words and ideas, books and articles instead of bayonets and guns, missiles and tanks. The principal casualty on the abortion front, the growing fetus, is largely unseen. Pregnancy by its very nature involves a certain symbiotic intimacy that no outsider, no government, nor any moral authority can directly disturb. The killing of the unwanted unborn draws a special and indisputable historical parallel with slavery. In contrast, slaves were visible. People could often see the harm that was being inflicted on them. They could witness the social disgrace of buying, selling, and trading human beings in the public square. Repeat performances were not necessary to tweak the social conscience of those who viewed this stain on the American Constitution and its Bill of Rights. The unborn, on the other hand, are basically hidden from view, with the sole exception of the sonargram, which is usually a private medical procedure. The unborn cannot hide, escape, or ask for assistance. They are at the mercy of their mothers and doctors. Two hundred years of slavery, bigotry, lynchings, segregation, discrimination and racial violence have taught us a lesson that we cannot treat segments of the American population with disregard, violence, and extinction. Human beings are human beings, no matter what the Supreme Court or the laws of our country say. In its 1857 *Dred Scott* decision, the Supreme Court defined black people as baggage, or chattel, the personal property of the owner who could dispose of his property at will. *Roe vs. Wade* granted American mothers the special privilege of being able to dispose of their unwanted children at will, as a matter of choice, just as their Southern forbearers had done to slaves in the mid-nineteenth century. The unborn have had the misfortune to be conceived in an era when the baby has literally been thrown out with the bath water. With the coming of the birth control pill, technology provided teens and adults with the necessary means to free themselves from the consequences of illicit intercourse. The unborn have become the pawns in a chess game of higher stakes than their human lives seem to merit. Many of these victims are the unintended consequences of a sexual revolution out of control. They are the unwanted results of the neo-pagan urge to seek pleasure at each and every opportunity without a care for the results, based on self-indulgent behavior, personal whim and immediate gratification.

Today, as a result of the rise of sexually transmitted diseases, including AIDS, growing concern over the Pill's side effects, the lack of aesthetic appeal of the condom, a wave of unwanted pregnancies has hit American society with the impact of a reproductive Hiroshima. Those women who decide to keep their babies send the illegitimacy rates soaring. Others seek the relief of the abortion safety net, to the devastating tune of 1.5 million abortions each year. By last count, the numbers have surpassed 38 million unborn killed.

Illegitimacy has had a deleterious effect especially upon the black population, where a full 66% of births occur to single mothers. This fact has generated a new subclass of poor women who have been impoverished by the moral and economic fallout of the Sexual Revolution. Thousands of fatherless boys have attained manhood, only to add to the social detritus by impregnating scores of teenager girls who have compounded the social pathology of the situation. This has also led to gang warfare, drive-by shooting and rampant crime. We may never grasp how deeply unbridled sexual practices have affected us as a people and as a nation. It is impossible to measure these negative effects on society as a whole. For those women who have aborted, it can only be speculated that they have undergone the natural pain of their loss, complicated by the fact that it was their own decision.

While many would agree that abortion is wrong, others, like President Bill Clinton, would say that the moral road is to make abortion safe, legal, and rare. Catholic theologian, Saint Thomas Aquinas, wrote seven centuries ago, quoting Saint Augustine, "Human law can not punish or forbid all evil deeds: since it while aiming at doing away with all evils, it would hinder the advance of the common good, which is necessary for human intercourse." Liberals use Aquinas to argue that abortion is one of those wrong acts that should be kept legal because of the personal nature of the abortion decision. The pendulum has swung both ways on the legality of moral wrongs. In the nineteenth and early twentieth centuries, the *Comstock Laws* and *Eighteenth Amendment* to the United States Constitution tried to outlaw evil while in our time we have said that whatever was legal was moral, effectively turning Aquinas on his head. What is at work is a social dynamic that has set up a priority system which devalues all human life and, in many ways, put us all at risk. America's social mores are caught in a moral vice that holds the simultaneous belief that abortion is murder but should be left to the mother's choice.

The most potent weapon the pro-abortion side has is the expropriation of the word "choice" for their purposes. Choice is as American as baseball, apple pie, and Chevrolet. It is the basic component that defines us as free Americans. We want to choose where to live, whom to marry, what clothes to wear, what church to attend or not attend, what school to go to. It is curious that the pro-choice movement balks at freedom of choice when it comes to taxation, hiring, club affiliation, and schools.

Choice and reproduction have been united in a discordant and violently unhappy union during the last quarter of the twentieth century. Until then, the propagation of the human species had never been the proper domain of government. Both Hitler and Stalin used the fascist powers of the state to encourage their citizens to increase the birth rate so that their respective countries would have more soldiers to send into battle. This new civil war has determined that extra people were an unnecessary burden which should be discouraged at all times. The choice to have an abortion is much more likely to degenerate into government's imposition of eugenics. The standard in the *Peoples Republic of China* is to have a coercive abortion policy for all couples who already have one child. Since liberals seem to favor the effectiveness of this draconian policy because of its value in population reproduction, can the loss of reproduction choice be far off in the US?

According to seven white males on the Supreme Court who voted in the *Roe vs. Wade* decision in 1973, women have the unique right of deciding what to do after they become pregnant. There was no rational or logical basis for this proclamation on the part of the Supreme Court. For nearly two hundred years, the Supreme Court saw no basis for justifying unlimited abortions in the Constitution. Such revered jurists as John Marshal, Joseph Storey, Oliver Wendell Holmes, and Louis Brandeis, saw no such right for women. The Court cannot and should not, invent, or discover penumbral rights that were not stated or even implied in the Constitution. All fundamental rights come from God. They can be defined basically as the right to life, liberty, and the pursuit of happiness. The Court should confine itself to protecting human beings from individual and group abuse, such as slavery and segregation. In the case of a woman's choice, all the Court has done is establish new permission or privilege, which is what the abortion right is today—the unlimited and uninhibited privilege of disposing of unborn babies. Before *Roe vs. Wade* became part of the public domain, each state had its own ideas about the necessity of protecting women from the fate of an unwanted pregnancy. In a pluralistic society this issue was quite properly in the public realm of debate. There was no talk of a woman's constitutional right. The issue was left up to each state, in a form of popular sovereignty, which unfortunately had the ante-bellum ring to it of Stephen A. Douglas' solution for the slavery issue in the last century. While the notion of popular sovereignty is noxious for its divorce of behavior from morality, we are in the analogous situation that slavery would have been if it had been legal in each state, a situation that did not emerge until the infamous *Dred Scott* decision in 1857, which defined black slaves as chattel, or personal property.

The *Roe vs. Wade* decision and its evil twin sister, *Doe vs. Bolton* in 1973 crystallized the debate and highly politicized it. Abortion went from a local issue to a national issue. Since 1976, great efforts have been made to influence presidential elections, with the goal of insuring a court that would eventually overturn these prior decisions. While the tenor of the Court improved under Ronald Reagan and George Bush, from 1981-1993, bitter debates within the Judiciary Committee of the Senate, beginning with the nomination of Robert Bork in 1989, forced the choice of stealth candidates, such as Arthur Kennedy and David Souter, who have been bitterly disappointing to all pro-life activists. The bitter and slanderous fight over the confirmation of Clarence Thomas underscored how far the pro-abortion lobby was willing to take this cultural fight. The false accusations of Anita Hill and the political machinations of Senators Kennedy, Biden, and Metzenbaum served as virulent examples of the depths to which the pro-abortion lobby would sink. The pro-life forces never did get that elusive fifth vote necessary for a reversal of *Roe vs. Wade*.

The election of Bill Clinton in 1992 has further complicated the debate. He overturned twenty years of pro-life activity in his first week in office with just a few casual strokes of his pen. Congressional Republicans were able to defeat the noxious *Freedom of Choice Act* (FOCA). Had FOCA been enacted, the abortion lobby could have imposed a national policy of abortion for any reason throughout the nine months of pregnancy. Once it became a federal law, it would have been extremely difficult to repeal. The National Abortion Rights Action League developed a marketing strategy that falsely stated that FOCA was a mere continuation of the last 19 years of legalized abortion. What they surreptitiously called "a codification of Roe vs. Wade," would have invalidated several laws that were upheld under *Roe vs. Wade,* such as parental consent and notification bills. The current laws of 29 states would have been invalidated by FOCA. Despite former Speaker of the House Tom Folly's strong promise that the House would quickly pass the bill, it never got out of committee. I found it hard to believe that Folly's strong support of this bill created no personal conflict with his Catholic faith.

With Clinton in the White House, the abortion lobby attempted to write abortion policy into Hillary Clinton's national health care plan. Under the proposed provisions, pressure would have been brought to bear on Catholic hospitals, doctors and nurses to perform or assist in performing the abortion procedure or suffer legal and financial penalties. The overt absence of many priests, and other religious from the front lines of the Culture War with regard to abortion has been a sad commentary on the clergy's commitment to the weakest of God's creations. Too many religions have put their love of political party above the unborn. Without the strong active leadership of the Catholic Church and its clergy, the pro-life movement will never be able to end this cancer on the American soul. By linking the fight against abortion to capital punishment or stressing other issues, such as the poor or the environment, the Catholic Church impedes the pro-life movement when it should be in the vanguard. The irony is that the Church has been singled out by liberals in government and their willing accomplices in the mainstream media, as the evil purveyor of un-Americanism and anti-choice rhetoric with a vehemence that makes one fear a return to the anti-clericalism of the French Revolution. They seem to have as their goal the virtual elimination of the Catholic Church as a relevant participant in this debate.

One need only read the letters to the editor printed in many of our liberal dailies to realize the vacuity and emptiness of the pro-choice philosophy. These letters often range from the trivial to the disoriented to the inane. Choice letters are usually filled with *ad hominem* assaults upon pro-life leaders and politicians, especially Catholics. It has often been said that bashing Catholics is the "Anti-Semitism of the Left." While most display a real ignorance of the majesty and beauty of the Church, some of their objections warrant consideration. One woman questioned the Church's infallible teachings, implying the Church was not certain of its teaching on abortion since it had not declared it to be infallible. It is obvious to the informed that the Church's teachings on murder, rape, suicide, stealing, or income tax evasion have not been defined or subjected to the tests of infallibility. Does this mean the Church is not certain on any of these other issues? 2000 years of consistent history provides a basis for the Church's defense of the unborn.

Another complained that the Church's pro-life stance fails to integrate the full goodness of human sexuality into its thinking. Perhaps it was a Freudian slip, but I assume that this writer believes the right to an abortion is part of the full goodness of human sexuality! Others complained that the Church forces women to become mothers through intimidation and fear. A more pertinent question seems to be how many women are forced to slaughter their children by boyfriends, parents, or husbands! Another writer questioned who should have children and why, betraying a eugenics approach to child birth, or what I call *Margaret Sangerism*. In 1934, about the same time the Nazis were launching their own eugenics abortion program, Margaret Sanger was pushing birth control and abortion as racial purification measures. More children for the fit, fewer for the unfit. (The unfit included all those not of Nordic descent.) Birth control to breed a race of thoroughbreds was among her favorite slogans. The April 1933 issue of her publication, *Birth Control Review,* was devoted exclusively to eugenics. It included an article written by Dr. Ernst Rudin, a leader of Hitler's forced sterilization/ euthanasia program. Later, the Nazis banned her books because they did not want Aryans to practice birth control. It was only the *Untermenschen* whose reproduction the Nazis wanted to limit. This policy of negative and positive genetics is partly reflected in the couples who will today abort their unborn female children because of the society's preference for boys.

Other letters in the *Post* follow in the anxious traditions of nineteenth century English clergyman and economist, Thomas Malthus. They often propose unlimited abortion as a means of controlling or eliminating social pathologies, such as drive-by shootings, wars, unemployment, political injustice and crime. Thirty years ago, *Planned Parenthood* said child abuse, illegitimacy, poverty and the common, cold would cease if we just had free, legal, and safe abortion. *Planned Parenthood* always blames overpopulation as the root of most social problems. I would argue that what the world needs is not fewer people, but better people. People should stop being concentrating on their own needs and desires and treat other people with more kindness and dignity instead of finding ways to eliminate them. We have endured years of social engineers talking about solving problems by limiting the growth of the world's population. Their solution to social problems has been an abject failure because it offers only death and dying as a cure for the social ills of the times. The numbers just don't add up. If each person had just one child, it would be centuries before the world population was significantly reduced. How would you enforce "voluntary" child limitation? What kind of penalties would people face? Will people's religious and moral positions be respected? What does this proposal do to the concept of "choice" as we now hear it? This notion is fraught with a danger that holds up more a promise of 1984, *Brave New World* and *The Night of the Living Dead* than it does Saint Thomas More's *Utopia.*

Jean Berg of the *Missouri Religious Coalition for Abortion Rights* has raised abortion to the sanctity of a personal sacrament. Berg's letter on 1 June 1993, in the *Post-Dispatch* pushed the bromide that every child has a right to be born into a welcome home. I wonder where that right comes from? I would think that the right would have to come from God. If her banality were accurate, there would not be that many people in the world which is perhaps what people like Berg really want.

Berg's letter also stated that women are created by God to make wise decisions. This notion is an exercise in feminist self-indulgence without any basis in reality. It glorifies the autocratic self, blindly assuming that just because a woman choose something, it is right and just. If everyone on earth applied the same ill-founded logic, there would be nothing but war, death destruction and moral chaos. You might hit her with a real religious idea, such as compassion, especially for the smallest of God's creatures; the Cross; self-sacrifice; charity; or love. She also calls the fetus a potential child. This notion of potentiality has long served to obscure and dehumanize the unborn child. What she is really saying is that a child is not a human being until its born. A growing unborn child is present in the womb. This child is not potential life. All unborn are potential children, just like all children are potential teens. She misses the point that life is an unbroken continuum that can not arbitrarily be divided. The child is alive in the womb, with all of its days and nights ahead of it. The baby is not a finished product but on the right track with its genetic road map all in place. It is all unfulfilled promises, an exciting and new beginning of a 70 to 80 year journey that hopefully will culminate in Heaven. Her letter made the formulaic case for abortion as a solution for social problems. Vice Presidential candidate Geradine Ferarro made this same point during the 1984 Presidential elections. I hear it all the time from my callers on WGNU. If killing the unborn were a viable solution for social problems, it would have severe and dangerous consequences for all Americans. Carry this logic a degree further and some will propose to end poverty, hunger and crime by simply exterminating all the sick, homeless, elderly, physically and mentally handicapped.

Adolf Hitler reached the same conclusion over sixty years ago. He tried to cure many of Germany's fiscal, social, and moral problems by exterminating Jews, effeminate homosexuals, the sick, disabled, unwanted and unproductive. For those who read closely between the lines, there is strong evidence of the same fascist ideology in the arguments of apologists for abortion who claim that a child does not have the right to live until it is wanted by its mother and accepted by the human community. Hitler's *T-4* program instituted an euthanasia project that started with defective children and eventually went to the elimination of all the unfit from the crippled, to the lame, to the deaf and mentally ill. The medical techniques, the facilities and the moral inversion of the Judeo-Christian ethic were in place for the *Final Solution*. The Germany company I. G. Farben evokes another example of the Hitlerian analogy. The very name conjures up horrid images of frightened human masses being herded into crowded showers of death. Forty-two years after its liquidation, the company is experiencing a revitalization. The general consensus is that the company has successfully shed it ignominious Nazi past. While it is a pleasant sentiment that evil-doers in history can regenerate and turn over new moral leaves, such is not the case. Deeper inspection has uncovered that one of the company's subsidiaries, Roussel-Unclaf, is the manufacturer of the equally nefarious abortion pill, RU-486. This human pesticide has the potential of ending more lives than its forerunner, Zyklon B. Some things just don't change! Zyklon B was used to kill Jews. I.G. Farben was the Orkin or Getz extermination company of its day in that they made the killing agents for household pests. Hitler employed their chemical technology for his diabolic Final Solution.

On a similar note, there is the case of Dr. George Tiller, the Wichita abortionist, who was nearly killed by an anti-abortion zealot. Tiller specialized in late-term abortions, performing about 500 per year. People who have picketed his abortuary tell me that he used an oven, visible from the street, to dispose of the fetal remains. It was small and unobtrusive—nothing like the spires of Auschwitz, but visible. Tiller had originally tried to send the fetal remains to the local hospital but the medical staff refused to participate. The medical personnel of the Wichita clinic suffered from comparable stress symptoms. Tiller decided to dispose of these bodies by burning them in his small but very effective oven. It has a familiar ring to it. Pro-choice people say these fetuses are not human. They are members of the American *Untermenschen.*

Another example of the physiological trauma of late term abortions relates to the so-called partial birth abortion technique. After assisting doctors in several of these procedure, Nurse Brenda Pratt Shafer said, "I never went back to the clinic. But I am still haunted by the face of that little boy. It was the most perfect angelic face I have ever seen." Late term abortions consistently have this horrible effect on people, causing many of them to fully comprehend what devilish work abortion really is. The sight of a dying or dead fetus, just a month or two from birth evokes a deep and powerful emotional experience that has been denied to the public. Late-term abortion is so graphic and apparent that most newspapers will refuse to expose its evil nature, partly out of the fear of offending pro-choice readers and advertisers and partly out of exciting an outrage among the general population.

Pro-abortion writers, however are not afraid to use emotional appeals to foster the abortion side of the Culture War. Anna Quindlen's column of 23 June 1992, in the St. Louis *Post-Dispatch* discussed the Sherri Finkbine incident of the early sixties. As a teenager in New York, I remember reading about her sad plight. The mother of four, Finkbine became pregnant with her fifth child. To combat some of the side effects of her pregnancy, she took the drug Thalidomide. Soon after, it was discovered that the drug was directly related to severe birth defects. *Life* magazine ran pictures of several babies with legs attached to their chests and web-like appendages for arms. It was a powerfully tragic sight. Concerned, Mrs. Finkbine immediately sought to abort her unborn child. She could not bear the thought of giving birth to a deformed child. To my knowledge, there was no sonargram or amniocentesis available at this time, so the mother sought the abortion on just the chance that her child was deformed. The Finkbine incident provides an important insight to the mind of a person who is willing to kill her unborn child on the chance that it might be defective. In Finkbine's case, the abortion found that the child had been severely deformed. This justified her decision in both her and Quindlen's eyes. The essential message here is that to be wanted and loved, you must be whole—perfect in the eyes of society. All our human defects should end up in the junk heap of human refuse. Implicit also is the message that a mother cannot take the time and energy to love a handicapped child. The *Life* pictorial was powerful photographic journalism. I still remember the eyes on this little blonde baby girl with a foot attached to her chest. Her eyes and her incandescent smile seemed to beg your affection, your attention. She was alive and happy to be here. So she'd never dance or run in a marathon. So what! It was obvious that her mother loved her. We are fast becoming a nation that will not tolerate any imperfection in our young. Can there be such a quantum leap from this to formulating a national policy that will imperil the nation's millions of disabled? Quindlen justified Finkbine's stance with the incredible and maternally blasphemous statement, "Loving mothers have abortions every day." I doubt that I have to tell how self-serving and loathsome statement this is. Even Adolf loved children: Aryan children.

Quindlen's appeal for sympathy is a plea for unequivocal approval of this act of abortion. This has become the nexus of the pro-choice thinking. They are not satisfied with an absolute right to an abortion through all nine months of pregnancy! The pro-choice forces also want personal and public approval for what they advocate. Pro-life advocates may eventually lose all support in Congress, the White House, the media, and the state legislatures but there is no way on earth that pro-lifers can ever allow pro-choice the luxury of the moral high ground. There is no way pro-choice can have the validation sedative that permits them to sleep nights, to rid themselves of the general state of uneasiness that goes with what they are doing of what they are advocating.

Another aspect of this issue that dramatically underscores its emotional nature is pro-life violence perpetrated on abortionists, their staffs and clinics. Numerous fire-bombings, and the murder of a few abortionists have grievously injured the pro-life cause. Fringe advocates have taken the law into their own hands and done far more harm than good. Firemen do not put out fires by pouring gasoline on an inferno. The murder of abortionist David Gunn in Pensacola put the pro-life forces on their guard. Like so many factors surrounding this issue, this one demands a certain amount of restraint, prompted by Christian charity. Though there is a human tendency to say *good riddance*—Gunn will not be killing anymore babies—no one who is really serious about stopping abortion can conscience his brutal killing. We are a nation of laws, juries, and appointed judges—not self-appointed assassins. What Michael Griffith did was dead wrong, no matter how much he cared about Dr. Gunn's victims.

Columnist Anthony Lewis could not refrain from using the Gunn killing to write a scurrilous attack on the pro-life movement. The crimes of a few have served his purpose in denigrating the entire pro-life movement. This blatant exploitation of the Gunn killing is an attack on all the peaceful pro-lifers who have been lining the sidewalks, busing to Washington, and picketing without a hint of disrespect for the law. Lewis also introduced a new theme in the pro-abortion legacy of disjointed arguments, the religious protection ploy. Abortion is now constitutionally sanctioned under the protective mantle of freedom of religion. I attended a debate in which the St. Louis *Riverfront Times'* publisher, Ray Hartmann, displayed this same defense. Since religions disagree on when life begins, you should not force your religious beliefs on me. This deviously creative argument is a little more difficult to dispel than arguments for personal choice or that a woman can do whatever she wants with her body. I pointed out to Ray that The Church of the Latter Day Saints has as one of its key tenets, the polygamous union of man and women, abrogated by the United States government. Mormons believe that the nether world is bursting with unbodied souls. God wants the Mormons to embody as many of them as was humanly possible. This religious tenet was annulled by the US Congress which denied Utah statehood until it eliminated polygamy from its state Constitution. In the 1890s, this was a classic case of the civil rights of women, who were not much better off than the unborn of today.

Though many churches today are divided over abortion, none would propose that human sacrifice is part of their individual credos. The churches were more divided over the issue of slavery in the 1850s. At Harpers Ferry in 1859, abolitionist John Brown staged an armed insurrection that left several dead in its wake, not unlike the actions of Michael Griffith and John Salvi who murdered two women in *Planned Parenthood* offices. The pro-slavery proponents used his extremism to cast aspersions on the Abolitionist movement. Brown, who quoted the Bible more frequently than Mike Griffith, was very much a part of the movement's lunatic fringe and probably, like Griffith, suffered from the frustration of being denied vindication of his views on all levels of government. John Brown was hanged for his crimes. I feel certain that Griffith and Salvi* will also be severely punished for their crimes. With the popular success and public acceptance of the *Civil Rights Act* of 1964, John Brown's memory was seen in the light of a crusading and avenging angel who was justified in taking the law into his own hands when it did not measure up to the higher standard of divine obligation. The case can be made that it is the pro-choice side that is creating an atmosphere of violence in their abortion clinics with the callous slaughter of millions of unborn children. The bitter irony is that they use every means to exploit the aberrant behavior of a few pro-life extremists, such as Griffith and Salvi, for their own ideological and financial gains.

Historical arguments notwithstanding, the religious defense is just another shallow example of pro-abortion rhetoric. I do not believe that any woman in her right mind seeks an abortion out of religious conviction. Abortion is not an issue of religion as Lewis and Hartmann contend, but of science. Dr. Bernard Nathanson, one of the founders of the *National Abortion Rights Action League*, admits to having performed or supervised over

---

* He later committed suicide in his cell. (hanged himself)

75,000 abortions in New York. Nathanson later changed his mind, not because he fell from his horse on the road to Damascus, but because of his research in Neonatology. He simply realized that these were human beings he was killing. Dr. Beverly McMillan became an abortionist in Mississippi for sincere humanitarian reasons. Her conversion experience happened one night, not because of a burning bush, but because she had held the severed limb of a five-month old fetus in her hand and noticed how perfectly formed was his deltoid muscle. She realized this was part of a human being that she held in her hand. It is not a question of religion but of anatomy.

The trouble with Lewis and Hartmann's religious argument is that it rejects the idea that there can be one immutable religious doctrine buttressing the law. All criminal law is predicated on a moral viewpoint: *Thou shall not kill, steal,* etc. If the pro-choice viewpoint were the rule then racism, rape, child abuse could not be outlawed. We have a single viewpoint on the equality of women that has outlawed polygamy in this country, putting us at odds with the Islamic and Mormon faiths as to the worth and function of women. Lewis and Hartmann's notion of religious relativity would create an atmosphere of moral anarchy to the detriment of Western Civilization. The sad irony here is that Ray Hartmann, a man who has been the tireless and unceasing spokesman for the downtrodden, the racially-oppressed, and the innocent victims of the system, is ideologically allied with abortionist profiteers who literally bleed their vulnerable and frightened female clients. He is a likable and talented man who is firmly dedicated to the choice ethic and all of its ramifications. I only wish he were on my side.

Columnist Susan Estrich, a proponent of abortion, queries why those opposed to abortion are not also opposed to tobacco since both kill babies. She contends that tobacco products kill 100 times more children than partial birth abortions do. What Estrich fails to recognize is that tobacco companies are aiming at profits and they do not intend the death of anyone, let alone innocent children. Illness and sometimes death are unintended side-effect of the smoking industry, while killing an unborn child is the main function of the abortion clinic. The death of the child in an abortion is the direct result and the direct intent of the abortionist. Turn it around and ask how can someone who is against the death incurred by smoking, not be against abortion which kills 1.6 million unborn children, 2500 times the number of children she calculates die from smoking. Estrich, a very bright and perceptive thinker in her own right, is too intelligent to resort to such specious reasoning.

The abortion debate has put thousands of Democratic politicians and millions of voters in a quandary. Do they desert the party of their youth—the party that has given meaning to so much in this country throughout the past three generations? Or do they look the other way and accept the spirit of the times, which encourages a mindless neo-pagan life of self-centered special interest group politics? This seems to be the choice perplexing Democrats around the country.

Many Catholic Democratic politicians have taken refuge behind what I call the *Cuomo Excuse*. In a highly celebrated speech, given at Notre Dame University in 1984, entitled *Religious Belief and Public Morality: A Catholic Governor's Perspective*, New York Governor Mario Cuomo expressed his viewpoint that, while he was personally opposed to abortion, he was publicly sworn to uphold the law of the land which had made free and unlimited abortion the right of every woman in the country. His speech was the rhetorical quintessence of equivocation. As governor of all the people, he could not let his Catholic faith dictate to all New York state residence. In reality, Cuomo's actions as Governor imply more than a public approval of abortion: he has denounced all attempts to restrain it. To define Mario Cuomo as personally opposed to abortion is to ignore his gleeful stance as fellow Democratic Governor Robert Casey of Pennsylvania was literally booed off the platform for his ardent pro-life views at Madison Square Garden stage during the Democratic National Convention in 1992.

It is not surprising that this same governor did not apply the same standard to the issue of capital punishment. Cuomo vehemently supported his Church's reformed stance on capital punishment. In light of the fact that fully two thirds of the citizens of New York wanted the death penalty, he has done everything in his power to thwart their collective will on this matter. The question than arises why Cuomo is so careful not to force his morality on the people with regard to abortion. But he had no moral compunction that prevented him from forcing his moral view on capital punishment on the voters of New York. His lust for the White House and the Democratic Party's abortion litmus test obviously had everything to do with it.

The notion of the seamless garment is at the heart of the Cuomo dodge. Professor James Hitchcock of St. Louis University asserts that Cardinal Joseph Bernardin's seamless garment has seriously hurt the anti-abortion cause. Bernardin argued that abortion should be considered only in the context of other life-related issues, such as war and capital punishment. Even though Bernardin stresses the Church's position that abortion is morally wrong, and is binding to Catholics because it expresses both Church law and the higher natural law of the dignity of human life, I sometimes think that Bernardin's idea trivializes the Church's fight against abortion. It allows many pro-choice Democratic politicians, such as Governor Cuomo, to hide under its protective mantel, By including abortion with opposition to nuclear energy, capital punishment and a host of other life issues, Bernardin's seamless garment waters down and camouflages the abject evil of a Catholic supporting legalized abortion in any way. The political connection is at the nexus of this dilemma. There is a historical association between the Catholic hierarchy, its flock, and the Democratic Party dating back over a century. The Democratic Party was the party of millions of Irish and Italian immigrants in this country. During Franklin Roosevelt's term, many Catholic union workers formed a lifelong alliance with the party that has lasted until this day, even as the Party has discarded many of the high moral principles on abortion, pornography, premarital sex and drug use, that once gave comfort to Catholics.

Many politicians, including former St. Louis Mayor Vincent Schoemehl, also a Catholic, have used the Cuomo dodge. Pragmatic politics seem to be a weak argument for implicitly supporting the abortion industry that thrives on the broken dreams, false promises and unrestricted freedoms involved in an unwanted pregnancy. Schoemehl and other Democrats of character could make a difference in this battle if they were to rid their party of this special interest group that goes against the very fabric of the party's great social history with regard to human rights and values. Unfortunately, the enticements of higher elective office seem too great or the character lacking for the Democratic Party to save itself from the moral cancer that has destroyed its integrity, just as slavery had done a 150 years ago.

The career of Abraham Lincoln is instructive in this matter of political conscience versus constitutional protections. (Ironically, Cuomo has published a book on Lincoln's thought.) In his book, *Abraham Lincoln and the Second American Revolution* (1991), author James McPherson relates President Lincoln's similar predicament. Though he had a personal disdain for slavery, Lincoln realized that the property rights of slave owners were protected by the Constitution. But unlike the New York Governor, Lincoln also did everything in his power to limit its expansion into the territories. In a speech in Connecticut in 1860, Lincoln destroyed the basis of what would be the Cuomo defense.

> You say that you think slavery is wrong, but you denounce all attempts to restrain it. Is there anything else that you think is wrong, that you are not willing to deal with as a wrong? . . . You will not let us do a single thing as if it were wrong; there is no place where you will allow it even to be wrong; there is no place that you will even allow it to be called wrong! We must not call it wrong in politics because that would be bringing religion into politics; we must not call it wrong in the pulpit because that would bring politics into religion. . . . and there is no single place . . . where this wrong thing can be properly called wrong!

All one has to do is substitute the word *abortion* for *slavery* and Lincoln's argument takes on an eerie relevance. Lincoln used his politics to serve his convictions as those like Mario Cuomo have ignored their convictions to serve their politics. Lincoln knew that the way to expose his opponents was not to advance an impossibly pure political position but to pin his opponents down on specifics. The same goes for abortion. The one question most Democrats fear to answer today is one question they are never asked. Name just one abortion out of the 1.5 million annual abortions in this country you would like to see restricted. They are afraid that once they allow the camel's nose in the tent, the rest of him will soon follow. Their determination for complete solidarity on this issue explains the obdurate opposition to the banning of the partial birth abortion procedure, passed by Congress but vetoed by President Clinton in 1996. This veto drew attention to another question. Clinton's mendacious rhetoric boasts that the Democratic Party is the party of inclusion, except for the fetus. He pretends to spout compassion for every human being but the unborn. The Democratic Party claims to represent the weak and the powerless in our society, yet supports the right of mothers to choose death for their innocent, unborn children.

Should not the government be compelled to protect the weakest and most fragile of all human beings? Is abortion not about sex but primarily an act of violence perpetrated on tiny little beings who have no voice, no vote and can not defend themselves? Paraphrasing the poet John Donne, does not abortion diminish us all, male and female?

Abortion advocates like President Clinton say they only want to make abortion safe, legal, and rare. Any of us with sense know that they have done little to make abortion rare. Proponents of choice oppose waiting periods, clinic regulation, developmental information about the fetus because they only care that poor women come in quick, kill their unborn children and get out before they have had any time to reflect on this most personal decision. Most surveys show that where 24-hour waiting periods are in effect, 50% of the women contemplating abortion change their minds, thus denying the abortion industry thousands of dollars.

Thanks to a lively book by Mark Crutcher, entitled *Lime 5*, it is apparent that the unholy trinity of death has been reduced to "legal." The book exposes, in graphic detail, how abortion clinics are often the site of forced sex, mutilation, and death. Many women are dying in these clinics.. It also explores the adverse psychological effects abortion has on the providers and their auxiliary personnel. *Lime-5* could be the *Uncle Tom's Cabin* of the abortion industry. Just as Harriet Beecher Stowe's moving ante-bellum novel exposed the underlying evils of slavery, *Lime-5* could have a similar effect on abortion. The book also focuses on the issue of breast cancer. Women should ask themselves if the abortion providers and their main promotional organizations, such as NARAL and *Planned Parenthood,* really care about their health. The *Journal of the American Medical Association,* (January 1996), featured yet another study establishing a strong link between abortion and breast cancer. There have been more than a few of these studies done in the past, all concluding that abortion will increase a woman's risk for breast cancer later in her life. The latest study of 16,417 women established that those who had undergone abortions had a 23% higher incidence of breast cancer than those who had never had a pregnancy termination. Women who had suffered a miscarriage during their first trimester of pregnancy also had an 11% higher risk. The pro-abortion lobby has done everything in its power to hide or discredit the results of these studies, which have great health implications for women who have had first trimester abortions.

There is also a strong influence of utilitarianism involved in this debate. People are valued in terms of their usefulness. Due to alleged population pressures, if an individual is not useful, and if this life is all we have, the world should be reserved for the fit, the well, and the productive. Too many people pollute and deplete the earth's limited resources. According to the beatitude of President Clinton's first Surgeon General, Joycelyn Elders, "Every child should be a planned, a wanted, and a loved child." Every one should have a high quality of life, a minimum standard of existence and if one falls short, life should be terminated. In remarks Elders made before Congress in May of 1990, she testified that abortion had resulted in a positive public health effect. Fewer children were being born with severe defects. There is a certain logic to Elders' thinking, since her brand of medicine had killed the unfit children before birth instead of finding a way to heal them after birth. On 18 January 1992, Elders told the Arkansas *Coalition for Choice* that she wished the right-to-life and anti-choice groups would get over "their love affair with the fetus." Her address was also infected with a virulent strain of anti-Catholic bigotry. In January of 1993, she referred to abortion opponents as non-Christians with slave/master mentalities. Elders personal invective directed at pro-life activists, the Catholic Church, and Christians in general, serves as a good illustration of how deep and how widespread the battle lines in this fight have been drawn. Pat Buchanan merely opined in his widely criticized speech at the 1992 Republican National Convention in Houston that there was a Culture War going on. He was vilified for stating the obvious. Dr. Elders can hurl bombshell after bombshell at the traditionalists in this battle and the media ignores the hostility and mean-spiritedness that characterizes cultural warriors of her kind.

Elders' comments also show that the country is on a collision course between the existential way of approaching ethical issues and that of the Judeo-Christian ethic. The latter recognizes the Biblical injunction of *Thou shalt not kill* and the transcendent value of human life. Existential philosophy focuses solely on the autocratic self, not on medical evidence, religious principle, or transcendent moral law or logical analysis. The only thing at issue is whether or not the mother has a choice. The content of that choice makes no matter in terms of the morality of her decision. Pro-choice is not only a rhetorical euphemism but a precise definition of existential ethics. Moral and religious beliefs are no more than personal constructs. Truth is relative, no matter if it goes under the name of values clarification or situation ethics. This philosophy was first formulated by existential theologian Joseph Fletcher. Prime values became those that served social utility. Existentialist John Paul Sartre felt that most people do not want the responsibility of making free choices, (i.e., accepting the consequences of their actions). This gnostic notion implies that men need to be dependent on an elite to think and decide for them. When the only ethical standard is that which is designed by an elite, there is the distinct possibility of fascist tyranny. It comes down to a matter of the strong controlling the weak and the dependent.

During the abortion wars, there have been many pretenders for the role of a gnostic elite. In the late 1960s *Planned Parenthood* revealed its goal of family limitation to one child, which is not much different than that of the People's Republic of China. One only needs to refer to any of the books or articles written by Stephen Mosher on China to experience China's progress in brutal population control. Mosher was the young man who was barred from finishing his Ph.D. at Stanford because he wanted to tell the truth about China's inhumanity to its people, especially its unborn children. His harrowing tales of truck loads of late-term pregnant women being dragged to the abortion mills is just another example of the sordid aspects of this issue that have been covered up or ignored. We have read of the horrors of the Nazi death camps, Bosnia, Rwanda, and Haiti. In the People's Republic, what we used to call Red China, we were gravely upset by the atrocities in Tinnamen Square. Where is the nation's moral outrage against China's coercive abortion policies? Why are not *Planned Parenthood, NARAL,* and NOW bombarding our State Department with their pointed messages about a woman's choice? What about the thirteen women that the Clinton administration returned to China because they had escaped because of their forced abortion policy and sterilization? Clinton's cowardly action was directly contrary to an Executive Order of President George Bush on human rights and a US law that prohibits any United States funding of any organization that supports or participates in the management of a program of coercive abortions. The Clinton administration has committed $50 million a year to the *United Nations Population Fund* which works closely with China to implement its abortion policy.

The Chinese have recently added another notch in their abortion belt. It appears that the Chinese are eating fetuses for their dermatological and other health benefits. The *Eastern Express,* a Hong Kong newspaper, in the 12 May 1995 *Human Events,* states that state-run hospitals and clinics sell fetuses for about ten Hong Kong dollars or a dollar and a quarter in American money. One doctor explained that the fetuses can make your skin smoother, your body stronger and are good for your kidneys. "They are wasted if we don't eat them . . . The women who receive the abortions don't want the fetuses." I thought the Chinese only ate dogs.

One thing is certain about this issue. It will not be swept into the dustbin of history. As Lincoln prophetically intoned, "A house divided against itself can not stand." It will either get better or the abortion mindset will further permeate the American soul, drowning any real form of civility; we will probably be finished as a civilization.

6 / Euthanasia
James Bond and the Last Taboo

> There can be no such thing as a right to assisted suicide because there can be no legal and moral order which tolerates the killing of innocent human life.
>
> —Cardinal Joseph Bernardin in a letter to the Supreme Court before his death in November of 1996.

I must admit that the issue of euthanasia is not as clear-cut as abortion. Unlike abortion, in euthanasia the victim is usually old, ill, probably near "death's door." Euthanasia literally translates to "good death." The term has traditionally been employed to refer to the hastening of a suffering person's death or as mercy killing. Every year two million people die in America— 80% in hospitals, hospices, or nursing homes. It is estimated that fully 70% of these die after a decision is made to forgo life-sustaining treatment. Most have lived a full life as successful business men, husbands, wives, fathers, professionals and good people. As heart attacks, strokes, and the ravages of age make them just shadows of their vibrant and healthy selves, their lives are all but over. Being old is hard, painful and very depressing at times. The so-called twilight or golden years, often do not bring what the travel and retirement home brochures promise they will. Often the elderly are surrounded by caring families who can not bear to see them suffer or who dread the financial burden that a slow and agonizing death could bring.

What the euthanasists are really about is that many people who should not exist, or do not meet their standards of a real quality of life, do not die quickly or easily enough. Many have a Messiah or Jesus complex in that they think it is their chosen role to hasten the death of many human beings who do not measure up, the so-called biologically tenacious. The aged, according to these doctors, are a burden to society. The members of this distinct but growing group include victims of strokes, multiple sclerosis, Lou Gehrig's disease (ALS), head injuries, quadriplegics and Altzheimer's disease. Pain is usually the excuse given for expanding euthanasia services. All doctors know how to control pain. If a patient is still suffering, then maybe he needs another doctor. A more insidious kind of pain is the emotional pain of despair, loneliness, isolation, loss of dignity, and a general weariness of life. It is this psychological distress, not physical pain, that is at the root cause of many who beg to be killed by family and friends.

Suicide among those with serious handicaps is almost non-existent. It is the normal people around those with illnesses or handicaps who judge their quality of life to be unacceptable and not worthy of continuation. With rare exception those who commit suicide are clinically depressed. Drug therapies can help this biological dysfunction. After four decades of decline, the elderly suicide rate has climbed nearly 9% from 1980 through 1992. Death has fast become a quicker remedy than pharmaceuticals. According to major studies, at least 94% of elderly suicides were found to have treatable mental disorders. The decriminalization of suicide was based on the recognition that people with suicidal wishes have severe psychological problems. That is why the law does not punish them if they fail in their suicide attempt. This is also a major reason to deny doctors or family members their right to assist in suicide. Government should help those who can not help or protect themselves. People in a clinically depressed state can easily be taken advantage of and coerced to do something fatal to themselves for the financial and emotional benefit of others.

This kind of thinking also has a corruptive influence on the American medical community. As with abortion, legalized euthanasia would be difficult to limit just to the so-called hard cases, once it becomes socially and morally acceptable. The camel's nose alludes to cases such as those for whom medication has been ineffective, patients in a permanent vegetative state (PVS) and others considered to be brain dead. All other forms of human suffering, disease and permanent injury or disability relate to the rest of the camel's anatomy. Entering into this situation are the children of the enlightenment, as personified by euthanasist, Dr. Jack Kervorkian and Derek Humphry, the founder of the Hemlock Society. These people, motivated by misguided humanitarianism, greed, or the satanic temptation to be godlike, prey on the dying and their families. They harp on the twin fears that live in the consciousness of everyone over fifty in this country, namely that of dying and being a family burden while dying. With the specter of Frankenstein, we have a medical economy that has learned to prolong life in the body, without curing the debilitating conditions old age often brings.

My wife and I attended my thirtieth reunion at Holy Cross in June of 1995. As part of the fun we attended a lecture given by former classmate, Dr. Leo Cooney, who is an expert in Gerontology at Yale University. At fifty-two, with his white hair and bulging middle, he looked anything but what I would call vigorously healthy. He joked that he did not jog or do any excessive healthy routine because he did not want the extra four months in a nursing home that exercise would bring. Getting old is no joking matter. I am at the age where my body gives me more pain than pleasure. I see physical fitness buffs and hordes of athletic cultists jogging in all sorts of dangerous weather and traffic conditions. It is as if they were trying to outrun the Grim Reaper. The only sure things in life are death and taxes. The idea of dying does not appeal to me at all. I prefer paying my taxes annually, no matter how painful, than contemplating the fact of my death. The very notion of not existing in this world, of being buried in the ground, or residing in a shelved tomb, as does my dad, is not something that I readily think about. I will cross that bridge when the time comes. I have placed my unequivocal trust in God and hope that He will strengthen me to face my death, no matter in what form it may come. On the one hand, I have no desire to have my life meaninglessly extended as is often the case with medical technology today. I want no extraordinary means utilized on behalf of my body. When my time is up, I want to be allowed to naturally journey into the next life. On the other hand, I do not wish to die prematurely in an auto accident, be murdered in a holdup, nor do I have any wish for some doctor or nurse to medically end my life before nature does. The ever-increasing incidence of euthanasia in some of our hospitals, nursing homes, and clinics is something that should worry us all. The ill-fated Clinton plan did not die in 1994. Its basic premises of cutting health costs by rationing care still exists and can only spell premature death for millions of elderly Americans. Pope John Paul II was right, on the culture of death we have created in this country.

With this in mind, euthanasia should have a more practical interest for all of us. Abortion affects a small percentage of men and women. But everyone gets old and everyone dies. The more people we have, the higher the cost of medicine and the more pressures there are on medical insurance companies and hospitals to provide care from a finite pool of resources. Eventually something is going to have to give. There exists now several social forces that are clamoring for ways of limiting our population. Those in the pro-life movement have been warning the public for twenty years that the culture of death is a two-way slippery slope that concerns not only the unborn but also the other end of the living spectrum, the elderly. In some ways, euthanasia acts as a diabolic complement to abortion—abortion's deadly twin sister. One reason there are dire predictions about the lack of funding for Social Security in the year 2020 is because abortion has left us with several million fewer people to contribute to the fund that will have to support the top-heavy baby boom generation led by President Bill Clinton. In 1990, there were four workers to support each Social Security recipient. By the year 2010, there will be only two. Today more people believe in extraterrestrial life than think that there will be anything left in the Social Security fund for them.

Many euthanasia proponents are already talking the talk that served the pro-abortion side so well! There must be quality of life! The Hemlock Society and its allies are quietly and subtlety conditioning their grandparents and their parents to fear that they will become a burden to their family.

They have not just a *right* to die but a *duty* to die. They are being led to believe that they should get out of the way and clear a spot on the planet for the young people who have not lived as fully or as long as they have. How a society looks at birth and death are often defining issues within the objective judgment rendered on a specific culture. In Roman times, the epitome of glorified and brilliant paganism, the act of self-immolation was considered noble and worthy of recognition. In ancient Japan, the notion of *seppuku,* ritualistic suicide that required the swift assistance of a trusted and loyal aide, evolved into the modern act of *hara-kiri* played out thousands of times during the Second World War. The fierce and deadly suicide pilots who selflessly crashed their *Zeros* into American battle ships and destroyers during the savage battle for Okinawa were considered so heroic that they were named *kamikaze* after the divine wind that had saved Japan from the Mongolian fleet in the twelfth century. The creed of Western Civilization that had enshrined man as the high point of creation could not sanction something such as this that flew in the face of a loving and forgiving God. In flirting with reformed thinking on euthanasia and assisted suicide, this country is in serious danger of denying its Judeo-Christian heritage. It is running the risk of slipping into some of the cultural excesses of countries like Japan where suicide was considered an honorable and a moral practice.

Although the perception of a right to die has interested philosophers since Greek antiquity, it has only been recently that the issue has taken on a life of its own. The Enlightenment philosophy of man as god is as much at work here as it has been in all our other issues. If man is God than he can act like God by making life and death decisions for people who can not make them for themselves. By the 1950s, advances in medical technology had allowed terminally ill and permanently unconscious patients, individuals who had once died quickly from complications or from an inability to eat and drink, to be kept alive dramatically longer than ever before. This new-found capability of medical science caused a rash of right-to-die debates that upset the delicate balance between medical science, care and religious ethics. Medicine could now alter the course of nature. Patients, families, and doctors now had to weigh several issues in order to balance medical care with practical economics. A few historic cases loom as illustrative of the problems, pains, moral dilemmas and consequences of modern age medicine and health care.

The first case involved Karen Ann Quinlan. In 1975, Quinlan suffered a respiratory arrest induced by drugs and alcohol. She drifted into a coma that left her in a permanent vegetative state, unable to breathe without a mechanical respirator and unable to eat without a feeding tube. Her family undertook a prolonged legal battle in which they argued that their daughter would not have wanted to be kept alive in this condition with no hope of recovery. She stayed that way for nine years until the courts allowed her parents to remove her from life support equipment. She finally died in 1985. It was during this case that the *right to die* entered the lexicon.

Another example is that of Nancy Cruzan. She died in December of 1990 after being in a persistent vegetative state since a 1983 auto accident in Missouri. The Supreme Court ruled in *Cruzan vs. Director, Missouri Department of Health* that she had a right to die after a five year struggle by her family to remove the feeding tube that had kept her alive. The Court recognized that the right to refuse unwanted medical care is a liberty interest and therefore is constitutionally protected. To define food and water as medical treatment seems to me a verbal stretch. It would seem that the Cruzan family wanted to bring to closure their own pain as much as that of Nancy. It was an overt act of playing God and the Supreme Court fed right into this situation with its ruling.

A more overt case that involved the withholding of food and water was Christine Busalacchi, a beautiful 22-year old woman who had been severely injured in an auto accident in 1990. She was deliberately starved to death at the prestigious Barnes Hospital in St. Louis after a neurological workup determined that she was in a persistent vegetative state and had no hope of any recovery. This was despite court testimony that uncovered that Christine could be fed food with a spoon by mouth, followed people with her eyes, laughed, sat up in a wheelchair and responded to her environment. According to the accepted definition of persistent vegetative state, patients are capable of none of the above. Mourners prayed and begged medical officials to feed her but their request were denied. Elizabeth McDonald of St. Louis attempted to intervene through the court system by being appointed her guardian, since Christine's father, Peter, was instrumental in getting the court's approval for her execution. But her requests were denied. Death by starvation is not a pretty sight. Christine died a painfully slow death on March 7, 1993. It was peculiar that not one of the many disability rights group came forward to file suit in federal court. Her death further muddied the waters as to what constituted a candidate for euthanasia. From Christine's death, one thing is grossly apparent. The length and suffering that a person being deliberately starved to death endures is a cruel and inhumane punishment. The pro-death lobby contended that Christine was going to die anyway because the hospital had refused to feed her. They have seized on the inhumanity of her starving to death to argue for direct euthanasia through lethal injection, the same kind of method now employed in several states to execute convicted murders. Decency and compassion demand that the patient receive a fast and speedy form of death.

Then there is the case of Gary Dockery, a policeman from Eastern Tennessee. He inexplicably came out of a coma after being shot in the forehead in September 1988. His recovery further complicates the situation. If there is any chance of recovery, even one in a million, should not more time be allotted before pulling the plug? It was like he had an electrical disconnect, said neurologist Dr. David Rankine, then suddenly the disconnect healed itself. Stunned and perplexed by his regaining consciousness, doctors were unable to come up with a medical explanation for his improvement. There was and still is no scientific rationale as to why he regained his vocal powers and seemed fully alert despite the loss of 20% of his brain function due to the shooting. Dr. Robert Daroff said that families should not hold out for miracles. The thousands of people who don't recover don't make the papers. The one person in a decade who does recover causes great public excitement and it usually involves a case like this in which there was no true vegetative state. Daroff seemed upset because he could not explain Dockery's miraculous recovery. To do so might force him to recognize a power higher than doctors or medical science.

An even more bizarre case involved Mark Newton, a 28-year-old diver, who awoke after being in a coma for six months. After a diving mishap off the coast of South Africa, he was declared brain dead and flown home to a London hospital. His case appeared hopeless. He had come up from a dive too quickly and had starved his brain of oxygen. A brain scan showed only a glimmer of activity was present, not enough to suggest the hope of recovery. His parents, Jo and George Newton of South Oxhey in Hertfordshire, grimly accepted the reality that they would someday have to give permission to turn off his life-support system. They had planned to donate his organs. On the day his life was to end, his mother begged the hospital to give him a few more weeks of life. Little did she know that he was listening to every word she was saying, even though he was unable to communicate. He opened his eyes a few days later and provided some great insight into his alter-existence in a comatose world. Newton said, "it was as clear as a bell. I heard you discussing this kid who was on a life support system. It never occurred to me that I was the kid you were talking about." He proceeded to recount several things, like the birth of his niece, told to him months before. He could remember the child's name and even her weight. His case raises the question of whether doctors know enough about the vegetative state to make such life and death pronouncements. The recovery of Mark Newton raises the chilling question of whether Kathy Cobb, the New York woman who became pregnant while in a persistent vegetative state, knows who the father of her child is. Injured in a car accident twelve years ago, she was raped while in the hospital. Her parents, staunch Catholics, will not allow the hospital to abort her baby nor will they turn off her life support system. Although Kathy is able to breathe on her own, feel pain, and her eyes follow visitors around the room, her doctors have always maintained that she is not aware of anything or anybody. The only conclusion to draw from cases such as these, is that our destinies really rest in God's hands. Physicians, medical support personnel and families have to refrain from speeding along or abetting the natural process of dying. That province belongs exclusively to God. To believe or do otherwise is to play God, even to be God. The film, *Malice,* with Stephen Baldwin and Nicole Kidman featured a physician with what is called in medical parlance, "a God complex." Baldwin shocked his colleagues by saying "I am God!" It is an arrogance that sometimes transcends the issue by assuming powers and controls that should be left for the real God.

The story of Derek Humphry and his second wife, Ann, is a good example of man as god with relation to death and dying in America. Humphry and Ann were active in the *Euthanasia Society of America*. It was their *Euthanasia Education Council* that had been attempting to effect legislation that would remove the stigma from suicide. In 1975, because of sensitivity to the word euthanasia, they decided to change the name to *Society for the Right to Die*. By the following year, the first *Living Will* law, called the *Natural Death Act* had passed and been signed into law in California. Two years later, the *Euthanasia Education Council* became *Concern for Dying*.

In the 1980s, the Humphrys captured a good part of the high moral ground. The council had adopted the abortion lobby's rhetoric, adapting such successful terms as choice and rights. They gained great support for what they called "the right to die". Derek and Ann felt there was a need for a new group since there was a great deal of infighting over monetary issues between the two active wings of the movement, the *Society for the Right to Die* and *Concern for Dying*. This led to the founding the *Hemlock Society* in 1980, Humphry took the name from the poison that Socrates used to end his life. Ironically, in Socrates' case, it was a forced suicide since he had been condemned to death by his fellow Greeks.

The origins of the Hemlock Society dates back to the Humphrys' book *Jean's Way*, which refers to the death of Humphry's first wife, Jean. According to the book's account, Jean and Derek made a pact during one of her hospitalizations for breast cancer. Derek promised his sick wife that if she ever asked him if it were time for her to kill herself, he would give her an honest answer. He also promised to provide her with the means when and if she decided to die. On 29 March 1975, Jean sat up in bed and asked Derek, *Is this the day?* He had mixed a lethal dose of drugs and put it into her coffee. He watched her drink as he sat by her bedside, ready with a pillow to smother her if the pills did not work. Derek did not have to use the pillows and she died peacefully that afternoon.

Humphry later met Ann Wickett, a young divorcee twelve years his junior who was pursuing a Ph.D. in English Literature at Birmingham University in England. Lonely and distraught, with a broken life and a failed suicide attempt in her past, Ann Wickett put an ad in the personals column. Derek answered it five months after Jean's death in 1975, and he and Ann were married shortly after. Almost immediately after their marriage, Ann was caught up in the romance of Jean's death. She wanted to turn it into a sacred cause. She viewed it as a love story and urged Derek to write about it and share it with others. The couple started attending meetings of EXIT, the *British Euthanasia Society*, founded in the 1930s. EXIT showed a great deal of interest in *Jean's Way*. This was accompanied by money, fame, and celebrity. A police inquiry began that could have resulted in Derek sentenced to a fourteen year jail term. This only increased interest in his book.

The book turned Derek into a symbol of a caring husband who could speak on the romantic and bittersweet realities of standing by a spouse through a terminal illness.

Derek's success drew greater attention to the circumstances of Jean's death. In her own suicide note, written in October of 1991, sent to author Rita Marker, whose poignant and heart-rending book, *Deadly Compassion*, details her own friendship with Ann Humphry, Ann Humphry told the real story of Jean Humphry's death: Jean actually died of suffocation. She had gone along with his sanitation of Jean's death because she thought he had acted out of love and compassion. Her own fatal bout with cancer made her realize what kind of a man Derek Humphry really was. In the early 1990s, euthanasia was not yet a real alternative. It made for a lively and interesting topic of both debate and conversation. The October 1980 edition of the *Hemlock Quarterly*, with Ann Humphry as its editor, was part of its purpose to make euthanasia more accessible and to remove the stigma attached to it. At this time, neither self-deliverance as Gerald Larue, one of the society's early directors wrote nor attempted suicide were illegal. What was unprecedented was the journal's attempt to legalize assisted suicide so that euthanasia would have an equal status with health for Americans. What really put the society on a firm foundation was the publication of *Let Me Die Before I Wake*, first published in 1981 and sold only to members of the society. This anthology of stories depicts how various people coped with the terminal illnesses of loved ones; in effect, it became their first suicide manual. Later on, with the use of a Hollywood publicist, the book brought in many new members and great infusion of money to push the group's agenda of death.

Humphry wrote another book, *The Final Exit*, which was highly acclaimed by critics in August of 1991. It topped the *New York Times* best seller list in the *Advice, How-to and Miscellaneous* category. The book's cover was adorned with endorsements from former Colorado Governor Richard Lamm, who expressed the notion of the elderly's duty to die, author Issac Asimov, and ethicist Frederick Abrams. Author Betty Rollins, whose own story about how she helped her mother to die was then in the filming stages of a made-for-TV movie. Rollins wrote the foreword to *Final Exit*. The book was published by Carol Publishing, a group which concentrates largely on sensational non-fiction. It is owned by Steven Schragis, who with his wife, were both Hemlock members. He took on a personal crusade to make this book the big commercial success it was. His one-man publicity campaign made it acceptable to mainline bookstores, even though it was an amateurishly-written, thin volume. Humphry had sent out 300 review copies without getting a single review. Sales slacked and the book was destined for the remainder heap until the *Wall Street Journal* ran a major story, entitled *Suicide Manual for Terminally Ill Stirs Heated Debate*, written by Meg Cox, who said that her article acted as a match to tinder. Humphry and his enlightened views about death and dying found willing accomplices within the mainstream media. From that point on, Humphry scheduled

interviews on CBS *This Morning, The Today Show,* and *Good Morning America.*
CNN and other networks devoted nightly news programs to it. Many commentators attributed the book's success to some great societal need to control death. University of Minnesota ethicist Arthur Caplan called it a statement of protest of how medicine is dealing with terminal illness and dying.

For virtually all the national interviews, Humphry stuck to his script of
self-deliverance. In an interview for a British newspaper, he made a slip of
the tongue that revealed a lot about the book's actual purpose. In an un-
guarded moment he admitted to the London *Sunday Express* that *Final
Exit,* tells you how, where and when to kill yourself or someone else. It
breaks the last taboo. That seems to be the true motivation behind euthanasia advocates. These children of the Enlightenment want to strike down
the last prohibition of Christian eschatology that links a personal God with
His people.

A sampling of some of the chapter headings indicate what kind of a
book it is. One chapter is entitled *Self-Deliverance via the Plastic Bag.* No
stranger to detail, Humphry discusses if one should use a clear or opaque
plastic bag for suicide. There is a chapter on *Going Together* discusses how
to arrange a cost effective final date. There is an etiquette section on final
preparations that includes *Letters to Be Written.* His pupils are instructed to
leave a note of apology for whomever discovers you and for any inconve-
nience you have caused. For the inventive, there is a section on *Bizarre Ways
to Die.* Self-execution can be committed with firecrackers, rattlesnakes, electricity, guns, and ropes. For those who are infirm, elderly or handicapped,
Humphry extends the promise that he was working to obtain a total acceptance and moral approval of euthanasia. Once the *Hemlock Society* get aid-
in-dying laws on the books, there will be a more tolerant view toward such
cases.

Not everyone heralded the need for such a book. Dr. Leon R. Kass, a
respectable medical ethicist, wrote a scathing review of *Final Exit,* for *Commentary Magazine,* in which he said:

> Adopting a tone and manner midway between the *Frugal Gour-
> met* and *Mister Rogers,* Humphry has written a book that reads
> like a "A Salt-Free Guide to Longer Life," or "How to Conquer
> Fear in Twenty-two Easy Lessons." The reader, blinded by his
> verbal blandness, nearly loses sight of the big picture: this self-
> appointed messiah is indiscriminately and shamelessly teaching
> suicide . . . to countless strangers. Humphry's book does include
> a few unspecified pages buried in the back of the book suggesting
> that depression is not a good reason to use his book. As an
> afterthought, he urged those who were depressed to get help.
> Where and how, he does not say.

It is impossible to gauge just how many strangers were led to pay the
full price for reading his book. Rita Marker's book does provide a few direct

examples of suicide victims found with a copy of Humphry's' book near by, including a thirteen-year-old girl from Southern California who found her mother dead with a plastic bag over her head. We know that from movies, newspapers and magazines that young people, especially teens, who go through periodic bouts of hormonal stress and even clinical depression, are often prone to these types of suggestions. I have had little personal experience with actual suicide. A classmate of my son's took his own life two months after graduation, using several methods to end his young and healthy life, including pills, and a razor blade. It was the carbon monoxide, which he had piped into the car that eventually killed him. This was not unlike the method used in the movie, *The Client.* The young man was unhappy because he would have few friends at his new school in the fall.

The football coach at Holy Cross in 1986, Rick Carter, had risen through the coaching ranks to give the school some of its best teams. His last season, 1985, the Holy Cross Crusaders had a lackluster 4-7 record. Carter, a young, dynamic and very popular coach, with the thick neck of a wrestler, had won a national championship with Dayton University in 3A, before coming to Worcester. There were other health reasons offered, but whatever the case, he hanged himself that February. The *New York Times* callously summed up his death by writing his phone had "stopped ringing." Whatever his motivation, it was tragic waste of a human life. The bitter irony is that his successor, Mark Duffner won his first ten games that fall of 1986, unveiling the athletic talents of Heisman Trophy candidate, Gordy Lockbaum. Duffner's Holy Cross teams went 60-5-1 in the six seasons after Carter's suicide.

It is into this changing moral climate on death and dying that doctors such as Jack Kervorkian, have entered. Though he has been the cause and focus of thousands of ghoulish jokes, the sobering reality of the situation is that here is a man, a doctor who has gone on an unholy crusade that views life, pain, and technology as the real enemies. He is a medical Luddite with the reasoning of the Unabomber, who views death as his assistant in effecting his ungodly will on the people who trust him. This angel of death is a deadly weapon whose messianic zeal for death has made him the worst nightmare of the medical profession. Jack Kervorkian first entered the battle for the soul of America as a sixty-two-year old unemployed (not retired as many have said), pathologist from Royal Oak, Michigan. "In person, Kervorkian comes across as an Old Testament prophet," wrote Max Hosenball in the 6 December 1993 issue of *Newsweek.* His obsession with death goes beyond his self-appointed mission of mercy. His flirtation with death started much earlier, while he was in residency at the University of Michigan. It was here that capital punishment caught his interest, arousing his curiosity. As he said in court testimony:

> While I was in my residency I was researching the idea of condemned men being allowed to submit to anesthesia rather than

execution. While under anesthesia we could do experiments from which they would not recover and then remove their organs. Now if you need a liver or a heart, would you like to see a young, healthy man or woman fried in the electric chair? No! But the Dark-Age school told me I would have to drop the project I was working on or leave. So, I left and spent my last two years of residency at Pontiac.

Kervorkian maintained his interest in death. He later corresponded with Westley Allan Dodd, the Washington state child-killer who was hanged in January of 1993. Kervorkian said that Dodd had wanted to donate his organs but was refused. When he died, six people died with him, Kervorkian said. He also discussed his experiments on newly-executed corpses, in an article for the *National Medical Association*. Of special interest was a nineteenth century experiment where French medical students caught heads as they fell from the guillotine. *Do you hear me?* they shouted into the ears of the newly-deceased. According to the article, there was no reply. While an associate pathologist at Pontiac General Hospital, Kervorkian ran afoul of the medical ethics board. As part of an experiment, this modern Dr. Frankenstein transfused cadaver blood directly into several patients. No legal action was taken but the medical community was shocked by his aberrant behavior.

In 1988, in a *Medicine and Law* article, Kervorkian explained his plans for combining medical experimentation with planned death. In a subsequent article, "The Last Fearsome Taboo: Medical Aspects of Planned Death," he transcended the notion of euthanasia or, "good death," to a higher plateau, *eutatosthanasaia*, or "best death." This concept is far broader than mere euthanasia or mercy killing as it is popularly known. The Kervorkian menu of planned death includes capital punishment, both involuntary and voluntary, obligatory suicide mandated by rigid theistic or philosophical principles. He also included on his death list a quasi-optional suicide for the relief of suffering resulting from illness, disability or old age. On the bottom of the page was strictly optional suicide for reasons not known to others, and finally justifiable infanticide or pedicide and feticide both intra- and extrauterine. What Kervorkian failed to discuss was the extreme powers over life and death with all of the financial and economic considerations that would be vested in the physician.

Though little has been written about any financial motivation behind his avante garde medical philosophy, Kervorkian did have a plan for harvesting and selling body parts. As Kervorkian wrote in an 1989 article for *Medicine and Law*:

> Sales to the rich could indirectly save more lives of the poor: because quality often erroneously is equated with price; wealthy donees might prefer to buy "high-quality" kidneys from donors

in the upper strata of society and leave most or all of the freely donated or very low-priced "low-quality" organs from "skid row" donors to the poor—thereby enhancing equity.

When Kervorkian was prevented from establishing a pathology clinic near Detroit prior to his new calling, he claimed that he was chased out of the business by other doctors who feared the competition. Years later he went to California to pursue a film project that never saw the light of day. He was reputed to have wanted to make a movie of Handel's *Messiah*. Later he commuted between two part-time pathology jobs at hospitals in Long Beach, sometimes sleeping in his rusty VW van. In 1985, Kervorkian returned to Michigan where he lived off canned food and Social Security. As he became famous, he turned down speaking engagements of $10,000, because he says he was conducting his campaign for humanity, not personal gain.

Dr. Death, as he has become known, was looking for the right person to test the killing machine he had made from scrap aluminum, the parts of a toy car and various other bits of material found at garage sales and flea markets. On 4 June 1990, Kervorkian parked his Volkswagen van near a campsite in suburban Detroit. With the help of his sister, Kervorkian hooked Janet Adkins to his primitive killing machine. The fifty-four-year-old woman from Portland, Oregon, had been diagnosed with Alzheimer's disease. She and her husband Ron were members of the *Hemlock Society* and had seen Kevorkian on the *Phil Donohue Show*. They contacted him to assist Mrs. Adkins in her self-deliverance.

Kervorkian's killing machine combined three solutions into a deadly mixture, including saline, a sedative, and potassium chloride. Similar solutions are considered as cruel and inhumane by opponents of capital punishment. Kervorkian hooked the woman up to the machine and started the saline solution. For her part she flipped a switch which started the lethal drip into her arm. One of the curious facts of this deadly scenario was that Kervorkian had never spoken to his patient until the week of her death. All the arrangements, and even the initial call, had been made by her husband. It was said that she did not want to be a burden to her husband and her family. The husband's overseer role seems to happen too frequently, leaving a large window open for abuse in these cases. There was also a good deal of trouble with this primitive method of self-deliverance. It proved cumbersome and ineffective the first number of times he used it, prompting this "Mr. Wizard of Death" to resort to carbon monoxide released through a facial covering that resembled a hockey mask.

On 22 April 1992, Kervorkian wrote an exclusive for the *Health Care Weekly Review,* entitled *A Final Statement from Jack Kervorkian, Great Minds Rule from the Grave: Dr. Kervorkian is Right.* Borrowing the words of Einstein, Kervorkian vigorously defended his killing spree by writing, "I will obey no injunction with regard to my humanitarian intent and actions, especially one that was maliciously inflicted by means of character assassination." In the true spirit of enlightened thought, Kervorkian is very much concerned with his self-image. In 1995, he filed suit against the *American Medical Association* for saying that he was a killer. Since Mrs. Adkins' death in 1991, Kervorkian has been in and out of jail as the state of Michigan has tried, unsuccessfully so far, to prosecute him under its law against assisted suicide. While this deadly cat and mouse game has been going on, Kervorkian has assisted in more than 100 other suicides. Kervorkian is a vivid example of the real meaning and impetus behind the euthanasia forces in this country. As in the case of the choice for abortion, how many of these clients, both young women and the elderly have been intimidated, coerced and forced into their choices? How many elderly persons, in the twilight of their long lives, are made to feel unwanted, in the way, and a financial and emotional burden to their children and their families? How many have sacrificed the remaining years of their lives so that they would not unduly hurt their families?

Derek Humphry came out in defense of Dr. Death, calling him a brave and lonely pioneer. If he is not stopped, his way of thinking may well become the wave of the future. In his twisted lifeboat mentality, Kevorkian truly believes that his methods of voluntary self-elimination of individual and mortally diseased or crippled lives taken collectively can only enhance the preservation of public health. He might be on the verge of winning public vindication, if not a great personal victory. It can not be dismissed that there is great support for him within the medical and legal professions. Newspapers and magazines often highlight doctors who agree with Kervorkian's philosophy, if not his sloppy methods. After four decades of steady decline. the elderly suicide rate has climbed nearly 9% from 1980 to 1992.

Geoffrey N. Fieger, Kervorkian's lawyer wrote an article for the 3 December 1993 edition of the *New York Times* that painted his client as a warm, fun-loving man who loves baseball, pretty girls, Bach, and big band music. According to Fieger, he is also incapable of being a hypocrite. Fieger says that Kevorkian thinks we are in danger of slipping back to the Dark Ages. Fieger also believes that this issue is not about death and dying because all people are going to die eventually. It is about suffering, he says with the implication that those who are opposed to assisted suicide are in favor of suffering. Such specious reasoning demonstrates how far the proponents of this kind of anointed behavior have gone in their attempt to remake human society in the image and likeness of the French Jacobins. To be opposed to assisted suicide is not to be pro-suffering but to recognize that doctors can control even the worst pain. It is also to realize that suffering does have a larger and deeper role in atonement for sin. Modernists, such as Fieger with their unbending loyalty to progress and enlightened thought, refuse to accept that pain is sometimes a necessary evil that must be endured in exchange for a higher purpose.

In the milieu created by Humphry and Kevorkian, the medical community finds itself caught between the duties and ancient strictures of centuries of medical practice and the pragmatic exigencies of a culture at war with itself. Many physicians have elected to ignore the morality of the past and adopt a relativistic approach to birth, death, and dying. The first casualty has been the Hippocratic Oath. Prior to the time of Hippocrates, in the fifth century B.C., the medical practitioner had a dual role. One was to heal; the other was to kill. Hippocrates, known as the *Father of Medicine*, was a Greek physician, who probably taught at Cos and is generally considered to have been the author of several of the 60-70 medical treatises that were compiled and edited at Alexandria in the third century, including the oath that states first, the physician should do no harm. Written by a pagan physician, this oath respects the life of the patient, even the unborn patient. It is now being challenged by those in the medical profession, such Kervorkian and many abortionists who would like it to conform to changes in modern medicine and values. According to *The Lancet,* these efforts must be resisted because the oath is a declaration of virtue based on faith and self-respect. It is still of vital concern for medical practice because it defends the patient's right to proper treatment, obliging the doctor to provide it with decency. Both Harvard and Johns Hopkins Universities issued a revised version of the Hippocratic Oath. According to former abortionist and now a pro-life activist, Dr. Bernard Nathanson, the new version has purged the oath of strictures against abortion, euthanasia and obligation to do good and avoid harming those in his charge. Medicine seems to have come full circle from paganism through an elevated sense of worth of each patient, to the more practical considerations of population pressures and the high cost of dying. Abortionists and euthanasists have all but reverted back to their pre-pagan days.

According to Nurse Nancy Valko, a nationally recognized expert on death and dying, there is a concerted effort to sell euthanasia to doctors and nurses by the hospital business community. There is a quiet seduction going on that is attempting to lure many doctors and nurses into medicalizing the termination of life. Valko stresses that there are two ways that euthanasia advocates are effecting this seduction. They are first lobbying medical and nursing associations nationwide, encouraging them to take a neutral stance with regard to euthanasia and assisted suicide. Secondly, they are couching this stance in terms of patient autonomy, with the implicit threat of litigation, which might cause medical personnel to take an unresponsive position. According to Valko this is still abandoning the patient. On the same issue Valko relates that the *Oregon Nursing Association* published guidelines in 1996 that included prohibitions against judgmental actions or words in case the patient did decide on death with dignity. The guidelines also included comfort and safety measures to be maintained during the suicide.

Euthanasia supporters insist that there will be conscience clauses to protect doctors and nurses who refuse to participate in the euthanizing of their patients. Making certain that patients receive information on end-of-life options is now considered a nursing duty. If nurses can not comply, the reality is that they may soon find themselves out of a job. Suicide has never required the presence of a doctor before. The right-to-die lobby is pushing for suicide assisted by medical personnel to add a patina of respectability to this evil process. True death with dignity, a swift and painless death without tubes and pain, cannot be achieved by doctors and nurses killing their patients or helping them kill themselves. While there may never be a total consensus on this issue, there must be a concerted effort to make certain that the integrity of the healing profession is not corrupted and vulnerable patients put at risk. It is difficult to believe that our medical community could be talking about the wholesale killing of its patients. The question is raised on how someone like Dr. Kervorkian came to be this ghoulish killer who sees a holy mission in the taking of life, the complete reversal of what the medical profession is supposed to be? This same question was evoked during the days of Nazi Germany. With the outset of the Second World War, the Nazis were no longer content simply to stop useless eaters from procreating. Starting in 1939, an estimated 275,000 Germans, mainly the insane, incurably ill and handicapped were put to death under the Third Reich's euthanasia program. This early program allowed the Nazi doctors to acquire the technical skills they would employ in the implementation of the Final Solution. Their defense at the Nuremberg trials echoes that of those used in current euthanasia debates. Lethal injections were a mercy to relieve hopeless suffering.

The historical parallel with Hitler's Germany raises another pointed question. How did the medical profession become so totally corrupt? The very thought that doctors and their nursing staffs might have a secret pact or tacit agreement with the forces of the Enlightenment shakes the very foundations of trust and honest upon which the medical relationship is often based. If patients lose faith in the hospital's mission to save lives from illness and death, it strikes right at the fundamental essence of the medical profession. Kervorkian is not an anomaly. When something alien to the American culture appears, it is always a good bet to consult Nazi Germany. One of the best books on the subject of the Nazis, *The Nazi Doctors: Medical Killing and the Psychology of Genocide* was written by psychiatrist Robert Jay Lifton in 1986. Nothing is more unthinkable than that physicians, men of healing, could subvert their delicate skills to mass murder.

As a sidebar to this issue, it is a fact that most of the historical attention of the Holocaust has been given to the six million Jews who perished at the hands of the Nazis. But what is not widely known is that the initial targets of the mass killings were the elderly and the mentally defective, since they were such a drain on Germany's limited resources in the 1930s. In 1996, the Discovery Channel aired a program entitled *Selling Murder: The Killing Films of the Third Reich*. One of the arguments the Germans used in an attempt to sway public opinion was that it cost 100,000 German mark to keep one of the defectives alive. Several euthanasia supporters say that a general policy of euthanasia will have beneficial social effects of lowering health care costs for both the patient and society at large. Today the papers are filled with examples of people taking the Nazi way out.

There are several factors at work here, including a pragmatic attitude that realizes that there is a dwindling number of health and medical resources available. Add to this the fact that too many families can not be distracted from the fast pace of their hectic and materialistic lives to adequately attend to the slow and eventual death of their loved ones. These attitudes combine to foster a national rationalization about the quality of life that is slowly conditioning the American people to accept the basic morality of the culture of death. The press, journalists, and other writers are gradually conditioning the American people to accept the notion of the dignity in dying, especially when helped by a physician. A 1995 book by Lonny Shaverson, entitled *A Chosen Death* makes the plea for allowing strictly regulated physician-assisted suicide as a legitimate medical option. His poignant and touching profile of breast cancer victim Mary Hall serves as the centerpiece of his book. Hall, who joined the *Hemlock Society* in 1992, was first diagnosed with cancer in 1989. When new medications sent her into remission, she knew that the cancer would eventually come back. She had saved a gun for her final exit when her cancer returned. Lacking a sense of God or the Divine, the book traces Mary Hall's long and painful odyssey into eternity. This basic liberal attitude is that society must help people end their lives instead of helping them meet their deaths. The author stated that this existential argument of choice was irrational and went against the grain of pro-euthanasia philosophy, which attempted to demonstrate that. The worst way to show that suicide at the end of a life can be a rational choice is to do something as irrational as killing yourself simply because you planned to do it. In the end, the pain, the discomfort became too much for her sagging spirit. There was no one else to talk her out of her decision. As the author watched, she took 30 Seconal tablets, one by one. An hour later she was deeply unconscious. She stopped breathing a few hours later. This story evokes the vivid images dramatized in the seventies movie with Jane Fonda, *They Shoot Horses, Don't They?* in which an attractive young woman, down on her luck and depressed by the sordid living conditions in the thirties, cajoles a young man into putting a gun to her head and ending her pain.

Shaverson has a personal interest in assisted suicide. When he was 14, his mother Roslyn, who was suffering from Crohn's disease, begged her son to help her take her own life. To his credit, he did not help his mother kill herself, but the experience left him scarred. He became obsessed with the ambition of being a doctor. He saw his role as either to cure her or kill her. He did earn a medical degree at the University of California in San Francisco in 1977 and went to work at the Kaiser Foundation Hospital in Walnut Creek, California. He became an early fan of Kervorkian, who had brought the issue of assisted suicide out of the closet. As a cultural warrior of change, Shaverson reasons that there are thousands of families dealing with this issue in secret. While his father could not understand his wife's depression, Shaverson nobly contends that her request would be turned down by pro-euthanasia advocates today because it was based on depression.

I have a brother-in-law, who has been married to my wife's sister for over thirty years. Six months after their marriage, while he was serving in the National Guard, he contracted a similar malady, then called Regional Enteritis, which, like Crohn's Disease, is a chronic inflammation of the bowel. I watched him suffer terribly over those early years. His weight dropped from 205 to about 130 pounds. We thought we were going to lose him a couple of times. Several surgeries, hospital emergency visits, tons of medication and a great deal of stress have left him with a perpetual grimace on his face. Yet not once did we ever hear of his wishing to kill himself and leave his wife and their three children alone in the world. Tony Ohmes proved through his faith in the Almighty, the support of his family and the prayers of everyone who ever met him that the individual can deal with pain without selfishly surrendering to the clarion call of Modernism. He will always rank as one of the bravest men I have ever known.

One case that calls assisted suicide into question is the report of a near forced suicide in Michigan. A Michigan physician, Gerald Klooster claims his father, a mentally incompetent physician, was almost coerced to submit to involuntary euthanasia at the hands of Kervorkian. His mother and four siblings insisted that the doctor, who suffered from Alzheimer's disease, had asked for suicidal assistance while still competent. After his illness diminished his mental capacity, the son literally had to kidnap his father from Florida to Petoskey, Michigan to keep him away from the deadly clutches of Kervorkian. Contrary to the rest of the family, the son contends that suicide is not the intention of his father and a lawyer appointed to represent the elder Klooster agrees. This ground-breaking case is the first time that a family member has gone to court to get help to prevent someone from getting help to kill himself. Not everyone agrees with the enlightened thinking of the pro-death forces in the new American civil war.

On 6 March 1996, a federal appeals court in San Francisco, in an 8-3 decision, ruled that Washington state's ban on doctor assisted suicide violated the constitutional rights of the terminally ill but mentally competent adults who want to hasten their deaths with drugs prescribed by doctors. The Washington law had been part of a ban on promoting or assisting suicide that had been on the books since 1854. US District Judge Barbara Rothstein ruled the law unconstitutional in 1994. Her decision was overturned in 1995 by a three-judge panel in a split decision that ruled the law protects the poor, disabled, and elderly and prevents doctors from being "killers" of their patients. The interconnectedness of the life and death issues now being decided in the courts was acknowledged by New Deal liberal Judge Stephen Reinhardt of the 9th Circuit. Writing for the majority in the euphemistically named *Compassion in Dying vs. Washington,* Reinhardt predictably equated the choice of suicide to the choice of abortion, noting that each involved the most intimate and personal choices a person may make in a lifetime. He added that prohibiting a terminally ill patient from hastening his death may have an even more profound impact on that person's life than forcing a woman to carry a pregnancy to term. Reinhardt also stated the state has a liberty interest in choosing a dignified and humane death rather than being reduced at the end of existence to a childlike state of helplessness, diapered, sedated and incompetent. When patients are no longer able to pursue liberty or happiness and do not wish to pursue life, the state's interest in forcing them to remain alive is less compelling. The culture of death that has been successfully forced on the unborn is now being slowly imposed on the sick and the aged. Citing the hard cases, of people on death's door, in great pain or in a persistent vegetative state, the custodians of our culture, the court system has allowed another vital fundamental principle to be violated.

Judges and legal scholars know that the sanctity of life is the organizing principle of American society. Even our children are familiar with the phrase: life, liberty and the pursuit of happiness. The 14th Amendment had been firmly grounded in an overdue recognition of the fullness of human life. Our legal system has degenerated because our law schools teach that objective truth is an illusion and the rule of law a farce. How many people would have thought this happy pursuit would include physician-assisted suicide? Now the argument appears that to complete the requirements of individual liberty, the Supreme Court must discover the right of a seriously ill person to ask a doctor to help him leave this world. It has created an atmosphere where the current argument in favor of physician-assisted suicide turns solely on whether it should be allowed because it qualifies under the due process or equal rights protections of the 14th amendment. Just as this amendment protects workers from discrimination on the basis of age or physical disability, it should also protect a dying person from unconstitutional discrimination. Just as the public was asked to consider how much society would save by not spending money on unwanted children, it is now being asked to accept the argument that certain classes of the elderly, the infirm and unwanted are readily and advisably disposable in order to enhance the bottom line. Unless something happens to stave off their momentum, the euthanasia lobby will win the day and then the American people will see death or one of its many euphemisms as a category in the Yellow Pages and an increasingly used option at hospitals and nursing homes.

The final question now is where is all this leading. If a constitutional right to die is upheld, then how long will it be before the state or one's heirs decides to mandate the choice to die? The right to die might sound enlightened until one realizes that legally it may mean someday that you can kill yourself or someone can kill you, even if you don't want to die. With an assisted suicide right, we would be living in a world in which the terminally ill were not thought of as moribund but prime candidates for assisted suicide. The issue is a complex one that the respective forces in the Culture War will battle over for generations to come. The right-to-die lobby has the practical consequences of illness—fear, pain and suffering—on their side while the pro-life forces have the less tangible, but no less powerful, forces of life, death, heaven, and hell on theirs. Living wills and the medical power of attorney further complicate the issue, as medical and legal definitions of *persistent vegetative state, extraordinary, and ordinary means of treatment* remain in flux. Contrary to the spirit of the enlightenment, absolute definitions of these terms have to be accepted by administrative, medical and ethical personnel to remove medicine from the battlefields of the Culture War. If something does not change quickly, acceptance of the next logical step, the obligation to die, will cause the American public to begin thinking of the seriously ill as inhuman. They will constitute a special category of citizenry—a *007 class,* licensed to kill itself.

PART III

GROUP
SOLIDARITY

7

Multiculturalism
The New Racism

Greece and Rome have robbed Egypt of her arts and letters, and taken all the credit for themselves.

—Marcus Garvey, 1923

One of my more lively discussions on the radio occurred several years ago with a regular caller named Bob Lawrence, who, like many of our WGNU regulars, would eventually have his own comedy show on Saturday mornings. I found it ironic that Lawrence, an articulate black man with a strong sense of history and culture, would specialize in black humor when so many of our heated discussions revolved around the idea of black solidarity. It was Lawrence who first introduced me to the idea of multiculturalism. During many of our phone debates on the air, he offered many of the same arguments that have become stale and hackneyed—ideas such as that the black past had been stolen by the Greeks or that most of the great inventions of the past and present had been stolen by white people. He argued that Western Civilization had dominated our schools and history for too long and that it would serve for a better education if all Americans could learn about the achievements and contributions of third world peoples, especially African-Americans (as the new nomenclature dictated). Lawrence also argued that young people in the black community needed to learn about their true past so that they would have a strong sense of who they were and where they had come from.

My initial reaction to this new way of thinking was perfunctory. The idea of learning about other peoples has always interested me. I told him that my own education was indeed multicultural. I had taken my masters degree in Asian history and had developed a strong intellectual interest in Southeast Asia during the Vietnam War. After many years of studying American culture, I found the subject of Asian history with its *Analects of Confucius* and the basic philosophical underpinnings of Buddhism fascinating. As our discussions of this issue became more intense over the course of several months, I began to research the notion of Afrocentrism which lay at the core of his argument. It surprised me that this issue was bigger and broader than anything either of us had touched. I realized that multiculturalism is part of the liberals' attempt to subvert and change the American culture as we have known and understood it for over two hundred years. I learned that Afrocentrism contends that the ancient Greeks stole most of their great intellectual discoveries in math, science and philosophy from their African originators, the Egyptians.

The Reverend Jesse Jackson joined the fray on the campus of Stanford University during one of the initial attempts to limit or eradicate Western ideas of freedom, equality and responsibility from the academic world, he could be heard chanting *Hey, hey, Western Civ has got to go!* Jackson and his followers decried the relevant merits of studying "dead white males," in the university classrooms. The inherent logic of this battle cry was that these men, such as Shakespeare, John Milton, John Donne, William Wordsworth, Ralph Waldo Emerson and Samuel Taylor Coleridge, had their chance. They professed that the canon of western thought had not to be expanded but replaced by the wisdom and knowledge in the works of Toni Morrison, Maya Angelou and Alice Walker. Jackson's involvement and the threat to traditional teaching took my discussions with Lawrence to a much higher level. He had been arguing for inclusion while these multicultural forces had cultural replacement as their *raison d'etre.*

As for the term "African-American," I offered Lawrence my strongest reservations in this changing of the nomenclature. I had grown up with the idea of black people being referred to as "Negroes." In some areas, the term "colored" was often applied. Epithets, such as "nigger" have never appealed to me and I can honestly say I have never used such derisive and offensive terms in conversation. The term "African-American" seemed to lack any basis in reality. The African root is too vague and indeterminate. Were blacks to call themselves Nigerian-Americans, or Kenynian-Americans, I probably would not have the same objections. In the seventies, ethnic identity seemed to loom large and other groups developed similar ethnic nomenclatures, such as Irish-American, Italian-American, and Chinese-American. But none really lasted very long in the popular parlance. Black leaders seemed to recognize the term's intellectual vacuity and introduced a phrase "people of color" aimed at creating political solidarity among other oppressed groups such as Latinos, Haitians, Cubans and other immigrants. When I heard a black student recruiter at Holy Cross College use this term, I quipped that there was not much difference between the sound of people of color and colored people, an opprobrious term deemed unsuitable for polite discourse today.

Afrocentrism is common place on many elite college campuses. Competent black professors and scholars are at a premium to teach the many courses that attempt to extend the myths of the Greeks pilfering of black intellectual property. It is common knowledge that white professors are not welcome in this discipline that has more a political and economic motivation than does it a scholarly one. Whole departments with exorbitant budgets have been established to serve as independent duchies with little or no restraint enforced on them by pedagogical governing bodies. Multiculturalism springs from the disjointed premise that Western Civilization, in general, and American institutions, in particular, are fundamentally racist because they elevate Eurocentric or white standards and values over those of other cultures. This fiction employs a standard of relativity in which each culture is unique and yet none is higher than the other. The Western idea of innate individual rights rests on a par with the practices of slavery, cannibalism and human sacrifice common in many third world cultures. According to their rubrics, the traditional curriculum teaches us to see the world through the eyes of the privileged, white European male so as to adopt his interests as our own. They argue that this is wrong because it denigrates other cultures as inferior when they are merely different. It is supported by a modish and moralistic liberalism that contends that whites are the villains of history. It professes that Western institutions are systematically racist, that, racism is so deeply ingrained in the very nature of these institutions that the only way to separate them is to destroy them and build anew. Multiculturalism is an unadulterated academic affirmative action plan to redress the wrongs committed by our ancestors on the so-called oppressed peoples of the world. Its proponents allow no questioning or debate on its fundamental premises. Multiculturalism's dependence on the sophomoric notion that one culture is as good as another, is a denial of all Western claims to transmutable truth and any absolute standard of right and wrong. As an educational philosophy, it has no use for timeless universals. Multiculturalism can only lead the United States into a state of moral and intellectual anarchy.

Richard Bernstein, the author of the *Dictatorship of Virtue,* points out that multiculturalism has already succeeded in making several basic changes in the nature of public discourse. First is the elimination from acceptable discourse of any claim of superiority or even special status for Europe, or any definition of the United States as derived primarily from European civilization. Second is the attack on the very notion of the individual and the concomitant paramount status accorded group identification. Third is the indictment of one group and the expiation of all other. In the true spirit of the Enlightenment, multiculturalists erroneously insist that slavery, pollution, and all the negative facts of American life are a legacy from our Western Civilization. They believe that the entire past culture must be disavowed and a new way of thinking be established that celebrates group identity or consciousness as opposed to individualism.

The multiculturalists began their assault on American culture on its very origins. On the 500th anniversary of Columbus' expedition to America, the multiculturalists came out in force. Columbus was vilified as a murderer, a rapist and his historic discovery was deemed as the origin of a sordid history of racism, Indian attacks, ozone depletion, earth warming, and the destruction of rain forests. An anniversary that should have served as a celebration, and even a glorification of the American past, was falsely denigrated and reduced to an excuse for national repentance and atonement. On another front, in San Francisco, a statue that was designed to show the compassion of the Catholic missionaries has been transformed into a confession of genocide by Christian and European civilization. One critic suggested that, "The Indians have all gone to heaven but rest assured the Christian missionaries have all gone to hell." What really has gone to hell is the proud appreciation for the country's European roots and traditions and, by association, a respect for the Catholic Church.

The most notorious of all the multicultural professors has been Leonard Jefferies, whose controversial career at the City College of New York finally ended in 1995. Jefferies had been teaching his own unique brand of eugenics to his predominantly black classes for over twenty years. In what can be best termed the theater of the absurd, Jefferies believes that black people are the sun people and white people are the ice people. This is a distinction based solely on skin color. Blacks have a much higher concentration of melanin and therefore they are warmer, unfailingly humanistic, and happier people. Because of a melanin deficiency, whites cannot exhibit the friendliness and happiness that black people can. Jefferies first made headlines when in a speech in Albany in 1991, he charged that rich Jews had financed the slave trade and had conspired with the Mafia to make anti-black movies in Hollywood designed to bring about the destruction of black people.

The sad irony of this situation was that Jefferies was allowed to teach for so long before crossing that indelible line that eventually led to his ouster from the CCNY faculty. Where were the guardians of decorum and interracial harmony for so long? No one had the courage to raise the issue that the toxic winds of racism blow in all directions. Blacks, like Jefferies, have used their racial past and sometimes, the threat of violence, to thoroughly intimidate a liberal white community into sanctioning the quasi-violent and anti-social behavior of black people in the classroom and on the job, on the grounds that it would be racist to stop them, or harmful not to indulge their activities. This is the depths of the long stream of anti-intellectualism that has characterized the multicultural issue in the nineties.

On the megrim of black racism, many black leaders contend that they cannot be racists, no matter how much they may despise and hate white people, solely because of their race. Since they are a minority and not in control of the major power organs and institutions of this country, they contend there is no way they can be racists. This is a totally disingenuous argument that really is a non-sequitur. Racism is in the heart and the soul. Power relationships have little to do with the color of one's skin. Many blacks are playing the race card to win more economic and political power for themselves. Power is based on money, education, and political connections. Racism is another in the long list of self-indulgent excuses that many people of goodwill have accepted from too many members of the black community. This attitude has been responsible for keeping blacks at the low level in which so many of them now exist. Nothing has been demanded of them. The disorderly and angry behavior of thousands of disaffected Blacks has been tolerated, if not encouraged, by the liberal press, black leaders, and government officials, at the expense of their schooling, their culture and their social assimilation into American society. The only true course for American unity and peace in this country. This is the only way that the racers can learn to live in relative harmony. The other choice is a bitter and angry situation that could very easily lead to a race war.

The search for racial bias takes on a life of its own in our hypersensitive society. While most complaints of racism center around jobs, housing, bank loans, and the redlining of insurance districts, other far-fetched examples, as evidence by the cultural writings of John Leo, a columnist in *US News and World Report*, underscore the discordant atmosphere that now exists between blacks and whites. During the O. J. Simpson trial, *Time* magazine was accused of racism for manipulating a cover photo of him so as to make him look more sinister. A black gay activist accused Greenwich Village gay bars of not having enough drinkers of all colors. A misspelled word in a high school yearbook drew fire because homecoming was spelled "hocoming." Since the homecoming couple that year was black, black students took great offense. An investigation proved that it was the printer's fault. Since he accepted full blame for the mistake and apologized, the chance that the mistake was racially motivated was next to zero. All these complaints seemed to stem from a false notion of equality. Paralleling the idea of cultural relativity is the notion that equality is an American right and that all people are created equal. This is a fallacy that cannot bear up under scrutiny. Empirical evidence and daily living demonstrate a wide variance of intelligence, ability, skills, talents, and efficiencies among people. People come in all shapes and sizes with a variety of values, vices, and motivations. Equality is just a union card to the human race—an entitlement to the basic rights of a human being to life, liberty, and the pursuit of happiness. Nothing more, nothing less.

The multiculturalists have taken the cultural issue a step further to argue that Western Civilization is vastly inferior to African culture. The myth of African cultural superiority started with the first installment of Martin Bernal's voluminous work, *Black Athena: The Roots of Classical Culture,* published in 1987. The author, a Sinologist at Cornell University, attempted to lessen European cultural arrogance by substituting it with an African arrogance of his own. His book led to a debate that made it, in the words of Italian architect Mario Liverani, "the most discussed book on the ancient history of the eastern Mediterranean world since the Bible." Bernal's original theories and his research of the late nineteenth and early twentieth century German classical studies have led to the speculation that modern classical studies have advanced a covertly racist agenda by elevating Greek culture over that of the Egyptians and Phoenicians. Afrocentrists have used *Black Athena* to support the erroneous contention that Greek civilization was actually the creation by black Egyptians, a claim disavowed by reputable Egyptologists. Bernal's false belief that Africa was the center of all civilization is essentially a left-wing conspiracy theory that believes Western scientists and academics have been distorting the fact that Cleopatra and Socrates were both black or the fact that all of Western antiquity descends from darkest Africa. These political and social myths trace their roots to the early twentieth century polemics of Marcus Garvey, the founder of the *Universal Negro Improvement Association.* He began his study of history while a teenager in Jamaica and the West Indies. He used his knowledge of Egyptian and African history to help promote racial emancipation as means to instill self-confidence in a people who had lost faith in themselves since they had been forced to give up their past. In his 1923 essay, "Who and What is a Negro," Garvey wrote that every student of history "knows that the Negro once ruled the world, when white men were savages and barbarians living in caves." When Garvey started this myth, he was creating a new historiography and a new mythology that has not helped black people advance themselves one bit in American society. The erroneous African origins of Greece is a dangerous myth of self-identification and self-ennoblement, the kind of noble lie that Socrates suggested was needed to achieve the utopian state he describes in Plato's Republic. The lie is neither necessary nor noble and can only lead to self-delusion and visions of non-existent grandeur. Many of Garvey's contemporaries disavowed his methods but the notion of a white conspiracy survived him. In 1954, George G. M. James' book *Stolen Legacy* repeated his wild assertions. Many of the black callers to my show make reference to James and his ideas of a white conspiracy.

Few scholars have had the courage to risk criticizing the excesses of multicultural programs, which are often devoid of much intellectual content. One exception is Mary Lefkowitz, a humanities professor at Wellesley College who has authored a fierce little polemic called, *Not Out of Africa.* She argues that Afrocentrists substitute pseudo history for what actually happened. As she writes: "the ancient Egypt described by Afrocentrists is a fiction." She systematically demolishes their basic contentions about ancient history through her rigorous examination of surviving testimony, putting to rest this form of academic quackery. The real problem with Afrocentrism, Lefkowitz concludes, is that false truths about Greece and Egypt are being taught in our schools and more dangerous to her perspective is the underlying premise that all history is fiction which can be manipulated at will for political ends. The Hitlerian overtones of her warning are hard to miss. Those who control the past can control the present and the future. This is precisely why liberals in the Culture War have placed such a high premium on fostering this anti-intellectual philosophy.

In the final analysis, not one of the multiculturalists' assertions about cultural expropriation and scholarly dishonesty can be properly documented. Writing in the 10 February 1992 issue of *The New Republic,* Lefkowitz stated it is simply untrue to claim that Greek philosophy was stolen from Egyptian sources. There is no way that James' claim that Alexander the Great could have taken a book from the great library at Alexandria, which was not founded until years after his death, is true. On a similar issue, she notes: "since Socrates was an Athenian citizen, he must have had Athenian parents; and since foreigners couldn't become naturalized Athenian citizens, he must have come from the same ethnic background as every other Athenian." With this statement, Professor Lefkowitz has thoroughly destroyed the linchpin of the Afrocentric argument.

Multiculturalism is not about learning or education. It is about power and money, control and politics. Bob Lawrence had made his point but at the expense of the black community which suffered most from this loss of intellectual experience and true learning. The black community desperately needs the educational skills to make up for the lost access to the resources of thought and intellectual structure that four hundred years of slavery and second class citizenship had denied it. Lack of marketable educational and social skills has furthered the gap between rich and poor, especially poor black children and their families. This attitude of cultural superiority, fostered by a condescending and patronizing white elite, has served to keep millions of blacks down on the liberal plantation, making their condition comparable with slavery days.

As John Leo points out in his 12 November 1990 column in *US News & World Report*, Afrocentricism is a fringe history of the world, patterned on the notorious "Baseline Essays," developed by Asa G. Hilliard III, an educational psychologist from Georgia State University. Hilliard developed these essays for the Portland, Oregon school system in 1982. Some of their fundamental beliefs include historical distortions, such as that Africa was the world center of culture and antiquity or that Ramses and King Tut were black. The most outrageous claim fosters the notion that Africa has a rich history of mathematics, scientific and literary accomplishment, mostly suppressed or stolen by whites. The "Baseline Essays" rely on a faulty logic to arrive at their erroneous conclusions. The African study of the electric eel might have led to the invention of the battery. To answer the objection of traditionalists why modern Africans have not demonstrated a similar level of cultural and scientific achievement, the multiculturalist stock answer is that if African traditions seem to be in eclipse, it is because of Western colonization. From an educational standpoint, multiculturalism tends to ghettoize or Balkanize the very people it is meant to serve. Black pride expressed through a unique language, indecipherable to all but a few, dress, rap music, and dance tends to exaggerate racial and cultural differences between blacks and whites, further dividing a society that has been beset for centuries with racial prejudice and strife. Dr. Martin Luther King gave his life so that there would be no significant differences between the races. He envisioned an America where there would be a colorblind society that would "not judge people by the color of their skin but by the content of their character."

Multiculturalism has clouded that vision, resulting in a backlash from all the progress made in the sixties and the seventies that has seen the races, especially the blacks in the colleges and universities, resegregate themselves at eating tables, dorms and clubs. Troubled by the snail's pace of reform and the need to preserve their own power, minority leaders have lost faith in the political and economic system, turning their backs on the goals of integration and a universal brotherhood. King's goals and methods are regarded as having failed, with the separatist ideas of Louis Farrakhan seemingly more central to the black way of thinking. This does not bode well for the future.

Professor Hilliard now believes that the Greek gods, the Ten Commandments, and the Olmec civilization in Mexico are all derived from black culture as well. It is difficult to understand how this kind of racially-distorted curriculum will prepare any young black students for a place within middle class society. The end result will be to further alienate young blacks from traditional education, turning them into isolated and basically uneducated islands of discontent that can only lead to fight or flight from American society. Perhaps that's what their leadership really intends. If they achieve their goals, they will lose their lucrative jobs.

One way the multiculturalists have attempted to establish a specifically black culture was with the implementation of the *National Standards for World History,* which were withdrawn in late 1994 amid a great deal of public indignation. The study was a veiled attempt to discredit or totally ignore the principles of constitutionalism and the great men who actually founded the country. Students were supposed to immerse themselves in the "wisdom" of different cultures and indigenous American societies such as the Aztec empire. As Gary Nash, the co-director of the rejected program explained: "We are trying to let children out of the prison of facts." He predicted that the classroom would be jumping with mock trials of noted figures from American history. In other words, this revisionary wave of educational thinking, was attempting to hold up the American past to scorn and indict its heroic leaders and venerated founders. This is a mockery and a repudiation of everything this country has ever stood for or proposed to be. How can the next generation of American citizens have anything but loathing and disrespect for what this country is and can be with this negative and erroneous pedagogic attitude? Of what value can the knowledge of other countries have if American citizens of all races have no true knowledge of their own history and culture. As Leo wrote in his 4 March 1996, column in *U.S. News & World Report,* ". . . through behind-the-scenes bureaucratic maneuvers and judge-imposed plans, we now have a vast and intrusive system of race and gender preferences that rests on no social consensus at all. It has all been done to and for the American people without bothering to get their consent. The multiculturalists have pulled another end-run by circumventing the traditional democratic practice of getting the people's consent before effecting drastic changes, thus providing another illustration of liberalism's fascist tendencies."

A multicultural curriculum can only contribute to what New York Democratic Senator Patrick Monayhan once called the "dumbing down" of America. Courses based on myth, historical lies, and fantasy can only result in the intellectual downsizing of the pool from where the next generation of leaders will emerge. I guarantee that multiculturalism will not prepare a population to meet the scientific and intellectual challenges of the twenty-first century. Multicultural education should be about empowering minorities not only through educating them about their own histories but through teaching them how they can use the current system to bring about a more democratic society. Multiculturalism should emphasize literary, reasoning, and mathematical skills that would allow blacks to assimilate into the white business world. As Lawrence Auster observed in his book, *The Path to National Suicide,* the American people have a shared story, which despite gradual modifications over the past two centuries, has provided them with a coherent sense of who they area and what their place in history is. Multiculturalism only negates the positive effects of this shared story, and impairs any legitimate attempt to bring Americans together. It is a deliberate attempt to tear down, discredit, and destroy the shared story that has made us as a people and impose a different story which tells us our civilization and past history are essentially evil. An even worse side effect, to multiculturalism and the politics of racial solidarity, is the long-range detriment to American society. Informed voters make good choices. Voters without a sense of their past—an honest assessment of American history, are doomed to fall for chicanery, the lies and false promises of demagogues, and succumb to unscrupulous politicians who say anything and promise anything to get their hands on the reigns of power and financial control.

Neo-racism is an outgrowth of the multicultural debate. Our country's racial past is a difficult one to defend. The South had built its own civilization on the forced servitude of millions of black slaves. Their lot did not improve much after the withdrawal of Union troops in 1877. In fact, Jim Crow laws and a culture of social, political, and legal segregation made their situation even worse. The Civil Rights movement, led by Dr. King, raised the social consciousness of millions of Americans, including the vast majority of Southerners. Things improved as millions of blacks migrated to Northern cities. The political considerations of the Democratic Party eventually led to affirmative action and job quotas. The after effects of Lyndon Johnson's ill-fated War on Poverty acerbated the relationship between the races as a noticeable white backlash became apparent. The social milieu and the status of the black family deteriorated under all the faulty promises of liberal politicians.

One of the most controversial books of the nineties was Dinesh D'Souza's *The End of Racism: Principles for a Multiracial Society.* The title is confusing and does as much to clarify the situation as did Michael Fukuyama's *End of History.* D'Souza's thesis is that race and racism explain less and less what is wrong with the black community. It is his belief that cultural pathologies are at the root of the problems in the black community, exacerbated by the federal funding of blatant antisocial behavior. D'Souza has taken sides in the Culture War by denouncing the Left for not being honest in repudiating the obvious barbarism inherent in the sickness of the poor areas. D'Souza brings to light the extraordinary idea of scientific racism that the enlightenment created, in addition to liberal politics. This view, subscribed to by Jefferson, Kant, Voltaire, and Franklin, served to explain why other cultures were so inferior to Western Civilization. A genetic explanation was the obvious conclusion. D'Souza's book argues that some cultures are superior to others. Liberals fear his book because they do not want to admit that they have fostered multicultural and affirmative action programs that have dissuaded many black Americans from obtaining the necessary intellectual and business skills they need to assimilate into middle class society. D'Souza believes there is a government-induced social pathology at work in the black community. Many central urban areas lay in ruins. Prisons overflow with young black men. More blacks are in prison than are currently enrolled in universities throughout the country. He does not spell it out but the inference is clear that it is black cultural inferiority that has caused this situation. D'Souza's book is the first comprehensive book on race since Gunnar Myrdal's classic, *An American Dilemma,* was published a little more than a half century ago. D'Souza airs just about every viewpoint on race from Jesse Jackson and Al Sharpton to those of white supremacists. The central theme of the book is that most of our basic assumptions about racism and civil rights are either wrong or obsolete. His leading assumption is based on a racial relativism that dates back to Franz Boas in the 1920s: all cultures are equally valid. They can only be different, not better or worse. This idea has become a key social science dogma that has wreaked havoc in racial policy and racial attitudes from the courtroom to the halls of Congress. If cultural relativism is valid, then any major cultural differences can only be attributed to discrimination or genetic differences. In the spirit of the Enlightenment, the theory of relativity began by dismissing both inherent cultural and genetic factors, as valid explanations for the apparent differences in racial behavior and achievement. Society and its basic institutions were considered to be the culprit.

D'Souza is correct when he emphasizes the pathology at work within the black community. More than two-thirds of black children are born to single mothers. More than one third live in poverty. The academic achievements of black students lag far behind that of Asians and whites. Black congressional representation depends on racial gerrymandering. Black separatism is making a comeback as more blacks clamor for separate dormitory rooms, lunch tables, year books, proms, and student union buildings. Can demands for separate drinking fountains and restrooms be far behind? Louis Farrakhan has replaced Dr. Martin Luther King as an icon in the black community. D'Zousa indicts much of black culture, saying that many black students seem to have adopted, with the help of their elders and civil rights leaders, a hostile stance toward the values of the white world, including the values of scholarship and study. Too often we hear the negative refrain that blacks do not want to be white or do what whites do to become successful.

This abject rejection of such white behavior is directly related to the terrible chaos that runs free in much of the black community. Black leaders and their followers have to adopt a more common sense view on this issue. Racial pride that leads to bondage and social devastation is a hollow ambition that can only result in defeat and failure.

The deplorable end result of multiculturalism and other assorted educational reforms is that many American students have become alien to and ignorant of their own culture and history. In 1987, University of Virginia Professor E. D. Hirsch, Jr. was appalled by the fact that too many of his students thought the Alamo was an epic poem by Homer and that Leningrad was a city in Jamaica. In response to this problem, Hirsch wrote a book, entitled *Cultural Literacy*, which emphasized putting the acquisition of information back into the curriculum. His appendix listed thousands of significant ideas, cultural figures and events, works of art, and literature that the ordinary American citizen should know after having attended high school in the United States. He provided a format and a sense of direction and purpose that had fallen by the pedagogical wayside. Unfortunately, test results since then have not proven encouraging for the future. The United States is fast become a culturally illiterate country. In one of the most controversial segments of his book, D'Zousa suggests that to right the racial situation in this country, we should amend the *Civil Rights Act* of 1964 so that its non-discrimination provisions apply to only the governmental employment. He reasons that any business that discriminates against the best talent available would eventually be penalized in our competitive marketplace. This view is somewhat naive. The United States has changed a great deal but not that much.

The Civil Rights movements, which originally focused on equality of opportunity, eventually led to the presumption of equality of result, an entirely different idea. Our failure to re-examine the basic premise of civil rights has led to a proliferation of inherently unstable and untested theories about racism—all used to justify affirmative action preferences or quotas. On the basis of this thinking, people and institutions began to be presumed guilty in courts of law when their statistics did not match the presuppositions of the racial Zeitgeist. United States Civil Rights policy has created what can be called a caste system in which people are privileged on the basis of their race and gender. To advance their liberal agenda federal bureaucracies and judges adopted this throwback to the status-based legal system They disobeyed statutory laws and redefined discrimination as the absence of proportionate representation without taking any demographic, social or individual explanations into account. The only way that businesses could avoid the wrath of the federal government was to artificially meet the numerical standards of the quota system. To accomplish this, they often had to resort to racial discrimination against their white employees, who were over-represented in the work force. This policy has led to other interesting breaches of common sense. To meet their quotas for female firefighters, the

US Forest Service specified in its job postings that only unqualified applicants will be considered. The Federal Aviation Administration instructed its supervisors that the merit promotion process will not be utilized if it will not promote your diversity goals. A Defense Department memo governing civilian employment specifies, "in the future special permission will be required for the promotion of all whites without disabilities." This is no way to run an airline and it is certainly no way to run a country.

According to D'Souza, governmental interference has created a new class of race merchants, a group of activists and bureaucrats who have exploited racial tension for their personal good. Even as the pillars and standards of American civilization began to teeter and totter, learned college and university professors made apologies for the uncivilized behavior in the major urban centers because of rage and racial hatred. Despite the title, D'Souza does not believe that we shall see the end of racism. Instead, he argues that the explanatory power of racism is very weak when put to the test and now that racism itself serves largely as a distraction from the hard work of dealing with other factors and very real problems, such as illegitimacy, family instability and unemployment. The author sees the ever more elastic definition of racism as both escapist and cynically exploitative in the hands of racial activists. As he succinctly puts it, no good is achieved by dressing these pathologies in sociological cant.

It is my own experience that the words *racism* and *racist* have nearly been invalidated by wrongful use and overuse. On WGNU I have been assailed many times for merely raising questions about black leadership, ideas, motivations, and behavior. It is the old story of the little boy who cried wolf. People, such as Al Sharpton, who are promoting positions not rooted in fact and reality often resort to this rhetorical device to distract from the issue or question at hand. It is a cowardly way to deflect the pointed question and demonize the critic or the opposing view. Liberals are experts at this. Victimhood is a deleterious consequence of this kind of thinking. Professor Christopher Lasch emphasized this point in his posthumously published book, *The Revolt of the Elite*. He felt that the social engineering that was initiated in the sixties has led to the rapid deterioration of race relations in this country, a process aided and abetted by the race merchants. D'Souza lists busing, affirmative action, and open housing as an explanation for the weakened condition of the black neighborhood. In the sixties and seventies, black militants, such as Eldridge Cleaver, Bobby Seale, Huey Newton, and Stokely Carmichael demanded a new politics of collective grievance and entitlement. Liberals allege that since blacks are victims of racism, they should not be held to the same traditional standards of honesty, self-discipline, and punctuality that white people were. According to D'Souza, liberals have also romanticized Afro-American culture as an expressive, sexually liberated way of life free of religious and middle class values, laying the core of the affirmative action mentality. Ironically, the Civil Rights movement which originated with the notion of equality and national brotherhood was hijacked by the same liberals who now attack the single standard as racist in nature.

With the eventual destruction of the ideals of Dr. Martin Luther King, the great debate of the sixties has degenerated into one of symbolic and imagined racism. The infamous Tawana Brawley case is illustrative here. Brawley was a young black woman in New York in 1990 who claimed that she was forcibly raped by two members of her local police force. Black militants and the race merchants, such as Sharpton and Alton Maddox, immediately jumped on the bandwagon, decrying white racism and oppression. When the resultant investigation resulted in Brawley's admission that her whole story had been a hoax, the notion of symbolic guilt for whites reared its ugly head. Her supporters concluded that even if it has not happened the way she had originally stated, it does not disguise the fact that a lot of young black women are treated the way she said she was treated. Symbolism, power politics, and fame had turned civil rights restoration into racial theater.

Dr. King would have been appalled by this situation. His humanitarian vision has deteriorated into the voluntary segregation of more militant visionaries, such as Minister Louis Farrakhan, the spiritual descendant of Malcolm X and his Nation of Islam. Farrakhan's twin goals of separation and reparations, as well as his flirtation with world dictators, such as Momar Khadafi and Saddam Hussein, put race relations in their worst situation since Reconstruction. Farrakhan wants more than a level playing field. He wants a part of the playing field. He has demanded that whites and Hispanics be forced to leave their lands and property in certain states as reparation for the four hundred years of black enslavement in America.

Farrakhan's movement, which crystallized with his Million Man March, which was actually closer to a 400,000 Man March, underscored his attempt to form a black solidarity that could unite millions of young, angry blacks against the white-dominated power structure. His notion of race solidarity, the belief that the group is more important than the individual, was the basis of the militant and coercive doctrines of communism and fascism that led to 170 million deaths in the twentieth century. Farrakhan could lead a bloody and violent sideshow to the Culture War, our own French Revolution in a racial motif. Another issue that has greatly contributed to black social and economic solidarity is affirmative action. To rapidly increase the incidence and the speed of black economic and social progress, anti-discrimination laws were unilaterally applied. Black educational deficiencies, or lack of necessary work skills and habits, were often overlooked so that their gains could more quickly approach the levels of whites in this country. The logic and intent behind affirmative action stated that if two workers—a black and a white—were equally qualified and both applied for a particular job, the black should get it in an effort to compensate for ground lost during slavery and segregation. The fallacy of this policy was the false assumption that all applicants would be equally qualified. Even if the white applicant were more qualified, experience demonstrated that the black applicant still got the job. Employers, faced with constant legal intimidation from black power groups such as the NAACP, found it more practical to adhere to a numbers system than argue over fundamental qualifications. The quota system was based on the idea that if the national percentage of blacks were 12-15%, each job should reflect that demographic percentage without considering merit or qualification. Equality of result was the goal, not equality of opportunity. This policy amounted to reverse discrimination with many whites discriminated against on account of their race.

Problems occur when there are not enough qualified women and minorities to fill quota numbers. To get around this dilemma, the social engineers came up with another pernicious notion, the idea of race norming. If there are not enough qualified candidates to fill the designated racial quotas in the fire department or police force, then the applicants are divided by race and gender. If the percentage to be arrived at for black males is 15%, then the top fifteen percent of the black candidates are given positions, no matter how their relative scores match up against those of white, Oriental or Hispanic candidates. Racial balance, in this case, is achieved at the expense of traditional fairness, honesty, and merit. One of the most dreaded and blatantly unfair residual effects of affirmative action policy is that it demeans and negates the dignity and accomplishment of those successful blacks, such as Justice Clarence Thomas or General Colin Powell, who are caught up in its tangled web. Would anyone want to be operated on by a surgeon who had attained his position through any means and not by his merit? This psychological undermining affects all professions and jobs that fall under the protective mantel of affirmative action. When someone who has ostensibly benefited from these programs, such as Justice Thomas, attempts to criticize or reform the liberals' distorted vision of equality, as did Thomas, he will be subjected to vicious and vile attack from the left. Thomas' status was mocked by the very powers that help lift him above others. He's the "house nigger" who licks the boots of his white oppressors. No fair due was given to how much hard work, diligence and honest effort might have contributed to his status. Affirmative action is the carrot liberals hold out for black people who will vote to keep them in office. Oppose the liberal agenda and blacks must suffer retribution and loss of position. The recalcitrant black is indelicately told to get back in line, keep his mouth shut, and stay down on the liberal plantation. I had one black caller who was so outraged at Thomas's defection to the enemy that he said, "if I had a son who I knew would grow up to be like Clarence Thomas, I would kill him."

The bitter irony is that many conservative white males feel more victimized by affirmative action than blacks. According to the cultural semantics, they are the oppressors, not its victims. Their fundamental beliefs, in religion, personal responsibility, charity, marital fidelity, and hard work, have been subtly attacked and demonized, as the laziness, dilatory lack of ambition of some blacks has been rewarded. Radical groups have made it very difficult for white men to feel safe and secure. This endangered species is faced with declining status in society, increasingly alienated from society. A white man often watches in muted anger as his leaders cater to and sanction these aggressively undemocratic groups, who are more concerned with a Marxist leveling than they are with human brotherhood.

As an alumnus of Holy Cross, I have been greatly disturbed by the school's handling of a racial incident that occurred in November, 1995. The incident revolved around the *Student Government Association's* 1995 ruling that white students should be allowed to hold elective office in the black Students' Union (BSU). The student government had struck down a provision in the black groups' constitution as discriminatory, a clause that required top elected officers to be of African descent. The student government contended that none of the 80 campus groups financed by student fees should be exclusive. The BSU included members who were white, Asian, and Hispanic who had been excluded from holding any elective office. In response to the ruling, a group of 68 black students, many of them athletes, took to the streets and boycotted football and basketball practices.

According to the *Times,* Father Gerald Reedy, the President of Holy Cross, caved in and overruled the student government on this issue, stating "there is a need to have black kids oriented by kids who are also in the minority and who can say it 's OK here." The real question should have been: *Why does Holy Cross need a black Student Union in the first place?* The school had always prided itself on creating a spiritual bond of unity that transcended the race, economic status and political affiliation of its students. At a St. Louis reception, held in March of 1996, I asked Father Reedy for his side of the story. After expressing doubts about the accuracy of most newspapers, he substantiated most of what had appeared in the *Times* article. He said it was only the three top offices that were limited to students of African-American dissent and that the student boycott was only of non-academic activities, such as football and basketball. The underlying reason for the college's posture centered around his innate understanding that a separately-run student union was necessary to ease the transition from a black cultural environment to the lily-white atmosphere of a school like Holy Cross. He asked, "What would a black student think if he went to the black Student Union and a white face answered the door?"

What Father Reedy did not seem to recognize is the fact that his action have allowed his black students to build a wall not a bridge to link them with the white community. This is just another step in the resegregation of America—another example of elitist egalitarianism. In understanding the depths to which the affirmative action/multicultural miasma has taken us, it is necessary to expound on the one idea that has been most disabused in this debate: equality. Just what does that word mean to any of us? The Declaration of Independence emphatically stated the revolutionary principle that all men are created equal. This seems clear enough. Yet the translation of the idea of equality into society has been all but litigated out of existence.

To me, the concept of equality is something that must be reduced to the basic common denominator. All men and women are equal before the law and before God. Simply put, we all have certain inalienable, though not absolute, rights that endow us with the freedom of speech, the right to practice or not practice a religion, and the right to accumulate wealth. We have the right to life, liberty, and the pursuit of happiness. After that, everything else is negotiable, particularly if it results in the loss of someone else's rights. Achievement used to mean something. There is dignity and self-worth in doing a job, completing a task or fulfilling a promise. True equality comes from doing something for yourself or those around you, not from sitting back and enjoying the fruits of your "victimization." Liberals have put the utopian ideas of equality before achievement. Under the rubric of welfare or aid for the poor and downtrodden, liberalism has relegated millions of blacks and whites to a federal plantation with its harmful and deleterious effects on the human soul.

I look around me and see people who are superior to me in talents, abilities, and intelligence. I also see many that are basically inferior to me in many things. I have often quipped that I have just two talents in life—a good memory and a big mouth. The undeniable conclusion here is that people are not equal in intelligence, athletic ability, and many mechanical and social skills. Education can make up some of the disparity, but for the most part there are basic differences that will always separate most of us from each other. The controversial book, *The Bell Curve,* based on several psychometrics studies printed the unspeakable, that there were as much as a 15-point differential in IQ scores between blacks and whites. The president of Rutgers nearly lost his job when he argued for the elimination of academic standards to offset this basic academic inequality. He spoke the unspeakable in private and was rebuked for it.

There is a vicious assault on this idea of equality that attempts to eradicate differences, stifle achievement and initiative in favor of a socially-engineered governmental assault on freedom of opportunity. In his book *The Death Of Common Sense,* lawyer Philip Howard points out how sympathy for the handicapped has resulted in an inordinate amount of power being used to thwart the majority will. He cites the example of the lack of public restrooms in New York City with its concomitant effects on public sanitation. The city once attempted to adopt the kiosk system in Europe. Of course, people in wheelchairs could not access these narrow cubicles. Their lobby demanded larger ones that could accommodate wheelchairs. The larger kiosks were unworkable since they blocked sidewalks making pedestrian traffic nearly impossible. Rather than admit the impracticality of their demands, the wheelchair lobby remained selfishly steadfast. The kiosks were thrown out, to the detriment of the entire city. In his book, *In Defense of Elitism,* the late William Henry III wrote of a deaf girl who wanted to enter a speech contest using sign language. When the contest officials failed to cooperate, her parents took the case to court. Somewhere along the line, people with handicaps or disabilities have to admit the truth of their situation: they are not equal. To say anything else is dishonest and a detriment to the rest of society. They should attempt to garner as much as they can from what they have but not expect society to bend over backwards at the expense of business and progress. I rue the day when blind people demand that they be allowed to drive on the highway. I have always believed that it is wise to help those who cannot help themselves but to labor under the false notion that people are entitled to be considered equal in all things is a misnomer that can spell nothing more than doom for this country.

The ideas of multiculturalism, affirmative action and universal equality do not hold much promise for the future of America. The sense of what it is to be an American seems to have been inexorably altered. Our country is slowly being fragmented into a collection of disparate tribal groups. Gangs, special interest groups, and lobbyists tear the worn notion that we are all in it together into shreds. The United States has not been so internally disordered since the Civil War. The depth of these ideas can be found in a statement made by Secretary of State Warren Christopher, just after NATO began its peacekeeping mission in Bosnia. He proudly described the war-stricken principality with its many diverse cultures as a model multicultural state. So it is. Multicultural states such as Bosnia can only be held together by tyranny or, in Bosnia's case, military occupation. This is a lesson that the United States should learn and learn well.

8 / Women
Hear Them Roar

We are not interested in social reconstruction—it's human reconstruction.

—Hillary Rodham, Wellesley
College Commencement, 1969

After my daughter's 1993 wedding, my cousin Pam asked my nineteen-year old niece, Ashleigh, if she were the next to be married. In the dulcet tones of her Southeast Missourian dialect, she pointed to her older brother as the one with the future nuptials. As I could never resist the opportunity for a clever remark. I exclaimed: "We'll have a hard time marrying her off!"

Without a moment's hesitation, Ashleigh remarked, "Uncle Bill, if you found someone to marry you, I won't have any trouble. "

Of course, she was right. She had evoked a wisdom beyond her tender years. I was extremely lucky to have married her Aunt Judy in 1966. The brunch incident reminded me of a sign I saw in a used car lot in Arlington, Virginia in 1963 that read "If women ever get equal rights with men, it will be a great step down for them." Times have changed! Too many women have subscribed to the Virginia Slims Myth, *You've come a long way, baby!* Certainly, there has been some progress in cracking the glass ceiling and attaining pay equity, but I wonder at what price. We now witness a decaying society, beset by rampant illegitimacy, pervasive drug abuse, spousal and child abuse, gun-toting marauders, and assisted suicide.

The word *feminist* is a derivative of the Latin *femina* which means woman. The feminist movement in America has sought in numerous ways to wrench women from their traditional habitat and connection to family fruition and wholeness and family life. The leaders of the modern feminist movement are rebelling against their very biological nature and all that womanhood stands for. The culture of death has not only made women barren in the physical sense but emotionally and spiritually as well. A feminist mindset that encourages and champions the killing of unborn children works against women's natural maternal instincts. As a man, I find the entire women's movement, regrettable, deplorable, and a tragic shame. I really love women in a *platonic* sense. There's a word on my vocabulary calendar, *philogynous*, that means just that. I have always preferred women's company to that of men. To paraphrase former President George Bush, women generally are a kinder, gentler sort who add something special to a room by just being there. It is not sexism, only honesty, that causes me to say that women are the hope of our civilization. It has always been that way. I can't see how the unbridled freedom that the women's movement has sought has really helped women.

In many ways, the unlimited access to abortion has had several terrible and devastating consequences for women. An unwanted pregnancy often is devastating and life-altering in itself but not nearly as devastating or life-threatening as an abortion. Once the woman realizes that she has killed her own child, she becomes another victim of the feminist movement. It is only pro-choice males, such as Hugh Heffner, who are really helped by legalized abortion. They can have the pleasures of unlimited sexual indulgence with easy legal extrication from any unwanted side effects. After all the talk in the 1996 election about abortion and the gender gap, it was the 18-35 year old males who most voted for Bill Clinton on this issue. *Back to the womb* used to be a phrase for a protected environment, a safe haven. Not any more. The abortionists have turned a woman's body into a bloody battle ground for profit, illustrating the worst possible features of our capitalistic society, killing someone else for money. The abortion lobby and its radical feminist allies want women to turn against their own bodies, scrape out the very distinction that makes them superior beings to men, the ability to create another human being, virtually on their own. For a few dollars abortionists often deny women the real right to choose by lying or hiding from them the fact of the human they carry within themselves. I seriously doubt that an expectant mother can view a picture of her bobbing fetus on a sonargram and proceed to let these butchers rip him or her into human garbage. An unwanted pregnancy is not the end of the world. There are thousands of caring individuals all over the country who will help these women. Just look up *Birthright* in the phone book. Unlike your standard abortion centers, which want cash up front, *Birthright* will provide medical care, clothing and everything the expectant mothers need, even after the baby is born.

The women's movement is quite possibly the single most dominant force on most college campuses. Enlightened feminists have replaced the term sex with the notion of gender. These terms are not interchangeable. Gender refers to the different roles that a particular culture has assigned or imposed on women while sex refers to biological differentiation. Modern feminists argue that gender always trumps sex, that biological differences are insignificant compared with the differences between men and women artificially imposed by society and culture. It is the male patriarchy that is responsible for the vast inequalities that exist between men and women in the marketplace and in the public square. If the feminists are correct in their beliefs, then I find it difficult to understand why women need abortion as their trump card. To assume the idea of sexual equality in the abstract is either desirable or realistically possible, one has also to assume that the basic differences between men and women are gender differences, culturally and historically imposed. Such differences are important, but in fact, the most important distinctions, between men and women, derive from sex and not gender. As Dr. John Gray's book says, *Men are from Mars, Women are from Venus,* stands feminist ideology on its head: sex trumps gender, as neo-conservative Irving Kristol extolled in his 6 March 1996 in the *Wall Street Journal:*

Traditional marriage has long been under assault and are now reaping the dire consequences of decades of narcissism. No-fault divorces and the right to choose have made paupers out of many women. It is apparent that the women who have followed the feminists of the sixties, have sold out themselves and their sisters at home. In many cases, they have exchanged respect, honor, love and security for sexual freedom and economic chaos. As much as women like weddings, marriage exists primarily as a civilizing institution for men. In his seminal study, "Men And Marriage," economist George Gilder contends that men need the civilizing comforts of marriage, even more than women. Their children, especially their sons, need a strong male presence to teach them how to discipline and control their nastier urges. Without marriage, men are free to satisfy their sexual urges at will, without assuming responsibility for their actions. Abortion may be the political tool of the radical feminists but even more importantly, it is the sexual security blanket of the libertine male, who now has a socially acceptable way of wantonly pursuing his own carnal pleasures without any apparent consequence.

The abortion issue has thoroughly permeated modern feminism. There is an uneasiness about this issue that has plagued many good and honest people who feel that a woman's choice is probably none of their business, yet there is a nagging doubt that just maybe it was wrong to kill whatever form of life the mother was carrying. Men shy away from this issue because they do not want to appear to be insensitive to a particular woman's unplanned pregnancy. This ambivalent attitude on abortion may lay at the root of why men have been more physically abusive to women in recent years. In their incessant need to exercise their individual freedom by throwing off the yoke of thousands of years of patriarchy, abortion attacks the fruitful bond that has united men and women since the beginning of time. A casualty of that has been a courtly respect for women, once considered a mark of the civilized male. That respect was doubled if a woman happened to be "with child," or in "a family way." Chivalry put this special gift of carrying, nurturing, and bringing forth life on a pedestal. The fact that only women could give birth put them on a higher plane than men who could only assist and take care of women. In the name of the god of feminism, women have sacrificed their pedestaled status on the altar of sexual equality. I thank God every day for the wife I have. She has taught me more about caring for people than I could ever have learned by myself. I am thankful for the best friend I have ever had, for her calming and sensible views toward so many everyday problems. Without her humanizing influence and the institution of marriage she represents, I would be less of a human being.

At the core of the feminist debate is marriage and the family. My daughter once had a little dog she aptly named *Murphy*. A modern women in every sense of the word, I called her the "Yuppie with a puppy." Unfortunately, her commitments to home, school, and work made it impossible for her to adequately care for the dog. He cried all day while she was gone and generally made a mess of her house. She did the merciful thing and put him up for adoption to a good home. Her brief tenure with the puppy reminded me of the infamous' Murphy Brown/Dan Quayle debate over family values. Murphy Brown's TV persona is that of an overbearing, arrogant proponent of every leftist cause, ever concocted by the apologists for Jean Jacques Rouseau, Karl Marx and John Dewey. Murphy conceived a child out of wedlock, though her coupling was confused by the fact that her lover was her ex-husband. She did choose life over the abortion clinic but merely as another life style choice. Murphy's decision not to abort trivialized and demeaned the sacrificial nature of motherhood. Even her act of giving birth was appraised within the narcissistic scope of how it impacted her life.

The sixty-four dollar question remains, what are family values? The essential building blocks of the family are trust, honesty, sexual fidelity, sobriety, and self-sacrifice. Other family values could include the twin virtues of self-control and respect for others. Anything that seriously threatens these values, such as divorce, alcoholism, pornography, drug addiction, premarital sex, adultery, or radical feminism, runs counter to the maintenance of American Civilization. Cynics will say that the above scenario bears little resemblance to the American family today. Perhaps, that is the trouble with society. Just because Ward Cleaver is as fictional as Murphy Brown does not mean that his ideal is not worthy of imitation. It is the larger context of Murphyism that underscores the Culture War that has permeated every social aspect. Too many women have willingly surrendered their traditional role as custodians of the spiritual and social good. Too many have decided to compete with men in all the negative facets of their lives, such as promiscuity, competitiveness, and debauchery, instead of remaining faithful to their own gender. Gender may not be destiny but it certainly has an overwhelming influence on what kind of people we become and what our society is. Murphyism has also made insurmountable contributions to the Sexual Revolution, with its twisted web of confused and indeterminate sexual roles. Unbridled feminism has unleashed a corral of social evils, such as illegitimacy and venereal diseases, including AIDS. It is incumbent upon society that it restore women to the elevated status they once enjoyed thirty years ago.

If one attitude is contrary to a smoothly-working society, it is the idea of Me-ness. The nuclear attitudes of the sixties, including *Me first, Do your own thing, I gotta be me,* and Frank Sinatra's old staple, *I did it my way* showered later generations with the self-indulgent fallout that whines for the instant gratification of each and every petty need or want. This anti-intellectual orgy of self-gratification, as personified by the feminist movement, is coming home to roost, as we have truly become a nation of victims, perpetrating violence and disease on the innocent, the elderly and the un-born. It is ironic that a generation that idealistically began with "Ask not what your country can do for you," has degenerated into the abject selfish-ness of what will you do for my needs?

Liberals, the evangelicals of the sexual revolution, never understood that by devaluing chastity they were devaluing women. Language plays an important part in this female devaluation. The word *bitch* has dominated much of the social interaction in the urban ghettos, reducing social behavior to that of a pack of wild animals. Many answer when challenged that they call females *bitches* because it's a natural thing and the boys often travel in packs, where they can engage in "whirlpooling" or "wilding." They think that twenty boys on one girl is males' nature. This attitude has successfully bid adieu to 5000 years of civilization that insisted human beings were created in the image and likeness of God, not mere dogs in heat.

Margie Janovich, a mother of nine, demonstrated what it really means to be a mother. A victim of thyroid cancer, Mrs. Janovich waited until her daughter was born before seeking radiation treatment. She was five months pregnant when she learned of her cancer. In a statement today's self-indul-gent culture cannot fathom, she said, "I would much rather give up my life for my baby, any good mother would do the same."

Our schools bear some responsibility for this sexual turmoil. Too often teachers impose their personal agendas on their students, seriously under-cutting parental authority. Ideally, sex education belongs in the home. If that is not possible, parents should be enlisted to work with teachers. Any sex education curriculum should be grounded on the idea that a person's body is sacred, not to be cheapened by the sexual promiscuity that is fostered by condom-distributing. The public schools implicit sanction of premarital sex is falsely predicated on the notion that our children are barnyard inhab-itants, incapable of self-control or sexual restraint. Too often school has ignored the concept of family values in favor of some nebulous doctrine of values clarification where the individual is free to create the morality of his or her own personal situation. Historical experience has demonstrated that heterosexual marriage, and there can be no other kind, must return to the center stage as the basic structural unit of our culture. To do this we must contradict the imposed attitude of tolerance for all divergent life styles. To praise marriage is viewed as the equivalent of condemning those persons who are divorced, living together out of wedlock, unwed parents, or homo-sexual, as if all of these other living arrangements were the moral equivalent of marriage. The epigones of liberation mock traditional marriage as an outdated relic of the fusty days of the fifties. One of the societal pillars that the French Jacobins attacked was that of marriage. The ceremony they devised to replace it was something akin to *gentlemen start your engines.* They coupled that with a divorce ceremony that congratulated the couple on starting a new life, deems them born again to pursue a new mate. This attitude toward marriage and divorce was resurrected in the seventies when it was argued that marriage was fundamentally incompatible with modern life. The marital virtues of fidelity, honesty and companionship seemed incompatible with the new wave of thinking that stormed the culture.

In his book *Future Shock,* Alvin Toffler, devised the modular marriage. According to Toffler, a man who had a wife and two children facing a transfer from Los Angeles to Pittsburgh could have the company arrange for him to move in with a new wife with two children instead of packing up the family and moving them across the country. For Toffler, marriage partners and family members were just interchangeable parts on the assembly line of the planned economy. The Swedish paradigm of benign socialism is another example of marital social engineering that is attractive to some intellectuals. Government and industry form partnerships which are centrally managed to ensure that every adult is employed while children are cared for primarily in communal settings by trained experts. Family privacy is shrunken to a minimum, while the moral and cultural formation of children, their nutrition, health care, and even their socialization become a public rather than family responsibility. This is a branch of utopianism which will cause the family to wither away as an institution, as central planning reshapes the economy to ensure a level of universal material comfort not unlike that envisioned in Aldous Huxley's novel *Brave New World.* The family will simply cease to have any relevant social function.

Columnist William F. Buckley once clarified this battle for civilization as an attempt to "immanitize the eschaton," that is to make material beliefs and values that are, by nature, spiritual and eternal. Phyllis Schfafly, a lovely septuagenarian who has probably done more to derail the radical feminist agenda than anyone, contends that modern feminism is dying because it seeks unattainable goals at variance with reality, common sense, and fairness. In the seventies and the eighties, she stressed the idea that feminists sought a gender-neutral society, in that they wanted women to be treated like men in every way, disapproving of Maurice Chavilier's ode to *Viva la difference!* The feminist reconstruction of historical gender roles is a fantasy doomed to failure. They might as well have attempted to pour the Mississippi River into a backyard swimming pool.

An unintended negative consequence of the modern feminist way of thinking, revolves around a definite male stratagem that has profited greatly from the women's movement. No one has benefited more from women's rights than irresponsible, pro-choice men. Women's lib has effectively set the stage for greater male exploitation of women. The Court has assumed that *Roe vs. Wade* enhances the dignity of women because abortion allows women to compete with men in the work force on a more equitable basis. The Court has not taken into consideration the opposing arguments that the abortion license has increased the incidence of abuse of women by irresponsible and predatory men. Their drive for legal equality has effectively stripped their human relations of many of the subtle moral and ethical underpinnings that women have enjoyed for centuries. Their denial of their own weakness has voided the internal need men have felt to protect, honor, and even obey them. This attitude has just relieved men of their historic obligation to respect and safeguard members of the weaker sex. Men now have another excuse not to commit to one woman. Abortion rights and no-fault divorce have allowed and even encouraged men to abdicate their moral and financial responsibility for their sexual activity. Feminism has provided men with a near-perfect stratagem that has allowed them to have the benefits of marriage without the full responsibilities of the institution. Men have used no-fault divorces to leave their wives and children in poverty while they pursued their own liberation and freedom with impunity. It is female *hubris* that has caused women to fall for male sexual trickery, as they have consistently through the ages. As strong as they envision themselves, too often they are easy prey for the vain promises of male predators, especially older ones, who stalk their quarry in bars, laundromats and health clubs. Perhaps female gullibility is a residue of the original fall. Women should wise up to this ideological trap set for them by their disoriented leadership.

With their efforts to gain absolute control over their bodies and the lives of their unborn children, feminists should have expected that someone like Mel Feit would have eventually surfaced. Columnist Don Feder related Feit's story. Feit's *National Center for Men* organization is a logical extension of *Roe vs. Wade*. If the choice to abort or not to abort is absolutely the woman's perrogative, without any input from the father, then if the woman decides to keep her baby against the wishes of the father the man should not have to assume any emotional or financial responsibility for his unwanted child. Feit's group challenges court-ordered child support. He sees it as a question of fairness. But what Feit and his association's members really want is reproductive freedom for themselves without being forced to pay child support. The *Men's Center* also contends that *Roe vs. Wade* violates men's right to privacy because the decision lets the woman live her life without the interference of an unwanted baby while it forces men to pay child support in those cases where the mother chooses to keep the child. If maximizing personal freedom is the goal of our legal system, Feit wonders why men should be forced to support the children they have fathered while women are liberated from theirs? A man who has to pay child support for 18 years will have his life diminished and his standard of living substantially lowered. Feit is onto something here. In his many TV and radio debates, Feit always asks his female counterpart, "Do you believe that government should be able to force someone to become a parent?" Women counter with the idea that the mother has got more of an investment in the child because she has to carry the child for nine months. Most women dodge Feit's trap by not answering his question. To me this sounds like the Freudian dogma, repudiated in the feminist community, that biology determines destiny. Many opine that Feit and men in general have a number of options— a condom, or even abstinence. Women have the same options, plus adoption. The implicit conclusion is that abortion is a freedom that neither men nor women should have. Too many Americans, men and women, want freedom without consequences. To paraphrase Richard Weaver, sex has consequences!

There is a pervasive fear in our culture of governmental interference in private moral decisions. The right to privacy has become a code word for sexual conduct. There is talk of a sex police from ultra-right wing conservatives who want us all to remain celibate our entire lives. Rape is ostensibly a sexual matter. Should it not be kept private? Should the government not stay out of a man's choice to have sex or not to have sex? Are not laws that outlaw rape, merely the first step in arriving at this right-wing police state? Women say that no man should have absolute power and dominion over any woman. They say the government can interfere to protect the weaker, at least physically weaker being in this case. They say that rape is far more than sexual in nature. It is really an act of violence. With this in mind, can it not be said that a mother should not have life and death control over her unborn baby? Should not the government want, be compelled to, protect the weakest and most fragile of all human beings? Is abortion then not about sex but primarily an act of violence practiced on tiny beings who have no voice, no vote and can not defend themselves? Does not abortion diminish us all, male and female? Rape is an act of human violence but in the psychology of the rapist, he is not hurting another person. He is not making love to a woman. To do what he does and live with himself, the rapist must depersonalize his victim. She's a piece of meat or a vagina. To define another human being in terms of her sexual organs is the most depersonalizing form of contempt a man can have for a woman. To depersonalize an unborn child by calling it a "fetus" accomplishes the same end—it affords justification for a heinous act of human violence. According to *Planned Parenthood*, the unborn are "products of conception," bits of tissue, not magnificent human miracles. A leading radical feminist, Gloria Steinem, has said that having an abortion is like having a tooth pulled. Some call these babies "parasites," another form of microbe that is not human. Before you can kill someone, you must make him a "slope," a "gook," a "Jap," vermin and less than human so that your killing does not stare you in the eye when you look at your own daughter, your loved ones. The argument is also made that abortion is acceptable because the baby is not fully formed and thus not worthy of legal protection. In rape, though most victims are fully formed women, this idea would seem to encourage the rape of girls ten or under. Their bodies certainly have not matured. They really do not look very much like women. They are more like "soft boys" as a friend's father once described little girls. Fully formed is such a relative term that almost anything or anybody could be defined out of existence. Consider the damage done to women who have been raped. They are emotionally scared, often required to go through long and painful physical and emotional therapy. Some women never get over the trauma. Can their lives be fully complete? What will be the quality of their post-rape lives? Of course the typical feminist response is that the above example is not valid because it does not take into consideration the victim's choice in the sex act. That is precisely the point! In abortion, the victim's choice to be or not to be is never at issue. It is only the rapist and the mother whose views and feelings are ever taken into consideration.

Given its stance on abortion rights, it is sardonic that the modern feminist party line hinges on the idea of victim, creating a dichotomy in its public persona that once heralded the strength of women. It is hard to fathom that the "I am woman" dirge of Helen Reddy has degenerated into the somber cries of weakness and victimhood. These radicals see our culture as a vast conspiracy of male domination and hierarchy that has created artificial barriers—the so-called glass ceiling—to their natural progression and economic success. No woman illustrates the *Big Lie* behind modern feminism better than First Lady Hillary Clinton. She has become an American icon, the purveyor of our conventional wisdom of what it is to be a woman, mother, and a wife. Her abject disdain for the cookie-baking proclivities of the majority of American women, like my wife, holds only women like herself as the paragon of feminine virtue. Right behind her is the *National Organization of Women*, with its large lesbian membership, proclaiming itself as the paradigm of female establishment. *Concerned Women of America*, a traditional family values group, dwarfs NOW in total membership yet does not merit a tenth of the publicity. Mrs. Clinton has said that we can not make our institutions more responsive to the kinds of human beings we wish to be and expect our institutions to respond. She thinks that the country must begin to see other people as they wish to be seen. This is a perversion of the Golden Rule that will lead eventually to thought control. Some contend that she is not a good example of a feminist role model because she arrived at the pinnacle of success not so much through her own efforts but like a female Horatio Alger, marrying the boss's son and leapfrogging her way up the ladder of success. Mrs. Clinton married a man with unbridled ambition and a strong determination to achieve his presidential aspiration. Granted that she helped in many ways, but it was still Bill Clinton who won the presidency twice. Feminists delight in touting Mrs. Clinton's individual skills. Incredibly, the *National Law Journal* ranked her as one of the 100 most important lawyers in the United States. Some of her allies in the media have privately scoffed at that idea, saying some doubt she was one of the top lawyers in Little Rock. She has often hidden behind the sham rubric that she is not liked by Republicans, religious people, and other critics because they fear strong women. In obdurate sarcasm, her apologists rail that next her detractors will have claim she was on the grassy knoll that afternoon in Dallas.

Nothing could be further from the truth. She is an imitation of a strong woman. She is the authentic phony. Every time the heat gets turned up, she runs from the kitchen to the bedroom. She is the nation's first hypocrite, wanting it both ways. She hides behind the insularity of the White House, while wanting to be a player without having to assume any responsibility or accountability, as in the case of her furtive *National Health Care Task Force*. Dressed in the chic robes of derivative status, waving her imitation scepter of power-by-proximity, she stands before a free country and tells people what they should do. Ever faithful to her liberal principles, Mrs. Clinton insists on controlling the terms and the language of the debate. Like most liberals, Mrs. Clinton has taken on the impossible task of redefining human nature and altering traditional concepts of truthfulness and integrity. She is a four star phony, with her familial pronouncements to her proxy book signings. Concerning her alleged involvement in the Whitewater/Travelgate scandals, the American public hears Mrs. Clinton and her allies mutter simplistic inanities about a systemic lack of sophistication or her befuddlement over the partisan accusations. The vacuity of some of her answers through the long legal and political ordeal betray either an unlikely naivete or a deviousness that coats itself in feminine and pristine innocence. Her amnesiac performances during the Whitewater and Travelgate hearings raise some serious questions about her memory and her personal integrity. This so-called strong woman with the raging temper, expects the American people to buy the idea that she was very important to the Rose Law Firm, had no knowledge of how her missing records came to be in the room off her office, had never intended to get Billy Dale and his aids fired, let alone tried for fraud, and was an innocent bystander in all the conflict of interest charges because of her high profile as the governor's wife. The American people are expected to believe that this tower of strength is, after all, merely a stereotypical, little housewife who is overwhelmed by all the fuss being made about her lies, noncompliance and verbal equivocations.

In a *Los Angeles Times* column, written in 1995, Arianna Huffington analyzed Mrs. Clinton as not attracted to the pure power and prestige of government policies, but inspired by a deeper and more complicated motivation. She thinks that the Clintons, especially Hillary, have been leading the country to the Promised Land, a utopia where human nature has been redone, so as to do away with the obvious evils of mankind. Mrs. Clinton cares passionately about saving the nation. Whether she will admit it or not, according to Huffington, her political salvation is rooted not in the American Revolution but in the French Revolution. After the storming of the Bastille in 1789, the French National Assembly proclaimed the "natural and imprescribeable" right of every citizen to liberty. Hillary Rodham told her Wellesley class in her 1969 commencement speech that "we are searching for more immediate, ecstatic and penetrating modes of living. Paralleling the European revolutionaries" political gospel, she has continued to talk of her burning desire not just for a new society but for a new humankind. This explains her constant involvement with such organizations as the *Children's Defense Fund* and educational reform. She can create a new human race by beginning with the children before they are corrupted by family and church. Huffington concludes that it is a thin line of apostolic succession from a government that guarantees security and equality of outcomes—as opposed to equality of opportunity—to a federal takeover of health care as was the case in 1994. A cliche used to read that the Vice President was only a heartbeat away from the presidency. As the personification of all the hopes and aspiration of modern feminism, Hillary Clinton is even closer to the presidency than Al Gore. She is feminism's dream come true. Having one of their own sitting next to the commander-in-chief has accelerated progress on another of the main battle fronts, upon which feminists have fought the Culture War. I have been amazed by how many women have blindly accepted identity politics of the gender war by wanting to integrate the military. Hundreds of young women, many of them who cast petite and frail figures, have flocked to the academies to get their share of its free education. Of course, when most did not measure to the strict physical standards of the military, instead of washing them out, as is the case with all the men who couldn't make the grade, the rules were changed, or shall we say, the playing field tilted to their side. Gender norming, or having a double standard for men and women, took care of the problem. Instead of ranking the women cadets in many of the physical categories, especially those involving upper body strength, the women were ranked, only with other women, or the standards were lowered to accommodate substandard performance. This same principle has been universally applied to the police force and fire department where maintenance of gender quotas has been mandated.

The infamous Tailhook incident of 1991 illustrates what I mean in this regard. Politely put, Tailhook was an annual wild party where members of the Navy went to unwind. There was excessive drinking, vomiting, carousing and now, with many fellow women officers in tow, a good deal of sex play that included grasping, pinching, stroking, fondling. What was not mentioned in most of the accounts is that many of the women were as raucous and as militarily unbecoming as their male counterparts. Still, a number of the women cried foul when they were set upon by a band of roaring drunks with their octopus-like hands. In the best traditions of modern feminism, they cried sexual harassment. Led by their comrade-in-arms, Congresswoman Patricia Schroeder, they demanded the heads and the careers of many of the senior and junior officers, some of whom were not even on the premises but who bore some systemic responsibility for this incident. This is not in any way an attempt to cite the old sophomoric adage that boys will be boys. I find this image of the men (and women) who are supposed to be guarding the safety of the American people, to be repulsive. The women movement's incessant demand that women be allowed, even recruited, to protect the security of this country leaves me with a deep feeling of insecurity. Female leaders, such as Schroeder, have politicized and denigrated the most basic function of a constitutional government, that of providing for national security and defense. In the sacred cause of identity politics, feminists have put all Americans at serious risk by weakening our military forces and undermining the chain of command. But these men in the military are about war. The Navy is about war! If these women can't handle the combat of something as relatively innocuous as Tailhook, what are they going to do in a real war? If they want to be soldiers, they should separate themselves from the traditional female ploy of tears. If there is no crying in baseball, there is certainly no crying in war! Their very presence on the front lines is a visible distraction to the service they claim to represent. During Desert Storm in 1991, one of the carriers was politely known as *The Love Boat* because of the high incidence of pregnancy. Could it be that the Navy has institutionalized the old notion of "camp follower" when it was forced to bring women to the front lines by the Pentagon's social engineers? Women have no place in combat. Armies are, as Rush Limbaugh says, designed to kill people and break things.

On another note, women demand equal pay for equal work when legitimate exigency has been the law of the land for thirty-three years. The pay discrepancy between professional men and women may be true but it is as conclusive as comparing apples and oranges. What they really want, according to Mrs. Schlafly is equal pay for unequal work. In 1994, only 55% of women worked 40 or more hours a week, while 75% of men did. Family and children also work into this equation. The more children a married women has, the less she works outside of the home. The converse is also relevant. The more children a man has the more he works. On the professional level, most women who earned advanced degrees, do so in teaching or education, not very high paying jobs, while men, ordinarily specialize in the more demanding and more rewarding science and engineering professions. As more women gravitate to these professions, the inequality will eventually lessen, if not vanish altogether.

Another issue where I think feminism has a legitimate complaint is the increasing violence in the home. Domestic abuse is one of the great tragedies of American life. The O. J. Simpson trial, with its revelations of how he beat his wife, is another sign that there will be a complete breakdown in the institution of marriage if something is not done to restore it to its predominant role as the major founding block in American society. Yet, the existence of real wife abuse has become another weapon in the feminist drive to unseat males from their patriarchy of power. Some feminists would have the public believe that all marriage is nothing more than legalized rape and that every male is capable of exercising his sexual power and control over his wife at the drop of a hat. Pat Stevens, a talk show host, said once on *Crossfire* that there were six million women who were battered by their husbands or boyfriends every year. That's true only if you extend abuse to include a push, shove or even loud language. If you clutch your spouse's elbow as she walks away from you, that counts as abuse. Stevens' statistics self-immolated when she added that only one in ten women actually report this abuse. That would give us a grand total of 60 million women who are abused every day—a neat trick since the Census Bureau tells us that there are only 56.8 million women in this country living with a man.

Feminists are very adept about cooking the books. They prefabricated the number that 10,000 women were dying from back alley abortions each year. This number helped influence the Supreme Court to invent abortion rights in 1973. Former abortionist, Dr. Bernard Nathanson later admitted that he and the other founders of NARAL made that number up because it was large and impressive. Numerical inaccuracy provided part of the inspiration for Christina Hoff Sommers' book, *Who Stole Feminism*. Feminists flatly and erroneously stated that 250,000 died each year from eating disorders. The inaccuracy, once pointed out, did not deter them from using the bogus information. What they meant to say was that 250,000 women suffered from these disorders, not died.

The exaggerated rate of female abuse has even filtered over to one of the last bastions of male comfort and fraternity—Monday Night Football. This night has become the official night of female abuse during the football season. Columnist John Leo sees it as a religious festival of the women's victim culture—a medieval morality play in which all the crucial things of your religion are brought on for display. Football breeds the violence that men foist on women. Another of the great pigskin myths to come out of the women's movement is the belief that on Super Bowl Sunday there is a great increase in the number of women who are forced to go to hospital emergency rooms because of the drunken, football-inspired violence of the no-good men in their lives.

Playwright David Mamet paints a dark picture of the extent of how social sexual mores have changed. In his play *Oleana*, a stark and frightening tale of a young woman, who ruins the life of a middle aged professor seeking tenure at a local university. Her ideological fanaticism plays off his good-natured desire to help what he falsely perceived to be a struggling young student. Her charges of sexual harassment, rape and assault break him in the end and he is forced to submit to her newfound power.

Naomi Wolf calls the successes of feminism a "genderquake." This is a false observation. The women's movement has actually resulted in the devolution of women. As vice-president Dan Quayle observed in his famous Murphy Brown speech in 1992, the apparently-so-desirable, sexually irresponsible behavior of privileged women, when it had filtered down to the lower classes, had an even more deleterious effect because they did not have the protection network to back them up. Poor or low middle class women only had the state and its bureaucracy to fall back on when they got in trouble.

The most influential residence of gender feminism has been college campuses where women were able to create cultural enclaves of feminism under the guise of liberal administrators and professors who provided them with special privileges and protections. They posted lists of suspected rapists, usually any male on campus. They demanded codes of behavior detailing how far a man could go on a date. At each "base," to resurrect the old dating terminology, the man would have to get explicit permission before proceeding. At Antioch college, this foolishness was even extended to a written contract. Legal sex had been added to safe sex in the lexicon of the ritual of modern wooing and lust.

There is another component of feminism that has served to pervert the language. While the term "politically correct" has wide spectrum that relates to many different avenues in the new American civil war, there is a special application that applies distinctively to women and feminism. My first experience with the ABC's of politically correct language occurred when I was teaching American History at Florissant Valley Community College in 1975. My office partner was a part-time psychologist who had subscribed to some of the earlier nomenclature debates over the pronouns him and her. She did not like the constant reference to committee chairmen, even though most committees were run by men. She preferred the unbiased committee person, even though the gender specifics of a committee chairman or chairwoman could have settled it simply. Partly in jest, she started referring to the President of Southern Illinois at Edwardsville, as "Dr. Rendelperson" instead of his real cognomen, *Rendelman.* I thought that was funny, though I have learned since then most gender feminist do not have any sense of humor. Imagine the fun that could be had if we were free to change the name of any person whose name was politically incorrect. The late band leader would have been Benny Goodperson, which has a certain bogus ring to it. Any name ending in son should also be changed. This would give us renditions, such as President Lyndon Johnschild. The late ecologist would have been Rachel Carschild and the great actor/director, Mel Gibschild. All of these have an Orwellian sense of the unreal. This notion of political correctness has further degenerated the language so that alternate history is now "herstory." Mankind is now humankind. Hurricanes, which have a dangerously negative connotation, have not been changed to "himacanes," though the names of these vicious storms now alternate between male and female names. I have no problem with this. All this is called language castration, or the cutting away of the phallus-centered value system imposed by patriarchy. A female professor at Washington University in St. Louis refused to teach seminars, naming her small classes on women studies, "ovums." This fine university, where my daughter has earned two degrees, has courses on *Radical Lesbian Studies.* I have often wondered if students could take courses in *Moderate Lesbian Studies.* Boston College Professor Mary Daly demanded extensive language revisions in the Bible in her book, *Theology after the*

Demise of God the Father: The Call for the Castration of the Sexist Religious.
This perverse and sacrilegious way of thinking has led Oxford University
Press to engage in the most egregious form of this movement, rewriting the
King James version of the Bible to change God from a male power figure
and all other "offensive ideas." This is a refutation of all Western history,
tradition, and culture.

The term *girl* has become a demeaning term, like *boy* is to black men.
The feminists prefer *pre-women* to any one under twelve and *women* to any
one else. I never really know what to call females. Heroines are now *she-roes*,
or *hera*. Thank God for Latin endings. Marriage is regarded as domestic
incarceration, or domestic rape. The greatest bane and distraction from
women attaining their goals is pregnancy, which is described as a disease or
being parasitically-oppressed. Babies have a way of doing that. No wonder
abortion has been raised to the level of a political sacrament by pro-abortion
feminists.

For the average red-blooded male, looking, even ogling, at a beautiful
woman as she saunters down the street is hard to resist. I am not talking
about leering, vulgar commentary, or sexual lust of the Jimmy Carter variety.
I simply mean a visual appreciation, with maybe a short prayer, thanking
God for making women so beautiful to look at. The first time I ever saw a
miniskirt, I nearly drove my car off Commonwealth Boulevard in Boston.
Girl-watching has also been a distraction, and sometimes even a preoccu-
pation for me. In simpler times, they used to say a woman is as old as she
looks but a man is old when he stops looking. This is the way nature
intended us to be and any feminist attempt to remake men into something
we are not and can never be without severe retardation of American civilization. In today's PC milieu, what I have just described is a crime—perhaps
a thought crime, which answers to the name of "lookism." Some women go
so far as to describe it as an amorphous example of sexual harassment. This
new idiom nearly defies description, though the 1999 *Webster's Collegiate
Dictionary* will probably define it by placing a picture of Senator Robert
Packwood in place of any verbal description.

The feminist movement would have had a field day with the 1954
Ernest Borgnine movie *Marty*, which garnered several academy awards.
Women in this film were referred to as "tomatoes" or "dogs." In saying,
"That girl is a dog," Marty's friend's Angie would have been guilty of several
unpardonable sins, such as phallocentrism—the belief that male generative
power should be and is the driving force in American society, not to mention sexism, lookism, and chauvinism. As is apt to happen in our increasingly litigious society, this issue eventually wound up in court. In 1995, the
court, in its own brand of unfettered wisdom, attempted to set a standard
legal definition of "lookism" that also recognized the male visual weakness
for a curvaceous figure. The court decided that men could look at women's
bodies for no longer than eight seconds. In this climate, the average male

will have to bring a stop watch and maybe even a lawyer while walking down the street where many women display their natural assets.

While magazines such as *Playboy,* and its more risque counterparts, *Penthouse* and *Hustler,* feature exposed feminine pulchritude in salacious and provocative poses, these publications are so overt in their raw sexuality, especially in the latter two magazines, they come close to my definition of pornography. A grayer area involves *Sports Illustrated,* a magazine known ostensibly for its highly literate features on prominent sports athletes, owners, and promoters. Their focus changes dramatically in early February when one half of the male population waits in eager anticipation for the annual swimsuit issue. The swimsuit issue has grown in popularity, since is was first inaugurated in 1966. The issue has been described as pornographic, salacious, and a symbol of our declining culture. As beach wear and styles have changed and in most cases, become more abbreviated, the daring of this issue has intensified. In the past there has been a hint of pubic hair. Many models have exposed nearly all of their breasts. The thong suit—what one pundit has described as dental floss for the bottom, leaves little to the imagination. The magazine has successfully launched the modeling and acting careers of two generations of beautiful women from Cheryl Tiegs, Christie Brinkley, Kathy Ireland, and the incredibly beautiful Swedish model, Vendela. Several years ago, the magazine hit on the idea of making a video of the making of their swimsuit issue that greatly enhanced its bottom line. (No pun intended.) Two to three weeks after each issue, there is a predictable flurry of critical letters about this issue, with several attendant subscription cancellations. In a letter published following the 1996 issue, one woman complained that "it nauseates me to see you continue this tired tradition. . . . you choose to devote 30 pages to women who have absolutely nothing to do with sports, teaching young girls the noble values of white teeth, tan bodies. . . . and lying in the sand." Women are not the only critics. A man from Norfolk, Virginia, opined, "The swimsuit issue is nothing more than a blatant sexist vehicle used to sell magazines on the newsstand. The connection between sports and bikini-clan women is, at best, a thin one. Take the high road and become an example for other sports magazines and society as a whole: sack the swimsuits." There are arguably men's issues at risk here. To sack the swimsuit issue, which in some ways, glorifies and underscores one of God's most natural and sensuously attractive creations—women, is to fall victim to the feminists distortion of the natural affinity the male sex has for its female counterparts. In the Culture War, anything that demeans women and men who solicit them or leer at them, is wrong. There are swimsuits and there are swimsuits. This is not a cut and dried issue, within the Culture War context. To enact strict guidelines and restrictive rules and regulations would be to fall victim to a false sense of elitist pride and vindictive repression. Dictatorships of virtues are nearly as bad as dictatorship of vice. Men and women should be free to speak, act and relax in the ways that they want, limited only by the Golden Rule and the spiritual pronouncements of the Judeo-Christian code of which we have lost sight.

Swimsuits have changed drastically and culturally over the last seventy-five years. What was shocking fifty years ago, is considered outdated and backward today. The idea of modesty has no doubt been changed and altered as women and men have become more conscious and in tune with the physical side of their nature. Obviously not all examples of bathing attire suits all women. Anything that enhances a woman's attractiveness, raising the spirit is a good thing. Anything that demeans her and engenders lust and misuse of her is an evil thing. Some men can turn even the most modest dress or swimwear into a seduction of spirit. This is not the woman's fault.

One feminist boasted that she should be able to walk down a street naked and not have any man notice her. Maybe in some utopian world that is not populated by human beings with a fallen nature that could happen. Men respond to sexual and physical stimuli much more quickly than women. It is a definite weakness that nature originally implanted in men, and women must recognize it and not do anything to provoke unwanted responses. Men and women need each other, not just for the sake of the species but because we each have something missing that the other can provide, not just in a physical sense, but emotionally and psychologically. Men need the softness and kindness of the feminine instinct, while women need the strength and decisiveness that men often bring. Together, especially in marriage, both sexes can achieve a civilization that is founded on religious and historical truth. Only in this way can American civilization really be saved from the dark forces that work against its very foundation.

9 / Gays
In Your Face Advocacy

We're here, we're queer, we're in the classroom.

—Gay activist Donna Redwing

I always look forward to my copy of the *Poop-Dispatch*, the annual update of the recent activities of my former classmates at Holy Cross. A recent enclosure included an article that appeared in the *New York Post*, written by one of our more controversial classmates, a fellow named Joe Nicholson. His commentary, detailing his personal outing and his banishment from a St. Patrick's Day Parade, left me shaking my head. What was the point on its inclusion? His view might be of interest to his readers in New York but why include them in our annual care package?

I started thinking back to what I remembered about Nicholson. He had a warm smile, and was a friendly enough sort of guy. I believe he was a linebacker, albeit a small one, on the freshman football team. I always admired him for that. I remember vividly a talk he gave at one of our weekly Sodality meetings in May of 1965. The prefect, the late Dan Stella, would pick a name out of a hat and the winner would have to meditate out loud on the week's readings. I will never forget Joey getting up there, beaming from ear to ear, and telling our august group of campus good guys about his participation in the Civil Rights March to Selma, Alabama, another thing I admired Joey for. Not only did he tell us of the march but also of his masturbatory proclivities and his casual sexual liaisons with a black woman on the march. I can still hear the silence now. Only one other evening in that auditorium matched it for the stillness and total attention, and that was the scary night in October of 1962, also a Sodality Monday night, when John Kennedy spoke about offensive missiles in Cuba—all but announcing the end of the civilized world. I thought our moderator, Father Joseph LaBran, was going to have a stroke or a heart attack when Joe finished. I don't remember if Nicholson suffered any consequences for his bold display of candor but he had quite a shocking impact. Funny thing, I was not upset by his self-revelation. It was an outrageous talk but I was not outraged. His article in the *Post* detailed his inner wrestling with his sexual identity. First, he was a heterosexual, then bisexual, and finally, a full-fledged gay. It seems to me that Joe is a sexual seeker, a pagan Roger Williams traipsing through the woods of his own inner doubts and physical urges, trying to find a niche were his body parts fit in. He seemed to be seeking his own self-definition, or more likely, searching for new ways to outrage his public and private lives. He reminded me of the toddler who has just had his first bowel movement unassisted and makes everyone rush to the toilet, under the gleeful pleading *See! See!* Or the little guy who pours his cereal bowl over his head and wants everyone to see how great he is.

His article was interesting but filled with the usual hyperbolic and twisted rhetoric that has come to characterize and even define the Gay Movement. Joe and his friends were not denied the right to be Irish and proud, just to hold up a life style that is patently offensive to the vast majority of people who view that parade. Cardinal O'Connor had not condemned him as a person—only his life style. It was the Christian standard of love the sinner but hate the sin approach. Like most advocates in the gay lobby, Joey wants public approval or an overt validation of everything he chooses to do with himself, no matter how offensive it may be. I think it is presumptuous that people like Joey should expect everyone else to suspend moral judgment on a life style that has historically been associated with perversity, disease, and social disruption. I am curious why the editors of the *Poop-Dispatch* saw fit to send us such a self-serving article. Maybe it was designed to be our post-modern lesson in tolerance. One thing I do know is that my reaction to the *Poop-Dispatch* was not a case of knee-jerk homophobia. This word is an artificial construct that was developed to demonize everyone who dared stand in the way of the gay agenda. It is a misnomer that means the fear of gays, lesbians, and bisexuals, as defined by Smith College Office of Student Affairs. Implicit in this definition, is the contention the person suffering from this phobia has an inordinate fear that he is really a homosexual himself. This notion is an arrogant display of ignorance and a self-indulgence—an inflated sense of self-importance that has not a shadow of reality to it. We have become a nation obsessed by sex and any nearness of men is misconstrued as sexual in nature. The motel scene in the hilarious movie, *Planes, Trains* starring Steve Martin and the late John Candy showed the reluctance grown men have to sharing a bed. Gays are guilty of imposing the agenda of the present on the situation of the past which was totally innocent.

The issue of homosexual sex will not go away. Nicholson's article was merely symptomatic of the larger issue of homosexual advocacy, which flies in the face of a culture that seems to be collapsing under the weight of excessive rights-creationism. Their public exhibitionism—their unrepentant in-your-face attitude toward all opposition and their general hatred of the Judeo-Christian underpinnings presents a great challenge to American society in the wake of the Civil Rights movement for blacks and the Feminist Movement for women. Neo-Conservative Irving Kristol believes that the legitimization of homosexuality flouts the Biblical injunction to be fruitful and multiply. He sees it in its philosophical context as a gnostic movement because they are always interested in sex since it is such a dominant human passion. Sometimes these movements become orgiastic other times ascetic. In gnostic sexuality, it is obscene for a woman to become pregnant at an orgy. The focus is on the sexual coupling and pregnancy is viewed as an undesirable result. This explains the tacit union that homosexuality and pro-abortion advocates have formed.

A new idea has been introduced into the national idiom—the myth that homosexuals are all cheerful, productive, poetic victims of unjust persecution. The book of Genesis and the punishment meted out to the inhabitants of Sodom because of their deviant sexual practices explains the Biblical and historical distrust of homosexuality. The Sodomites were not the least bit interested in sexual relations between consenting adults. They were aggressive and forceful in their erotic pursuits. They were also vengeful and violent in their actions toward Lot, threatening to do worse to him than their intended victims because he criticized their sexual aberrations. Nothing has changed with this element in the population. Militant homosexuals are not enlightened civilized people who are far removed from barbaric behaviors. Many serial killers, such as Jeffery Dahmer and John Wayne Gacy were homosexuals. The top six serial killers in US history were homosexual. Gacy raped and killed 33 boys and buried them under his Chicago house. Patrick Kearney murdered 32 young men, cutting them into small pieces after sex and leaving the bodies in trash bags along Los Angeles freeways. Juan Corona, the migrant worker in California, was convicted of murdering twenty-five fellow migrant workers. He testified at his trial that he made love with their corpses. This is not to argue that being gay makes one a serial killer but it does imply the unnatural attraction these men felt for the bodies of other men and boys led them to deviate from the most basic of civil liberties—the right to life.

The goal of the homosexual subculture is to influence public consciousness until homosexuality is accepted as the norm. Homophobia is regarded by traditional standard bearers in health and religion as a deviancy, a neuroses that is in need of psychological and spiritual counseling. Few remember that it was in 1973 when homosexual intimidation forced the *American Psychiatric Society* into removing homosexuality from its *Diagnostic and Statistical Manual of Psychiatric Disorders*. Sexual *perversion* became sexual *orientation*. This raises the question: will pedophilia and incest someday be regarded as orientations also? Will there be any recourse against child molesters? The homosexual lobby plans to accomplish universal acceptance of them and their life style by exposing the general population to an assault of positive messages, in movies, on television and in magazines. They plan to establish the homosexual lifestyle as an attractive choice by further confusing young men and women about their own nascent sexual roles and feelings. Their assault on the general consciousness will also condition the average

American into thinking that gay behavior is allright—just a different lifestyle, like being left-handed or a bird watcher.

TV has discovered gay acceptance as an emerging positive social trend and plans to exploit it. In doing so, TV can condition the viewing audience to accept and tolerate homosexuality as just another life style choice, as good, if not better than, heterosexuality. Transvestites, homosexuality, bisexuality, and gay bars are all the rage these days on network TV. In what has been called the gayest TV season in memory, as labeled by *USA Today* in late 1995. People are coming out, moving in and making jokes about homosexual life. To prove they are in the vanguard, if not actually promoting social change, television programmers have brought the gay wedding to the small screen. The 12 December 1995 episode of that bastion of liberal social commentary, "Roseanne," featured a raunchy ceremony between two men, with several double entendres by the eponymous Ms. Barr. In January of 1996, Candace Gingrich, the lesbian half sister of the Speaker of the House, officiated at a TV wedding of two women on NBC's *Friends*. Most of this gay repartee has been shown during the so-called family hour, from 8-9 P.M. A number of other shows feature homosexual characters, including CBS's *Courthouse*, NBC's *The Pursuit of Happiness*, and *United Paramount's Live Shot* were all canceled. The American public is apparently not ready for this quantum leap in social transformation. Despite these failures, according to the Media Research Center, transvestites are hot. *So are lesbians.*

Television presented only the sanitized side of the gay lifestyle. There's a bifurcated dark side to their agenda and that has created widespread fear and distrust of homosexuals, especially gay men. The homosexual community is propelled by the selfish desire of individuals who seek sexual gratification from as many sources as they can with no thought to the welfare of the rest of society or even to those in their own community. If homosexuals had any real compassion they would do everything in their power to help stop the spread of AIDS, including closing down the bathhouses and providing random testing and informing all sexual partners of being HIV positive. Homosexuals refuse any genuine help in this matter, such as behavior modification. They constantly demand more money, ostensibly for research as the only viable solution. Many of the same politicians who demanded that the Catholic and public schools spend millions to remove asbestos from their schools, in the name of public health, cripple efforts to control the spread of AIDS by protecting and promoting the absolute privacy of infected individuals..

The other side of the gay coin is what scares heterosexuals of the gay agenda. That is the relationship of gay men to young boys and the seduction of a generation of sexually confused adolescents. Gay sex usually begins at an early age. Articles in gay newspapers stress the connection between pedophilia and gay sex. An editorial in the *San Francisco Sentinel* for 26 March 1992 proclaimed that the love between men and boys is the foundation of homosexuality. A survey done for *Focus on the Family* in May of 1989, revealed that 79% of homosexuals had a relationship with a person under the age of 19. Young male children have the characteristics prized by many gay men. They are clean, usually disease free and easily seduced. Homosexual pornographic magazines are profusely illustrated with sex acts involving male children. An intergenerational (men/boys) sexual relationship could be and should be character building, says Wayne Dynes, a Hunter College Professor and editorial board member of *Paidika: The Journal of Paedophilia*. Also in *Paidika* is the following from John Money, Ph.D., a retired professor of medical psychology and pediatrics at Johns Hopkins in Baltimore, "If I were to see the case of a boy age 10 or 11 who's intensely erotically attracted toward a man in his 20s or 30s, if the relationship were mutual, and the bonding is genuinely totally mutual, then I would not call it pathological in any way." The question then is how can pedophiles be stopped from preying on children? Since the gay population cannot reproduce itself, except occasionally through some artificial inseminated lesbians, in order to sustain their numbers, gays often have to rely on recruitment. Like the United States Army, which attempts to get young men before they have formed many of their attitudes, the gay population cannot continue to exist unless it is constantly fed a new supply of young boys and girls.

A headline in a San Francisco newspaper read, *If no sex by eight, it's too late!* Supported by the 1948 findings of the *Kinsey Report,* a deeply flawed study with a strong homosexual bias, gay lobbyists argue to lower the age of sexual consent in many states. The *North American Man-Boy Love Association* (Nambla) has been a part of the United Nations' apparatus. Pedophiles have already learned to speak the language of egalitarianism. A Nambla representative said his group's main function was to allow adults to have sexual relations with children. Citing ancient antiquity, Nambla members emphasize that men who love boys need quiet time to express their feelings about a society that does not understand the forms of love esteemed in ancient Greece and many other cultures throughout history. Consider the following statement from an article by Michael Swift, a radical homosexual activist, writing in the *Gay Community News,* in February 1987.

> We shall sodomize your sons, emblems of your feeble masculinity, of your shallow dreams and vulgar lies. We shall seduce them in your schools, in your dormitories, in your gymnasiums, in your locker rooms, in your sports areas, in your seminaries, in your youth groups, in your movie theater bathrooms . . . wherever men are with men together. Your sons shall become our minions and do our bidding. They will be recast in our image. They will come to crave us and adore us.

Lesbianism also has a direct interest in children. A coven of lesbians in Louisiana distributed candy in school yards to introduce young girls to the joys of female sex.

Mary Eberstadt explored this idea in her *The Weekly Standard* article entitled, *Pedophilia Chic.* She described a new consciousness to desensitize the American public to the notion of consensual sexual relations between adult males and minor children. She extensively quoted novelist Edmund White, the author of *A Boy's Own Story,* who wrote "Sex may be the one way children can win serious consideration from adults." White feels it is the youth who aggressively comes to or seduces the innocent pedophile in these cases. He also believes that society has historically exploited children—telling them what they can and cannot do. They have to go to school, sometimes church. They can't vote, drink, or run away. The waters of sexual liberation for children have been boldly explored by ad campaigns for Calvin Klein, who first gave us an underage Brooke Shield seductively telling us that nothing comes between her and her Calvin Kleins. Klein's most provocative offering was the unsettling and much-reviled jeans ads which featured young boys lounging around semi-dressed—suggesting a body ready for pleasure.

In 1990, the *International Lesbian and Gay Association* passed a resolution that recognized pedophiliacs as a sexual minority. The ILGA calls on all members to treat all sexual members with respect and to engage in constructive dialogue with them. This has become a very important part of the gay agenda. By claiming minority status, pederasts can essentially follow in the footsteps of homosexual activists and demand legal and societal changes to guarantee their rights. Pedophilic rights would follow in the footsteps of gay rights. In 1993, the United Nations awarded consultative status to the *International Lesbian and Gay Association,* a gay umbrella organization. That same year the United States and 21 other member countries of the *UN Economic and Social Council* (ECOSOC) in Geneva, Switzerland listed Nambla and other gay and lesbian groups, even some sadomasochistic groups, among its members. This seems to imply that the UN is putting its moral force and exalted position to advance lesbian and gay rights around the globe. Another ILGA resolution arising from their paedophilia workshops states that in many countries, with regard to minors existing laws on sexual coercion and rules of evidence also operate to oppress and not to protect. This parallels the Nambla belief that laws such as the age-of-consent law exploit and limit the sexual freedom of young boys and girls because they infringe on their right to be sexual beings. Nambla offers free membership to prisoners, that is, pederasts incarcerated for child molestation and other sex crimes. Its newsletter, *Bulletin,* runs photos of scantily clad prepubescent boys—often in swimsuits. In its advice column, it advises boys to decide that you like having sex with men without becoming their friend or lover. The real fact of the matter is that these laws protect young children from the kind of sexual predators that populate organizations such as Nambla.

As with many other minorities, the homosexual movement, is about power and money. Gays, lesbians and bisexuals have joined hands in a sociopolitical alliance across America and throughout the civilized world to overthrow the traditional approach to sexual relations. The homosexual lobby is using the 1964 *Civil Rights Act* and the 1992 *Disabilities Act* to gain for themselves the status of protected minority status. They want to stifle all opposition to their activities by making opposition to them illegal. President Clinton nominated Roberta Achtenberg for a top position in the *Housing and Urban Development Department,* making her the first openly gay person ever nominated to a top job in government. A bitter opponent of the Boy Scouts, she was defiantly confirmed in the presence of her lover and her rabbi.

Christian churches are the target of most militant gay organizations. Their aim, as that of other pagan cultural warriors, is the complete overthrow of the Christian moral order under which Western civilization has existed and flourished for hundreds of years. The problem—a real philosophical dilemma—is that the egalitarian philosophy that has been widely extended to blacks and women is now being extended to homosexuals, on the basis of chosen behavior as opposed to traits like race and gender. According to the liberal tenet, all men are assumed to be of good will except those who are infected with the twin evils of theism or patriotism. The further you stand from God and country, the more righteous you are assumed to be because of your tolerance, acceptance and open-mindedness. Applying this liberal paradigm, churches, governments, and businesses must not discriminate against homosexuals. Anyone who discriminates against gays because of their behavior is, in effect, a criminal. Gays want to see the legacy of affirmative action, which has worked so well with blacks and women, applied to them, so they can secure special legal protections that will enable them to deeply instill their beliefs into the social fabric.

Like blacks, and women to a lesser degree, the gay lobby sees the United States military as a vehicle towards their gradual acceptance into the mainstream of American society. The US military has been the focal point of the opening wedge for gays to gain official sanction to their lifestyle. Gays also serve as a weapon in the new American Civil War for the left to weaken what has been traditionally considered a bastion of conservative sentiment and patriotic feeling. By forcing proud and principled officers and enlisted men to accept the gay life style as equal to their own undermines the traditional notion of family, military male bonding and camaraderie that is psychologically so important to a fighting force. More so than the abortion issue, gays in the military raises a serious privacy issue. If gay men and women are to be bivouacked with straight men and women, living in close quarters, it creates an air of immodesty, the same type of unsolicited familiarity that women soldiers would feel if they had to dress and shower with men. The gay susceptibility to the protected disease of AIDS is also a factor. During combat, soldiers are often called upon to give blood to their wounded comrades. This would undermine faith in the medical corps' ability to save lives if the wounded feared they might get a fatal disease from contaminated blood during the course of their recovery. There is also an effort being made in the military to condition its officers and men into accepting the gay life style of buggery, fisting, rimming, and water sports as normal and equal to heterosexual activities. The Navy sponsored *Diversity Day* program in 1994 featured a video, *On Being Gay*. In the film, a homosexual described and promoted his sexual practices. Compare this to the case of General Edwin Walker who tried to indoctrinate US troops in Germany with his anti-Communist beliefs during the Kennedy administration. In that instance, all hell broke loose and Walker was swiftly cashiered. Even more graphic films are winding their way into sex education courses all over the country where the gay life style seeks equal treatment with the traditional family. Both soldiers and school children represent captive audiences. There is little opportunity for soldiers or students to forcefully voice any opposition to this form of governmental indoctrination.

Borrowing a leaf from the black multicultural handbook, homosexuals have attempted to rewrite history to suit their claim to exalted status in American life. The alleged gayness of presidents Lincoln and Buchanan, as well as the heroic exploits of gay soldiers, have been highlighted to bring homosexuality further into the mainstream of American cultural acceptability. Following the lead of black and women's groups, gays are also pushing for a special month for Gay History Appreciation, an idea proposed by Rodney Wilson, a gay high school teacher from suburban St. Louis. Not one school district signed up for it.

Gays don't expect the schools to teach the actual mechanics of gay sex, even though some already do that. Most would be satisfied if the fact of Julius Caesar' and Michealangelo's gayness were recognized. Some advocates want to detail the long history of homosexual persecution. They want students taught that Thomas Jefferson sought—unsuccessfully—to liberalize Virginia's sodomy laws by reducing the punishment from death to castration. They also want it known that George Washington was homophobic because he kicked soldiers out of the Continental army for gay activities, that in 1953, President Eisenhower required government employees to take an oath that they weren't communists or gays. The problem with this gay historical intrusion is that there are few verifiable sources existent because of the social stigma and penalties against homosexuality. Most records of liaisons have been destroyed. Consequently the gay lobby has striven to find legitimate examples of outstanding gay personalities in American history, often at the expense of historical accuracy and intellectual honesty. The far-fetched rumor about Abraham Lincoln, who was the father of four boys, came from an article by a Tufts History professor, *Was Abe Lincoln Gay, Too? A Divided Man to Heal a Divided Nation*. Gays claim President Lincoln as their own because of this oblique reference to his having shared a bed with a friend at a time when a soft bed was a luxury. The fifteenth president of the United States, James Buchanan, was the only bachelor president. Gays have linked him romantically to an Alabama Senator, whom Andrew Jackson often called *Miss Nancy*. Most historians agree that Buchanan was a heterosexual who had suffered a broken heart at an early age and had taken a personal vow never to marry. There is also the cruel irony of the attempt by gay activists to tie into the Holocaust, seeking representation with the Jews as the targets of the German genocide. Gays are attempting to increase their profile within the context of the Holocaust and its many museums exhibits within the United States, further lifting the group's self-esteem and leading to full acceptability and inclusion. They want to use the moral authority of being victims of the Holocaust to attack Christian and Jewish homophobia.

Many who have been repelled by the lavender lobby's hypocrisy do not fully understand the historical, social and intellectual links which bind the contemporary gay rights movement to the early Nazis. There is a strong homosexual connection to the Nazi ideology. Hans Kahnert was the founder of the German-based *Society for Human Rights*. He was also a member of the *Thule Society* which served as an incubator for the most violent element of Nazism. Ernest Roehm, the homosexual leader of Hitler's thugs, the notorious SA or the Brownshirts, was a member of both the SHR and the Thule Society. Until it was forced to assume a facade of respectability, Germany's Nazi leadership took a progressive position on homosexuality. Hitler only condemned his party's homosexual wing when it hurt him in general elections or when he need the support of the German military in 1933. In fact, Hitler's high echelon was staffed with many active homosexuals, including Magnus Hirschfeld. Hirschfeld founded the *Sex Research Institute of Berlin* that was later sacked on 6 May 1933 by Hitler's orders because *der Fuhrer* feared the exploitative information that Hirschfeld had collected on his subordinates. Until the final purge in 1934, known as the *Night of the Long Knives,* when Hitler murdered his most public homosexuals, such as Roehm, his SA officers and many other opposition leaders who were not gay, Hitler demonstrated an amazing flexibility with his homosexual party members.

The Pink Swastika, a book by Scott Lively and Kevin Abrahams has thoroughly investigated this issue. The authors contend that not only did the majority of the SA homosexuals survive the purge, but that the massacre was largely implemented by homosexuals. They found that the kinship between nascent Nazism and the violent direct action wing of the present homosexual movement was acknowledged by Eric Pollard, a founder of the Washington, DC affiliate of the *AIDS Coalition to Unleash Power,* better known as the *Act-up.* Pollard admitted the fascist nature of this militant group, stating that many of its tactics had been drawn from Adolf Hitler's *Mein Kampf.* The *Act-up* leadership relied on the enlightened view that there are no objective standards of right and wrong: there is only the naked quest for power. Lively and Abrahams both point out that the task of creating the American homosexual movement fell to the Communist wing of the Socialist movement. In August 1948, Communist Party leader Marty Hay created the nucleus of the modern *Mattachine Society,* a group which took its name from the occult underground of pre-revolutionary France. Hay was also a communicant at the Los Angeles lodge of Aleister Crowley's *Order of the Eastern Temple,* an occult group that descended from Adam Weishaupt's Bavarian *Illuminati.* Hay's *Mattachine Society* was designed as a vehicle to destroy social restraints against homosexuality in American culture. Hay is regarded as the father of the gay movement.

The Clinton administration has also shown a fondness for the gay agenda. The homosexual march on Washington, DC in April of 1993 carried the queer clamor to a higher decibel level. By some estimates, 300,000 gay, lesbian and bisexuals invaded the nation's capital and demanded their civil rights. The movement was in full flower as lesbians strolled topless, men pranced totally naked, and both sported anti-Christian and anti-capitalist signs replete with vile language. Two members of the Clinton entourage were prominent in this march. Larry Kramer, one of the founders of the militant *Act-up* ousted or exposed the alleged homosexuality of Secretary of Health and Human Services Donna Shalala, denouncing her for failing to join the march. Similar accusations were directed at First Lady Hillary Clinton. No comment came from either of their targets. One of the masters of ceremony, a lesbian, declared: "at last there is someone in the White House I can have sex with." She did not mean Bill Clinton. No presidential administration in American history has opened itself more to the gay agenda than that of Bill Clinton. He has allowed gays into every bureau of the government, allowing his gay supporters to force America to accept homosexuality as a normal alternate lifestyle. Under White House mandate, all government bureaus must add sexual orientation to their employment policies so as to desensitize other federal employees to their activities. Permitting homosexuals in the military was only the tip of the iceberg. Federal workers, especially Christians, who objected to this indoctrination and infiltration were harassed, censored and persecuted. The president has required each cabinet secretary to implement HIV/AIDS education and prevention programs and develop workplace policies for employees with AIDS. Jesse Helms has incurred the wrath of the gay lobby for his bill to eliminate federal agency programs that promote and condone homosexual practices. Helms wished the legislation was not necessary but feels that the Clinton administration "has conducted a concerted effort to give homosexual rights, privileges and protections throughout federal agencies—to extend to homosexuals special rights in the federal workplace, rights not accorded to most other groups and individuals." No other group in America has been given special rights based on sexual preference. One of Helms' bills would prohibit agencies from spending appropriated funds on programs that compel, instruct, encourage, urge, or persuade employees or officials to recruit—on the basis of sexual orientation—homosexuals for employment with the government or embrace, accept, condone, or celebrate homosexuality. Another bill would prohibit removing employees who criticize the government's policies on homosexuals without first giving them a public hearing. This bill grew out of the removal of Agriculture Department employee, Karl Mertz, who, while on personal leave, criticized the administration's policy on gays. Helms held up confirmation of five administration nominees and threatened to delay the Agricultural Appropriations bill until former Secretary Mike Espy eventually agreed to reinstate Mertz.

About 22 federal agencies have their own *Globe* organizations, that is *Gay, Lesbians, or Bisexuals Employees* groups. They are allowed the use of E-mail, voice mail, and bulletin boards to promote their events. The Agriculture Department has its own Globe manager within the Foreign Agriculture Service. This position involves promoting the gay, lesbian, and bisexual employment program. FBI director Louis Freeh has adopted a new policy to admit more gays into his bureau. Attorney General Janet Reno has issued orders that the Department of Justice will recognize sexual orientation when granting security clearances. In 1994 she stirred up a hornet's nest when she let thousands of HIV-infected foreigners participate in New York City's Gay Olympics. Secretary of the Department of Health and Human Services, Donna Shalala sponsored a Multicultural Day in Dallas where an employee was given official permission for his exhibit *Highlighting our Gay and Lesbian Culture.* Energy Secretary Hazel O'Leary made it mandatory for all her employees to complete a three-hour AIDS training session called *Walkin' the Talk,* that graphically described homosexual acts. During the Cherry Jubilee in April of 1996, a pair of fund-raisers for AIDS, took place first in the historic Andrew W. Mellon Auditorium, across from the Smithsonian's Museum of American History, followed by a Sunday brunch at the Rayburn House Office Building. Described as a New York-style gay circuit party, several hundred gay men attended, including homosexual Steve Gunderson, a Republican Congressman from Wisconsin. Video footage showed that many engaged in an orgy of sexual and drug activities that defaced the public nature of the government buildings in which they took place.

The *National Endowment for the Arts* (NEA) is a prime supporter of gay art and theater. In 1992, it paid over $170,000 to underwrite the *LaMaMa Experimental Theater Club* which provided the venue for *Lesbian Bitches Who Kill* for its 1992-93 season. The NEA reversed a Bush Administration decision and awarded $17,500 to the *National Alliance for Media Arts and Culture* for three homosexual film festivals featuring titles such as *Why I Masturbate,* and *We're Talking Vulva.* The NEA also contributed $25,000 toward the production of the film *Poison,* which dealt with deviant sexual behavior and graphic homosexual sex.

Gays have also made great strides in advancing their agenda with the willful cooperation of many in the mainstream media. The *New York Times, Sports Illustrated* and the rest of the liberal media go out of their way to promote homosexuals as normal people. In December 1995, the *New York Times* magazine profiled lesbian activist, Dorothy Allison whose work has been labeled by many as pornographic. Hollywood plans to make a movie from her book. The *Times* raved that one of her subjects was "the joys of raunchy sex between women." It carried a photo of Allison, her lover and their son. The child was described as someone who insists on gnawing bones while watching TV.

Sympathetic journalists have helped by vilifying gay opposition as extremist or intolerant. The press has adopted the homosexual cause because it fits right in with another liberal tenet of *do it if it feels good* way of thinking. Gay staff members are often showcased to show how the various news services have counteracted the prejudices of the past. Leonard Downie, executive director of the *Washington Post* boasted that he had several gay staff members who made his paper just that much smarter. Tim Russert added to this debate by saying reporters at NBC are taught to be sensitive to gay concerns and that an association of gay journalists is active at his network. Many journalists criticize the Catholic Church for its homophobia. There is a growing trend by major newspapers and news organizations to recruit openly gay men and women. The *Washington Post,* the *New York Times,* as well as the *Gannett Foundation,* the *LA Times,* the Hearst Newspapers, and CBS News contributed several thousand dollars to sponsor the *National Lesbian and Gay Journalist Convention* in Washington in October 1995. Though gays comprise no more than 1 or 2% of the general population, it is certain that they have infiltrated the mainline journalism in a much greater proportion.

The gay lobby has dealt with its perceived enemies in a severe and thorough manner. In the seventies, popular singer Anita Bryant was destroyed by her opposition to the gay movement that was just beginning. The media ridiculed her religious-based opposition, causing her to suffer both in her professional and private lives for speaking out. Other direct targets of straight bashing include Senator Helms of North Carolina, who has been quite vocal in his condemnation of homosexuality, and Cardinal John O'Connor of New York's St. Patrick Cathedral. One AIDS activist, writing in an art catalog funded by the NEA, called Cardinal John O'Connor of New York *a fat cannibal from the house of walking swastikas up on Fifth Avenue.* Neither of these men have ever bashed a gay but homosexuals do annually parade naked in front of St. Patrick's Cathedral, perform lewd acts on the parade route, disrupt Sunday masses, desecrate the Holy Eucharist and vandalize churches. The media and the police often stand idly by in a stance of benign neglect, either afraid to get involved or because they support this bold and brazen behavior. One misguided group that evokes sympathy is the *Pro-life Alliance of Gay and Lesbians.* They were understandably excluded from a pro-life convention and the annual January *March For Life* in 1996. Organizers refused to allow their participation because they did not want their shameful banner to besmirch the overall tenor of the events. In 1995, they had to flee for their lives as they were literally attacked at a gay pride festival by a horde of screaming abortion rights activists.

The AIDS epidemic is another issue in which gay activists have attempted to influence popular opinion. AIDS ranks as our first politically driven disease—a tribute to the homosexual lobby. An ad in the *New York Times* blames deaths from AIDS on homophobia, not gay behavior: "irrational prejudices like homophobia have obstructed public health efforts to prevent the spread of AIDS, the Public Media Center charges." This is a desperate claim, bordering on the kind of paranoia the late Richard Hofstadeter said had permeated McCarthyism in the 1950s. In 1994, AIDS took the lives of 42,000 people. That same year 730,000 Americans died of heart disease and 520,000 of cancer. Not counting Medicare and Medicaid under the President's 1996 budget, Washington will allocate $1,134 for each heart-disease death, $4,808 for every cancer victim and $71,429 for each AIDS victim. There are no cancer or heart disease activists beating their fists and feet on the floor over inadequate funding for their ailments. At Academy Awards ceremonies, celebrities do not wear tiny insulin bottles to identify with diabetics even though diabetes killed more people in 1994 than AIDS did. Unfortunately much of the money allegedly allocated for AIDS research goes to foster the homosexual lifestyle, possibly causing more people to contract the deadly disease. The 6 April 1994 Trentonian said a $100,000 federal AIDS grant was used to sponsor a drag queen ball in Newark, New Jersey. There is another dark side running through the AIDS controversy. Homosexual victims of AIDS are often reckless in their behavior. One wonders if they are really sincere in finding a cure for AIDS. Were a cure to be found, the gay movement would suffer a commensurate loss in status, much like the curing of poverty would throw thousands of Health and Human Service bureaucrats out of work. The gay population has a vested interest in the continuation of AIDS because it is the only thing, outside of the Clinton presidency, that gives legitimacy to the movement.

While most gays believe that condom distribution in the schools is the only way to stave off the spread of the disease, many do not follow that advice. Much of the behavior that transpires at massage parlors, bath houses, and other homosexual trusting places is riven with sordid and reckless behavior. *The Washington Blade,* a gay newspaper, sermonizes about safe sex, the mantra of the gay movement, while running display ads for orgies and wild parties. Wally Hansen, who was working for a gay San Francisco newspaper in 1992, felt no compunction about giving the disease to his partners: "I can only think positively. I do anything I want. I feel like I'm doing more damage to myself by stressing my system out of worry."

Gays are also notorious for fighting the very methods that have worked for stopping the transmission of other sexually transmitted diseases, such as syphilis and gonorrhea: testing and contact tracing. In July 1994, the Senate rejected an amendment to the reauthorization of the *Ryan White Act* that would have required HIV testing for all mothers and newborns. Under the protective mantel of privacy, gays complained vehemently that this amendment was an intolerable intrusion, never mind that the children's health might be jeopardized. For the AIDS lobby a mother's privacy jeopardized the health of her baby.

The homosexual population hit upon an impressive strategy in an article for *The Guide*, a homosexual magazine. The article, "The Overhauling of Straight America," instructed its readers first to desensitize the public so they'll view homosexuality with indifference instead of emotion. It also encouraged the regular media to continue to portray homosexuals as victims in need of protection, hoping to gradually change the public's perception of gays from hatred to concern. Another aspect of their grand design for cultural acceptance focuses on the school system. In early 1995, the Des Moines Public School District unveiled its *Multicultural Non-sexist Education Plan*, prepared by its *Sexual Orientation Advisory Committee*. This plan established comprehensive long-range and short-range goals for using the schools as a conduit to impose the gay/lesbian lobby's value system on schoolchildren. The most revealing part of the 900-word document is its repeated use of the word "infuse" and its plan to develop gay/lesbian information modules that can be fully integrated into a wide range of courses. This plan hopes to include in the elementary, middle, and high school curricula a discussion of the nature of families, including same gender families and parenting. It hopes also to include the evolution of modern gay/lesbian/bisexual identity and cross-cultural representations of homosexuality in psychology and sociology courses. The curriculum is determined to use the public schools as an agent of change to create student awareness of homophobic thinking and behavior, comparing these with other forms of prejudice and oppression. One means of doing this was New York Chancellor Joseph Fernandez's outrageous choice of elementary school readers, *Heather has Two Mommies*, and *Daddy's Roommate*. Fortunately the plan was defeated by the City Board of Education. The strategy also calls for a ban on heterosexual bias in language and for increasing their materials in school libraries and multimedia centers. This curriculum also calls for the presentation of information on gender/sexual orientation and the natural diversity present in human beings. Diversity is the code word for homosexual propaganda. According to talk show host, Jan Michelson, "this is not an agenda for tolerance. This is an in-your-face gay agenda seeking taxpayer support to target your kids." This gives lie to the liberal cultural belief that one should not impose one's own morality on others. This is precisely what the gay agenda, working in concert with liberal moral philosophy, has in mind for generations of American students. Phyllis Schlafly believes that the schools are just one skirmish in the Culture War.

One of my regular callers on WGNU, "the Prisoner of Love" was obsessed with pedophilic priests. It is definitely a problem that falls within the context of this chapter. St. Louis University professor James Hitchcock thinks the Church is too preoccupied with its AIDS ministry and those who claim their homosexuality as the main part of their self-identity. He cites for special attention those gay priests for whom "their orientation ought to be nobody's business but that of their religious superiors and they may well have a higher place in the Kingdom of heaven for practicing the heroic chastity of the celibate life." This should be the essential Christian view point. Pat Buchanan opined in a 1994 column that it is not the right which has started the Culture War with reference to gays and lesbians but "the relentless drive by homosexuals and their allies to use schools and media to validate and propagate their moral beliefs, to convert all of America to those beliefs and to codify them into federal law." It is the gay lobby's relentless quest to reform American society that has given rise to contentious debate that is an integral part of the Culture War. When traditionalists attempt to salvage their culture they are demonized for being intolerant, homophobic, and mean-spirited. It is the gays' unfettered grasping for the reigns of power that will lead to violence. It is a given law of power that once they receive the preferential status they demand with its attendant money and power, like most left-wing groups they will not give it up without a fight. Buchanan continued by giving the best way that gays should be viewed:

> no one is for gay bashing for deliberately and maliciously taunt-ing gay men and women but while homosexuality is wrong, gays and lesbians are children of God and citizens of this republic. That entitles them to all the constitutional rights of citizens, and to be treated with decency, and yes, compassion. But their con-duct cannot command respect, because it so violently contradicts our beliefs. If that be "homophobia," make the most of it.

Gays have taken Buchanan's statement as an act of war when it is nothing more than a statement of principle.

Gays have a very committed ally in former Surgeon-General Joycelyn Elders who called gay sex "wonderful and normal . . . and a healthy part of our being." In an issue of the *Advocate* magazine in 1994, she opined, "We can't write off 10 percent of our student population." She criticized the Boys Scouts for their ban on homosexual members because it had a negative effect on the mental health of homosexual youth. She publicly agonized about the alleged ill effects of secondhand tobacco smoke yet gave the green light to dangerous sexual practices.

A 1995 study by Dean Hammer, a molecular biologist at the National Cancer Institute, revealed new evidence of a gay gene. This news was re-ceived in the liberal/gay community, with the same enthusiasm as if a cure for cancer had been discovered. Biological determinism has quickly become a powerful weapon in the gay lobby's moral arsenal. Hammer's highly touted 1993 gay gene study is currently under investigation for fraud by the federal *Office of Research Integrity*. One could raise the question why money ear-marked for cancer research had been diverted to the more politically-correct gay research. Nor did the newspapers report Hammer's own homosexuality, which could serve as a conflict of interest under these guidelines. Hammer once told a meeting of *Parents and Friends of Lesbians and Gays,* "you tell the press what to write about a scientific study, they'll write it." Once he told the media that being gay was analogous to being left-handed. Most journalists subscribed to his argument without question or verification because it fit in with the pro-gay media agenda. On the same note, there has been research done that hints there may be a similar gene that affects alcoholic behavior. But the disease of genetic predisposition to alcohol would not excuse someone from getting drunk and then killing someone in an auto accident. Even if this study were conclusive, it would not excuse their kind of sordid behavior.

The standard debate over nature versus nurture has been used to discuss everything from eye color to IQ. Its application to homosexuality has had significant repercussions. The scientific search for the elusive gay gene preoccupies many researchers, hoping for that biological element that would nullify choice. Are homosexuals born that way or do they learn or acquire this behavior? Proponents of this view argue that if it is nature's fault, then homosexuals should not be blamed for whatever they do. If gays are born that way, like being redheaded, there is little that should be done to discourage or condemn that behavior. There are hundreds of support groups that believe gayness is learned if an adolescent is exposed to an environment where gender models are confused or absent. To relieve thousands of gays and lesbians from the chains of this sexual life style with all of its attendant physical and psychological dangers, there are groups such as *Exodus.* This group mixes a love for the Bible and religion with an honest assessment of who these people really are. They have had an impressive success rate and have a number of cases where gay men have married lesbian women with great relief to their spiritual lives. In addition to *Exodus,* there are several other organizations that attempt to counsel gays out of their homosexuality. They include *Homosexuals Anonymous, Love in Action, Desert Stream,* and *Whitestone Ministries.*

The case that brought the gay power issue to the forefront was *Baehr vs. Lewin* which first reached the Hawaii Supreme Court in 1993. Three gay couples sued for their right to marry, stating that a denial of their marriage licenses amounted to unconstitutional discrimination on the basis of sex. In an effort to bolster the state's arguments, the Hawaii Legislature passed a law in 1994 that defined marriage as a union, solely between a man and a woman. Baehr was the first significant challenge to the principle of heterosexual marriage. The case was carefully crafted to raise no federal constitutional challenge because gay legislation has always fared best when directed at state laws. Not since *Roe vs. Wade* has there been the potential to so adversely impact the way Americans live.

With this early success, gay advocates have attempted to break the barrier to their union under the full faith and credit section of the federal constitution which reads that all states must recognize the public acts, records and judicial proceedings of every other side state. In short, if gays get married in Hawaii, they are recognized as being married in all the other 49 states. While the principle of full faith and credit has never been explicitly applied to the institution of marriage, there are some precedents. New York does not allow common law marriages, but it does recognize those in other states. Many Southern states, which had miscegenation laws on the books, still recognize the marriage of racially mixed couples from other states.

State divorce laws provide a better example of just how full faith and credit effect the gay agenda in this context. Las Vegas developed a large and profitable industry of quickie divorce, which had a very positive effect on its hotel and entertainment industries. The same could happened to Hawaii, which is already planning to do for gay marriages what Las Vegas did for divorce. Legalized gambling got its foot in the door with Las Vegas. If this decision is eventually upheld, despite federal legislation, the Rainbow State will serve as the conduit through which the gay agenda on marriage will be recognized in all 50 states. The argument for recognizing homosexuals marriage rests on the relativistic assumption that marriage is nothing more than an arbitrary social convention that can be changed or altered or reinvented in light of changing times and social thinking. It is this way of thinking that contends that law makes things right—if a court chooses to make homosexual marriage legal, then it follows that there is no absolute truth about marriage to prevent them from doing so. Some libertarians, such as John Leo, oppose gay marriages yet think that committed gay couples, should have the same health plan coverage as straights. In his 24 May 1993 column in *U.S. & World News Report,* Leo suggested that this could be accomplished through domestic-partnership legislation or registered bonding ceremonies. I thoroughly disagree with his arguments. They support special privileges for gays that straight friends of the same sex or even the opposite sex would not be allowed by law. Leo's thinking assaults the notion of equality before the law. No matter how much gay men and women may care for one another, to allow or compel the law to recognize sodomitic unions is a grievous attack on the most basic and culturally necessary institution of American society.

Another libertarian, Stephen Chapman attacked religious opposition to gay marriages in a 1996 column. Chapman failed to recognize that the law has great moral power and to legitimize and is, in effect, to approve and encourage the targeted behavior. While St. Thomas Aquinas wrote that everything that is wrong should not be outlawed, the converse is also true, everything that is not wrong should be made into law. While few want to return to the days when sodomy and gay sex were illegal, that kind of behavior should not be elevated to legitimate status of approved or acceptable behavior. For the sake of the social mores, there are still some things that should be stigmatized in this country without necessarily constituting a crime. Gays are asking for a complete divorce of the moral and legal. No society can exist, based on a purely amoral legal structure. Without proper moral strictures, antisocial behavior will be the order of the day.

Traditional society originally defined marriage as much more than consent for sexual pleasure and companionship. Marriage occupies a special place for American society. To Catholics it is a sacrament, and to Protestants a holy office. The institution not only seeks to create mystic bonds between husbands and wives but also to ensure that humans rear children in ways that guarantee the survival of society. As columnist Tony Snow points out, "contrary to a popular, recent book title, it doesn't take a village to raise a child. It takes a mom and a dad." The assumption that procreation is a societal good has come under attack because of fears that population pressures will result in cataclysmic disasters. The crusade for gay marriage would reduce matrimony to a contractual arrangement, shorn of its sacred nature and its child-rearing obligations. Gays and lesbians who adopt or resort to artificial insemination will further weaken the special bonding between natural parents and their offspring that is essentially important and socially beneficial to future adults.

Phillip Lawler, the editor of *Catholic World Report,* wrote in the *Wall Street Journal* that a four-year-old he encountered instinctively knew what marriage was all about: *papa loved mama so they got married and had babies.* No more depth of explanation is required for understanding the essentials of marriage. Like it or not, gays cannot enter into this kind of psychological, sexual and mysterious union of souls. In marriage, a man and a woman (only a man and a woman) promise to love one another; in the marriage act they extend that love toward the next generation. Childless couples know the pain and frustration of not being able to reproduce. It has been our common cultural understanding that romantic love implies the promise of marriage and marriage implies the promise of children. Once that link in the chain was broken—once the prospect of begetting and raising children was reduced, in the manner of Murphy Brown, to just another lifestyle option—our understanding of marriage was destined for a radical change. Once sexual intercourse is overtly denied its procreative purpose then there is no real reason to limit sexual intercourse to heterosexuals. As logic would have it, if the sole purpose of sex is pleasure then the anatomical qualities of the partners would seem to be indifferent to the nature of the act.

It might take the Supreme Court to settle this debate. Perhaps, though unlikely, it will employ the same logic that the court did in 1878 in *Reynolds vs. United States.* Discounting the Jeffersonian ideal of the wall of separation between church and state, the court ruled that Utah's Mormons could not practice polygamy because it had always been odious among the northern and western nations of Europe and because it is impossible to believe that the constitution was intended to prohibit legislation in respect to this most important feature of social life. This is a viable historical parallel and could very well prevent the gay lobby from perverting the institution of marriage for the aggrandizement of additional political power.

In his book, *Virtually Normal, New Republic* homosexual editor Andrew Sullivan argues that "the heterosexuality of marriage is intrinsic only if understood to be intrinsically procreative; but that definition has long been abandoned by Western society." I would argue that it has been altered rather than abandoned. Couples have used many chemical and artificial means to limit the size of their families because of the increasing number of educational, material and psychological demands society has pushed on the family. Sullivan also argues that gay marriages will benefit society because marriage data show that married couples are healthier, live longer, and are financially more successful. But *Catholic World* editor Phillip Lawler counters that "it is not the possession of a marriage license that transforms impulsive young men and women into mature and responsible adults; it is the presence of children in the household." This is a salient point that gays cannot refute.

The issue of marital fidelity is also a key consideration in this argument. The average homosexual has over 100 partners in a lifetime while the average heterosexual male has about 15-18 and the average female about 7-8. This pervasive promiscuity leads to diseases of all natures and nearly certain premature death for the vast majority of homosexuals. Most gays do not live past their mid-forties. Due to their frequency of anal intercourse, gay men often suffer from a variety of intestinal and rectal disorders, known simply as "gay bowel syndrome." They are also more susceptible to Hepatitis B and any other illnesses. Michael Fumento created a furor when he wrote his book, *The Myth of Heterosexual Disease,* which downplayed the notion of HIV virus as the cause of AIDS. Fumento put forth a great deal of documentation that painted AIDS as primarily a disease of the gay and drug subcultures in America. His efforts were met with a scurrilous hate campaign conducted by the gay lobby that made his book as hard to find as the writings of *Planned Parenthood* founder Margaret Sanger. The main difference here is that proponents of Sangerism don't want her views known and have hidden or destroyed as many copies as they could find. The gay lobby does not want the truth of Fumento's book disseminated since it would undercut their attempts to normalize gay disease patterns and remove the stigmatization that rightfully belongs to their perverse behavior. The homosexual campaign to stop the book was so successful that Fumento's publisher, Basic Books, embargoed all unsold copies. *Forbes* magazine inspired the wrath of gay activists from *Act-up* after the business periodical gave the book a favorable review. The late publisher Malcolm Forbes recanted his role in the issue and said he would have killed the article had he not been traveling at the time. There is no evidence that a marriage license will lessen the homosexual's urge for multiple partners. Sullivan is widely quoted for his remark that gay unions would be tolerant of extramarital outlets. In other words, a gay marriage would not include the heterosexual idea of sexual fidelity, which is one of the defining conditions of marriage itself. Joseph Sobran has wondered out loud, *Just what would the partners be promising at the altar?*

The Hebrew Bible unleashed an intellectual and cultural revolution over 3000 years ago when it defined marriage as a union between a man and a woman. As Dennis Praeger noted in his book, *The Public Interest,* most ancient societies condoned, even exalted, homosexuality. The Hebrew innovation sublimated man's sexual drive, raised women from chattel status to partners, and established a new sociological building block for society, making civilization possible. Fortunately for society, the logic and the metaphysical links between love and marriage, sex and babies, are still unbroken—if not in the popular best-sellers, at least in millions of American homes. One thing is certain that gays can not fathom is that the human reproductive system is designed to reproduce and as a result human, will always reproduce. Once absolute principles and standards have been torn asunder there is no stopping any sort of sexual and human perversion. If we expunge the presumption of procreation from the marital formula—if marriage only sanctions the power of love and carnality, what principle prevents states from demanding tolerance of consensual arrangements that are now taboo? Why limit a man to just one wife or a woman to just one husband? Will state age requirements hold up under this? Will not gay marriage include young boys or young girls? Will not incestuous fathers and mothers demand their right to marry their offspring? Why stop there? I have seen some people so attached to their pets, that bestiality might need to be raised to the level of holy matrimony. Sexual crusaders will darken the doorsteps of every Las Vegas-style preacher in the United States because we will have no legitimate reason to prevent such unions. I admit the latter is patently absurd but in a society without moral standards, the old adage of anything goes does really ring true. The only true fact is the institution of marriage will cease to exist as we now know it.

10 / Word Power
Newspeak for the Nineties

> A dictator lurks in every forceful writer. Power over words leads easily to longing for power over men.
>
> —A. J. P. Taylor on Leon Trotsky

The fifties were not the best of times nor were they the worst of times. My youth was characterized by a clear understanding of what was morally right and morally wrong, with little leeway for discussion or exception. Though this is a quality of that time which is often subject to criticism, the direct approach to the inestimable problems of youth, also provided a comfortable sense of security. Saturday afternoons at the movies served as a perfect metaphor for growing up in the fifties. The good guys always wore white hats. The bad guys had facial hair and dressed in dark clothing. The Indians behaved as savages, grunting and slaughtering innocent white settlers on the frontier. Predictably, the cavalry rode up on the horizon, flying the banner of good and signaling the inevitable triumph over evil.

With avuncular Dwight Eisenhower in the Oval Office, we felt safe even with the threat of nuclear annihilation hanging over our heads. We were confident that the world would still be there when we got up the next morning. There were few co-dependents in the fifties. While we knew divorce existed, most parents stuck it out, and dealt with their problems without drugs or painkillers. Their outwardly stable unions provided the attendant sense of familial security that seems to have vanished from the face of the American culture in the 1990s. Collecting bubble gum cards, which were a nickel a pack and had that memorable aroma, was a fond memory of my adolescence. So was an afternoon watching the Brooklyn Dodgers play at Ebbets Field. I can still recall the distinctive smell the old ball park emanated. It was a curious mixture of spilled beer, smoke, sweat and peanuts that made the game even more enjoyable than listening to Red Barber or Vince Scully on the radio. The grass was real and the fans did not need any escapees from an aviary to cheer for the home team.

Sex on the screen or in music was implied rather than crudely consummated. Sexually explicit magazines were virtually unattainable for adolescents. What few there were often contained nothing more sinister than some black and white photos of happy nudists frolicking on the beach. Priests and nuns sternly moralized on just how far on a girl's body you could tread before entering sinful waters. Wally Cleaver religiously did his homework and cheerfully helped his mom and dad with the Beaver. Ward Cleaver demonstrated all the paternal skills a father needed. His calm counsel and unruffled demeanor, made him the paragon of parental behavior for the times. The fifties had a pristine innocence that made the scars of acne the only damaging remnants of adolescence.

The assassination of President John F. Kennedy in 1963, coupled with the televised horrors of the Vietnam War, served as a watershed that separated the innocence of adolescence from the painful reality of daily life. Children born since 1963 have had few of the protections that buffered a young person on the verge of adulthood in 1958. The nation's moral vision has been so blurred that it is nearly impossible to tell the bad guys from the good guys anymore, the Indians from the cowboys. Our national mores have become submerged within a moral relativism, whose twin gods, Chaos and Insecurity, still reign supreme. Today's hero has welded himself to the status of a victim as the nation's traditional Gatekeepers—government, the news media, the churches and the schools, invent every imaginable physical, social and mental handicap to deprive millions of flawed human beings from accepting the responsibilities and the consequences of their behaviors. Basketball star Magic Johnson astonished the world with the revelation of his HIV positive status. The public reaction was overwhelming. How could this happen to one of the gods of sport? The royal Gatekeepers declared that the hero on the court had become a victim off the court. He paraded around from talk show to talk show, the public confessional of the nineties, detailing how he had accommodated some 2,000 affectionate women in the bedroom since the start of his professional career. His gospel message of safe sex, which could be treated as the oxymoronic bromide of the ages, raised the question of culpability and responsibility among a small and ineffective coterie of critics. A bone fide hero would have shown a sense of personal responsibility for having acquired the deadly disease. A drunk driver, especially one worth millions of dollars with a pregnant wife and a big house, who accidentally kills himself is certainly not a heroic figure in the traditional understanding of the term.

Forty years ago, heroes were tall, quiet men who shunned the limelight for the sake of real privacy. John Wayne, Alan Ladd, and Randolf Scott epitomized the quiet grace under pressure that carried the day, saved the maiden and always saw to it that good triumphed over evil. Many of us growing up in Queens had affection for Brooklyn Dodger shortstop, Pee Wee Reese, a modest man of heroic proportions who led by example and a calm, genteel manner. Quiet and unassuming, the Kentucky Colonel performed with skill, dignity and aplomb, earning the respect of all his contemporaries, including many opposing players. No athlete epitomized the fifties more than the St. Louis Cardinals' legend, Stan-The-Man-Musial. Stan

Musial was a genuine family man whose unfeigned goodness, gentle good humor and unpretentiousness created this special aura. Today's heroes are often aloof, so taken by their own vaulted sense of self-importance that they are unable to relate to their fans in any meaningful way. The Willie Mays' and the other greats of the past all had the same human nature as the Jose Cansecoes and the Darryl Strawberries. But with the publication of *Ball Four* a raucously funny kiss-and-tell book, written by Seattle Pilots' iconoclastic pitcher, Jim Bouton, in 1970, many of the players had their private faults, vices and anti-social behavior exposed to the general public. Bouton's book and a legion of imitators, had a revolutionary effect on the public's perception of its sports heroes. Prior to *Ball Four*, sports writers had fashioned a protective mythology that properly kept the fans' focus on the game between the lines, without any inference of their off-the-field activities, such as Wade Boggs adulterous affairs or the Yankees' Mickey Mantle's midnight "beaver shoots" on the roof of a Washington hotel. Because of this loss of innocence, heroes and their relationship to the fans would never again be the same.

The American paparazzi contributed to this gradual alienation of the public from the fans by fostering the petty jealousies among owners and fellow players. A story, probably apocryphal in nature, illustrates this radical departure. Babe Ruth, a good-natured libertine in the twenties, was seen running naked through the dinning car on the train from St. Louis to Cleveland. He was followed by an irate, semi-nude woman, wielding an eight-inch butcher knife. Sports reporter Fred Lieb looked dispassionately at his comrades and said shaking his head, "Whose deal?" Sensing a loss of economic enterprise should sports slip in popularity, journalists conspired in preventing the fans from knowing too much about sports heroes' imperfections and shenanigans, much to the good of the sport involved.

The tide turned in a post-Watergate flourish that witnessed an overzealous press, hell-bent on investigative reporting, feeling compelled to publish, print or broadcast every blemish on our sports figures. This journalistic license eventually pervaded all public forums, including movies and politics, creating an internal animus that has poisoned much of social discourse in this country. With the fame often came the shame. Real heroes abound if we just can transcend the media hype. They serve in the hospitals, nursing homes, high crime areas and fire departments. Men and women who each day put their lives on the line for other people, such as the soldiers of Desert Storm, deserve recognition for their consistent heroism. Mother Teresa and other clergy who give up the pleasures of the flesh for the sake of others and volunteer doctors in violence-torn Haiti often go unnoticed and unappreciated. The alcoholic wife who not only quit drinking because it was destroying her life and her family but also stopped smoking because she wanted to get well for them is another kind of unheralded hero. A scientist at MIT who accepted the challenge of the loss of his limbs to invent and develop prosthetic improvements that will make his life and those of other handicapped people more productive can easily be added to this list of heroes. In exemplifying virtue and fair play, all of the above expressed what Edmund Burke called "the unbought grace of life."

Those like Magic Johnson, who bring plagues on their own houses, have no one to blame for their troubles. Their self-destructive attitude would not have survived in the fifties because people had more personal and religious values. They did not listen to the clarion call of a culture in despair that urged them to do it if it feels good with little regard for the rights or concerns of others. People in the fifties did not gratify their every whim or desire without heeding the spiritual or physical cost. The mindless self-indulgence that has permeated the nineties, distorting the traditional perception of Cowboys and Indians has turned society into a sewer of filth and despair, polluting the eyes and ears on all levels of our society. Since words and ideas are intricately linked, the idea of the hero has led me to a consideration of words and their meanings. Many alterations in word meaning, such as the word "hero," have led to mass confusion in society about the fundamental values of its American heritage. I have always been fascinated by words, especially those rich in meaning and sound. The polysyllabic musings of William F. Buckley, William Safire, R. Emmett Terrell and Richard Lederer continue to impress me. My daughter, who also has a great love of the lexicon, passed on her favorite word to me recently: *sesquipedalian*, which means "one given to the use of long words."

Words can also be fun. People delight for hours in crossword puzzles. Families pass time on vacation travel with all kinds of innovative word games. Words can also hurt, cause pain and break hearts. Words of rejection have caused more than one teenager to go over the deep end. When Robert Louis Stevenson wrote, "Words are power!" he implied that the person who had command of the language would go far because people are usually impressed by people with strong vocabularies. Words are to the intellect what height and strength are to the athlete.

Words have power, and this power must be used carefully. In his book, *The Inarticulate Society: Eloquence and Culture in America,* Tom Schachtman explored the uses of profanity or male dicta in social situations. These words, mostly copulative or excretionary in meaning, are now what substitutes for writing in many of our movies today. Because of their connection with sex or the bodily organs, our culturally anointed are attempting to win the social acceptance of these words as part of their effort to liberate the ordinary person from the repressive strictures and inhibitions of the Victorian past. As the public becomes more and more desensitized to these words, the social mores will sink to a new level. Some of these words are already making their way onto prime time with the excuse that the major networks need them so as to compete with the cable stations that broadcast R-rated movies. Song lyrics, especially from rap-artists, are riven with vulgar and profane expressions that we are told are realistic renditions of ghetto rage, engendered by four hundred years of slavery. To use Senator Patrick

Moynahan's phrase, we are quickly "defining deviancy down," with all the negative social consequences that idea entails. Profane words have, according to researcher Vivian de Klerk, covert prestige value. They often masquerade as power speech with assertion of dominance, interrupting, challenging, disputing and being direct. When used in arguments, profanity points the loss to verbal and argumentative skills in our society. When words fail in explosive situations because of a lack of verbal reasoning skills, violence is often just a step away. Civilization is on the road back to the caves.

It has also been written that whomever controls the language, controls society. Every high school student should have to read George Orwell's prophetic vision as outlined in *1984*, where a tyrannical government controls the thoughts, feelings and minds of its subjects by not only controlling language but by deliberately distorting it. The language in *1984* was called *Newspeak*. Its use of blatant contradiction and constant change in word meaning gradually reduced the people's thought processes to mush. As one of the characters gleefully proclaimed, "It's a beautiful thing, the destruction of words. Orthodoxy means not thinking, not needing to think."

There is a real danger here. Reduce a people's ability to clearly reason and logically think and you have the bases for fascism, which relies more on images than reasoned logical arguments. Marshall McLuhan's dictum, the medium is the message, had this in mind. He wrote of the global village as an exercise in communal group-consciousness, based on a more primitive tribal way of thinking. A society with limited skills in verbal communication will eventually be reduced to a headless mob controlled by their emotion and not their reason. This was the concern of Benjamin Franklin and the other founding fathers who feared the potential mobocratic tendencies of a pure democracy.

To find a good example of the use and abuse of a nation's language, one need only look to Adolf Hitler and his propaganda minister Joseph Goebbels. This process was known as the *Sprachlenkung*—a word that was later used to describe similar attempts to manipulate language in the Communist-led German Democratic Republic. According to literary and social critic, John Wesley Young,

> the ultimate aim of these Nazi language alterations was to produce a citizen who partly because of his constant exposure to the emotional and manipulative rhetoric of the Party and his addictions to dogma and catchwords would never—could never—exert himself to think critically about the regime and the manner of society it was creating.

According to Hitler's *Mein Kampf*, the only thing that this national brainwashing had to do, was to unforgettably brand the Nazi way of thinking in each individual's mind. Nazi speeches used such words as fate, conditioned, and predetermined which evoked an image of an individual devoid of free will and frozen into one spot in an unchangeable cosmic pattern.

Nazism sired a lexicon of euphemisms that will ring familiar to many people in this country. The invasion of Poland in 1939 that marked the official beginning of World War II, was called a "police action." The withholding of money from the workers' paycheck for government programs was touted as a system of "voluntary contributions," a tautology that was last heard echoing in the Clinton White House. The razing of a Protestant Church was called "urban renewal." The SS did not arrest people and confiscate their property. They took them into "protective custody" for the purposes of "securing their property." The verisimilitude is apparent at this moment. Politicians have commandeered the native tongue with a nefarious spirit that often has obscured the nature of things. President Clinton talks of contributions when he means new taxes. He boasts of investment when he means more government spending. Affirmative action is really just another name for quotas.

Our educational bureaucracy has contributed to this intellectual confusion. Some call it the "dumbing down" of American students. I see it as a mental downsizing that bodes ill for this nation's future. When schools devalue student education by replacing traditional disciplines of science, math, foreign language, history, literature and government with self esteem, value clarifications, and feel-good-about-myself courses, the finished product will be much less able to intellectually discern the different nuances of words and ideas. This educated public will find itself easily swayed by the emotionally-laden jargon of the spin doctors. Unfortunately, we are fast becoming a nation of feelers and introspective weaklings who put more credence in an EST encounter than an afternoon at the local library. I sense that Americans are losing sense of the language. There was a town Shinar in the book of Genesis which degenerated into a land of noise and confusion. When verbal distortions and feelings reign, how long will it be before America is like the city of Babel, where no one is able to communicate because they do not have a common language? Thinking individuals must guard against taking words at their face value. Everyone is selling something and individuals must resort to the basic principle of *caveat emptor,* let the buyer beware in the marketplace of words and ideas.

Probably the most sinister agency in this battle for the language is the abortion lobby, who has expropriated several of traditional American ideas and bastardized them to support a hidden agenda of social disruption and family breakdown. No greater abuse is evident in this issue than the bastardizing of the word choice. We are all pro-choice when it comes to the choosing of whom we marry, where we work, what we read, eat, or do with our leisure time, where we send our children to school. The genius of this verbal expropriation ranks with the author of the term final solution in its euphemistic hiding of the evil involved. Yet even these choices are often limited by law, talents, parents, consideration for our neighbors etc. This clever verbal machination has allowed basically good and honest people to believe they can hold morally conflicting principles and still sleep nights.

Substitute rape, slavery, or incest within the basic context of choice and see what happens to this phony mental construct. "I would never rape anyone but I believe a red blooded American boy has the right. I would never own a slave, but I will not interfere with a Southern property owner's choice to own one." To oppose these evil acts, according to current philosophy, would amount to imposing our morality on someone else. If the issue at hand is a moral abomination, it is easy to understand why they have to hide behind such an innocuous and popular word choice.

Catholics for Free Choice is one group that really pushes the envelope with its use of choice. It has the same moral suasion that *Jews for Hitler* would have. This group traces its origins to a coterie which opposed the Catholic Church's opposition to New York State's extremely permissive abortion statutes. Most of the group's early funding came from a Unitarian Universalist Church in New York. The CCFC is a virulent anti-Catholic front group sponsored by such prominent opponents of the Catholic Church as *Planned Parenthood* and the *Playboy* Foundation. By 1980, the organization had moved to Washington, D.C. and vastly increased its budget with generous grants from such groups as the *Sunnen Foundation,* a St. Louis group built on the manufacture and sale of contraceptive foam, the *Ford Foundation,* and the *North Shore Unitarian Universalist Veatch* Program. The CCFC's sole purpose is to attack and misrepresent Church teachings and sow dissension and moral confusion among Catholics on behalf of its enemies. Only 3% of its annual income of $221,900 came from membership dues. While the organization claims about 5000 members, there does not seem to be accurate data to back that claim up. No one denies this group its constitutional right to support any side of the abortion issue but their appropriation or perhaps, misappropriation, of the word "Catholic" is something one can readily protest. Though the term is not copyrighted and is open to general use, it does represent the core beliefs of hundreds of millions of people around the world. For a divergent group to attach the term "Catholic" to its movement, gives grave scandal and causes serious confusion as to the propriety of the term.

In 1983, CCFC announced that it was a voice for conscience for the 79% of American Catholics who believe in abortion rights. They arrived at this outlandish figure by counting every Catholic who supports a less than exclusive ban on abortion as an ally, including such groups as the *National Right to Life Committee* which endorses a ban on abortion, except when the life of the mother is at stake. This is just another flagrant example on how the pro-abortion lobby manipulates and distorts the language. They refer to the religious ceremony we Catholics attend faithfully each Sunday as "a religious service." Practicing Catholics call it the Holy Mass. This oxymoronic group would have us believe that choice is one of the original 10 commandments and any sermonizing or letter writing protesting it in Church is an abrogation of their religious liberties. If the right to an abortion is protected under the Mosaic and Christian concept of moral law, then it must have been evident to only those who are able to see the penumbra surrounding the tablets of stone.

The logical argument of this *Committee of Concerned Catholics* seems to be that since the First Amendment to the US Constitution protects each citizen's right to freely speak his or her mind without jeopardizing citizenship, that same protection is extended to their roles as Catholics. A person deserves the title of "Catholic" only if he or she fully embraces the Gospel and the doctrinal and moral tradition of the Church. To publicly contradict that teaching or to pretend that opinions opposed to official teaching are equally viable is to jeopardize one's membership in the Church. The rules for citizenship and membership in the Catholic Church are not the same. As a citizen I am free to say that Jesus was not God, but as a Catholic I am not. Though the Catholic Church is universal it does not boast of having a big tent when it comes to moral perversity. In the January of 1994 edition of *The Catholic World Report*, C. Joseph Doyle profiled Frances Kissling, the Executive Director of CCFC. Kissling is highly favored by the mainstream press. She effectively markets her apostate group as a legitimate voice of Catholic dissent, a theologically respectable and authentically Catholic alternative to the teachings of the pope and the American hierarchy on issues of public morality. She has been hailed by the *Washington Post* as the "Cardinal of Choice."

Frances Kissling was born in 1942 of Polish ancestry, grew up in Flushing, New York, not far from where I spent my youth. Her father was Thomas Romanski and her mother moved back to New York, and following her divorce she married a wealthy Protestant, Charles Kissling. After two years at St. John's University, Kissling joined the convent of the Sisters of St. Joseph as a postulant. Six months later she departed the convent and the faith. Her anti-Catholic tradition credentials are impeccable. In 1979 she joined CCFC, becoming its executive director in 1982. When she joined CCFC in 1979, she said, "I no longer considered myself a Catholic." She later told feminist writer, Annie Lay Millhaven, "When I came back to the Church, I never came back on the old terms . . . I came back to the Church as a social change agent. I came back to woman-church . . . I am not talking about coming back to Sunday Mass, confession and all these things that are memories of my childhood." Kissling is guilty of defying the Catholicism in her own terms. In effect, she is perpetrating a fraud for anti-Catholic objectives, working as a fifth columnist within the Church's wall, in the Culture War.

Many pro-choice advocates refuse to acknowledge the basic humanity of the unborn child by referring to the fetus as a potential child. Just what is a *potential child*? Is not a child a potential teenager, still human by conventional standards? In this twisted metaphysics of choice, the pro-abortion lobby says that the child has the right to be born into a welcoming family. Where does the child get this right? From the parents? Humans can not confer rights on any other being. They are either with them from the moment of their being or they do not exist.

It is apparent that the abortion debate has influenced the way we perceive the elderly. The word fetus allowed people to believe that the unborn child was not yet fully human. The language of the culture of death has already infiltrated the national discussion. We hear that the comatose, the sick and dying, and people with long, yet not terminal diseases, are not living full lives . They are not really human. I submit that the death with dignity lobby needs only more time before they adopt or construct a word such as *senilitus* to further this practice of elderly impersonalization. It can be defined as the condition of aging, whereby the formerly active person, was not living up to the acceptable standards of human social intercourse and therefore, can be determined to be not fully living.

On a grander scale, beginning with the academic community, there is a widespread and pervasive attempt to totally rewrite the language so as to destroy it as one of the basic pillars of American social and moral stability. The term is known as "Deconstruction." It starts with the existential doctrine that meaning is a human construct, fabricated through language which is meaningless in itself since it can never reach beyond itself. Because of the gap between meaning and reality, hateful crimes can be rationalized. Its pure subjectivism increases the margin between objective reality and subjective influences, giving the individual a great leeway in moral culpability.

The patron saint of Deconstruction is a French intellectual, Michel Foucault. While a professor at the prestigious College de France, his book *Madness and Civilization* was published. He had long been fascinated by the subject of madness. He believed that the concept of insanity was a modern invention. Before this, the mad were accepted as a part of society, even valued as an interesting part of the human landscape. In the eighteenth century, the term madness was invented with all its negative connotations and since then, society has routinely set people apart, isolating and institutionalizing them. He believed that the world was a richer more interesting place before doctors tried to separate the mad from the sane. Foucault's notion implies that there are no such thing as facts . The mad are just another example of the variety of the human species and our view of them determined by historical context. This is much more than a mere sense of moral relativity: it is the annihilation of objective and transcendent moral and intellectual standards.

His writing, especially that found in his novel *I, Pierre Riviere,* about a young man who murders his family provides another insight into Foucault's thinking. The novel effectively establishes different regimes of truth as the norm. Riviere's willingness to wantonly violate the accepted social order by murdering his parents appealed to Foucault. He was fascinated by the story, saying that we fell under the spell of the parricide with the reddish-brown eyes. Foucault's intellectual musings allowed him the freedom to cross over the line that separated traditional morality from barbarism and rationalized immorality.

Foucault also had a profound effect on the Paris student population leading to the riots of 1968. Because of their nihilistic disdain for rules and regulations—any rules and regulations, Foucault's students attempted to subvert the old social order without having any idea on what to replace it. His ideas were successfully transplanted in the United States. American students and intellectuals saw the best and the brightest of the Johnson administration tailor facts and events to suit their purposes in the Vietnam War. They concluded that information carried ideology and that there was no "pure" knowledge. Foucault's ideas and perception of reality became nothing less than an assault on Western civilization. In rejecting an independent reality, he was rejecting the founding principles of the West. No other idea underscores the powerful effect that the deconstruction of language can have on the continuing ideas and principles that shape the reality of American society. As Dr. Lynne Cheney says in her book, *Telling the Truth,* this is revolution by other means.

One of Foucault's spiritual disciples, Yale professor J. Hillis Miller, summed up the impact of this way of thinking when he wrote, "a deconstructionist is not a parasite but a parricide. He is a bad son demolishing beyond hope of repair the machine of Western metaphysics." These assassins of objectivity, such as Foucault, Jacques Derrida, and others, have had a great impact on our American campuses. As Cheney points out, "anyone who wishes to understand the origins of a way of thinking that has turned American campuses upside down and begun to change the larger society can no better than start with Foucault." His thinking is largely responsible for the anti-intellectual unrest that has dominated the American college scene since the late sixties. The belief that reality is nothing more than a social construct, has had a profound impact on both the civil rights and women's movements. Foucault's thinking lay at the heart of the shift from logic, consistency, factual accuracy, and absolute truth to emotional and subjective feelings. While the goals of these groups had once centered on acquiring equal opportunity and achievement, the new social construct now focuses on equality of result. If test scores and aptitude tests stand in the way of black or female success, then the tests and the scoring criteria had to be changed or removed so as to allow for minority empowerment. It is a pernicious type of relativity that argues that standards have no objective reality but only serve to perpetuate the preferences of the entrenched. Proponents of this way of thinking want only to substitute other touchstones that perpetuate their own preferences. The traditional Western standards, they argue, such as a concentration on success, achievement, and objectivity, are white masculine in origin and merely perpetuate the subjugation of minorities in this country. They feel it is their turn and white power structure should step down and get out of the way. To replace society's existing power structure they have established new categories, such as cooperation, subjectivity, and political correctness.

This subjective way of thinking is clearly in evidence in the Clinton administration. No political office holder has ever demonstrated more of a mastery of Foucault than Bill Clinton. While Clinton delights in likening himself to a powerful combination of the best features of Franklin Roosevelt, Harry S Truman and even Ronald Reagan, he conjures more similarities with Richard Nixon than any other chief executive in history. "Tricky Dick" and "Slick Willie" have more than a few things in common. The most salient similarity is their inability to consistently deal with the truth. Nixon was the object of more criticism since there was still such a thing as objective truth in his day. As columnist Joseph Sobran succinctly points out, "we are now in a post-Nixon phase of history, and what used to be called demagoguery is now called marketing. If enough people believe or 'accept' an assertion, it is therefore 'validated'." This is the golden age of the con man and Bill Clinton is the epitome of a flim-flam man. In the absence of immutable principles, the Decalogue, Ciceronian natural law, the Ten Commandments, the code of the gentleman, and the Hippocratic Oath, are all irrelevant. The con man himself makes the laws and decides the morality of each situation on a case-by-case basis.

Another perversion of the language advanced by the Clinton administration involves his Americorps. The President calls these 24,000 government employees "volunteers" whose purpose is to strengthen local charities and show how government money could stimulate private giving. The Americorps actually allowed the federal system to interfere in local situations. Even though these volunteers did accomplish a modicum of good by painting houses in some poor neighborhoods and restoring some wilderness trails, each participant cost the taxpayers $27,000 in 1994, roughly $10,000 more per worker than had been estimated. The program also had its own liberal agenda, like sex education programs, self-esteem enhancement projects, and advocacy groups for liberal causes. Paying volunteers confuses the genuine contributions of the 90 million unpaid Americans who give of their time and energy to support their local communities. The very premise of Americorps contradicts the principle of responsibility that is at the heart of self-government. Yet the Americorps is just the tip of the iceberg. Politicians are the biggest proponents of this kind of constitutional verbal manipulation. They promise and demand the right to fair housing, the right to a job, the right to health care, without specifying how these rights are to be financed.

It is very easy to lapse from quota talk into rights talk. When merit and demographic forces are ignored a raw statistic becomes an entitlement in the name of group identity and solidarity. The newest wrinkle in the fabric of society is professor George Gerbner's contention that blacks, women, and the disabled are not proportionately represented on television. We have finally reached the point in our society where it is almost impossible to discuss any problem or desire without someone hollering that their rights have been infringed or they have been discriminated against.

Another example John Leo mentioned in his 28 June 1993 column involved a battered wife who felt that it was her right to live in a safe, loving home, transcending an issue of public safety into what he has called "the spread of rights babble." Unfortunately there is no right to a loving home to be found, outside of a gnostic utopia. Life can be hard and even unfair. Politicians cannot guarantee a perfect world, a life without hardship, pain and misery.

Sensitivity serves as an adjunct to the idea of word manipulation and deconstruction of the traditional way of understanding and defining issues. As our country has become increasingly desensitized to verbal and visual profanity, the qualities of tolerance and sensitivity are being heralded as core values. Verbal sensitivity has risen to the level of an ideology. An entirely new nomenclature that was thought to be playful, cute, innocuous, and devoid of any double meaning has now been singled out so as not to offend people who may be fat, short, bald, or ugly. All of these terms, which are implicitly negative value judgments, have been deemed to cause social pain, distress, and embarrassment to many of the so-called outgroups in society. To offset this negative group identity and create a solidarity among those displaced peoples, a new language of social sensitivity has been developed to wash away this sediment from the vestiges of the past. At one time, it used to be considered a cardinal social sin to give odoriferous offense via the breath or the body. Billions were spent annually to ward off these human olfactory crimes. This way of thinking has given way to a fear of committing verbal offense. In the liberal notion of morality, words that hurt are more dangerous and more pernicious than actions that maim and even kill.

Henry Beard and Christopher Cerf have compiled a witty book, *The Official Politically Correct Dictionary and Handbook,* to educate all of the ignorant, make that the "knowledge-challenged" dealing with the proper and sensitive way to deal with the diverse people we meet in everyday life. Their book would be comical if it were not a fact that too many people have blindly attempted to adapt their verbal behavior to the anti-cultural spirit that permeates their book. To use the word fat in a pejorative sense would make one guilty of the social crime of "fatism," "sizeism," or perhaps "weightism." These victims are "horizontally-challenged," while short people are "vertically challenged." Political correctness (PC) refuses to impose any judgment on people's abilities or their behaviors. Tolerance of a panoply of pathologies, such as abortion, euthanasia, pornography, and homosexuality has reigned as the cardinal virtue in the PC morality. The Post Office refers to its driver's skills as the "least best." The walls of academia have not been safe from this artificial tampering with the language. Many PC terms relate to testing, evaluations, and academic judgments. Grading and evaluation systems must be so geared as not to offend anyone who might not measure up, which in itself is judgmental. Testing is used for needs assessment, not as a gauge of achievement.

This overt silliness is regarded with great seriousness on some college campuses. At many citadels of higher learning, there is an Orwellian thought police that report any university code violations against minorities, women, and gays. According to author Charles Sykes, the heart of this totalitarian disregard for the First Amendment, is the fact that PC is Marxist in origin. PC attempts to redistribute power from the privileged class (white males) to the oppressed masses. It is a spurious form of linguistic corruption where everything is seen through the prism of race, gender or sexual orientation.

What began as the attempt to politicize psychology has led to the emergence of a therapeutic culture whereby medical standards have been substituted for what has traditionally been regarded as moral and spiritual questions. As a society we have been too ready to say a person is "sick" or "morally different" instead of saying he is *bad* or *evil.*

The homosexual lifestyle is the moving force behind some of the changes in the way Americans talk and think. It is the noveau-doublespeak of political correctness that has reclassified sexual deviancy as an alternate lifestyle choice, and sexual perversion becomes sexual orientation. *Gay* used to be a nice word. Today it is loaded with a cornucopia of twisted and perverse sexual activities. The central vision of artificial equality behind PC is extremely biased, not only against white males but against mankind in general. Animals are now to be treated with the same respect we afford humans, including individual rights. Perhaps the corollary speaks more to the truth in that we are now treating our fellow humans with the same disrespect we have often reserved for animals. If people descended from apes, then it is perfectly logical to treat other humans, especially weaker females, as just pieces of meat. In some circles, pets are no longer just pets. The ordinary puppy or cat is now a "nonhuman animal companion." People are by definition human animals, just a shade above the other kind. This national social obsession with rights does not end with animals. Amitai Etzoni's book *The Spirit of Community,* documents some startling examples of people who believe that even inanimate objects have rights. Professor Christopher Stone, for example, once argued that rocks and streams should be treated like human beings who have rights but cannot speak, such as infants and legal incompetents. A pet rock is now a "mineral companion." This does more to lower personal regard for fellow humans than it does to elevate the status of rocks or plants.

One aspect of college life, where the PC forces have truly amalgamated their forces is that of athletic team mascots. The most obvious offenders of newspeak current on many of today's campuses, are the twenty or thirty schools that have adopted the Native American, (nee American Indian) as their mascot. The first school to cry foul in favor of America's Aborigines was Stanford University which had developed an aversion to anything that promoted Western culture. The students demanded that their mascot be changed first to the ridiculous "Thunderchickens." This was later dropped in favor of the Stanford Cardinal, in honor of a color, not a bird, so as not to offend any members of the People for the Equal Treatment of Animals (PETA). Several other schools, such as the "fighting Illini," of Illinois University, the Marquette Warriors, and the St. John's Redmen, all received derision and complaint from representatives of Native Americans. Marquette and St. John's Universities did change their team mascots to Golden Hurricanes and Red Storm respectively. The Indian or warrior classification was not the only target of these rebels of nomenclature. The University of Massachusetts at Amherst Minutemen came under fire from this band of verbal revolutionaries. The Minuteman, which stands at the entrance to Lexington, Massachusetts, is a proud symbol of the citizen soldier and his spirit of defending hearth and home. These students regarded him as a mascot which was racist, sexist, and promoted violence. The school's faculty and students obviously could not discern between a harmless mascot and a burning cross on a hilltop. At Auburn University, the students waged a campaign to remove the school's Senator mascot because it struck the school's politically correct element as not only racist and sexist but because it also resembled what some called a white plantation owner. At the University of Alabama, at Birmingham, their Norseman struck the students and faculty as too masculine to represent female students. Others objected because he was too Aryan, or too violent. An even more sophistic example involved Emory and Henry College in Emory, Virginia. The school's athletic teams are known as the Wasps. The school's African-American Society was afraid that visitors might get the wrong impression that their teams were glorifying White Anglo Saxon Protestants, not insects. It seems to me that these students have too much free time and are not being adequately challenged in the classroom.

Professional teams, which have long adopted the Indian or his derivative, as a mascot because of his ferocity and bravery in the heat of battle, have also come under fire. The Chicago Black Hawks of hockey, the Kansas City Chiefs, and especially the Washington Redskins professional football team, have all suffered opprobrium for their respect for the American Indian. The PC police nearly had a fit when the Cleveland Indians and Atlanta Braves squared off during the 1995 World Series. Who but one of the most politically correct of them all, Jane Fonda, was busily doing the popular tomahawk chop with her husband, liberal mogul Ted Turner, the owner of the Braves in tow? Most of these owners, like Turner, have all but ignored the rabid demands of these disaffected groups. In a fit of illogic, the owner of the NBA Washington Bullets, has decided to drop his team's name in favor of the occultic "wizzards," because it might encourage more killing in the nation's capital.

The PC police also have an affiliate branch deeply embedded in the newspaper industry which has also been unduly influenced by this Orwellian attempt at language control. In 1994, the *Los Angeles Times* promulgated its guidelines on acceptable language for all of its reporters. As verbal gatekeepers, the Times attempted to purge its lexicon of all insensitive and ethnic terms. Noxious terms included "hit list," "Chinese fire drill," and "to welsh." It is ironic that a newspaper's traditional role has centered around communicating the news of the day. The PC way of thinking makes communication much more difficult as newspapers and other media are forced to invent phrases and literal meanings that spoil the richness and beauty of a language.

Artificial word creations ultimately lead to a loss of meaning, robbing words of their poetry, their implicit message, and harm accurate and intelligent communication. A society that has lost its sense of language is well on the road to moral, economic, and political slavery. I first noticed this phenomenon in the new translations of the Catholic Bible used at Sunday Mass. The poetry of the Bible has disappeared amid the flood of politically correct sanitation. We seldom hear of the "lilies of the field," and other forms of metaphorical content. The "good thief" who died on Christ's right hand has been replaced by an "insurgent," a term more appropriate for an exercise in liberation theology.

Author Thomas Shactman, in his trenchant book, *The Inarticulate Society*, writes of how the narrowing of our language has decreased society's ability to understand and communicate with one another. He writes of this in terms of what he calls *reification*, which he contends is rife in contemporary culture. Reification emphasizes the literal meaning of words, eliminating any metaphorical dimensions. A population, couched in this limited range of thought, will have great difficulty in thinking on an abstract level. This will make them more susceptible to political hucksters and economic con men. Even Halloween has succumbed to notions of PC. Some parents and schools will not let children dress up as witches, angels, or even hoboes.

The historical pendulum may well be ready to swing back to simpler times when there was a clear distinction between the cowboys and the Native Americans. Lucid and objective language can bridge the communications gap that Deconstruction-ism and PC has helped to create. While Orwell's ultimate vision is encapsulated in the book's final image, that of a boot stomping on a human face, the author places more weight on the importance of language manipulation than he does the threat of brute force. War is peace and freedom is slavery, has a more devastating effect on the human spirit than all of Big Brother's police. We have to be ever vigilant or we may not be too far from our own version of an Orwellian dystopic vision.

PART IV

SOCIETY'S
SHAKEN PILLARS

11 / The US Constitution
From Camelot to Clinton

The advanced world may well be like, and feel like a closed and "guarded palace," in a city gripped by the plague.

—Connor Cruise O'Brien in
On the Eve of the Millennium

One of my favorite movies is the Mel Gibson film, *Braveheart,* which won the Oscar in 1996 for *Best Picture.* It is the epic story of a Scottish patriot, William Wallace, who spent his adult life fighting British tyranny in his native land. It was a marvelous film, filled with political and social intrigues worthy of a LeCarre novel. But, most of all, I liked Gibson's character, Wallace, a shy, quiet man with a great sense of honor and virtue. Unfortunately, it was his same sense of trust and loyalty that led him to his brutal and barbarous death. Wallace was the quintessential Conservative. All he wanted was to be left alone to live his life in freedom and decency. In the summer of 1995, during a trip to the British Isles, I rode past the site of the great battle of Sterling where Wallace defeated a large English Army. The following afternoon, I stood in Edinburgh Castle next to a life-size statue of the great Scottish patriot. I could sense his presence and in many ways drew inspiration from his edifice on the power of freedom. The film majestically underscored one of the most vital issues in human history— the inexorable quest to be free. Wallace's energetic equestrian charges before his downtrodden men, screaming *Fr-eee-dom! Fr-eee-dom!* underscored the vital importance freedom has had for this nation.

Freedom is not to be mistaken for license. Central to the Culture War is the notion professed in the *Planned Parenthood vs. Casey* decision in 1992. At the heart of liberty is the right to define one's own concept of existence or meaning, of the universe, and of the mystery of human life. This notion of freedom resonates with a ring of subjectivism: existence means what I want it to. In effect we are all freshman composition gods in a universe where all assertions are equally sincere and equally meaningful. To understand liberalism with regard to social issues, one must only fathom the concept of the autonomous self. The history of mankind can be reduced to a conflict between different entities, over who will have power and control of the other. It is both a natural inclination and a powerful idea that has launched many men to risk life and limb in attaining or maintaining that right.

The May 1995 issue of *Culture Wars Magazine* opined that part of the inner architecture of the American idea of freedom has been the profound conviction "that only a virtuous people can be free." I would agree that it is not only an American belief that only a virtuous people can be free or that free government is inevitable. Freedom is possible when the people are inwardly governed by the moral law with absolute standards. M. Stanton Evans reminded us of this in his book, *The Theme is Freedom*, that Western liberty and the country's free institutions are products of our own religious faith and that neither we or our freedom can survive without it. He sees the multiculturalism and its ideological sisters as a direct threat to the country's historical liberties. Evans puts the battle in the perspective of the Enlightenment, warning us that the secular religions of the modern epoch are actually species of neopaganism. Reverting to the French Revolution, Evans reminds us that Rousseau was an ardent neopagan, as was Hegel. He adds that both Engels and Nietzsche were devotees of pagan doctrine concerning nature. It is true that both Hitler and Rosenberg made paganism a center of the Nazi cult. If the United States persists in the elimination and disregard of its religious underpinnings, then the same can happen to us that happened to France and Germany. With Evans' dire warnings in mind, it is important to realize that the idea of freedom has flourished in the United States like nowhere else in the world. Freedom has served as the cornerstone of our government, history, and civilization but it is a precious commodity that requires eternal vigilance. Economist Frederick Hayek warned in 1944 that the statist policies of Franklin Roosevelt would lead us down the road to serfdom. I do not know how long Hayek's road is but I doubt we'll have to pack a toothbrush to get to our statist destination.

The gradual loss of individual liberty in this country and the creeping specter of a growing federal government poses a great threat to our historic notions of freedom. The past fifty years has witnessed an unparalleled period of increased federalization and militarization of American law enforcement. The nation has suffered a gradual erosion of many of its internal safeguards to our liberty that our Founding Fathers had bequeathed to us. The Bill of Rights, and the 10th Amendment, have been decimated while power has gradually been assumed by the Beltway in Washington D.C. James Bovard's book, *Lost Rights* detailed several instances of citizen abuse by a legion of the government's alphabetical agencies. The Waco Massacre and the Randy Weaver incident have served to increase the general distrust and fear of the coercive might of Big Government.

Attacks on the White House, the rise of local militias, and the deadly Oklahoma City bombing have created an atmosphere of paranoia that has permeated much of the population. President Bill Clinton has exploited the situation by turning the White House into a bunker, demanding anti-terrorist legislation and demonizing the NRA and conservative talk show hosts, such as Rush Limbaugh. The message from the White House is that to criticize the President or his policies is tantamount to criticizing the institutions of the country. That has all the indications of an American form of fascism. Clinton's 1996 State of the Union address was described as conservative because he raised such themes as crime, family values, and morality on TV and in the movies—all of which he talked about as if their reform or control was the proper purview of the federal government. Of course his record with regard to abortion, the federalization of crime and great increase in federal regulations, is anything but conservative. Operating on the practical assumption that the American public is practically deaf, dumb, and stupid, he has risen to the highest office in the land. President Clinton's 1995 appointment of abortionist, Henry Foster, to head the president's abstinence program has just reminded us of why he is the most pro-abortion president in the nation's history. In addition to the obvious message to all pro-lifers who helped defeat Foster's nomination for Surgeon General last year, is the fact that his efforts generally resulted in an increase in teenage pregnancy rates. This is akin to pouring gasoline on a fire.

Other liberal messages from the Clintons include Hillary's "novel" approach to sex. Postpone sexual activity until you are older, she says—but if you're going to do it anyway, here is how to protect yourself. They apply the same mixed message to drugs—if you are going to use them, here's how to sterilize your needle. Drug use is also up. The Clintons at the helm during the Culture War, can only weaken and, quite possibly, sink the ship of state. The reach of law enforcement today is much greater and has approached a state of siege between the President and his enemies. According to Mr. Clinton's logic, pro-life groups, the religious right, the NRA, and radio talk show hosts bear intense scrutiny. Al Hunt of the *Wall Street Journal* has written that "the desire to destroy valuable institutions, like welfare, Medicare, and legal abortion is both the object and the matrix of terrorism, implying that the full extent of the federal government can be brought against such dissidents." President Clinton jumps at every opportunity, such as the explosion of TWA Fl #800 and the pipe bombing at Centennial Park in Atlanta during the Olympics to extend the protective mantle of federal legislation over a grief-stricken people. Under the pretext of increased national terrorism, Clinton plays on the population's growing fears to increase the power of the federal government, lessening the freedom of the American people. This is really no more than a blatant power grab.

Government regulations now total 202 volumes and run over 132,000 pages. As one federal prosecutor has quipped, we can indict a ham sandwich. The practice of civil forfeiture allows the government to seize homes, cash, possessions, or farms, without ever filing a charge. The IRS has started an audit of the National Rifle Association, echoing the dictum of Chief Justice John Marshall (1801-1833) that the power to tax involves the power to destroy! What is really at risk here, is not our institutions but our freedom. The Bill of Rights was written to protect us from our government not from each other. The real enemy of freedom is not the president, but the socialistic imperatives of Big Government. William Wallace would have understood.

The Father of the United States Constitution, James Madison, recognized the inevitable conflict between freedom and government in Federalist Papers #51 when he wrote:

> in forming a government of men over men, the greatest difficulty lies in this: You must enable government to control the governed; and in the next place oblige it to control itself.

A proper understanding of this perpetual battle between freedom and control is at the heart of the Culture War, for it is the government's loss of accountability and its proclivity for handing out "rights" wily nily, such as the right to choose, that is at the root cause of this internecine struggle for the soul of America.

This civil war naturally involves an understanding of the much-abused terms, liberal and conservative. There are probably no more misunderstood terms in the English language today. The controversy between liberalism and conservatism dates back to the Enlightenment—the intellectual movement of the sixteenth to seventeenth century that replaced God as the center of the universe with man and a philosophy of natural rights. While the American Revolution was founded on the natural law, God was not absent from its intellectual underpinnings. The American revolutionaries maintained a fervent belief in a combination of both the Christian Bible and natural rights philosophy of the English Enlightenment, making it basically a conservative revolution with the aim to preserve American society. The period from 1650-1763 has been described as a period of salutary neglect. Since the mother country was preoccupied with the Seven Years War, (1756-1763), analogous to a working mother today, it did not have time to mind its thirteen children in America. When the mother country defeated her enemies, England had more time and energy to devote to governing her colonial brood. Like any rebellious teenager, the colonies fought to thwart English re-assertion of control, at the expense of local autonomy and individual liberty. The revolutionary period from 1770 to 1776 can be seen in the light of this internal struggle between colonial freedom and imperial control. The American revolutionists believed that mankind was basically flawed. Colonial leaders, who believed that human beings needed restraints, legal and social, sought to effect a federal system of government where powers were separated and diffused in a sophisticated system of checks and balances. The division of powers over a broad system of governmental entities was their special genius. Before the colonists would accept this unique system, Jefferson, Madison and the other founding fathers had to buttress the United States Constitution with the Bill of Rights, a series of functions that protected the citizens from their government, not the other way around.

This insured that one branch of the government or one element of the citizenry would not be able to centralize enough power to coerce and control any part of the body politic.

A number of American intellectuals, especially Thomas Jefferson, were enamored of the French philosophy. But Jefferson had a more fundamental faith in the will and mind of the people, especially the American farmer, because of his relationship with his farm land. He believed that the nature of farming brought man closer to his Creator and instilled in him virtues that inspired moral behavior. Jefferson viewed government as nearly unnecessary, espousing his dictum of that government is best that governs least. His *laissez-faire* manner of thinking has given rise to what is known today as Libertarianism. When it comes to a fundamental agreement on the basic goodness of mankind, libertarians have a lot in common with twentieth century liberals, especially when it comes to moral freedoms and lack of restraint, issues such as abortion and the legalization of drugs. I believe the libertarian would be scandalized at the direct involvement of liberal government into the mundane activities of the ordinary citizen.

Since the American Revolution, the spirit of American politics can be described as a battle between the thinking that typified Jefferson and his opposite among the founding fathers, Alexander Hamilton. Hamilton despised the philosophy of the French Revolution. He did believe in a larger role for the federal government, especially in support of manufacturing and new industries. As the first Secretary of the Treasury, Hamilton proposed bounties for new patents and manufacturing innovation, higher tariffs to protect the so-called infant industries, and deficit spending to enlist the economic and emotional support of the American people. He stretched the elastic clause that allowed the government to do whatever was necessary and proper for the successful fulfillment of the US Constitution. He even ordered the use of the federal troops to put down the first internal rebellion against the American government, the ill-fated *Whiskey Rebellion* of 1794. Bigger government was his strong suit—ideas and proclivities that you would think would align him solidly within the liberal camp today. Or would Hamilton more likely side with the conservative camp because of his pro-business stance? That's where the confusion comes in. Hamilton's thinking, taken to its logical conclusions, would result in fascism or communism, while Jefferson's would lead us to social and political anarchy. This internal struggle provides the backdrop for the larger context of the Culture War.

It has been a long-standing misconception that big business is by nature, conservative. This myth emerged from the scandals and greedy confrontations of the so-called *Gilded Age* of unfettered industrial growth from 1865-1900. The names of Carnegie, Rockefeller, and Vanderbilt often dominated the newspapers and their *laissez faire* spirit of little government dominated American commerce. While it is basically true that big business blanches at the thought of government regulation, what is not widely realized is that big business will often solicit the positive involvement of government, employing a highly aggressive and well-paid lobby system. Business wants government protection of their interests issued in the form of subsidies through tariffs and the limitations of rival business through excessive, regulatory, and fiscal policies designed to stifle competition, rather than foster it. For those who delve into the dynamics of NAFTA and GATT it is apparent that a collectivist mentality is at work which will more than likely cut competition, not increase it. As a result, it should not be surprising to learn that big business often supports causes and policies that are a far cry from any conservative positions. According to a report from the *Capital Research Center* in 1994, and again in 1995, the *Children's Defense Fund*, a darling of Hillary Clinton's, received over $700,000 from corporate grants in 1992. The following year it was increased to nearly $950,000. The nation's 129 largest corporations contributed $36 million to 300 nonprofit organizations that year. Liberal groups received $3.42 for each dollar the conservative groups did. In 1993, the latest years for which records were made available, the figure was up to $4.07 for each dollar. The bottom line is big business is willing to play both sides against the middle, proving that the appellation "conservative" is often misleading.

The research of St. Louis University history professor James Hitchcock comes to the conclusion that many business men forsake their moral sense, in favor of only the almighty bottom line. David Rockefeller said he would deal with any country, no matter what its policies were, as long as he made money for his corporation. This view echoes the sentiment of Vladimir Lenin, who once boasted that the "capitalists will sell us the rope with which to hang them." With regard to the Culture War, Hitchcock also emphasizes how liberal most corporations are. He believes that corporations will often distance themselves as far as they can from conservative ideas, especially the pro-life movement because principled, though unpopular, stances will hurt their businesses. Many corporations support the population policies of sustainable growth of the UN and its related agencies. They lavish millions on *Planned Parenthood*, which is viewed as a respectable organization with worthy goals. Right-to-life groups are regarded as controversial. Controversy must be eschewed at all costs because it hurts profitability.

According to Hitchcock, corporate culture is primarily liberal. It rests on no fixed moral principles—just the bottom line of textbook economics. Morally conservative people—those hard working men and women who are motivated by obligation rather than desire—may make good workers but they are rotten consumers. The vast machinery of corporate marketing aims to turn people into hedonists who consider pleasure their ultimate goal and who reach impulsively to attain it. Modern corporate life seems to turn around process as opposed to character—a willingness to "reinvent" oneself repeatedly for the sake of one's career. Business defines the ideal employee as one who is flexible in all things—lifestyle, attitude toward others, loyalty and convictions, etc. Principled people often become a liability because of their lack of tolerance or flexibility. I know of many pro-life people who have lost their jobs or businesses because of their unwillingness to remove religious or anti-abortion articles that "offended" the sensibilities of coworkers who did not share their ideals.

The rise of big business, with its government protection, has created a rift in society. It has given rise to the countervailing forces of the labor movement and the farmers' movement. Populism was a grass roots movement begun by farmers in the 1890s who wanted the government involvement to protect them from big business, specifically the railroads. While Populism attempted to return government to the people, their reforms actually enlarged the scope of the federal government. The 1892 Populist Party Platform included such radical proposals as the graduated income tax, a Central Bank, and universal education for children, all extracted from the writings of Karl Marx. While the notion of Populism today carries more the connotation of being for the little guy or supporting the small farmer against big economic combinations in effect, Populism has served as an instrument of advancing the reach of big government. In 1997, the tragic irony is that there is no greater big combination than big government.

Progressivism, the intellectual urban heir to Populism, was a bipartisan movement that included Republican Teddy Roosevelt and Democrat Woodrow Wilson. Progressive politicians, under the intellectual tutelage of Socialist Herbert Croly, the founder and first editor of the New Republic, performed the ideological marriage of Hamiltonian means, that is big government, with Jeffersonian ends, namely the welfare of the American population. The statist child of that historic union was the very welfare state that President Franklin D. Roosevelt godfathered into existence during the 1930s. As president, Wilson provided us with a glimpse of the New World Order, a plan for one world government, spearheaded by the League of Nations, and eventually leading to the United Nations and its panoply of global involvements.

The evils of big business were exposed and propounded by the social writers of the day, the so-called muckrakers, like Upton Sinclair, Ida Tarbell, and Lincoln Steffens. These reform-minded writers encouraged the extension of the Federal government into industries through regulations, etc. Once government, espousing the civic good, got its foot into a sector of American life, like the uninvited guest, it just wouldn't leave. With the smell of power in the air, the government usurped many former state functions, such as education, Social Security, and care of the elderly. This set a dangerous precedent. Several government bodies and institutions came into effect, such as the Sixteenth Amendment, which established the federal income tax in 1913, then the Federal Reserve Act, which set up a national bank, the Federal Reserve System, in 1914, as well as many other extensions of federal power into everyday American life. The Tenth Amendment suffered a hit and run blow that would prove to be fatal fifty years later. It was during the critical times of the Great Depression that President Franklin Roosevelt drove another stake in the heart of the Bill of Rights. With the development of his notion of the "guarantor state," Roosevelt used the power of government, under the rubric of national emergency, to assume the mantle of guaranteeing the pursuit of happiness in the United States. It unilaterally assumed responsibility for what usually had been up to the individual, the churches, or the state government. The American people began to look to government for their basic needs. They reluctantly accepted the dole in defiance to their historic faith in their independence, self-sufficiency, and their personal repulsion to taking something for nothing. Husbands and fathers who had been once proud of their strong and vital strain of rugged individualism were now taking government handouts, admitting their own failure to provide for their wives and families. After Roosevelt's New Deal, Americans bought the basic fallacy that the individual serves the needs of the state. Roosevelt's thinking was predicated on the idea that government should be directly used to make people's lives better—progressivism on a much larger scale. Fifty years later it has nearly bankrupted our country.

Since the sixties this selfish attitude had started to erode the essential of the American character. Millions of Americans started looking to Washington for help, sustenance, and relief. This radical change in the American attitude is best illustrated by John Kennedy's challenge during his presidential inauguration in January of 1961: "ask not what your country can do for you! But ask what you can do for your country!" Thirty-one years later, Kennedy's noble attitude had degenerated to that of the young man with the ponytail who admonished President Bush during the Richmond debate with Governor Bill Clinton and industrialist Ross Perot in 1992 when he said: "what do you plan to do for our needs?" America has come a long way from Camelot to Clinton. Freedom was sacrificed for the security that government offered. Voters became more inclined to cast their ballots for the politicians who secured these financial rights and credits. President Johnson extended Roosevelt's leitmotif with his daring and ill-fated War on Poverty. The term *entitlement* became institutionalized. Roosevelt's boastful predictions that government subsidies would be virtually impossible to repeal started to ring true with the election of Bill Clinton to the presidency. His abortive attempt to nationalize the American health care system in 1994, which would have amounted to a government seizure of 14% of the United States economy, demonstrated how far the federal government's usurpation power had gone.

Liberalism, as illustrated by the above trio of big government presidents, is a way of thinking that holds the government as the solution to virtually every human, social, and political problem under the sun. But freedom, real freedom, has nothing to do with political liberalism. Liberalism utilizes social engineering, social planning, and the enactment of sociological plans for people's lives and futures at every opportunity it gets. It encourages people to trade their individual freedoms for group security. Genuine liberals believe that they can better manage your life than you can and for this expect to be kept in power and enriched from the public coffers. Every government entitlement comes with strings and hidden catches that compel the receiver to continually re-elect the giver. Consider the chant of President Franklin Roosevelt's chief advisor, Harry Hopkins, who said "Tax, tax, spend, spend, elect, elect!"

Ever since Roosevelt, personal responsibility has been replaced by the notion of victimhood. According to liberalism's founding father, Jean Jacques Rousseau, society, not man, is responsible for man's negative behavior. Guns kill people, not people. The common refrain was that hate, not individuals, was responsible for 19 April 1995, bombing of the McMurray Federal Building in Oklahoma City. Liberalism encourages misplaced empathy. It feels the pain of the inmate on death row. The liberal will often recognize the guilty as the real victim of a poor background or stress the root causes of crime—poverty, ignorance, drugs, child abuse, and any other social malady that can be used to expiate the guilty of the criminal. There is too much empathy for the alleged victim of society and not enough for the real victim, creating, yet another divide in the Culture War.

This empathy is the result of a guilt for the sins of their fathers. This idea has also made great inroads among Jewish people and Catholics, especially fallen-away Catholics. They project their sense of personal guilt for their personal behavior onto feeling bad about the anonymous poor or the dead and dying in Bosnia. It is a sense of personal relation, which allows them the luxury of being unattached and impersonal. The liberal spirit, while empowering the State with expanding governmental controls, has caused a rapid deterioration in local law enforcement on the local level, by its eagerness to assuage the guilt of many career criminals. The easy availability of guns and the proliferation of drugs in American society have also served to worsen the problem. In America today, good people seem to be at the mercy of bad people. This is an unenlightened view because calling anyone "bad" is judgmental and betrays one as some right-wing fanatic. Calling someone else "bad" is inadvisable because it misses the whole point of the root causes of crime which in light of Rousseau's philosophy are caused by institutions, economic conditions, poor toilet training, and a host of other excuses. In accordance with the reigning psychological and sociological philosophy of the moment, we no longer punish bad people—we rehabilitate them through departments of correction. Our concern must not be if it is a fair punishment but with criminal's needs. The root cause of the failure of our penal system is the search for the root cause of the criminal's behavior. We should do criminals the honor of assuming that they are human beings such as ourselves, endowed with free will and moral responsibility. They are bad because they chose to be bad. The solution is very simple. Bad people must be made to fear the wrath of good people. The courts should adopt an attitude that refuses to sanction the notions of victimhood and coddling of criminals that has nearly led to the total breakdown in societal control.

On the opposite side of the intellectual lever, conservatism, or better put, *neo-traditionalism,* is actually a product of nineteenth century economic liberalism. Here, Darwinian rugged individualism and self-reliance, are tempered with the Biblical imperative of helping those who can not help themselves. Many would also add the Hippocratic oath, joined with the Confucian Analects: *Do not do to others what you do not want them to do to you!*

Conservatives believe that America's matchless society was the result of a volunteerism that only government could spoil. They also believe that men are basically flawed and have to be protected from the excesses of each other through the diffusion of governmental power. They believe that government's basic function is to provide security for their homes and shores and after that, it should limit itself to doing what is specifically provided for in the Constitution, the so-called delegated powers, of treaties, revenue collection and national defense. Government should foster businesses through trade agreements, tariffs, and bounties, but not at the expense of the small entrepreneur. It should provide tax incentives and other positive things to encourage people to invest in the nation's economic future. Government should employ common sense in dealing with the environment. Preserving jobs should be balanced with health and natural issues for the greater good for the greater number of people.

Lawyer Philip K. Howard's short book, *The Death of Common Sense* details several examples of how the legal system is suffocating America today. A nation which had set up a near-perfect and flexible government is now finding common sense more endangered than the snail darter. Lawyers have hamstrung society with nit-picking minutiae. There was the case of Mother Theresa, beloved by all (except socialist Christopher Hitchens), who wanted to start a halfway home for victims of AIDS in New York City. She acquired an old building, had it renovated but was told by city engineers that she had to install elevators. She answered that this was cost-prohibitive. There was no money for elevators. She argued that her sisters would be willing to carry up the stairs anyone who could not climb them. The city said no! The project was canceled. This lack of common sense has led inevitably to a rights revolution, where only selfishness and personal interest seem to reign supreme. In 1993, a judge in Rhode Island found special rights for obese citizens, while Mari Matsuda, a feminist advocate has advocated rights for those who are discriminated for having an unusual accent.

Government should refrain from being overly involved in the ordinary affairs of its citizens. It should only intervene where the lives, property and safety of its citizens are concerned, including the unborn. There are only three basic rights protected in the Constitution: life, liberty, and the pursuit of happiness. The emphasis is on the word "pursuit." Unlike liberalism, conservatism does not guarantee success. There must be a dedicated effort. As a result, conservatism heralds personal achievement and successful people. Governmental policies often discourage or even negate personal achievement and the enjoyment of the fruits of one's industry. In his book, *Lost*

Rights, James Bovard enumerates literally hundreds of examples of the con-
fiscation of private property under the guide of wetlands or environmental
extinction acts. In his second book, *How the Government Screws You From A
to Z,* Bovard writes on such contentious issues as affirmative action, zoning
laws, and HUD's breakup of neighborhoods through its Section 8 Proper-
ties. In page after page, the author demonstrates how the government treats
those on welfare as if they were self-reliant, productive members of the
community, there is little or no accountability. In many cases, welfare recipients live better than the tax payers who pay their bills, such as in La Jolla
where the "poor" get ocean front apartments. The FDA refuses to approve
a machine that gives CPR to heart attack victims because the victims can
not give their informed consent. In New York State, a woman was accused
of abusing her daughter because she breast-fed. It seems that the woman
admitted that she became sexually aroused while her daughter nursed. The
social welfare people thought this was tantamount to having sex with the
infant and arrested the mother. Probably the most ludicrous example the
author could find regarded a Los Angeles strip club which was cited for a
violation of the 1990 *Disabilities Act* because it had a shower stall in which
young women shed their clothes for their male patrons which was not
wheelchair accessible. Though I have never been to one of these establishments, I seriously doubt that there will be any dancers in wheelchairs willing
and able to perform in these strip stalls. The American people have unwittingly allowed our legislators to bind us to a ponderous system of jurisprudence that is neither just nor prudent.

The government's long arm has also reached into the national culture
and the fine arts. The National Endowment for the Arts (NEA), has funded
many exhibits and projects that run afoul of our country's erstwhile moral
tenets. The most egregious projects include performance artist, Tim Miller,
who has taken money to disrobe on stage and sexually stimulate himself.
Holly Hughes has accepted NEA money for her performance of the *Well of
Horniness.* The Kitchen Theater used some of their NEA funds to pay
Annie Sprinkle to invite her audience to explore the mysterious wonders of
her genitalia with a flashlight. Frameline used taxpayer money to organize
and host the pornographic offerings of the annual *Gay and Lesbian Film
Festival* in San Francisco. Ron Athey appeared in the Walker Art Center
which also produced Karen Finley, known for her smearing of chocolate all
over her nude body on stage. Athey's act features his slicing artistic designs
into the flesh of another man's back, soaking up the blood with paper towels
and throwing them over the heads of the audience. Some say that he has
used assistants who have tested HIV positive.

Health care is another area that government has meddled without
legitimate constitutional authority. The *Health Security Act* that Hillary and
Bill Clinton proposed tried to federalize a broad range of routine crimes and
torts that previously fell under the aegis of the state. It federalized ordinary
fraud cases because they were perpetrated on an organization that provided

health care. Some of the penalties included the newest federal method of confiscating private property. This notion worked well under federal drug laws and so it was to be applied to health crimes. The list of criminal and civil penalties laid to rest the administration's false claim that their plan was based on choice and market conditions. A sick patient could get several years in jail for attempting to bribe or influence health care personnel. In a system that was designed to create shortages and limit the availability of care, this bill would have established a new category of federal criminals: the sick and the elderly.

Conservatives and liberals have their most pronounced debates over the United States Constitution. In his book, *Constitution: Fact or Fiction,* Dr. Eugene Schroeder, has advanced his erroneous belief that the Constitution has been suspended since 1933 through a declaration of national emergency by Franklin Roosevelt. Thought his thesis is obviously a fallacy, the Constitution has devolved into a position where it is often ignored, as in the case of a declaration of war. Conservative columnist Joseph Sobran, an expert on the nature and scope of the United States Constitution, compares this document to the Royal Family in England—a nice symbol but practically devoid of any real meaning. He also quips that the Constitution is "no threat" to our current system of government. Sobran adroitly strips the protective mantel of the rubric, a living document from liberals who have consistently disregarded the internal safeguards against usurpation of power. The status of the document has so deteriorated that none of the founding fathers would recognize it were they alive today.

The Bill of Rights was designed to provide for a limitation on the powers of the federal government. The First Amendment reads Congress shall make no law; combined with the reserved powers in the 10th Amendment; this limits Congress' authority to interfere with religious activities on the local level. When President Clinton expressed his opinion in July of 1995 that the First Amendment does not convert our schools into religion free-zones, he evoked the disdain of both the NEA which believes that religion and religious values have no place in American schools and the conservative philosophy that holds that our schools should be a Congress-free zone. Clinton's statement also implies that rights come from the federal government, which in turn suggests that these rights can also be taken away. This false notion that a person's rights come from government has totally perverted the United States Constitution. Federal usurpation of power and the near-exclusion of the United States Constitution has effectively eliminated without due process the 10th Amendment. Individual states have lost much of their individuality. The country is slowly melding into one amorphous geographic political structure. The separation of the Tenth and First Amendments makes no sense. The First Amendment has been used not as a limitation on federal power but as an excuse to eliminate religion and, with it religious men and women, from the public square.

According to Sobran, who quotes from an incisive article by Professor Ilno Graglia in the *National Review,* given its rulings on segregation, pornography, contraception, abortion, capital punishment, defendant's rights, and many other questions outside the constitutional purview of the federal government, "the Court has become a powerful but lawless council, unelected and virtually unremovable for the making of social policy." Sobran has accurately portrayed the court's increasing intervention into the daily lives of United States citizens. Its judicial dictates, have effectively derailed the democratic process in this country. Judicial activism can best be illustrated by its surreptitious path to the *Roe vs. Wade* decision that set states' rights on its back once and for all. The case began with Estelle Griswold, who ran an eight-room birth control clinic on the second floor of #79 Trumbell St., in New Haven Connecticut, in November of 1961. She effectively laid the cornerstone for the *Roe vs. Wade* decision, that would come twelve years later. A highly respected member of the Junior League, she performed social work during and after World War II. She set out to deliberately challenge a Connecticut law that barred doctors from giving married women birth control devices. She was promptly arrested and her clinic closed on the charge of assisting, abetting and counseling married women in using drugs, medicines, and other instruments for the purpose of preventing conception. Griswold received a $100 fine for her offense. Griswold sued and four years later, the Supreme Court ruled 6-2 to overturn her conviction. This case effectively established the constitutional right to privacy. It was under the rubric of privacy, which is not mentioned at all in the Constitution, that the abortion right was established.

On 6 April 1967, a leading advocate of legal abortion, Bill Baird, took the next logical step down the slippery slope. The Griswold case had only applied to married couples. Baird directly challenged a Massachusetts Chastity Law that forbade giving any form of contraception to an unmarried woman. At a public lecture before 2000 students and faculty at Boston University, he handed a can of contraceptive foam to a young coed. He was arrested and jailed for 34 days. In 1972, the Supreme Court overturned his conviction and nullified the state laws of twenty-five different states. The Court stressed the belief that if the right to privacy was to mean anything, it should allow married or single individuals to be free from unwarranted government intrusion into matters so fundamentally affecting a person as the decision to bear a child or not. This ruling undermined the essential right of local officials to safeguard the moral tenor of their communities.

One of the principles in the *Roe vs. Wade* decision was a young attorney, Sarah Weddington, from Austin, Texas. As a young attorney in the late 1960s, she was concerned with the number of Texas women who were seeking abortions in Mexico, only to be butchered by Mexican abortionists. Some never came back and others came back with severe medical complications. Weddington wanted someone to test the state's restrictive abortion laws and she found that person in Norma McCorvey. A high school dropout with little prospects for the future, McCorvey was unmarried and pregnant with her second child. She was afraid that she would lose her job if she carried the baby to term. Her mother was raising the first child. McCorvey told Weddington that she had been gang raped. In truth, the baby was that of her boyfriend—a fact she did not admit to the public until 1987. The suit was filed against Henry Wade, the District Attorney for Dallas. The Supreme Court had been looking for a case like this one so it could establish an abortion right for all women in this country. Justice Harry Blackmun wrote the majority opinion that set up the trimester system. During the first trimester, the doctor and the woman privately determined whether or not to pursue abortion. In the second trimester, the state would have some interest and could set up certain limitations to safeguard the health of the mother. Since *Roe vs, Wade,* it has been the general consensus that the state could bar abortions during the third trimester. The question of the mother's health was extremely vague. This term was not defined until *Doe vs. Bolton,* (1973) which painted the term *health* with such broad legalistic strokes that a woman's health could mean anything imaginable. There was the story of two twenty-five year old women who elected to have abortions, one because at twenty-five she felt too old to have a baby and the other who, at twenty-five, felt too young. *Doe vs. Bolton* effectively by-passed the third trimester provision, making abortion legal until the moment of birth. Blackmun did admit to having some problems balancing the rights of the mother with the life of the unborn during the last few months of pregnancy. He was astute enough to realize what this decision would do to the moral landscape of the country.

Justice William Douglas provided the philosophical underpinnings for the *Roe vs. Wade* decision, stating that the right to privacy including the taking of innocent unborn children, was contained in the penumbra of the Ninth and Fourteenth Amendments. Most people would not know what a penumbra was if it bit them on the foot. But it sounded convincing and few were able to dispute his reasoning. The penumbra or dark shadow emanates when the light of truth is hidden from the American people. Aside from the incalculable damage unrestricted abortion has done to the American soul, the *Roe vs. Wade* decision also usurped the state's right to regulate abortion within its own boundaries. A number of states, led by New York, already had liberal abortion policies. However the court's peremptory abolition of abortion law in 1973, eliminated the accepted practice to provide, with a few exceptions, for the legal protection of the fetus. That is nearly impossible today and many women have paid dearly in loss of health, fertility and sometimes, even their lives, because of the court's decision.

During the Reagan-Bush years, the Court took a decided turn to the right on the abortion issue. The obstructionist and slanderous tactics of the Senate Judiciary Committee, led by Ted Kennedy, Joe Biden and Howard Metzenbaum, prevented Reagan from appointing the strict constructionist justices his strategy had called for. He had to settle for stealth candidates Anthony Kennedy and David Souter who proved to be liberals in conservative robes. The Webster decision of 1987 laid the foundation for returning the abortion issue to the states as it had been prior to *Roe vs. Wade.* But before pro-lifers could celebrate, the pro-abortion forces roused a backlash that unleashed millions of dollars of support to combat the pro-life gains. All their major supporters reported a vast increase in recruits, especially celebrities who jumped on their bandwagon. The pro-life side had won the legal battle but lost the public relations battle. William Webster, the heroic Attorney-General of the state of Missouri, paid dearly for his pro-life support. Irregularities from his office and spurious charges of financial mismanagement led to his conviction and a two-year prison term. Had Webster been pro-choice, he would have been the next governor of Missouri.

While the Supreme Court was originally designed to protect individual citizens from the tyranny of the federal government through judicial review, after 1945 a noticeable change in the court's philosophy became apparent. The liberal court began to strip the states of their reserved powers and more government control was extended over the various state capitals with impunity. Through a creative application of the "incorporation" clause of the 14th amendment, the court has accused various states of violating individual rights, whether by segregation, school prayer, the death penalty, or banning abortion. The Court then let the federal government force its way into these issues in the breech that was opened. As Joseph Sobran points out, "instead of obeying the Constitution, the federal government was pretending to enforce it . . . instead of preventing federal usurpation of power, the Constitution itself had become the instrument and pretext of federal usurpation." Put another way, he added, "the Constitution has ceased being the voice of 'We the People,' and had become the oracle of the federal government, which solely controls its meaning and is prepared to impute to it any absurdity necessary to maintain and enlarge federal power." Under the guise of public welfare, the states have supinely allowed their Constitution to be stolen from them. Most people falsely assume that the Constitution is federal property, which only the Supreme Court can interpret with authority. Nobody in 1789 could foresee that one day Congress would claim 95% of its powers under the Commerce Clause.

The *coup de grace* of the right-to-life federal strategy occurred in 1990 with the Casey decision. It was assumed that this decision would be the one to overturn *Roe vs. Wade.* A lamentable coalition of centrists, led by O'Connor, Kennedy, and Souter took the impetus out of the abortion debate. The Casey decision reaffirmed the *Roe vs. Wade* decision on the ludicrous grounds that the Court's own authority would suffer if the people thought it was bowing to political pressure from the religious right. On this manifest example of judicious arrogance and self-indulgence, Sobran opined the court "was treating itself as a party to the controversy and deciding in its own favor, in defiance of every principle of jurisprudence." It was confessing that it could not admit that the *Roe vs. Wade* decision was a bad decision comparable to the *Dred Scott* decision or *Plessey vs. Ferguson* because its own prestige and historical importance was paramount.

The Court waxed metaphysically and endorsed the radically individualistic notion of the self-constituted self. It asserted that the abortion liberty was necessary in order to define one's concept of existence, of meaning. Evidently, not only does personhood require freedom from the state but from all other potentially encumbering communities, such as the Church or even spouses. Casey confirmed the belief that abortion is necessary for women to order their lives. The court also added that the abortion license has been a critical factor in securing greater dignity for women. In attempting to re-establish its own credibility, the court had taken sides in the Culture War and demanded that the nation follow its choice. It reinforced the Hobbesan notion that we are a nation of strangers, perhaps "enemies" and the chief business of government is to prevent others from, interfering with or obliging the sovereign self. The end result is an atomistic and potentially totalitarian doctrine that claims society is comprised of only two actors, government and the solitary individual. The four dissenters from Casey were not alarmists but they did raise an alarm. Conservative Justice Antonin Scalia wrote that "the twin facts that the American people are not fools. They will not forever, they will not for long, be denied democracy and treated like fools." Kennedy, O'Connor, and Souter said that right or wrong precedent must be upheld so it would not appear they were bending to the political demands of the pro-life side while they simultaneously bowed to the demands of the pro-abortion side. To anyone familiar with the Casey decision, it is apparent that the court had put its own self-image above the truth of the abortion issue. *Roe vs. Wade* was bad law yet the court shamefully hid themselves behind the diaphanous shield of precedent, rather than overturn it. The decision without a doubt signaled the end of the pro-life strategy of judicial overturn of *Roe vs. Wade*.

The result is that a woman has an undeniable right to obtain an abortion at any time during her pregnancy. Any remaining regulations can be circumvented for reasons of health, including psychological health as in case of emotional distress caused by being denied an abortion. The fact remains that after Casey, as before Casey, not one unborn child in America is legally protected from being killed by abortion. The most glaring weakness of any of these decisions is the Court's failure to recognize the other party in the abortion debate: the fetus. The court under *Roe vs. Wade* defined the fetus as potential human life in which the state has a legitimate, but not a compelling, interest. The question of human life is not a question to be resolved but a fact to be acknowledged. Human life is not a value judgment. The strange case of Nancy Klein underscores the lack of rights that the fetus has under the US Constitution. Klein was four months pregnant when seriously injured in a 1988 auto accident on Long Island. Her doctors gave her little hope but said it might help her chances if she aborted her fetus, since there would be less strain on her body's ability to stay alive. Since she was in a coma, her husband Martin elected to seek the abortion. Two members of the Long Island Right to Life sought a court injunction to prevent the abortion. Klein had to fight this through three state courts until the United States Supreme Court finally dismissed the two men's case. Her baby died during the subsequent abortion.

Since the court recognized the fact that as many as 40% of abortions were used to back up contraception that had failed, they dubiously reasoned that 1.6 million abortions were the price society had to pay in order not to interfere with diverse lifestyles. The Casey decision attempted to establish *Roe vs. Wade* as a precedent that should not be tampered with by future courts. Justice Scalia noted such arrogance with contempt. The Court's majority, he says has concocted an Orwellian decision that rules out the possibility of political compromise on the most agitated question of the day and then declares it the duty of the American people to accept it as resolved. It is instructive to compare this Nietzschean vision of unelected, life-tenured judges with the more modest role envisioned for these lawyers by the founders. If the policy of the government upon vital questions affecting the whole people is to be irrevocably fixed by decisions of the Supreme Court, the people will have ceased to be their own rulers, having to that extent practically resigned their government into the hands of that eminent tribunal. Mary Ann Glendon of Harvard Law School is the authority on abortion law in the Western world. She notes that of all democratic societies, the United States is far and away the most permissive in terms of abortion. In the very week the Casey decision was handed down, the newly united Germany adopted a new abortion law, providing significant protection for the unborn. The German decision serves as a noted contrast to the direction our court has been going.

The abortion decisions have created a federally protected aura around abortion clinics and abortionists, making them impervious to public scrutiny and democratic protest. The police have seen fit to physically abuse pro-life demonstrators, severely restricting their picketing and rights of free speech. RICO, a federal law with sharp teeth, was originally enacted to combat the Mafia. The government has also been skillfully using it to combat pro-lifers in the Culture War. As the democratic processes have been cut off concerning this issue, it is not surprising that there have been an increasing number of violent incidents, initiated by individuals claiming to be pro-life.

The seriousness of this court-inspired situation draws an interesting parallel with *Dred Scott* decision from 1857. In a similar 7 to 2 vote the court ruled that black people, slaves, were not legal persons and that they were in effect the property of the slave owners. Abolitionists protests were met with the popular refrain: we understand you oppose slavery and find it morally offensive. That is your privilege. You don't have to own a slave if you don't want to. But don't impose your morality on the slave owner. He has the constitutionally protected right to choose to own a slave. Abraham Lincoln might have explained to a "modern" Stephen A. Douglas, that Casey is not the law of the land. It is one wrong decision of the court affirming an earlier wrong decision of the court. The Constitution is the law of the land and, contrary to some judicial activists, the Constitution is not whatever the court says it is. In the constitutional order of this country, it is the people through their elected representatives, that define the laws of the land.

Cheryl Richardson went to jail in November of 1995 for 54 days because she refused to testify at a Justice Department hearing to determine if there were a nationwide conspiracy involving violence against abortion clinics. Senator Christopher Smith, who heads the Pro-life caucus in the House of Representatives, said it was a witch hunt and misuse of scarce resources, a political payback given to *National Abortion and Reproductive Rights Action League* and *Planned Parenthood* by the Clinton administration. The Richardson case demonstrates that the abortion issue is part of a much larger picture. Her imprisonment clearly shows how much arbitrary power the federal government can muster against its citizens if they deviate from the established way of thinking. It must be remembered that the Russians had a Constitution extolling the same rights as the United States Constitution. It was just that the Soviet government chose to blatantly ignore its provisions. The same thing is happening here.

12

The Catholic Church
Saturday Night Fever

The human race does not need a Church to complete the state as an instrument of human betterment in this world.

—Msgr. George A. Kelly,
The Battle for the American Church Revisited, 1995

The Catholic Church is a two-thousand-year-old institution with a storied history, rich in drama, controversy, and divine spirituality. Its indelible sense of mystery, supernatural ritual, and public presence has made it a source of warmth, satisfaction, and sanctification for its members. At the same time, to some, it has appeared as a superstitious enigma and target for caustic aspersions. Today, a particularly virulent form of anti-Catholic bigotry, what I call *Christophobia,* prevails as the most acceptable form of prejudice in American society. A number of anti-Catholic groups flourished in the late nineteenth century, namely the *American Protestant Association,* the *Christian Alliance,* the *American and Foreign Christian Union,* and the *American Protective Union.* The mutual hostility of Protestants and Catholics had its roots of the Reformation in sixteenth and seventeenth century Europe. The split between Catholics and Protestants created a historic and cultural rift that has lasted for centuries, abetting in the choosing of sides in the Culture War.

Traditional Catholic bigotry resurfaced in the 1980s as a result of the Church's orthodox and consistent stand against homosexuality and abortion. While the Church was a welcomed participant in the Civil Rights struggles of the 1960s, it quickly lost favor with the homosexuality and abortion movements, causing a resurgence of the country's historical intolerance. Unlike prejudice towards blacks and Jews, attacks on the Catholic Church were often sanctioned, overlooked or even encouraged by the mainstream media, giving rise to the axiom that anti-Catholic bigotry was the anti-Semitism of the left. I have been a Catholic since my baptism in 1943. All I have known since then is the Catholic faith. It has given me hope, emotional and spiritual comfort, fostered a sense of charity and concern for other people, and, at times, been the source of deep feelings of guilt and confusion. Priests have been my role models, friends, and have even put an unhealthy fear of hell in me at times. What I know of the Church is probably typical of most practicing Catholics today.

During the summer of 1963, I stayed with a friend in Washington, D.C. While touring the nation's Capital, I struck up a spontaneous conversation with a Catholic priest on the steps of the Capitol Building. During the few minutes we exchanged pleasantries, I informed him that I had attended separate lectures by the controversial theologian Hans Kung and presidential hopeful, Barry Goldwater, at Holy Cross College during the past year. He offered the candid observation "Oh, you're conservative in politics and liberal in religion." I really liked the ring of his succinct comment. I decided that I could be faithful to both precepts without fear of contradiction since politics was founded on power and religion, on love and faith. The priest's astute observation has been a philosophical underpinning in my mindset ever since. That is, until now! I have undergone a radical transformation in my thinking, not because of any specific conversion experience but because the etymological distinctions between conservative and liberal seemed to have become blurred, if not totally obscured. Conservative used to mean preserve, slow to change with an emphasis on the country's historical traditions. Conservatism is a perfect intellectual and moral supposition when men's lives and daily existences are the focal point. A liberal was someone who worked for more personal freedom, with an implicit emphasis on individual responsibility. Today, however, it is conservatives who are calling for change, a return to the Judeo-Christian traditions that have become all but obliterated in our culture. Religious liberals have become more closely allied with those in politics whose main goal is a Leviathan increase in the paternalistic power of the central government. This change in religious posture is unnatural and can not work

There have been many other significant changes over the past thirty years. My old hero, Barry Goldwater, later came out for abortion and gay rights while Kung has nearly vanished from the great doctrinal debates. Other religious leaders have forsaken their divine mandate to minister to the poor and tend the sick, by pandering for the financial support of government to accomplish its ends. Too many members of my own Church have unwittingly attempted to mate power with charity. Like the Exxon Valdez, this religious/political mixture will result in a moral ecological mess! Government may say it is interested in caring for people, promising anything under the sun, but historically it has consistently failed to accomplish anything of substance. President Lyndon Johnson's efforts to end poverty, became a five trillion dollar exercise in futility. Marvin Olasky's perceptive book, *The Tragedy of American Compassion* elaborates this gradual loss of the private need to help people as more charitable functions have been absorbed by the state. He documents the gradual seduction of the private charity sector by the all-encompassing federal government. Since 1913 we have seen the gradual erosion of our basic charitable instincts. The government's incessant need to extend its federal arm into ordinary lives has negatively impacted the churches. The latest promise of herculean and potentially statist consequences is that of providing affordable and efficient health care to all Americans. Very popular among church leaders, this campaign for universal health coverage was but another pipe dream, fueled by a power grab that will blur the important distinction between private benevolence and public charity.

It is into this governmental lust for power and control that the Catholic Church has unwittingly been absorbed. A new order or way of thinking has permeated the Church. I cannot read the Catholic *St. Louis Review* without being accosted by the term "social justice." When I was reared in the Church forty years ago, the words I so often heard were *charity, fidelity,* and *love.* All of these ideas stressed the altruistic giving of oneself and one's worldly goods. It was this belief that compelled me to spend a year of my life in the home missions in Charleston, Missouri, as a member of the Catholic Lay Extension. It was my early Catholic training that prompted my service in the pro-life movement, *Birthright,* and the *Foundation for Special Education for Children.* The moral obligation has always been on me to help out in whatever way I could. That's not what social justice says to me.

The emphasis is now on the legalistic notion of justice for the oppressed poor and minorities who have suffered past slavery and discrimination. In the 10 December 1995 edition of our parish bulletin, the *Dear Padre* column, written by Father Michael Parise lamented the state of the oppressed poor. In terminology reminiscent of Karl Marx, the article stated that God sides with the oppressed. While Parise's sentiments smack of a love of the underdog, he continued to plead for all those who are burdened by economics, politics, hopelessness, and sin. I would argue that this would include just about everyone. Oppression and injustice were introduced into the world by Adam and Eve. But Father Parise urged his readers to show a preferential love for the poor. He quoted Saint John Chrysostom, who wrote that not to enable the poor to share in our goods is to steal from them and deprive them of life. The goods we possess are not ours but theirs. This tangled logic has a strong flavor of Gnosticism that was all right for monks, such as St. John. Priests like Father Parise make it seem as if race or economic status entitles the poor to some special treatment by way of a legal obligation with all the coercive power that the law can bring. This is a gross perversion of the Gospel message of placing a moral obligation on the shoulders of the rich to help those who cannot help themselves. The poor and racial minorities are neither owed nor entitled to anything of themselves, especially those who can help themselves. Help from others is not their right. True help has to come from each individual's heart without coercion. When governmental coercion and legalism enters the equation, spiritual growth and true holiness disappear for both the rich and the poor because both have been denied the Christian freedom of doing for themselves or doing for others.

Neo-conservative Irving Kristol says that Christianity began as a gnostic movement with the attitude that poor people are holy in a sense. I have studied the Bible faithfully, and its teachings seem to be more concerned with the rich. Christ felt that they were the ones in jeopardy. The poor, He felt, would always be with us! The poor were God's children, even though in most cases their poverty was involuntary. Like the agrarian myth of Thomas Jefferson, an enlightened notion that erroneously held that farmers were inherently better than anyone who lived in the urban areas, there is no reason to think that poor people are any nicer or wiser than other people. In many cases their lack of education and basic greed and jealousy are more pronounced. In the Dostoevsky's novel, *The Brothers Karamazov*, the Grand Inquisitor says that when the Anti-Christ comes his message will be to feed the people of the world and then ask of them virtue.

Look at the poor in this country. Many own their own modest homes, have cars that work, color televisions, refrigerators, and even air-conditioners. Many live better, relatively speaking, than did the middle class of just fifty years ago. Poverty is a relative term. Poverty to me is what happens in Bangladesh, Calcutta, and Rangoon. Former deputy assistant Treasury Secretary, Bruce Bartlett did a study, predicated on data from the Census Bureau's 1990 census, which appeared in the *American Enterprise*. Bartlett found that 93% of Americans living below the official poverty line owned at least one color television set. Sixty percent of those classified as poor owned microwave ovens and VCRs—72% owned their own washing machines. The percentage who owned their own dishwasher was as high as the general population in Great Britain, the Netherlands or Italy. In Great Britain only 48% of all households and 37% of Swedish households owned microwaves. Britain is the only country where general ownership of VCR's exceeded that of the American poor. It is axiomatic that our poor today live far better than our middle class did in the 1940s or 1950s. Irving Kristol believes that economic growth solves the problem of poverty through redistribution. In a dynamic society, everyone improves his condition—all boats rise in a good economy. Christianity has always frowned on a materialistic society where there is dynamic economic growth and everyone improves his condition. It prefers a static society, the Christian virtues of self-sacrifice, charity, and prudence predominate.

Given our government's propensity to run up exorbitant deficits, waste taxpayers' money, and commit abject fraud, should not the Church, as a matter of real justice, be urging the government to provide accountability, justification and fiscal responsibility for the billions of dollars it demands from its citizens before encouraging its faithful to blindly pour additional hard-earned money down the government sinkhole? At a certain point, does not the word "contribute" metamorphose into "confiscate?" The health care plan mentioned earlier serves as a splendid example to illustrate the rift within the Catholic Church. I was disturbed by the overall naive acceptance of the Catholic clergy, press, and general population of the abortive Clintons' health care plan. No doubt, many of these good-hearted people wrung their hands in genuine agony over the fact that this bill was deeply flawed in its implicit support for both abortion and euthanasia. Yet I would wager that they had no concern for the basic statist philosophical underpinnings of the bill.

As a Catholic-American taxpayer, I have done some soul-searching over this matter. Why universal coverage? Who pays for it? I hear that health care/coverage is a right and yet I read the brilliant analyses of this concept by Professor Walter Williams, of George Mason University, who says that no right can ever impose a financial obligation on another person and I wholeheartedly agree. You may have the right of free speech or the freedom to practice your religion but that does not mean I have to buy you a radio station or build you a church. Of course, I believe Catholics have a moral obligation to help those who can't help themselves but out of the virtue of charity, not out of some obligation to a nebulous right. It worries me that while the Catholic hierarchy think a mandate for abortion is wrong, they consider a mandate for universal health coverage, an expensive, and perhaps bankrupting social entitlement, is praiseworthy. Who is our government, and associatively our Church, to tell all Americans they must have this? The bishops say that health care is a fundamental right, making it incumbent upon the federal government to entitle everyone to health care at the taxpayers' expense. The Catholic Church has surrendered its divine imperative to care for the sick and minister to the poor to the federal government. This ideological merger of church and state is dangerous to the Catholic Church and its 59 million members.

Our central government has spent nearly five trillion, since 1964 on the inner-cities in the so-called *War on Poverty.* I ask you, are things today any better for the urban poor, especially the blacks? If anything, government control has nearly destroyed them by making them dependent on Big Brother. What makes the bishops think big government will do any better with health care? Since the government developed Medicare, medical costs have soared. Our Church leadership should be cognizant of this causal relationship. It is as if the government is in the business of self-fulfilling prophecy. They helped to cause the crisis that they now say justifies their nationalizing one-seventh of our economy. This is a dangerous precedent and I am disturbed that my Church is siding with people like the Clintons and Democratic minority leader, Richard Gephardt. I do not think these people really care about health care or universal coverage. Power, unadulterated power, is the name of their game. Control over you and me and finally, the effective elimination of the Catholic Church from all debates on moral issues is what motivates these people. It reminds me of an old definition of peaceful coexistence. That's what the farmer says to the turkey until Thanksgiving. Since the Culture War has replaced the Cold War, the analogy fits perfectly.

On a tangential note, price controls will lead to a reduction in health care. Most Americans still remember the gas lines we suffered through when President Nixon instituted price controls on gas and oil in 1973. The same will be true of health care. Then we will really have a crisis. If you are seventy years old and need a heart bypass, the Clinton Plan's medical boards, not your doctor, might well have reasoned that you are old, so why waste our limited resources on you. It will lead to the indirect and even direct euthanizing of the elderly, the infirm, and the mentally handicapped. The right to die will gradually devolve to the duty to die. I seriously wish that the Church would reconsider its position in this matter and go back to being a Church, with all that entails, instead of an unwitting partner in the Leviathan state. I know of many fellow Catholics who have decreased their church donations in proportion to the increase in taxes for these ill-fated government programs. They reason that if the Church is going to join with government in these utopian social programs, which will inevitably raise their taxes, why should they donate to the Catholic Church.

This merger of a Catholic/Liberal state reminds me of a story told by William Bennett. Shortly after he went to work for the Reagan administration, he was told by Liberal Republican Senator, Jacob Javitts, not to make any deals with the Democrats. If you dance with someone he was told, you will have to dance with the whole crowd! In his timely book, *Slouching Towards Gomorrah,* Robert Bork opines that the president of Notre Dame would much rather have the approval of the presidents of Harvard and Yale than that of the Pope. He also paints the American Catholic bishops as "Democrats in robes." Reflecting his prescient view, I believe that the Church has caught a bad case of Saturday Night Fever. It is dancing too closely with the very people who have been holding it up to scorn as an obstacle to their secular agenda. Unless the Church stands firmly on its traditional spiritual and salvational principles, it will cease to have a voice of authority on any spiritual issue within the public debate.

The embryonic roots of the church's secularization trace back to the 1960s. While the Church has always been a leader in the fight to defeat the tyranny of Communism all over the world, two events drastically changed the Church in the early sixties. The first was the election of the first Catholic, John F. Kennedy, to the presidency of the United States. According to John Cooney in his *The American Pope,* Kennedy had chosen to associate with that segment of American society which is either unwilling or unable to regard Communism as more than a childish bugaboo. After such a historic event as the election of a Catholic to the presidency, most Catholics did not want to jeopardize the social gains Kennedy had given Catholics with his election. They cooled the heat of their anti-Communist rhetoric. Even more importantly was the election of Pope John XXIII, replacing Pope Pius XII, who had been an ardent anti-Communist. Pope John immediately started redefining the Church's relationship to the modern world.

He started an open dialogue between Catholics and Communists. From the Russian Revolution in 1917 until the 1960s, the Catholic Church and most of its members exuded a vigilant and consistent opposition to Communism and Socialism as typified by the attitude of Cardinal William O'Connell of Boston who, in 1918, warned his flock there can not be a Catholic socialist. Since so many of their flock were laborers, the bishops feared that the socialist doctrine would destroy the faith of their flock. They established the *American Federation of Catholic Societies* to fight the destructive propaganda of Socialism.

This Church's attitude toward statism changed with Pope John XXIII's first major encyclical, *Mater et Magistra* in July 1961. It dispensed with the traditional denunciation of world Communism, arguing that colonialism was the true cause of the third world's plight. From that moment on, anti-Communism became less important for Catholics. A new spirit of detente, or international reconciliation, became the order of the day. Pope John XXIII regarded anti-Communist as an obstacle to the Church's influence in a world where Marxist philosophy seemed to be a permanent fixture in both politics and culture. Socialism has a natural attraction for Christians because of its emphasis on the community, as distinct from a liberal society's emphasis on individualism. Socialism, like all gnostic movements, has a morphological structure. There is a group at the top, what Thomas Sowell calls the "Anointed." The trouble, according to Irving Kristol in *Neo-Conservatism,* lies in the fact that socialist societies offer a redistribution that only looks like Christian charity when in fact these societies offer nothing more than grotesque parodies of a Christian community. It offers both abundance and redistribution and it can not deliver.

Since Vatican II, there has been a noticeable shift in the Church's emphasis on eternal salvation to the immediate social ills of American society. Generated by the call for civil rights for minorities, clergy and laity alike have embarked on an idealistic attempt to make everything on earth fair. As the Church demanded that injustice and unfairness be reconciled on earth, fewer Catholics concerned themselves with the afterlife. The Church seemed to have sacrificed the hereafter for the now. The Church adopted much of the liberal agenda that Vatican II spawned with Civil Rights serving as the vanguard for greater secularization of the faith. The Church had a new vigor and enthusiasm that sparked its growth and devotion. Many older Catholics were scandalized by this new and fresh approach toward world Communism. When the Pope's *aggiornamento* opened the windows, he let in a lot of dust, dirt and moral pollutants that have beset the Church ever since. The culture's creation and support of abortion rights in 1973 created a chasm within the Church. Pope Paul VI's poorly-received encyclical, *Vita Humani,* which reaffirmed the Church's teachings on artificial birth control, split the Church into those who felt in strict conscience they could disobey the Pope on this personal matter, those whose freedom of conscience turned into license with respect to all forms of sexual misbehavior, including abortion, and those who felt conscience-bound to remain absolutely faithful to the Church's magisterium.

It was my understanding that the Second Vatican Council was supposed to purge the Church of its old concepts of legalism. It appears that magisterial legalism has been replaced with a social legalism that implies it is within our power to create some earthly paradise, free of poverty and war, on this earth. To paraphrase T. S. Eliot, where is the faith we have lost in justice? Where is the love we have lost in faith? In the Church's laudable effort at reform, it has thrown the proverbial baby out with the bath water, creating a host of new problems for its faithful members. I think Pope John Paul II should consider calling Vatican III.

In a column he wrote for *King Features* in November of 1994, Charley Reese observed that the Reverend John Ricard, the auxiliary bishop of Baltimore, had said the state has the obligation to care for those who can not care for themselves. The hierarchy had come a long way since Cardinal O'Connell's warning about socialists in 1917. Reese called it the "bumper sticker approach to religion," adding that a religion which can not effect change in the lives of people without the help of the government is a dead religion. There is no place in my Bible that says that Jesus advocated a Roman welfare state. Baltimore's new Cardinal—William Keeler—added fuel to this fire when he said we in church stand with the unborn and the undocumented, the poor and the vulnerable. The bishops argue that the nation's economic policies have become so unfair that the rights of the haves outweigh the rights of the have-nots. Many of them preach that economic justice is not an ideological choice for Catholics but a requirement of Catholic teaching. The bishops boast that every one of them was the son of a working man. Since most of them were weaned on FDR, it is no wonder they have such an egalitarian view on so many things. Coercing taxpayers to subsidize people, who have no legitimate rights to the fruits of their labor is the height of liberal arrogance and moral preening. This way of thinking represents a liberal infusion that has effectively altered the fundamental message of the 2000-year old Gospels.

The bishops seem to be forgetting the Catholic principle of subsidiary which formulates the right of free exercise of one's functions and responsibilities in personal care and living. Socialist arguments violate this principle by transferring these responsibilities to a superior order, the State. The entire society is turned into a monstrous public assistance system and its members are reduced to the status of children, forever beholden to the nanny state. For many the welfare state represents the transition to the utopia they envision for future society. In the December 1995 issue of *The American Spectator*, Tom Berthel profiled Dr. James Hitchcock, a professor of history at St. Louis University and one of the Church's most articulate and prolific writers. In an article for *The Catholic World Report*, entitled *Conservative Bishops, Liberal Results*, Hitchcock painted a saturnine picture of a church hierarchy that has been infiltrated or captured by gnostic and feminist forces who have distorted the papal message from Rome on issues such as birth control, abortion, women priests, and liturgical practices. He recounted a situation where men applying to the priesthood were washed out when they did not give the politically correct answers in response to the question of female priests. It is quite possible that the current shortage of priests in this country is in part being created by the very people who propose themselves as the solution for this shortage.

The infiltration of the liberal mindset appears to stretch to the highest echelon of the church hierarchy in this country. Cardinal Law of Boston, who has apparently surrounded himself with assistants more concerned with placating the gnostic dissenters in their midst than upholding true orthodoxy, was eager to promote the feminist English translation of the new *Catechism of the Catholic Church*. This ill-advised move was eventually stopped by Fr. Joseph Fessio of Ignatius Press and Cardinal Ratzinger of Rome. Closer to home, Hitchcock asserted that Archbishop Justin Rigali, who worked with the Vatican and John Paul II for many years, had been smothered in St. Louis by the liberal prelates who shield him from opposing views. He called Donald Wuerl, the Archbishop of Pittsburgh, "the David Souter of the Church." Wuerl had a reputation as an orthodox figure but has run a very liberal ship since assuming control of his diocese. In San Francisco many of the church workers drive to work with pro-choice bumper stickers on their cars. Hitchcock says the biggest disappointment in fighting this infectious trend within the Church has been New York's Cardinal O'Connor. While still doctrinaire on abortion, he has taken liberal positions on labor, education, welfare, and the care of those with AIDS. He has also adopted a *laissez faire* approach toward liturgical and doctrinal non-conformity. Hitchcock attributes this liberal epidemic within the Church to the belief that the bishops do not want to antagonize the feminist and liberal dissenters within their ranks. Hitchcock believes that these dissenters are everywhere and well connected to the leftist media. This situation has put the bishops in a moral conundrum of following the traditions of the Church or bowing to the progressive fervor of the present. The dilemma for the Church and the people in the pews is that they have been presented with the unenviable choice of deciding between a system that undercuts the family, promotes illegitimacy, and lifelong dependency on the federal government and a reform package that might increase the number of abortions in the short term, though designed to improve everyone's lot down the road.

A spokesman for the *United States Catholic Conference* said we disagreed with Reagan and Bush on some things and its the same way with the Clinton administration. This is an obvious moral relativity that lumps opposition to fetal tissue testing and abortion in the same group as its opposition to trade with Japan and health care. Their policy of win on a few issues, lose a few issues, it's all part of the game underscores why there is so much dissension within the Catholic Church. The Catholic Church says that abortion is its leading issue of concern but its actions do not support this contention. Abortion is all but ignored in many parishes throughout the country. Pastors have other things to do. They have money to collect and many are afraid of angering a volatile parish membership with moral strictures against something that has become deeply ingrained as acceptable in our society. The Catholic Church has not only failed to persuade the vast majority of the faithful on the abject evils of abortion but also to communicate the most elementary facts about its nature to its parishioners. J. P. McFadden, who writes a cogent and intellectually stimulating newsletter, the *Catholic Eye*, put the church's moral dilemma in proper perspective when he wrote in a personal letter to the author, on 10 November 1995,

> the Catholic liberal clergy know in their guts that what they demand of the pew-sitters they despise goes against the human grain. It is a form of gnosticism: only they know the truth, which isn't available to 'ordinary Catholics'—they're too dumb.

Gregg Cunningham, the dynamic founder of the *Center for Bio-Ethical Reform*, has noted another indication that the America Catholic Church has lost its moral compass. In the August, 1992 issue of his *In-Perspective*, Cunningham mirrored the thought of Italian Communist, Antonio Gramsci when he opined that secular culture was influencing the Church more profoundly than the Church was influencing secular culture. Abortion advocates have disingenuously persuaded naive pro-life Christians that the constitutional wall of separation between church and state deprives the church of any right to participate in the formulation of public policy. Christians may act justly at a personal level, but not collectively at a societal level. Many church leaders reflexively accept this fiction, however, because it provides convenient cover for their embarrassing tendency to cower in the face of evil.

The founding fathers wisely prohibited the government from mandating religious practice but this is very different from the liberal contention that public policy may not reflect a particular moral value. A country's laws will always reflect someone's perception of moral values. These values are going to be either Judeo-Christian or secular humanistic. Religiosity does not disqualify a value as a proper foundation for secular law. Respect for human life is an indisputable Judeo-Christian value that provides the basis for our society's prohibitions against murder in secular law. No one attacked the Church when it supported a nuclear freeze. There was no talk of the wall of separation between church and state when Catholic priests and nuns marched in Selma in 1965 to protest the city's segregationist practices. Liberals only evoke proscriptions against Church involvement in political issues when it goes against their political and social agenda.

On a broader level, the national media has prided itself in portraying the Catholic Church as a deeply flawed institution. I agree with this attitude but for different reasons. The media says the Church is too intolerant on abortion and homosexuality. This is just part of what is good about the

Church. The Church's flaw, as illustrated through groups like its *Human Rights Commission,* is that it seems to have discarded its traditional role of independent minister to the poor, sick, and the helpless, in favor of an unholy alliance with big government, whose main concern is not helping the disadvantaged, but the naked aggrandizement of power. In pushing its statist agenda of social justice, the Church is placing its historic and divine mission at great risk, not to mention doing a great disservice to its faithful in the pews. If Catholics are to help the poor and the downtrodden, not through the charity in their hearts, but through the coercive tax policies of government, what spiritual joy is there in giving? Of what value is forced contributing to the soul? Or does that not matter in the new order of things? Another deep flaw in the Church is its reliance on the social philosophy of the sixties. In his book, *The Thirty Years War,* Republican administrator, Thomas Pauken, a Catholic from South Texas, laments over the intellectual invasion that the Church has suffered. While he was the Director of Action in Texas during the first Reagan administration, he told of Saul Alinsky, from Chicago, who wrote *The Leftist Organizing Bible, Rules for Radicals.* According to Pauken, Alinsky was personally responsible for the student demonstrations that thoroughly disrupted the nomination of Hubert Humphrey at the Democratic National Convention in 1968. After his defeat, Alinsky provided an over-the-shoulder acknowledgment to the very first radical who rebelled against the establishment so effectively that at least he won his own kingdom—Lucifer. Pauken contends that over the years several young nuns and priests have fallen under Alinsky's demonic spell. His objective was to employ many young and idealistic Catholic recruits to drive a wedge inside the institution of the Church in order to change it. He has several disciples within the bureaucracies of many of the Catholic orders.

Many of the Church's so-called human rights organizations, such as its controversial *Campaign for Human Development,* are highly politicized and do nothing to address the problems they were established to meet. The ordinary Catholic in the pews are told every November that their money will be used to support self-help projects designed to give the poor a hand up not a handout. What they do not know is that some of this CHD will go for radical groups, such as the *Association of Community Organizations for Reform Now* (ACORN). It was a busload of their people who forced cancellations of speeches by republicans, including Speaker Newt Gingrich in 1995. Even worse is that some of this CHD money may wind up in the coffers of pro-abortion groups. In 1993 and 1994, CHD made donations of $60,000 to the *Massachusetts Senior Action Council,* an affiliate of the pro-tax, pro-spending *National Council of Senior Citizens.* They supported the liberal health care plan the Democrats tried to ram down the nation's throat in 1993. This is extraordinary in light of the fact that the bishops opposed the bill that included abortion as a prominent feature. As far back as 1972, *Triumph* magazine was reporting that CHD was funding pro-abortion groups. In the 1980s CHD gave money to the national health care campaign, a clearinghouse for several pro-choice women's groups. In 1994 it was reported that CHD gave $100,000 to the *National Committee for Responsive Philanthropy*, a Washington D.C. group that seeks to direct charitable giving to liberal nonprofit groups. According to NCPR's literature, its work has benefited such pro-abortion groups, such as the *NARAL Foundation, NOW Legal Defense and Education Fund, Planned Parenthood-World Population*, the *Religious Coalition for Abortion Rights Education Fund, and the Women's Legal Defense Fund*, as well as the *Lesbian Resource Center for Lesbian Rights*. CHD also refuses to fund projects that promote school choice, which is on the bishop's recommended list. The bottom line is that CHD's method of trying to end poverty by funding so-called community based organizations is outdated and ineffective. Government and foundation anti-poverty programs have been funneling money, Acorn-style, for thirty years. Often these organizations are simply modern versions of old ward-based political machines. The main goal of these local groups is not to help ease the burden of the poor but to elect their political benefactors and operate modern patronage mills.

The Church's revised stance on the issue of capital punishment has also created some difficulty for the faithful. I say "revised" because throughout my upbringing, it was always a given that in certain cases a vicious and violent criminal could be put to death under the aegis of the state and local government. Lynching and anything constituting personal vengeance or mob violence was ruled out. Punishment was not inflicted without ample time for the guilty party to ask for forgiveness before leaving this world. My ethics text in college, written by a Jesuit, spoke of three instances when one could morally take the life of another human being: in a just war, in self-defense, and in the proper and legal function of the state to maintain order and justice. The death penalty was appropriate for heinous crimes. The Church seems to be rewriting my ethic text's exceptions as if they had inspired Christians for centuries. Granted, there have been innumerable theologians who would have liked to have outlawed the death penalty over the centuries but never as a matter of Church or canon law. The Church had no qualms in executing hundreds of agnostics and heretics during the crusades and later during the Spanish Inquisition in the fifteenth century.

But as part of the seamless garment professed by Cardinal Bernardin, Catholics are being made to feel that we may never protect society from some of the vicious and sociopathic vermin that prey on it. We are told that to execute a vicious killer is vengeance, which totally misses or distorts the proper frame of reference involved in capital punishment. If the families of murder victims were after vengeance, they would not stop at killing the murderer of their loved ones. They would go after the families and friends of the guilty party in the manner of the Corsican vendetta.

I was at a dinner with Archbishop Rigali when the subject of capital punishment came up for discussion. One of the other dinner guests asked the Archbishop, a quiet man whose spirituality radiates from his bright and lively eyes, about his involvement in a recent capital case. An eighteen-year old man had brutally abducted a middle-aged woman, bound and gagged her, and then summarily thrown her off a bridge to her death. He was caught, tried, sentenced, and condemned to death. The Archbishop was asked to intercede, which he did, privately asking the state to spare the young man's life. The matter was leaked to the press and the new Arch-bishop was put on the defensive. He told our gathering that he never intended his interest to be publicized but when it was he had no choice but to defend his plea for mercy and his belief that even a vicious killer should be given every opportunity of repenting for his sin. Most of us agreed with his sentiment but pointed out that the average killer on death row spends well over ten years before any sentence is actually carried out, ample time for a spiritual penance.

My wife lost her sister Jan, and nearly her sister's three children, to a black man who had a bad day on one of Kentucky's two lane highways several years ago. He had taken enough muscle relaxers and tranquilizers to sedate a horse, causing his vehicle to sideswipe another car before putting a fatal obstacle in Jan's path. Though it was not anything near what I would judge to be a capital crime, we all felt a deep personal loss. The man worsened the situation by focusing on his own petty life. Jan and her three children meant nothing to him. They were like ants on a hill that had impeded the progress of his foot. In a way, we experienced the loss that must befall anyone who has had a loved one die at the hand of another. There was no cry for revenge. No demand for his blood! Our only plea was that this man recognize what he had done and attempt to atone for the injustice he had committed. He was sentenced to one-to-three years in prison.

I am not a strong proponent of the death penalty but I have to laugh when the subject is capital punishment. Our bishops' talk of justice is quickly replaced with the ideas of forgiveness and wholeness, not to be confused with holiness. I certainly would not like to pull the switch on anyone, even though he may have done harm to me or my family, but I believe that it does have a valid and possibly necessary function to play in American soci-ety. To callously and viciously take another being's life, I believe a person should forfeit his or her own life, as a means of restitution. While the victim cannot return, the execution of the guilty retires that debt to society in kind as a measure of value. A deliberate murder is an affront to human society and the debt must be paid in kind. I learned this basic belief in my Catholic grade school. The Church now seems to be rewriting this principle, suggest-ing that its moral teachings are not all immutable.

John Ashcroft, the former Governor of Missouri and now a United States Senator, supports capital punishment. He has severe reservations with Cardinal Bernardin's seamless garment. Ashcroft believes that the support of capital punishment is a pro-life view, in that by eliminating convicted murders who can, will get out of prison and kill again, we are actually saving lives. There is a plausibility to the Senator's logic with which I can not find fault. Economist Thomas Sowell echoed this view when he wrote, "I am prepared to admit that the death penalty does not deter if the opponents of the death penalty can show me just one case where a murderer who was executed then committed another murder." Archbishop Rigali wants murderers to have ample time to repent of their crime against society. But how much time is enough? Consider the case of Crazy Joe Spaziano. He has been on death row in Florida for over twenty years. In 1976, he was convicted of murdering an 18-year old girl. Now a number of liberals who are opposed to the death penalty are arguing that he is an innocent man. The witness who testified at the original trial has, under duress, changed his testimony. No rational person believes that Spaziano is not the kind of man who is capable of murder. He has also been convicted of raping a sixteen-year old girl and then gouging out her eyes with his knife. His own family has said publicly that they are terrified that he will be released and will kill them as he has threatened to do.

The case of Paul Hill, a zealot convicted and sentenced to death for the murders of an abortion doctor and his body guard, raises the question of capital punishment again. Obviously many pro-choice people are encouraged by his death sentence. I have mixed emotions about the decision. Hill did approximately what John Brown did in the antebellum period in the last century. John Brown had executed six slaveholders who were perfectly within their legal rights, in the practice of their peculiar institution to own slaves, at peace with man's law, but at odds with God's law. The law of the land demanded that he pay with his own life, even though what he tried to do, led to the eradication of an historic evil. Who is to say Paul Hill will not be regarded in a similar vein by future generations? As for my discussion with the Archbishop, I added that killing another soldier in battle is probably less moral than executing a threat to society because the soldier is probably no worse a person than the one who kills him. The Archbishop's silence spoke volumes of the logic of the Church's current position. I got the distinct feeling that he did not like the acceptability of war either, not that I do, but sometimes to prevent violence or lessen the incidence of violence, violence is needed. I wish I had asked him if there were anyone in history whom he believed did warrant the death penalty. Liberals are great at using anecdotal and individual examples to argue for their general assumptions. The obvious choice here is Adolf Hitler, who was personally responsible for the second World War and the extermination of over 11 million people, including six million Jews in hundreds of concentration camps all over Europe. Would anyone, even those who believe in the seamless garment, not make an exception here and sanction the public execution of this evil monster? What about the greatest mass murderers in history, Joseph Stalin or Mao Tse-tung? Would men of God make an exception for these kind of mass murderers? Or would they remain consistent with the Christian principle that motivates their seamless garment? Was Hitler not a human being, worthy of an opportunity at repentance? Joseph E. Perspico in his fascinating book, *Nuremberg: Infamy on Trial*, recreates the Nuremberg trials from start to finish. Of the twenty-two men who originally went on trial, eleven Nazis received the death sentence, including Herman Goring and Julius Streicher. Ten died on the gallows while Goring cheated the hangman with a cyanide capsule on the eve of his execution.

My favorite Nazis, in that I find him an example of the German *Everyman*, was Albert Speer. Speer was a talented, well-liked, upbeat man with a professional future as an architect ahead of him. Yet he was seduced by Nazi promises of a better world for Germany and for the German people. He made compromises with principle throughout his relationship with Hitler and just missed the executioner's noose by a hair. To study Speer and his life, as well evidenced in his memoir *Inside the Third Reich*, and the lengthy biography, written by Gitta Sreny, *Albert Speer: His Battle With the Truth*, is to understand Germany and its fatal attraction. If a man like Speer can fall for the Nitzschean message of the will to power, anyone can be seduced. The historical Hitler does make one come to terms with the nature of taking another person's life. These men did not wear horns. The Nazis were not devils incarnate but ordinary men, who during a period of great power, chose to exercise that power to the tune of murdering millions of people. The fact that one of the United States' allies, the Soviet Union, was guilty of similar crimes against humanity, sat in judgment of the Nazis, lent a satanic irony to the situation.

The executions were vividly described. Perspico profiled Master Sergeant John Woods, the Army's expert who had already hanged 347 men, and what pains he took to carry out his job. He secretly smuggled his men into Nuremberg at night and secluded them in the courtyard as unsuspecting GIs played basketball in the gym that would house the executions after midnight. Woods was very professional. He asked for the weights and heights of the men, properly waxed his ropes but was unable to use proper weights to test the scaffolding before the appointed time. Joachim von Ribbentrop was first, followed by Field Marshall Wilhelm Keitel. It was many minutes before the first two were declared dead. After the other eight had been hanged, it became known that something had gone wrong with several of the executions. Woods had not built the gallows high enough. Many of the prisoners had strangled to death. Was this cruel and inhumane punishment, even for Nazis?

Hollywood is usually known for its blatant attempt to inspire mercy for the guilty in capital crimes, no matter how heinous the offense. When I saw *Dead Man Walking*, with Susan Sarandon and Sean Penn, I expected the usual. I was pleasantly mistaken. Rather than appeal to the pure emotion of the state taking a human being's life, this movie had a Christian flavor to it that is little seen in most of what passes for religious themes from Hollywood. Sarandon played a realistic nun who, though opposed to taking Penn's life, resigned herself to the will of the state government with all of its political and unequal dealing—there are no rich men on death row, something that O. J. Simpson bears witness to. That being said, she urges Penn to repent, to confess his part in the crime and wash away his attempt to play the poor victim. More importantly she gets him to focus on the abject evil of what he had done. He went to his lethal injection asking for forgiveness from the families he had robbed of their children, expressing his hope that his death would relieve them of the pain he had caused them. Like the good thief Dismas on the right hand of Christ on the Cross, he literally stole heaven. Instead of offering some gnostic muttering about the inherent evils of capital punishment, the film presented execution as a necessary thing that governments must sometimes employ to provide real justice and closure for the victims. As his lethal cocktail started taking its deadly effect, the camera flashed back to the brutality done to the teenage couple, Penn's character had shot, stabbed, and raped. Opponents of capital punishment may view this juxtaposition as a commentary on the barbarity of the taking of any life. I saw it as a contrast. Young, innocent lives are viciously terminated in the naked inhumanity of a quiet woods while the murder is executed in front of serious and reflective witnesses, granted all the dignity of a last meal, spiritual reconciliation and tearful parting with relatives, none of which he and his accomplice allowed to the real victims in this case.

I could not help thinking that many members of my Church are misguided on capital punishment. The threat of execution and the fervent prayers of worldly nun caused Penn to ask for forgiveness. Instead of life in prison, he got eternal life. We should all be so fortunate. If there actually is a seamless garment for Catholics and other pro-life advocates, would there not be a similar unity among pro-choice people in favor of capital punishment for unborn children and convicted criminals? My experience in this matter has revealed an obvious inconsistency among pro-choice advocates who are opposed to the death penalty for anyone except the unborn. I find this glaring distinction much more curious than that of pro-lifers, like myself, who have few reservations about the death penalty. Research has finally established an indelible link between the pro-choice movement and anti-capital punishment lobby. In each case, the real victim of the action, whether the fetus or the murder victim, are cast aside and replaced in the spotlight by a woman's choice and the sanctity of the felon's life. Both the mother and the murderer are described as the real victims in these matters. Bona fide innocence is not relevant in the new moral order that dominates public discourse today. As in Orwell's *Oceania*, light is dark and dark is light.

Pope Pius IX's *Syllabus of Errors* was especially far-sighted in this matter. The Pope condemned modernity which makes up much of the basic social gospel that has so influenced the modern Church since the Second Vatican Council. The declining interest in the Church, as evidenced by a decline in attendance at mass on Sundays, may be attributed to the Church's choice to go modern in much of its thinking. In a prescient essay written in 1979, by neo-conservative Irving Kristol,

> young people do not want to hear that the Church is becoming modern. Tell them that the message is to wear sackcloth and ashes. The Church has turned the wrong way. Young people are looking for religion so desperately that they have invented new ones because the established churches have given way to modernity at the very moment when that spirit was about to self-destruct.

Kristol was right on target with this view point. Liberal doctrine encourages excuse making and a shying away from the hard realities of life. Young people want and seek the truth as much as anyone else. To coddle them from the pulpit will leave their spiritual hunger for God unsatisfied. They will turn to other sources of comfort for their solace and redemption.

On another front, the Bishops' liberal perspective has fueled public debate about the Church's tacit union with government with a noxious pamphlet they published, in 1995, entitled "Political Responsibility: Proclaiming the Gospel of Life, Protecting the Least Among Us and Pursuing the Common Good." I eagerly read it only to be dismayed by its liberal contents. It boasts that it has no partisan platforms or ideological agendas. It says that the pamphlet is not conservative, liberal, Democrat, or Republican. With a few exceptions, such as abortion, school choice, and opposition to assisted suicide, the document could have been written by the members of the Democratic National Committee. The document's opposition to abortion was raveled in with other threads of the seamless garment. There is as much Feurbach, Rousseau, and Marx in it as there is Jesus Christ. Political responsibility calls for DNC agenda issues, such as a raise of the minimum wage, more environmental controls, nuclear disarmament, and the progressive income tax. It says it is against discrimination for sex, race, ethnicity, or age, yet in the same breath it states support of affirmative action. It calls for an end to welfare as we know it, yet decries Republican attempts to make valid reforms. Another very troublesome aspect called for continued membership in the United Nations. Given this world body's population programs and attempts at cultural imperialism on the real poor of this world, it seems grossly inconsistent. The pamphlet includes the code phrase, "sustainable development," which refers to the United Nation's plan for reducing world populations through a reproductive cocktail of condoms, abortion, and possibly, infanticide. The specter of Antonio Gramsci looms largely here.

The problem facing the bishops is that too many Catholics are liberal Democrats who judge social policy by its intentions not its effects. This has led the bishops to adopt the belief that welfare reform is harmful and even cruel. They do not accept the idea that welfare morally undermines its recipients. The number of people who simultaneously retain in their minds a belief in New Deal liberalism and the traditional moral standards of the

Church is small and shrinking fast. I quickly tire of the usual bromidic refutations offered in response to accusations of disloyalty to the Church's teachings. Apologists offer the same hallow sentiments—war, poverty, crime, the homeless, and the spotted owl in fending off criticism from his fellow Catholic in the Democratic Party. There is no excuse for Catholics being mindless robots or docile sheep when it comes to the political and moral undercutting of American society. The current occupant of the White House has actively done more to advance the pro-abortion cause than anyone else in history. Yet so many of our hierarchy, priests and the faithful in the pew, tend to blindly follow him because of the gnostic legacy that he proposes on behalf of the poor. Before the 1992 election, the Catholic press fawned over Clinton's Catholic education. We were implicitly reminded that Catholics should be proud that he is one of us. Clinton had graduated from Georgetown University and had some Catholic grade school education which helped lead him to the top of his party and ultimately the White House. We are now to believe that the word *Catholic,* instead of universal, means an inclusive big tent philosophy where verbal support of the social gospel excuses an overt and aggressive stand on the violent disposition of the unborn.

What good is it to espouse the Catholic social gospel if one's private life spits in the face of Catholic teaching? To claim such a man as our own does both a disservice to the ill-informed Catholic adult and gives grave scandal to the young who will see in Mr. Clinton a man to be admired and emulated. Such stupid and blatant religious chauvinism probably accounted for many of the 47% of Catholics who voted for Clinton in the general election. Another 20% voted for the pro-abortion Ross Perot. In the 1996 election his support among Catholics rose to 54%. My Jesuit education taught me to be honest in all my dealings with my fellow man, analytical and thoughtful in my intellectual positions, faithful to my spouse, and generous to those who were less fortunate. It also provided me with a sensitivity to the weakest in our society, those who have had no powerful lobby to speak for them. To cast off this endangered portion of our human species, namely the unborn, in a mere perfunctory paragraph gives lie to every pronouncement on helping the poor, the homeless, and the elderly. I fear too many Catholics have put Party over Church. My question for these Democrats is how they can continue to trust a man, who has sold himself to the abortion lobby to be compassionate and caring to the poor or the homeless? The sanctity of all life, especially innocent life, is at the core of any theological argument. I fear the problem with these clerics and their faithful is the fact that they still think Franklin Roosevelt is in the White House.

This subservience to the Democratic Party, among Catholics it is noticeable in many Catholic schools, universities, and charitable institutions, who have sold out in effect and now are so dependent on the government's largess that they can not consider voting against where their next check is coming from, even with the possibility that the whole structure will eventually come down on their heads. They have effectively put party or pocketbook above Church and that does not bode well for the future of either this country or the United States Catholic Church. There's a nun at my mother's nursing home who said she had voted for Bill Clinton. When I asked her how she had balanced her Catholic faith with his views on abortion, she snapped, "There are other life issues!" She was angry because George Bush had bombed Iraqi soldiers during Desert Storm, a clear and hollow rationalization.

The Church could use an infusion of courage here. *Planned Parenthood* attempted to get the Church's tax exempt status revoked in 1987. Their legal efforts were unsuccessful yet their suit caused the Church to cower in face of their continued threats which effectively limited the church's stand on abortion. While pro-abortion Democrats paraded their agenda in front of the Protestant denominations, the Catholic clergy has to watch each and every word it says with regard to politics and abortion. New York's Cardinal O'Connor has been one of the few who have dared to fight this form of political blackmail. I would like to see more of the Church's hierarchy dare the government to revoke its tax exempt status. The United States Cardinals did so in response to Clinton's noxious veto of the Republican Congress' partial birth abortion ban in 1996. With all the legal and financial firepower the laity could muster, it would be political suicide for Democratic politicians to risk such a rupture in their traditional voting bloc. I do not expect that to happen. Too many prelates have been emotionally and traditionally wedded to the Democratic Party and could never suffer an alienation from that allegiance. Fortunately, millions of Catholics have realized that the Democratic Party, the party of their family's legacy, had deserted them. They should be applauded for their ability to recognize the truth of what has happened since their church backed George McGovern in 1972.

Father Richard John Neuhaus in his *Public Square Commentary* for the May 1993 issue of *First Things Journal* wrote that the leadership of the major churches, including the Roman Catholic Church, was in the war between political freedom and tyranny woefully inadequate and more attuned to siding with the appeasers in a sort of peaceful coexistence—much like that condemned by Pius XII. Pope John Paul II was not one of them. He was called pejoratively a "Cold Warrior." With admirable individual exceptions, the American Catholic bishops have wasted their credibility in the endless weaving of a seamless garment with ethereal threads of liberal prescription. Laudably, the bishops have had as their mission, the infusion our common life with a sense of the source, the end and the dignity of the human person. Their approach has been all wrong, as Neuhaus opined: in what they have tried to do, weaving a shapeless garment of evasive consistency and trying to become players of consequence in Caesar's political games, they have shown themselves to be foolish and inept. We can only pray for them and for ourselves.

13 / Walking the Tightrope
The Media's Balancing Act

Slanting the news comes naturally to most reporters.

—Bernard Goldberg, defrocked
CBS Evening News reporter

There is a consistent and widespread dissatisfaction among the American people with the major media organizations in the country. The traditional press has philosophically distanced themselves from the general population. They tend to represent the values of the anointed Thomas Sowell so brilliantly discussed in his book, *The Vision of the Anointed.* Their elitism, fed by an unadulterated celebrity status, has made them more the stars of the news than merely its reporters. Sam Donaldson, Tom Brokaw, Peter Jennings, Dan Rather, Cokie Roberts, and a host of other opinion-shapers have risen above the masses and like many of the enlightened, degrade and condescend to those below them.

News stories are often filtered through a legion of associative editors who twist and shape the evening news to fit their pervasive agenda. The correct word or phrase leaves behind in its wake a desirable result. Listeners or viewers are coaxed into believing the latent interpretation of the journalists. In a myriad of subtle ways, the public is often fooled about issues and deliberately misled under the banner of it's good for the cause, the liberal cause that has created a social cleavage in American society.

We live in an age of sound-bite intelligence. Everyone familiar with this process has honed his or her message down to a pithy ten to twenty second bits of pointed information. The incessant demands of work, family, and recreation have reduced the average citizen's news gathering to these short bursts of information. There is no time for substance or depth. TV producers recognize this facet of American life and exercise great power in what they choose to present on the ten o'clock news. They can slant positions on social issues, politics and economics to support and enhance their own liberal agenda. The media also distorts the truth by what it does not cover. Had the media been more balanced during the 1992 election, George Bush would have been re-elected. They would have explored the outlandish claims of Governor Clinton, such as, "We have the worst economy in fifty years," or they would have relentlessly exposed his financial machinations in the Whitewater land deal. The media's lack of investigative curiosity evidenced their ideological duplicity with the Clinton campaign.

On another note, the media does not police itself. It employs no truth detectors to check the veracity of its stories or the claims of liberal politicians. My study of the news and those who cover current events convinces me that most so-called journalists are not interested in a search for the truth—they only wish to foster or maintain a liberal agenda because liberalism enhances their power and feeling of personal status. Journalists are more akin to the legal profession, in that winning the argument or pushing their agenda is more important than their concern for accuracy and fact. The major schools of journalism in this country, Northwestern, Missouri University, and Columbia in New York, like so many other universities and colleges have been infected with the liberal way of thinking. Those who do not conform, by concealing their traditional principles are forced to exit such programs by either social or academic pressure. There is no room in these classes for people with anything except the prescribed mode of thought. The real message is truly the medium. Studies show that 85 to 90% of journalists and journalism faculties admit to a liberal way of thinking.

As a result, millions of Americans have turned away from the major media in favor of the so-called alternate media offered by C-Span, Rush Limbaugh, and Gordon Liddy. Others resort to picking up their news from the internet. Some subscribe to secondary publications, like the *National Review, Human Events, The Conservative Chronicles,* or the *American Spectator.*

James Fallows, is the former Washington editor of *The Atlantic Monthly,* and commentator on public radio, has taken his profession to task for trivializing the news. Fallows likens the demise of the news industry to that of the United States military after the Vietnam War and the auto industry in the seventies. His book, *Breaking the News: How the Media Undermine American Democracy* attempts to rehabilitate an industry that is top-heavy with its own arrogance and distortion of the truth. His parallels with the Pentagon and Detroit will fall on deaf ears unless the media changes its philosophy as did both of these giants. Liberalism and its corrupt message is why millions have turned away from the mainstream media. Fallows' worst fear, with an implicit reference to Nazi Germany, is that a public estranged from the press is also disengaged from the institutions and newsmakers that journalists cover and will understandably look outside the system for both information and leadership, whether to a Rush Limbaugh or a Ross Perot or worse, might have already happened. Given what is controlling the minds of the population now, could turning off Brokaw and company in favor of Limbaugh, be such a bad idea?

The media's treatment of abortion can serve as an illustration of the lack of balance in major media today. In his book, *The Press and Abortion, 1838-1988,* Marvin Olasky argued that aggressive news coverage of the abortion industry combined with crusading anti-abortion editorials, contributed to the general strengthening of abortion laws throughout the United States in the 1870s. Abortion opponents have grave concerns that media support for abortion rights will make it nearly impossible to reaffirm those laws once again. Part of the problem is that the dominant media has treated all pro-lifers alike, lumping the few extremists who have killed together with the millions of peaceful and prayerful witnesses to the evils of abortion. They have never attempted to understand the grass roots opposition to abortion, patently dismissing it as the futile exercise of religious fanatics. They have showcased such pro-life leaders as Judy Brown, whose devotion to her church and opposition to artificial birth control has sometimes obscured her opposition to abortion. They also have frequently profiled born-again Christian and former used car dealer Randall Terry. His more extreme opposition through *Operation Rescue* has attracted a certain kind of follower. The *Wall Street Journal* and a handful of other reputable publications have editorialized against this twisted logic while the dominant media have all but ignored Terry's plight. Police brutality, sexual abuse of women prisoners, civil liberties violations, and special torture techniques, have nearly been totally ignored. Media moguls, such as millionaire Ted Turner, have not tried to hide contempt for pro-life activists. Turner has shamelessly used his TV cable empire to portray pro-life demonstrators as bozos and idiots. David Shaw's eighteen-month seminal study of how bias seeps into news coverage of abortion, written as a four-part series for the *Los Angles Times* which first appeared on 1 July 1990 and ran through Wednesday, July 4th, began with the story of science editor Susan Okie. Susan wrote, on page one of the *Washington Post* in 1989 that advances in the treatment of premature babies could undermine support for the abortion rights movement. She swiftly received a stern reprimand from pro-choice leaders and her newspaper colleagues and was told to cool her articles because they hurt the pro-choice movement. Okie was taken aback by the implicit message that women reporters were expected to write only stories that reflected favorably on abortion rights. "I was being herded back in line," she said. The truth of the matter according to Shaw is that most major newspapers support abortion rights on their editorial pages and two major media studies have shown that 80 to 90% of US journalists personally favor abortion rights. Shaw lists the major ways a pro-choice bias is most evidenced in the nation's major newspapers. First, the news media consistently use language and images that frame abortion in terms that favor the pro-choice side. This has been most evident with the use of the word choice for those who support abortion and anti-abortion, or even worse, anti-choice to describe those in opposition. The *Post* usually relegates its coverage of the St. Louis Archdiocesan Pro-life Convention each year to its back pages. In 1989, reporter Cynthia Todd even changed the name of the convention to the "Anti-abortion Convention," a blatant distortion of its Pro-life nature. As much news coverage was given to the 15-20 Catholics picketing outside the convention site as was given to the thousand people inside. In 1994, the *Post* did mention the newly-installed Archbishop Justin Rigali's bold statement reiterating the stand taken in 1989 that no Catholic can reasonably take a pro-choice stance. One does not have to think too hard to come up with a list of prominent politicians who have been saying this for years. There should have been a story in that but the *Post* did not want to bring unwanted attention to the hypocrisy of many of the pro-abortion movement's leading supporters. Dr. Wanda Franz, the Director of the *National Right to Life Committee*, took the same high road with regard to the fundamental right to life in the womb. That also failed to make the newspaper.

The *Post's* quiet dismissal of Kevin Horrigan revealed their deep prejudice in this matter. The portly Horrigan, at that time a co-host of KMOX's popular show, *The Morning Meeting*, is a liberal on most issues—but when it comes to abortion, Horrigan, who has adopted three children, has also adopted a conservative pro-life stance. Horrigan appeared at the convention and no one covered it. If his appearance at the convention was not news, then nothing was! Seldom will there be a more blatant example of man bites dog. Another example of media bias is the fact that abortion rights advocates are often quoted more frequently and characterized more favorably than abortion opponents. Many news organizations have given more prominence to rallies and electoral and legislative victories by abortion rights advocates than to those of abortion opponents. When the Republicans scored a surprising upset of the Democratic Congress in the 1994 elections, scant mention was made that in every election where a pro-life candidate squared off against a pro-choice, those against abortion won in every case. Columns of commentary favoring abortions outnumber those opposing them. Newspaper editors and journalists long sensitive to First Amendment violations, such as those inflicted on the marchers to Selma, Alabama in 1965, have largely ignored these breaches when members of *Operation Rescue* and other abortion opponents have had their rights violated during a civil protest.

Shaw does not believe that this bias is conscious or the result of a conspiracy but that the cultural environment of the press room is one of approval for abortion. Douglas Johnson, the legislative director of the *National Right to Life* in 1989, said the insular culture that produces network newscasts create an implicit bias that is more pervasive than in the print media. Most denizens of the liberal news rooms admit to not numbering pro-lifer people among their friends or having any idea of what makes them tick. John Buckley, a long-time spokesman for various conservative politicians, said abortion is the first issue since the Vietnam War in which some journalists' instinctive allegiance to their own world view is stronger than their professional allegiance to objectivity. Surveys show that the more money and education a person has, the more likely he or she is to favor abortion rights. Most newspapers like to typecast all pro-lifers as religious fanatics who would gladly sit down in front of trucks and buses to save the fetus. The press has had a field day with this kind of dedicated pro-lifer. Shaw's study drew attention to cover stories on abortion that appeared in *Newsweek* and

Time. In the *Time* article, the cover showed a drawing of a woman. *Newsweek* depicted a pregnant woman. Neither magazine made any indication of the presence of the unborn child, giving the impression that abortion is strictly a woman's issue. Women buy magazines, fetuses don't. As in any debate, perception is everything.

Language is an important tool in establishing the proper perception. When the *Washington Post* wrote about proposed anti-abortion legislation in Louisiana in June of 1990, it spoke of the bill in terms of a women's reproductive rights. Discussing abortion in these terms was tantamount to adopting both the paradigm and the polemic of the abortion lobby. The *Washington Post* referred to the law as restrictive taking a negative view when they could have described the law as protective for women and their unborn children.

Shaw relates the story of Ethan Bronner, who wrote an article for the *Boston Globe,* in which Bronner describes the abortion procedure as destroying the fetus by crushing forming bones and skull. His editor forced him to soften his language as otherwise it would appear as if he were taking sides in the issue. According to the editor, until that thing is born, it is really no different from a kidney or a liver.

The use of proper abortion language has always been a troubling issue for the press. On this issue, the press reveals schizoid tendencies. When it is obvious the mother does not want her baby, the press always refers to it as a fetus. But they forget their PC attitudes when a mother tragically loses her unborn child or displays some pride in her pregnancy. Then, almost without fail, the reporter or commentator refers to the women's baby, as in "she's having a baby." When Roman Catholic bishops individually or collectively speak out, threatening to excommunicate Catholic politicians who support the abortion rights platform, the press attacks them, grumbling about the church's privacy intrusions. When all the Cardinals of the Catholic Church in the United States assembled in Washington in the Summer of 1996 to lobby for a Congressional override of President Clinton's veto of the bill outlawing partial birth abortion, the *New York Times* ran a front page picture of the august assembly but neglected to include any explanation of the gathering. But when the bishops speak out in support of the liberal agenda or attack Speaker's Newt Gingrich's "Contract With America," the press has nothing but praise for them. Gone are the pretenses of giving both sides of the issue. With a president advancing the pro-abortion cause, the mainstream media act as if pro-lifers are nothing more than petty irritants that can best be handled by near complete disregard.

Because of the Shaw series, most newspapers and their editorial staffs have agreed to use the neutral and balanced terms of abortion rights for pro-choice and anti-abortion for pro-life. The Associated Press wire service, the largest news agency in the free world still refuses to be fair in this. They will use the term pro-choice but not pro-life. The AP's Ed Petykiewicz has stated that: we use pro-choice because we decided that it was an issue of choice, not when life began. That's an issue yet to be decided. What Petykiewicz fails to see is that by employing the choice rhetoric, he has already determined their side as the more valid and accurate. Petykiewicz personifies the pro-abortion propensity for self-delusion. Abortion opponents are often identified as conservative, a word that has carried with it journalist opprobrium and equivalent to evangelical, Catholics, fundamentalists, or the Religious Right. Abortion proponents are never identified liberal or any other code word. When applied to the political realm, the above terms take on an even greater negative impact. The Religious Right is called militant or strident, denoting negative impressions. The media address only the few pro-life extremists and never those who favor the equally extreme support of abortion in the final minutes of pregnancy. President Clinton's sustained veto of the so-called partial birth abortion ban, underscoring this propensity to ignore choice extremists.

On the national level, the dominant media culture has made no pretense of its effort to influence the basic cultural issues. Abortion strikes at the very core of the liberal belief in the autocratic self which is deeply entwined within the cultural context of the last thirty years, making journalistic objectivity is a veritable impossibility. Our culture has defined sex as self and to surrender the liberal freedom of sex would be a counter-cultural surrender of self. This modern attitude has been best evidenced by the press' coverage of the 1989 Webster decision. Several journalists put aside any pretext at journalist impartiality in this issue and marched in the abortion rights parade in April of 1989. For the first time since the Vietnam War, supposedly objective journalists were seen prejudicially supporting the agenda of one side of a major cultural issue. One such reporter said defiantly: "this is not about building some bridge downtown. This is about my body!" Supreme Court Reporter, Linda Greenhouse of the *New York Times* had marched. The *Washington Post* admitted that several of its reporters had joined the marchers as participants. This was a violation of the *Post's* traditional policies. Managing editor, Leonard Donne Sr. said: "some people found it shocking that they are called on not to exercise some of their personal rights, so that the paper can vigorously defend its own First Amendment Rights." David Broder, the *Post's* venerable political reporter agreed: "when you decide to become a journalist, you accept a lot of inhibitions that come with the responsibility of being part of a private business that performs a very public service."

No abortion rights leaders has suffered the close scrutiny and dedicated journalistic opposition that *Operation Rescue's* Randall Terry did. They harp on his propensity for quoting the Bible and the fact that he has little formal education and used to sell used cars for a living. In contrast, articles on NARAL's Kate Michelman are veritable examples of Orwellian wordsmithery. The news media compare her stand for abortion rights to that of the blacks in the Civil Rights movement in the sixties. Faye Wattleton, a statuesque black woman, was during her long reign as the National Director of *Planned Parenthood*, lionized as a nubian princess with Martin Luther Kingesque qualities. Terry has a different opinion of the media. He believes that most of the secular media has become the lap dog, the ideological slave, of the death industry. The fervor of their commitment to abortion makes them blind to the abuses and injustices that regularly occur.

With legal and judicial power apparently in pro-abortion hands for years to come, it seems only fair that the major newspapers provide pro-lifers with a fair and open forum to express their ideas. Such is not the case. A few years ago, the *St. Louis Post-Dispatch* refused to publish a $25,000 ad submitted by Missouri *Right to Life*. The ad depicted a broken baby doll, representing the horror of abortion. It could have just as easily used a dead fetus submerged in a jar of formaldehyde. The *Post's* management found the broken doll offensive. They argued that the doll did not look like a fetus. It did not look like a baby either. A picture of what an aborted fetus looks like would have been the best visual reproduction of the real horror of what abortion really is. But the *Post* would never have allowed that in its family newspaper. If they had run an ad on the Holocaust, would the *Post's* censors delete the images of stacks of dead bodies? The *Post's* action was a blatant form of news management at best and overt censorship at worst. Censorship is a term the *Post* can only apply to some parent group trying to stop humanistic sex education courses in the public schools or women fighting pornography. It is never applied to its own advertisement policies.

The irony of the rejection of the Missouri *Right to Life's* ad was the *Post's* opposition to the use of real abortion photos that has led MRL to use a broken doll. The *Post* was responsible for this apparent breech of truth in advertising. Not only had the *Post* refused to let MRL use real pictures of butchered unborn children, it prohibited the use of the broken plastic doll. And how can a broken baby doll be offensive, unless of course it reminds the *Post's* editors of the nature of what their editorial policy advocates?

As the director of the Archdiocesan pro-life committee's *Media Watch,* I have followed the *Post* and other members of the St. Louis media with concern and scrutiny. In January of 1993, the broken doll controversy embroiled me in a long debate with the *Post's* publisher, Nicholas G. Penniman. Penniman had been interviewed on KSIV radio, where he adroitly side-stepped the host's pointed questions about the controversial ad. His conclusion that the ad was rejected because it was not suitable for a family newspaper prompted me to begin a prolonged correspondence with him. His paper has run a series of other ads the *Post* deemed suitable for a family newspaper consisting of scantily clad women in seductive poses advertising for the strip shows that dot the east side of the Mississippi River. I told him as one of the 5000 signers of this ad, I feel that my constitutional voice, my free speech under the First Amendment had been severely curtailed. I was unhappy that my name and those of my family had been censored from his newspaper. I told him that the *Post's* bimbo ads were far less suitable for a family newspaper than the pro-life ad which had already been sanitized.

Penniman weakly attempted to defend the bimbo ads. I guess that beauty or lust is in the eye of the beholder. Penniman claimed he had consulted several of his women employees on the suitability of the abortion ad. I wondered if these same women were consulted on the relative merits of the bimbo ads. It is difficult to understand how Penniman and those who dominate his profession can find nothing offensive in the bimbo ads that relegate women to the status of sex toy but regard a broken doll to be in poor taste. Readers of the *Post* have been subjected to a daily dose of horrible pictures of twisted corpses in Bosnia, bloated bellies in Somalia, and the crushed bodies of auto, train, and plane wrecks. Graphic pictures can be very powerful. But the carnage of abortion seems to be the one evil in American society that the press can ignore with impunity. Consequently, the media makes special rules to squelch a movement that cries out for public attention. Penniman also made the point that the ad was rejected as false advertising. I took issue with his statement that MRL's original ad was filled with inaccuracy and untruth. Many medical and ethical experts supported the assertions in the ad. As a point of contrast, I checked the ad from the *Religious Coalition for Abortion Rights* published in the *Post* and found their ad had some very serious and offensive statements in it.

In Penniman's last letter to me, on 9 February 1993, he said our differences on these issues was akin to apples and oranges. He accused me of arguing from a combination of the philosophical and scientific/technical perspective, while for him the matter was one of merely taste. I disagree. Mr. Penniman's newspaper would have seen its obligation to fairly report the news on any other issue and show the abject evil of abortion as an example of man's inhumanity to man or child. Whether he understood it or not, he had granted MRL and people like me the moral high ground.

In 1995-96, I engaged Edward Higgins, then the editor of the *Post-Dispatch's* highly leftist editorial page, in a bitter debate concerning his paper's consistent stance in favor of free and unrestricted abortion. Higgins had made a series of distortive remarks about the Catholic Church's failure to actively support women in crisis pregnancies. As gay Congressman Barney Frank quipped, "pro-lifers love the fetus from conception to birth." Much of his 26 June 1995 editorial was inexorably wedded to subjective polling data, and the fire of his own ideological biases. I reminded Higgins of the famous *Boston Globe* poll of years ago which found, depending on how the questions were worded, 65-70% of the people polled approved of a woman's choice but a similar number thought abortion was murder. This demonstrates that there is a strong strain of cognitive dissonance, coupled with moral ambivalence on the abortion issue. Special care must be given to the nature of the questions asked to find an accurate understanding of current sentiments on this issue. The press too easily selects just that data that appears to supports its prior conclusions. Higgins believes that there is a pro-choice majority in this country. I wondered how he came to that conclusion. I reminded him that every pro-life candidate that went up against a pro-choice candidate in the 1994 congressional elections won. Not one Republican pro-life defeat in nearly 30 different contests! Higgins had also called the Republican bill to outlaw what is commonly known as the partial birth abortion or in medical terminology, "the D&X" procedure, unnecessary because it was a rare procedure. I raised the question, "Just how rare is 'rare'?" Higgins used the term rare to mean a procedure used in less than 0.04 percent of all abortions. Six hundred forty abortions per year. That's not a small number. It sounds much like the number of abortions Dr. Henry Foster did or did not perform. That's more people than were in my graduating class in Xavier High School and Holy Cross College combined. I would have trouble dismissing 640 people that easily. There were only 169 killed in Oklahoma City in 1995, only 230 killed on TWA Flight 800 in the summer of 1996, and 241 marines killed in Lebanon in 1983. The American people were rightfully upset about all of these incidents. We later discovered that there were thousands of these abortions each year.

Partial birth abortion is hideous. The fetus or unborn child is rotated so that the feet come out first. The abortionist pulls the baby all the way out of the womb with the exception of the head. Scissors are then inserted above the spinal column and opened so that a catheter can be inserted to remove the brains from the unborn child's skull: a painful and horrible death. Kate Michelman of NARAL has erroneously tried to obscure the horrors of this procedure by saying that the fetus dies from the anesthesia. This is a blatant falsehood that many doctors have attacked. Former Colorado representative, the pro-choice queen, Pat Schroeder quipped in pure liberal insensitivity, when someone mentioned the pain these babies must endure, "Well so what, child birth is painful too!"

Higgins, who retired from the *Post* in 1997, is representative of most editors who have little understanding of the pro-life movement. Just because the left hand is picketing the abortion clinics, writing letters, etc., it mattered not that the right hand is helping women in crisis pregnancies to the tune of 9000 each year in St. Louis alone since 1982. I reiterated my belief that if newspapers and editorial writers such as Higgins really did believe in a woman's right to choose, they would try to make certain the woman knew all her options. The fact that there are thousands of people willing to help her through difficult times. In a subsequent letter, Higgins argued the fact that since the Catholic Church has always had these agencies to serve women in crisis pregnancies, their antecedence to the anti-abortion movement does not count, so to speak, since it was not a direct by-product of the movement.

The Church has always been anti-abortion. Its universal and historic opposition to abortion has been the guiding spirit for the formation of its crisis pregnancies centers. *Roe vs. Wade* and *Doe vs. Bolton*, in effect, necessitated the expansion of this long-standing charitable imperative and the greater application of aid and assistance to these women. These centers have always been and will always be intrinsically connected to the anti-abortion movement. Higgins' exclusion of the church's organizations conveniently ignored the dedicated service of a legion of pregnancy care centers, such as *Birthright* and *Care Net*, which are neither owned or operated by the Catholic Church. I referred Higgins to Frederica Mathewes-Green's prescient article, *Embryonic Trend* in the Summer Issue (1995) of the *Heritage Foundation's Policy Review*, which states:

> about 90% of the women surveyed said the main reason for the abortion was to please or protect some other person, usually a partner or parents. When asked 'What would you have needed to continue the pregnancy?' The answer was consistent and emphatic: "Just one person. If I'd had only one person to stand by me, I would have had my baby." I seriously doubt that anyone in any of the abortion agencies, *Planned Parenthood* for example, would have been there to help these women through their personal crises.

There have to be moral standards in our society, not just vain exercises in intellectual relativity. As the only newspaper in St. Louis, the *Post-Dispatch* has an undeniable duty to print both sides of an argument without bias. In 1993, I witnessed a woman grieve for her grandson, Andrew, who died just two days after he was born. He was 22 weeks in gestation when he was prematurely born. He was not a potential life! He was alive! After his death, his parents, grandparents, and many others missed him. Andrew had about 50 to 60,000 brothers and sisters of similar gestation throughout this country, who were brutally killed that year—victims in the name of "choice."

One reason the abortion holocaust has paled in comparison with the Final Solution of Adolf Hitler, is that there has been a handful of survivors of abortion. There is nearly a 100% kill ratio in this violent procedure. One of those survivors is a young woman named Gianna Jessen. Not willing to leave anyone alive, some pro-abortion activists have tried to savage her reputation and impugn her motives for witnessing the accident of her birth. In one of our community newspapers, an anonymous writer attacked her story as a cruel and unsubstantiated hoax. Gianna, who was a victim of a saline abortion—she wasn't really born—developed palsy as a side-effect of the trauma of her partial abortion. The major newspapers have treated her remarkable story with silence and abject indifference. Gianna was never featured in the mainstream press. It was as if she had never really been born and if some of them had their way, she never would have. Gianna, is an abortionist's worst nightmare—living proof that abortion is about real people, not just some globs of protoplasm. Her doctors did not give her any real hope of survival. She was not supposed to sit up, walk, or do anything that you would expect in a normal child. Given her violent entry into this world, Gianna is not a normal child in the strictest sense. She is a very special

person, a fighter, who beat all the medical odds. She was later adopted by
the daughter of her foster mother. To this day, she does not know who her
natural mother is.

As a youngster Gianna always wondered why she was sick, had trouble
walking and why she was the way she was. No one would tell her. She
describes her rump-exaggerated movement with good humor as just "Gianna's
walk." She thinks other people walk funny. On a California beach, when she
was eleven, her adoptive mother finally told her the truth of her birth. Word
of her background traveled slowly around the country through religious
groups who urged her to bear witness to her unusual birth experience. The
dominant media will not touch her at all because of what it does to their
special pro-abortion agenda. CBF really should ask herself the obvious question, *what if I am wrong here and what if she is really telling the truth? What
does that say about the abortion right?*

I, along with 20 other pro-life volunteers had dinner with Gianna, in
late October of 1993 after our annual Pro-life Convention. I can tell you for
a fact that she does not have any hidden agenda. I found her to be a warm,
wonderful young woman, whom any man would be proud to call his daughter or wife. She bore no hate nor malice toward anyone. She was still a little
girl in some ways—she had just learned to ride a bike for the first time at
the age of fifteen. All Gianna wanted to do is have a honeymoon in Ireland
someday, ironically the last country in the world where she could have
suffered her mother's pregnancy termination. She is never going to be on
Letterman, Leno, or *Koppel* with her story. An abortion survivor is the last
person on earth anyone of them would want as a guest. Pat Robertson and
the religious right do not have the power to make her rich and famous. To
be on *Donahue, Oprey,* and the like, Gianna would have been better off
being a transsexual nun or a lesbian metermaid. Now twenty-two years old,
Gianna Jessen serves as a poster girl for all the victims of choice who never
had the chance to tell their story.

There are other examples of survivors. The Chairman of *Planned
Parenthood's* board, a doctor named Kenneth Edelin, was initially convicted
in Boston in 1973 for killing a child that survived his mother's abortion.
There is the little girl, baby Ana Rosa who survived the 1992 abortion
attempt of "the Butcher of Avenue A" in New York City, currently serving
a jail sentence. This doctor used a knife on the unborn girl, permanently
severing one of her arms. I hope some insensitive writer will not question
her legitimacy when she's fifteen by saying she was hurt in a hunting accident. When a baby such as this survives an abortion, the newborn is usually
put in a pail which is placed in a closet where the infant is left to die. That
probably would have been Gianna's fate had not some angel of mercy in-
terceded with the usual policy and taken her to a real hospital. To make
certain that these anomalies, these survivors, would not continue to plague
the conscience of abortionists, the partial birth method of abortion was
developed by Dr. Martin Haskell. Haskell has performed over a thousand

of them, 80% of which he states are elective. This would seem to discredit the notion that this procedure is used only on those babies who are seriously deformed. Had Gianna's mother's abortionist used this method, Gianna would have been just another nameless victim of choice.

The callous disregard for human life, exhibited by some of the abortionists described above goes a long way to explain why some pro-life advocates go off the deep end with regard to taking the law into their own hands. During the infrequent times pro-life advocates violently violate the law, liberal newspapers, such as the *Post-Dispatch* are quick to condemn, deplore, and demand federal sanctions for the protection of their secular sacrament. The *Post-Dispatch* was correct however in denouncing the murder of abortionist, David Gunn, and the attempt on the life of abortionist, George Tiller outside his abortuary in Wichita. Even more difficult to fathom is the late John Salvi brutal murder of two *Planned Parenthood* receptionists. Naked violence, even in the name of life and innocence, is never justifiable. Anthony Lewis' column in the *New York Times* usually suffers from an excess of scurrilous negativity on this issue. In a 1994 column, he exhibited the worst prejudices imaginable. The crimes of a few have served his purpose in denigrating the entire pro-life movement. This blatant exploitation of the Gunn killing is an attack, not only on all the peaceful pro-lifers who have been lining the sidewalks, bussing to Washington, and picketing without a hint of disrespect for the law but on religion itself. When the shoe is on the other foot, newspapers, like the *Post*, are really not bothered by the moral violations of these doctors. They only denounce violence that does not suit its ideological ends. Gunn and Tiller, like the rest of Americans, are little more than pawns in the power struggle that dominates the Culture War. What is really important is that the power elite use them to maintain their precarious foothold on the moral agenda of the American conscience. Another example of media bias involved its reaction to the violence following the first Rodney King jury verdict in Los Angeles in 1991. The press' failure to express outrage at the violent actions of the unbridled criminal element implicitly gave sanction to the scores of blacks and other minorities, who looted and killed with near impunity. When the media allot blame, it pointed to the blacks' historic rage and unhappiness at the hands of white racism. Applying the media's logic, it could be said that rage, based on a higher law, inspired these killings, justifying them, in fact, because all legitimate means of stopping the evil of abortion in this country, had been cut off. When legitimate means to effect reform are denied or frustrated, as they were to the abolitionists of the antebellum period in our history, then violence is a definite possibility. The modern day abolitionist—the pro-life volunteer—is not an ideologue when it comes to saving the unborn and their mothers. He will not commit a wrong to right another wrong. John Brown was wrong in murdering slaveholders. But his bloody extremism did not diminish the evil of slavery. On the same token, it is pharisaic for newspapers like the Post-Dispatch to focus on a few random acts of violence when their policy for twenty years has been to sanction the abject violence that has left us with 32 million dead. If the press were consistent, it would denounce abortionists like Tiller and the savage butchery he and his colleagues have inflicted on their innocent victims.

The abortion bias of the press can best be seen in its coverage of federal and legal issues, such as the ill-fated *Freedom of Choice Act*. This act did not merely codify *Roe vs. Wade* as it promised, but would have undone the few restrictions and regulations on abortion that had been established by consensus over the past twenty years like 24-hour waiting periods, parental notification and sex selection. None of these restrictions were the work of a religious-crazed right-wing group but rather reasonable limitations on an outright evil. This act underscored the fact that the abortion rights proponents want the cultural approval of their abortion policies, including the underwriting of each procedure as part of the American string of entitlement. In 1993, the pro-abortion forces launched a new drive to push for government funding of abortion, fetal testing, and the nationalization of the abortion movement, hoping that abortion on demand would be locked as solidly in our governmental apparatus as Social Security and Medicare. Their methodology was nearly as severe as the abortion procedure itself. When they failed to win the battle of ideas, they resorted to *ad hominem* attacks on the character and family of the leading pro-life politicians and their allies.

Newspapers do not have a monopoly of liberal bias. The only other major news media outlet in St. Louis is KMOX Radio, now a Westinghouse affiliate. Years ago it was a bastion of pro-life support and objective reporting. Headed by its stern captain, Robert Hyland the regional vice-president of CBS, KMOX was a tight ship. An indefatigable taskmaster, who functioned on 2 to 3 hours of sleep, Hyland listened attentively to his station's programs throughout the day and night, often calling employees to account for themselves. I worked for him part-time over a two year period and can honestly say he was intimidating. Despite his archaic solutions to problems, he was a man dedicated to the truth and was said to be fair and honest in his judgment. Hyland prided himself on balance and was dedicated to the eternal verities, especially to family values and the unborn. He was a good man who had an enviable dedication to his religious faith, his family, and the radio station he established as one of the greatest in the nation. Since Hyland's demise from cancer, KMOX has gravitated to the left with its news and features increasingly voicing support for the conventional cultural perversions. It does not have a single reputable conservative on its full-time staff and more and more of its hosts exhibit the statist bias that blankets the industry. KMOX's only known pro-life female seemed fearful of rocking the boat or making waves before leaving the station with Kevin Horrigan and others, for the lesser but more lucrative WIBV in Belleville, Illinois in January of 1996. After this shakeup, the station moved even farther to the left.

As a profession, journalism has come full circle. In the Federalist period, as Richard Brookshire points out in his illustrious biography of George Washington, the first president loathed journalists. Virtually all who labored for newspapers were bitter partisans who used their writing skills to ridicule and assault the character and actions of the other side. It was the dichotomy between editors Philip Frenau of the anti-Federalist *National Gazette* and Federalist John Fenno of the *Gazette of the United States* which led to the foundation of the political party system, something that Washington did not believe in. The period from World War II through the Watergate investigations of Woodward and Bernstein serves as the high water mark of journalism. After that, investigative reporters gradually abandoned decorum and ethics and the profession started on a long downhill slide that has seen it merge in function with the entertainment section of the media. In becoming celebrities themselves, news people and television anchors have lost any sense of fairness and objectivity they might have shown in past eras. They have become team players, gravitating mostly to the left-wing of the political strata. In ejecting their professional objectivity, they have gotten too close to the game of politics and the public has, not without cause, identified the Sam Donaldsons and the Peter Jennings with the establishment that is at the root cause of so many of society's ills. Journalists think it is good reporting to seize the political issues from the candidates, give it their gnostic spin, and then tell the people that the result is what they really saw and heard. Many journalists today hold a self-righteous contempt for many of the people they cover. They cherish the notion that their ideals are purer and higher than those in government or business. Most in the media elite have long wised up and dismissed objectivity, says ombudsman Joann Byrd of the *Washington Post,* as a pretension fantasy.

Perhaps unknowingly, journalists wear their cultural and moral prejudices on their sleeves like many talismans that render them impervious to the cognitive dissonance their writing often creates. In sort of a passive conspiracy, while they are openly respectful and even sycophantic to the feminist left, reporters openly display a blatant disgust, if not hostility for the religious right, deriding them to the point of caricature. Even though the majority of Americans are believers in some deity and organized religion, few journalists believe in any religion. This anti-religious bias is enforced not so much by a conscious effort but a news room culture that is becoming increasingly monopartisan and monocultural, even while it espouses diversity and openness. A 1996 Roper poll revealed that 89% of all active journalists had a liberal bias that could not be separated from their work. A liberal Democratic bias has been obvious in the press' coverage of American issues and candidates. There has been no greater, nor more consistent, lie than that the Republican eighties was the decade of greed. Mark Levinnson of *Newsweek* consistently compares it to a second Gilded Age, evoking memories of the infamous Robber Barons. Jeff Greenfield wrote in *Time* that it was a time when the rich got bigger yachts, the middle class foundered, and many of the poor went under. The statistics do not bear up these demagogic claims.

The press had a field day with the 1992 Republican National Convention in Houston. The Republican delegates were frequently referred to as conservative, or ultra right, hard right, or far right. They centered on the mean-spirited speech of Pat Buchanan who opined that there was a Culture War going on, not that the Republicans had declared war on the culture as was widely reported. No such mention of comparable degrees of extreme liberalism were heard in New York. Distortions, such as these have a great impact on public perception. George Bush narrowed the race to under ten points after Houston. After the media spin, his gains evaporated. Before that it was the Anita Hill affair. During Clarence Thomas' controversial confirmation hearings, the general public feeling on him was about 65% favorable. A year later, after a fusillade of liberal bashing of Justice Thomas, his approval rating had slipped to 35%. Over 70% of the American people approved of the Republican "Contract for America" in 1994. Months later, fewer than 27% of the American people agreed with it after the press had "exposed" all of its weakness. When the Republicans surprised even the most astute among the mainstream media with their recapture of both Houses of Congress after a forty-year hiatus, the press went to work on Speaker of the House, Newt Gingrich. Six months after the November elections, Gingrich's popularity had tumbled to less than 20% approval rating. Since when does the Speaker's office warrant a poll? I cannot remember any similar polls taken on the merits or demerits of Thomas Folly or James Wright. A Nexus search revealed that 100% of the stories on him were negative. The press has taken every opportunity it could to savage any politician, clergyman, business leaders, or citizen that appears as a threat to their liberal agenda. Pat Buchanan was subjected to one of the most scurrilous media campaigns in recent history because of the threat he posed to the liberal status quo. Charges of racism, nazism, bigotry, and protectionism dominated virtually all the news stories covering the Buchanan presidential bid.

As has been illustrated throughout this book, the abortion issue demonstrates the liberal bias of the mainstream media. The abortion lobby's allies in the gay rights and environmental movements all have received strong and consistent support from the media in fostering their left-wing agendas on the benighted American public. Had the press been more honest and curious about these issues, the country would not be in the social and intellectual disorder it now finds itself. The press has historically been the guardian of the truth. Attracted to the enlightened agenda of liberalism and the fame attendant it, journalists has sold out the integrity of their profession. Today, too many of them are no more than the sordid promoters of a twisted and outdated ideology that threatens to bring the walls of American civilization tumbling down like a modern Jerrico.

14 / School Wars
America's Intellectual Downsizing

> If this is what they do to the language, think what they do to the children.
>
> —Flannery O'Connor

Historian Henry Adams marveled at the dynamo on display at the Chicago Centennial Exposition in 1876. To him it served as the technological symbol of the advancements of American Civilization. A hundred and twenty years later, the scientific advances represented by the dynamo is dwarfed by the microchip and the information highway. To those of us who are technophobic, this cyberspace world is fraught with danger, misgivings, and deep-seated anxiety. Machines, toys with instructions, and anything requiring electricity or a battery has always sent chills up and down my spine. As a small boy, I think I was frightened by my mother's new vacuum cleaner. Along with this fear was a pathological lack of mechanical dexterity that has alienated me from the world of amps and volts, let alone bytes and megabytes. In high school, I remember with vivid horror taking the *Kuder Preference Test*. My scores on the KPT suggested I would make a good clerical worker. In basic mechanics I scored in the third percentile—that's three from the bottom. That was in a world without calculators, where the word Apple still meant fruit .

As a writer with indecipherable handwriting, the demise of Smith-Corona nearly left me without any visible means of communicating my written word. With the advent of new technology, the myriad of entertainment and educational diversions that have emerged have hastened the decline of the use and enjoyment of the old-fashioned book. Most books bought today are destined to rest ornamentally on the family room bookcase or take up residency in the dusty archives of some misanthropic academic.

Reading has become an obsession with me. Though not in Bill Clinton's league of 300 books a year, I read about seventy to eighty a year. The constant need for more books was not only expensive, but intrusive on my family's living space. Books lined the entrance to my den, stacked three feet high, like rows of colorful stalagmites, forming a narrow path to my desk. Yards of shelves bristled and groaned with the excess weight of more books, stacked and stashed with random abandon. Tables and chairs lay cluttered under more books—some read, others just waiting for their initial perusal. It was my love of books and lack of mechanical skills that prompted me to think of becoming a teacher. I had contemplated law school or business but the arduousness and personal toughness those professions demanded frightened me off. Even then, I perceived that law was obsessed with winning. It was the laudable idealism, evidenced in an old James Whitmore television show, *The Law and Abraham Lincoln Jones,* that attracted me to the law but as I grew older I determined that his kind of lawyer did not really exist. My dad was a retired physician. He quit medicine in the prime of his career because of government restrictions. The world of corporate finance was his second chosen profession and he was very adept at it. Yet he always seemed grumpy, as if he had the weight of the world on his shoulders. He was concerned with making money and that did not appeal to me. I thought it would turn me into a hardened person and I really did not want to become like that.

With this abject sense of naivete, fueled by an anxiety of finding my niche, I gravitated to the wonderful world of academia with my boyish enthusiasm. I had observed many teachers during the course of my education and like the younger brother in *Chorus Line,* I was convinced I could teach as well if not better than most of them. My love of reading provided me with the ideas and information I needed to teach. As many other dreams we have, the reality of life proved otherwise. The world of education is not what I thought it would be. It has become another battleground, perhaps the most vital battleground, in the Culture War. The real enemy here revolves around the idea of secular humanism, the educationally pernicious philosophy initiated by John Dewey. In the true spirit of the Enlightenment, Dewey hoped to create a new secular religion that would do away with traditional religion.

In a speech in Philadelphia celebrating the Bicentennial in 1976, Leo Pfeffer, a lawyer who has represented several left-wing groups including the ACLU, discussed the role of secular humanism in the Culture War. His vision was for an America "in which individuals enjoy maximum freedom of thought and expression, sexual freedom, no unwanted children, and control the population of the poor." Pfeffer singled out Catholics for their repressive social morality opposed to contraception, abortion, and homosexuality as wanting to force their beliefs on the rest of society. The secular humanists have a great fear of the Catholic School system because parochial schools have a significant impact on the culture. From that impact there is a possibility that a society would come into being where there were "no divorce, no contraception, no abortion, no obscene books or pictures, no homosexuality." What the secular humanists fear is a society "where social mores were congruent with moral law, specifically the moral law regulating sexual behavior."

Since secular humanism has dominated the typical public school curriculum, academic and moral standards have tumbled. Poor people and lower middle class parents cannot afford to send their children to private schools as do more than half of the children of public school teachers in some communities. To help these people break the shackles of poverty through education, Republicans have attempted to institute the concept of school choice. According to liberal Democrats, choice is good when it involves the dismemberment of an unborn child, but bad when it concerns allowing school children, many of them poor and black, to go to better schools. Without fully understanding the ironic applications of his language, President Clinton's Secretary of Education, Richard Riley, has described those who want school choice as people who seek nothing less than dismemberment of the public education system. Parents who lobby for the choice of better schools for their children do not want to bring down the public school system. They are simply sick and tired of the violence, miseducation, and ideological brainwashing that passes for education in too many of the public school systems across the nation. It has been the public schools' monopolistic control on their children that has inspired them to force this vital reform.

No one opposes school choice more than the *National Education Association*, a power-laden union with great lobbying ability. It is more concerned with raising teachers' salaries and establishing itself as a political force on the national level than it is in educating the nation's children. The NEA is a federally charted corporation that is uniquely privileged. As a professional organization, it is exempted from property taxes. It has a near monopoly status in that it is a supplier to the government-enforced monopoly consumer. It is dominated by the left-wing ideology that emanated from the works of Dewey. School choice is a direct threat to the NEA's power and influence. In 1994, they spent over 15 million dollars to defeat a school choice initiative in California. In 1996, they lobbied Democratic and Republican senators to defeat a program in Washington D. C. that would have given school choice vouchers to a few thousand parents so their children could attend local private schools. Coupled with Clinton's threatened veto and Senator Kennedy's plan to filibuster, the plan was defeated on a procedural vote. As John Leo wrote in his 11 March 1996, column in *U.S. News & World Report,* Democrats routinely argue that the poor should have the same options as the middle class and the rich, even if it takes public funds to provide them. All these party instincts are suppressed when the subject is schools and the lobby applying pressure is the major teachers' union, the NEA. According to Leo, the NEA, the giant dinosaur of educational policy, is the largest single reason why the public school system seems almost impervious to real reform. It is no surprise that the President of the United States has served as standard-bearer in defeating school choice. The NEA has exercised great power within the Democratic Party. One of every eight delegates at their National Convention in New York in 1992 was a member. The NEA has a symbiotic relationship with Bill Clinton. On his way to the 1992 Democratic National Convention that nominated him, he stopped off for a visit with then NEA president, Keith Geiger, and promised to invite him to sleep in Abe Lincoln's bed at the White House. In effect, the NEA's agenda is hidden behind the much abused wall of separation that has been erected between religious and public schools. Former Assistant Secretary of Education Diane Ravitch points out that both the Head Start program and public scholarships to college provide models for choice—in both cases public funds legally follow students even to sectarian institutions.

During the Eisenhowers years, the educrats of the public schools realized that what they needed to guarantee their power and control of the public school system was a large infusion of federal funding. Federal money would serve as the lever through which the NEA could consolidate its power and control over each school district. Funding would provide a nearly limitless supply of money that would not suffer from the local control of school boards, parents, and local taxpayers. Once local control by school boards passed to the centralized offices of the Washington bureaucracies, the NEA was free to coalesce its own dominions of power without the interference of parents and local boards. The educrats who run our schools are engaging in what may be termed educational fascism, the merging of the business of teaching, as represented by the NEA, and the federal government through the Department of Education. The federal government's control over education began in earnest during the Eisenhower administration after the Soviet Union launched Sputnik, the first earth-orbiting satellite on 4 October 1957. The nation's educators went into immediate shock at this crisis. Within the context of the Cold War, Sputnik was a grievous defeat for the country. Our military leaders and politicians feared that this seminal event would herald the Soviet Union as the leader in the space race with all of its military and scientific ramifications. Science had not enjoyed a primary seat at the education table. I never had a science course of any kind during my eight years of primary education, which incidentally ended in June of 1957. Since then billions of dollars have been expended and America's education seems to be in worse shape than it was in the fifties.

In 1976, Democratic Presidential candidate Jimmy Carter promised the 1.8 million members of the NEA that he would lead the charge in forming a National Department of Education in return for their support. The NEA delivered and Carter is rightfully credited with being the midwife at this department's birth in May of 1980. Opponents of this new department immediately pointed out the unconstitutional nature of this new bureaucratic contrivance. They stressed the idea was not new and had actually been recommended by former National Chairman of the Communist Party USA, William Z. Foster, in his 1932 book, entitled, *Toward Soviet America.* He boldly predicted that the schools, colleges, and universities will be coordinated and grouped under a National Department of Education and its state and local branches. The studies will be revolutionized, being cleansed of religious, patriotic, and other features of the bourgeois ideology. Foster also recommended that students be taught internationalism and the general ethics of the new Socialist society. Sounds like the beginnings of the global village school room.

The NEA was founded by a group of socialist educators that included John Dewey in 1857. These educators firmly believed that schools should be owned and controlled by the government. The original founders preferred the old Prussian system of education that was strongly committed to spiritual neutrality and statism. They demanded that parents surrender the rights of their children to the state because young minds were easier to mold without parental interference. With this in mind, it is not difficult to realize why there is no room for God in the public school classroom. John Dewey expounded his belief that existing classrooms were too rigid and detached from reality in his book, *Progressive Education.* He stressed that children learned better by doing in a less structured, more flexible educational setting where students and teachers had more of a casual relationship. The goal of the progressives was to define "useful" subjects and then create schools that taught those subjects. Over the years it would appear that progressive teachers did not consider subjects like math or reading useful. They were more intent on implementing more practical items, such as driver's education, sex education, and moral relativism. Dewey was also instrumental in introducing behaviorism into the public school classroom. We now know this as "Outcome Based Education." In devaluing cognitive thinking, Dewey and his associates emphasized telling students what to think instead of teaching them how to think. Education, or the fostering of authentic learning, was not the goal of his philosophy. He wanted to demonstrate that by manipulating children's minds teachers could get them to behave in a specific way, even to the point of changing the way they viewed society. Teach the child, not the subject became the catalytic tenet of Dewey's philosophy.

In 1896, Dewey became the head of the Departments of Philosophy, Psychology, and Education at the prestigious University of Chicago and enjoyed a broad and widespread influence in the molding and shaping of generations of elementary and secondary school teachers. His influence literally reached into every community in the country. Dewey created the Laboratory School, where the curriculum was adjusted in order to test all of Dewey's theories and ideas. Dewey's thinking was a boon to secular humanism by undercutting the basic tenets of the Judeo-Christian faith but replacing thinking subjects with feeling subjects.

From the very beginning, these humanistic founders of the NEA carried on Dewey's tradition of dislodging the Judeo-Christian way of thinking from the halls of learning. True descendants of the French Enlightenment, the NEA still insists that humanism is a philosophy and not a religion. The true definition can be found in Dewey's own *Humanist Manifesto I,* which states "Humanism is a philosophical, religious, and moral point of view." This would seem to place the implementation of humanism in direct violation of the Constitution which prohibits an establishment of religion or at least a violation of the wall of separation of church and state that has so obsessed our educators and jurists today. The federal government doles out $70 billion a year for what it euphemistically calls education. The Department of Education spends $33 billion a year in administering nearly 250 different programs. The rest is allocated between 300 programs by 30 other federal agencies. The educational system, which has nose-dived since the 1950s, is top heavy with the bureaucratic weight of duplicative and redundant programs, caught in a maze of waste, mismanagement and governmental inertia. Federal spending imposes a costly burden of paperwork on local schools. A 1991 survey showed that in the Ohio school districts, each school must complete 173 federal forms and reports.

While the weight of government red tape and paperwork is making it increasingly more difficult to teach, illiteracy has reached epidemic proportions. The more money spent on education, the worse the education seems to become. *Borst's First Law of Education* reads: "Money drives out true education!" By shifting the focus away from teaching to money, school boards and teachers' unions foster a management/labor conflict that short changes student education. There is a diabolic plan now working its way through the public school system that threatens to turn the nation's schools into Orwellian institutions that will limit the freedom and choice of Americans. The national and state governments will decide for our children where they are to go to school, for how long and what professions they may attempt to enter. In 1994, the Democratic Congress passed the Federal *School-to-Work Opportunities Act.* There was scant mention, let alone analysis, of this bill by the national media. This act set up a national structure, requires the 50 states to implement its basic provisions of downsizing intellectual content, tying schools in with jobs, providing the infrastructure for the socialization of all labor in this country. This was followed by the *Goals 2000 Act,* which Clinton also signed that year. *Goals 2000* requires schools to adopt standards and the *School-to-Work Act.* This laid the groundwork for using high schools to train students for occupations selected by the local labor market. The federal government is now gearing itself to exert power over every individual's ability to earn a living. If Americans let the government decide what jobs young people may be trained for, what certificate qualifies them to be hired, and then track each individual's performance and behavior in school and in the workforce on a national computer data, they will suffer a precipitous loss of personal freedom. *School-to-Work* is about creating a planned work force for the 21st century—one which is politically correct, which won't expect a lot out of life, won't ask a lot of questions, and won't challenge their masters. Their ultimate goal is centralized control of all labor in the United States under the guise they are preparing them to compete in the global economy that's sure to dominate the next century. The creation and control of human capital is to be used as the state sees fit. If this model seems familiar, it is patterned after the Soviet system idea of centralized control of labor. The state will teach American children only what it wants them to learn. Once our children's abilities have been molded, the state will determine what jobs or careers they may enter, based on the needs of the society.

In the state of Missouri, the ball was put into motion by Governor Mel Carnahan and several of his cohorts that included Marc Tucker president of the *National Center on Education and Economy*, a think tank that pays board member Hillary Clinton an annual $100,000 fee. Carnahan signed *Executive Order 95-11* on 12 May 1995 on the final and busiest day of the 1994-1995 Missouri General assembly. No more than a handful of Missouri legislators were even aware of this sweeping executive action. He did it in this manner, so the full intent and scope of this bill would remain a secret for as long as possible. Once Missouri's plan is in effect, federal moneys will follow to the state coffers and there will be no turning back. This plan, dated June of 1995, is a 116-page document entitled, *School-to-Work—Missouri's Roadway to Success*. Under this plan every child in America will have to have a *Certificate of Initial Mastery* (CIM) in order to continue their education beyond the 10th grade. This includes everyone in private, public and home schooling. To get this certificate, the student has to pass certain standards, politically correct standards that have more to do with psychological/social engineering than academic achievement. If a student fails to meet these standards or rejects the indoctrination, that student must continue a re-education process until he or she gets it right. After graduation, students will have to have another certificate—a skills certificate, as a prerequisite for hiring, promoting, doing business overseas, etc.

Work force or job placement boards are being put in place across the nation. Their purpose is to identify all future jobs that they perceive to be needed, then special mentors will direct students towards occupational training to fill those needs, whether this is what they want to do or not. Everyone must participate in this closed ended system for it to work. Another feature of this bill is that its sponsors intend to devalue college education. About 30% of America's college age youth attend college and universities today. This plan attempts to reduce it to about 15%. So much for school choice.

In an 11 November 1992 letter—a summary of his meeting with David Rockefeller, and John Sculley of Apple Computers—to Hillary Clinton, Marc Tucker of the NCEE explained how involved this new system would be. He stated that "his system is interwoven with a new approach to governing that we create a seamless web of opportunities, to develop ones skills that literally extends from cradle to grave and is the same system for everyone." They planned to establish this within an intricate web of supportive legislation that will be so complicated that once the entire system is in place, nuclear weapons could not dislodge it without destroying the entire educational system. The group's master plan was to remold the public schools into a national human resources development center which would be guided by clear standards that define the stages of the system for the people who progress through it. Tucker's seamless web effectively establishes the government's authority at every stage of an individual's education. The labor market boards would decide which jobs would be allowed. The schools would train students for jobs selected by these boards and the new general education standard would be a prerequisite for enrollment in all professional and technical degree programs. Under his system, schools would be required to provide information to government agencies in a uniform format. This all has the making of establishing the *Socialists States of Amerika*. Not only could this happen in America, it is happening in America.

There is a *Careers Bill*, now pending, that expands the *School-to-Work* program, perfectly tracking the Tucker letter. The bottom line is total government economic planning with students as the pawns in their social engineering exercises. This will in effect give the federal government the power over every individual's ability to earn a living. Combining the American labor system with the failure to teach children to read and the intellectual downsizing process, known as *Outcome-Based-Education*, American children will get a third world education and third world wages. The establishment wants public school graduates to be content to compete with workers in foreign countries who work for 1/40th of American wages. That's what they mean when they say Americans must compete in the global economy and become citizens of the world. The reasoning and philosophy is closely akin to that Ira Magaziner put into the First Lady's health bill.

Through OBE, the NEA is attempting to reinvent society by radically changing what is taught and how it is taught, in our public schools. *Goals 2000* is the culmination of years of careful planning by humanistically inspired educators in the mold of John Dewey. Like Dewey's Laboratory School, this program is designed to manipulate thought and de-emphasize the cognitive skills that are really needed for advancement into a more complicated world. Government call the *Goals 2000*, a lifelong learning plan. President Clinton let some of the truth out of the bag when he said that our schools, would become laboratories of democracy with American children as the guinea pigs. The real intent of this program is to shift allegiance of our children away from family and country and redirect it toward global citizenship and one world government. As President George Bush said, "We are preparing our children for the *New World Order*." When First Lady Hillary Clinton writes about our children, *It takes a Village*, she does not mean literally the village of the old African proverb but the modern version of the state *in loco parenti*.

Under *Goals 2000*, the federal government would determine national standards for school spending, create uniform requirements for schools and class size, and dictate the curricula for all public schools. The plan is to eventually mandate these standards for all schools, including those students privately and home educated. Once this happens, the notion of school choice or the need for local school boards will be rendered moot. While our educational bureaucrats' rhetoric states that compliance with this plan will be voluntary, scrutiny suggests something less. Any state wanting federal funds must submit standards to the US Department of Education, explaining what students are expected to know and do. If these state standards do not meet the federal government's own criterion, funding will be most likely refused. So the message will be for these states to conform or suffer the loss of tax money.

One of the objectives outlined in *Goals 2000* is that students will project anti-racist, anti-biased attitudes through their participation in a multi-lingual, multi-ethnic, culturally diverse curriculum. The use of the word project demonstrates that *Goals 2000* is not about learning or understanding but about brainwashing students with what these educators think is the proper way of looking at the world. Sadly absent from this program is signs of any moral training. This values-neutral curriculum dictates that students teach themselves. They are told that they must determine what is right and wrong through experience and experimentation. Given their age and lack of rules and regulations on morality, it is not difficult to see why students are confused about premarital sex and drug use. Their limited experience has not prepared them to make moral decisions on many of these issues. They need the adult guidance of teachers who can warn them of the various pitfalls that their undisciplined behavior might lead them. In place of real teaching, their educrats tell us that their system is values-neutral, which is in a pluralistic society an oxymoron.

There is also a constitutional question to be considered: where in the United States Constitution is education mentioned, let alone delegated to the federal government to legislate the schooling of the nation's young? The federal government has no legal right to impose curriculum requirements or dole out funds according to the whims and the political aims of federal officials. This is just another example of the government's usurpation of state power and jurisdiction. *Goals 2000* and its allied plans have particularly ominous consequences for the education of minorities. According to Dinesh D'Souza's book, *The End of Racism,* the educational bureaucracy's prescription for students of color is that need to be clustered in class to give each other moral support. Blacks learn in groups and have trouble dealing with individual one on one teaching. There is strength in numbers is the real underpinning here. There is more of a chance to use loud language, profanity and the threat of disorder to stave off the intellectual corrections of an overwhelmed teacher.

These educational bureaucrats also had a special concern for the education of homosexuals. The *Chronicle of Higher Education* devoted thirteen consecutive pages to AIDS and homosexuality in a 1994 edition of its publication. People infected with AIDS were elevated to the holy status of saviors of the Republic. As Thomas Sowell pointed out in his 19 December 1994 column in *Forbes* magazine, no such beatification comes to those suffering from cancer, Alzheimer's or other diseases that kill far more people than AIDS. Sowell goes on to state that this is only "the very tip of the gay iceberg." Sowell underscores the fact that from kindergarten to the universities, propaganda for homosexuality has become one of the hallmarks of

American education, and double standards favoring homosexuals have not been far behind. The brief flurry caused by the use of books like *Daddy's Roommate,* and *Heather Has Two Mommies,* in New York's elementary schools might have made it seem that such vain attempts at indoctrination were the exception and not the rule. The gay life style was put on a par with that of traditional heterosexual relationships. Films showing naked couples of both heterosexual and homosexual relations have been shown to elementary school children in sex education courses all over the country. Ostensibly, these sex education courses state they are designed to reduce teen pregnancy and stave off the epidemic of sexually transmitted disease among the young. Behind the outward exterior is the hidden part of their agenda which is to lessen and eradicate moral revulsion and resistance to gay practices. By falsely emphasizing the heterosexual's risk in contracting the deadly disease, the proponents of these courses, especially *Planned Parenthood,* have used the fear of AIDS to infiltrate and propagandize the homosexual lifestyle when it is that lifestyle that has been largely responsible for the spread of AIDS.

While public schools show gay and pro-choice propaganda in their classrooms under the rubric of education, they will not allow any information about the nature of contradictory views, many of which have a religious or moral foundation, under the misdirected Jeffersonian principle of separation of Church and State. Try to keep *Heather Has Two Mommies* out of the schools and it is censorship. Any attempt to introduce films, advocating pro-life and pro-family views as did Westchester County teacher, William Wienecke did by showing "Ultrasound: A Window to the Womb," to his seventh grade class and you can get relieved of your teaching duties. Progressive teaching methods are behind the decline in academic standards and performance within the public schools. One philosophical culprit here is the so-called "Whole Language" method. This system was in place when I learned to read in 1949. Our "Dick and Jane" readers were infantile attempts to make us learn words by recognition. We would read the same words, run, see, look, jump, and play so many times in the course of a story that eventually we would recognize the words by sight. The overwhelming disadvantage is that this limits students to recognizing, not understanding words. That's how the Chinese language is taught, since it does not have a phonetic alphabet. The only way to learn the language is by memorization and sight recognition. It takes ten years of devoted study to become literate in Chinese. I spent eight weeks in the Summer of 1965, studying it at St. John's University and I realized how difficult the Chinese language really is. The English language has a phonetic alphabet, containing 44 different sounds. There is no need to teach reading as if it was made up of thousands of different ideographs.

The summer before my last year at Holy Cross, I volunteered to teach a third grade boy who had been struggling with the basics of reading. To prepare myself, I took out Rudolf Flesch's seminal book, *Why Johnny Can't Read!* from my local library. Ironically, my student was a shy, chubby, little boy whose name was not Johnny but Walter—Walter Reed. Once I started running him through the several lists of sounds and sound groups in Flesch's book, as hard as I tried, the little boy just did not seem to get it. To this day, I do not know if my efforts were in vain, but after that experience I became hooked on phonics. All of my children studied phonics in school. My daughter was reading well when she was five-years old. In kindergarten they wanted to accelerate her because she could read rings around people in the third grade. I thought phonetics was here to stay.

Since the Department of Education came into being during the Carter administration, phonics has been devalued. Pedagogy has demanded that teachers go back to "Whole Language" to teach students the proper way to read. The Whole Language method teaches children: (1) to Guess what the story is about by looking at the pictures on the page and thinking about them. (I do not remember seeing any illustrations in Tolstoy's *War and Peace*.); (2) to predict what will happen next by looking at the picture; (3) to skip over words they don't know or recognize; I could have used this method in "whole math." Students are given books with lots of pictures and told to look for clues. Under no circumstances in this absurd educational system is the student ever asked to sound out the words. That would be heresy under this backward philosophy. Teachers are encouraged to take a constructivist approach to teaching. What this means is that each individual student must inevitably develop or construct his or her own meaning from the content. To these facilitators, education is not mere reading, listening, and repeating what others tell them. Each student must subjectively derive meaning or make sense of his own world.

This approach is a lowly handmaiden to situation ethics or values clarification. It is really a low-budget form of deconstructionism which is so popular in higher education. The research and writing of "Investor's Business Daily's" Matthew Robinson, who reported that there was a new high in educational theory making the rounds in California—subjective mathematics, supports this contention. He found that a guide to teaching math advised teachers that "their job is not to judge the rightness or wrongness of each student's answer. Let those determinations come from the class." This view has turned democratic education into intellectual anarchy where truth is thrown out the window in favor of some group dynamic of social conformity. Actress Tracey Ullman was so upset by this approach to learning that the British film and television star sent her young daughter back to England for her formal education. According to Ullman, her daughter Mabel could not spell her own name but knew who she was. Ullman was afraid that she would end up as "dumb as a mudflap." At the root of this nonsensical education system is the belief that competition is bad for the student psyche since their feelings will be hurt if they are not among the brightest. This is a patronizing egalitarianism that says it is protecting the child, yet its end result is that students are not at all prepared to deal with the inevitable hard knocks that will cross their paths for the rest of their lives. It is akin to the racists attitude that assumes blacks are unable to fend for themselves, are endowed with so little natural and intellectual skills that they need the guiding elite to run interference for them. Games, whether in gym or with other schools, spelling contests, any kind of physical or intellectual competition are frowned on because of this attitude. Basic facts have no place in this attitude. This is not a content based method of teaching. Teachers of OBE believe that it is not as important to know when the Civil War was fought or what the capital of Georgia is as long as the student can establish priorities to balance multiple life roles. As a result, the public school system is producing millions of students with diplomas that only mean that they have not been in trouble with the police for four years. They are often worthless pieces of paper that represent an education devoid of any substance or factual content. Highly skilled in their own feelings, this illiterate subclass of students will be lucky if they can find their place in the unemployment line without difficulty. As intended by the reigning pedagogy, they will become dependent on their liberal masters for their subsistence and their self-worth. Their own responsibility is to re-elect, their liberal mentors who maintain them in their dependent existence.

When I was in college, the ruling philosophy of Holy Cross, primarily a boarding school, was that the college was to serve *in loco parenti*. Since my parents were 165 miles away, the college would be responsible for my welfare, health, and well-being as long as I was under their supervision. Holy Cross was even a little less demanding then my parents. I remember there was bed check during freshman year but they never made me clean my room or told me what clothes to wear. I once wore the same light tan pants for 21 consecutive days. I liked the way they fit and after a few weeks they could stand up by themselves in the corner of the room. By the seventies, most colleges and universities had divested themselves of this responsibility and the college campus was forever changed. In an effort to create a freer and a more open academic atmosphere, these institutions of higher learning threw out the baby with the bath water. By transforming privileges into rights the university lost much of its special ardor and ambience by allowing for the free association of men and women in their dormitory rooms. The absence of rules and regulations, without corresponding virtues and responsibilities turned quickly into chaos and anarchy. The dorm became an impossible place to study, sleep, and rest. Dirt, filth, and squalor often became the rule, rather than the exception as civility and respect for school property hit a new low. Frequent sex and near orgies dominated campus dormitories around the country. Freedom ruled at the expense of harmony, morality and fraternity.

In many ways, the public school system is maneuvering to serve *in loco parenti* to students of all ages. While this was acceptable and even laudatory at the college level when parents were far removed from the college campus, on the lower levels it is an approach that is fraught with danger. Behind the failure of our schools could be that the reigning pedagogical philosophy views the school not solely as an educational institution but as a social service institution. Educational leaders seem intent on converting the schools into a one-stop community/health/training/employment centers. The public schools' mission is to serve as the government nanny, that is, as a provider of round-the clock services, including counseling, infant care, drug abuse, domestic violence, sexual practices, medical care, and job placement. Schools are not for education any more but for government welfare, government medicine, and job placement. Their goal today is not to turn out educated citizens but welfare recipients, medical and psychiatric patients, and worker ants for the global economy.

The purpose of the health portion of the schools' new mission is to prepare students to accept socialized medicine as the standard course of medicine in this country. The federal government is establishing the public schools as beachheads in leading the American people to be dependent on government for their health care needs. The Clinton health care bill had 40 pages devoted to comprehensive school health education, that would have provided $400 million a year for school-based clinics, popularly known as condom clinics. It would have included funds for all kinds of health and social services, counseling, and even abortion referrals. To get the money to open a clinic, the school had to agree to set up a local community partnership that had experience with providing services to at-risk youths. This language was designed to allow *Planned Parenthood* and its odious philosophy to pollute the school system and operate these condom clinics. Even though the Clinton plan failed to pass, the partnership between schools and the Department of Health and Human Service continues to provide the schools with enormous amounts of money to pursue these goals without official legislation.

The key to catching almost all school children in this tangled web of socialized deceit is the categorization of "children at risk." Schools have a financial incentive to classify as many students as at risk because the more students a school has that come under this heading, the more federal cash the schools' coffers receives. In conservative Utah, 47% of its public school children are classified as at risk. An at risk child includes any student who, because of his or her individual needs, requires some kind of uniquely designed intervention in order to achieve literacy, graduate, and be prepared for transition from academia to post-graduation. This could and does mean just about anything school administrators want it to mean, from a lack of goals to gender disorders, to students working part-time jobs. In effect, this broad definition reveals that this policy is just a device to bring most if not all children into the social service web, to hire more social welfare personnel, and to demand more tax dollars. The Clinton administration wants to start the socialization process as early as preschool. Former Surgeon-General Joycelyn Elders wanted to get children as early as three years old into this system so they could be trained and molded into whatever the government wants them to be. Adolf Hitler knew the value in brainwashing the impressionable youth of the Uaterland before reason, maturity, and good judgment developed. The Marc Tucker letter included this cradle-to-grave agenda that these social planners have for the American public. This might also explain the government's high regard for establishing day care centers around the country. In this way beleaguered middle class parents can drop off their impressionable children for brainwashing without parental interference.

The mantra for co-opting infants and preschoolers into the social service web is, "it takes a village to raise a child," the African proverb Hillary Clinton filched for her 1996 book on children. Incurable utopians, such as Mrs. Clinton, do not believe in a permanent human nature. If they did, they would have to give up their notion of the evolutionary nature of mankind. A constant in all utopian thinking is the necessity of removing children from the care of their parents. From the early days of Communism in France in the 1840s, it was accepted that the Communists wanted to remove all children from their parents before the age of five because parents would teach their offspring moral values that would hinder the formation of the Party's collective ideals.

These utopians have lost faith in God. They substitute the love of mankind to fill that void, substituting the modern social gospel for those of Matthew, Mark, Luke, and John. This is the same intellectual underpinning that has been witnessed in the ideological aspirations of the Hillary Clinton's pet project, the *Children's Defense Fund.* By village, Mrs. Clinton and her allies do not mean the extended family, unless we include our figurative Uncle Sam and Big Brother into this sociological equation. Raising a child requires a mother and a father and most parents do not want their roles co-opted by impersonal, mostly anonymous, government employees. Their village system is designed to include everyone within its sticky web. It is only a matter of time until legislation will attempt to bring the private schools and the homeschools under the federal mantle. Bills such as these usually include language, such as "all children deserve to be cared for," or "children will be healthy and contributing members of society," or "health and wellness are responsibilities shared among individuals, families, communities, local governments, and the state." It is just another example of the statist mind, vowing to bring everyone together under the big tent of dependency. Of all the subjects that have been devalued under this federal and union assault on education, it is History, especially American History, that has suffered most. A 1996 report about the American public schools students' general ignorance about American History revealed appalling, but not surprising, results, given the fact that many social studies teachers, products of the countercultural, anti-American animus of the sixties, have nothing but disdain for the country that gave them opportunity and freedom. Half of the 22,000 students surveyed by the Education Department were unaware of the Cold War and nearly six of ten knew little, if anything, about the foundation of our republic.

People who are unaware of their past are disconnected from the temporal flow of things. They can not have any understanding or bearing on the forces that propel their society. I have always loved history. Having taught history for several years in colleges and universities, I have sometimes put myself inside the subject, looking almost outward from the past. The factual side of history is the easy part. There is little doubt that Lincoln was shot on 14 April 1865, or that the United States dropped the atomic bomb on Hiroshima in 1945. What is difficult about history is determining what it all means. Interpretations confound historians as much as trends confound economists. On the first day of class, I usually enumerate several theories of history, starting with the cynical denunciations of Henry Ford who termed all history "as bunk." I have always taught that history is the study of man's human nature in time and space. In the first volume of his herculean study, *Order and History*, Eric Voegelin wrote that, "History is the revelation of the way of God with man." There are other major schools of history that include the evolutionary beliefs that events have flowed into each other without purpose or reason. I believe that history is the study of the effects of man's fallen nature or original sin. Another school, based on gnostic assumptions, believes that history has been the progress toward some grand terrestrial culmination and perfection—a progress sometimes impeded but certain of ultimate victory. This futurism advanced by the positivists, such as Condorcet, Comte, and Marx, has dominated the writing of popular history for many years until the wars, genocides, and terrorism of the 20th century made many rethink its basic assumptions.

When I was in elementary and high school, much of what was taught bordered on American propaganda, especially with relation to the subjects of slavery. But I seriously doubt if I would ever echo the sentiment of Stephen Decatur, who said, "may she always be in the right; but our country, right or wrong." The same idea also applies to our schools, local communities, political parties, and even the Catholic church. Loyalty and patriotism must never be confused with a blindness that automatically resists any criticism. The truth is what makes us free from such automatic attachments.

What usually passes for American History in the nineties classroom is a propaganda of another nature—one more virulent and negative tone that ultimately destroys the basic concepts of nationhood, patriotism, and citizenship. My criticism of my country's history has always been tempered by a profound respect for the men and women who, though fallible and imperfect, created and established a country that has had no equal since the beginning of time. The United States has had the soul of a church. It has always recognized its spiritual roots and has made honest and sincere attempts to right the many wrongs of its past. America will always inspire in me a profound love and a deep respect, though not a blind faith, to the country's past as I understand it. History as it is taught today is a far cry from these sentiments. Today's universities are largely staffed with liberal and Marxist historians who seem to hate the country they write and teach about. As if on a holy quest to correct all the wrongs of the American past, they make no excuses about destroying any patriotic faith their impressionable students might have for their nation. They contrast this stark and audacious combination of falsehood, innuendo and fact, with a subliminal respect and compassionate overview of the socialist states of the world. Their ideological annihilation and deconstruction of American ideals create in their students the worst kind of emptiness and hostility toward their own heritage. It is analogous to the outrageous ideology that has turned a generation of American women against their own children.

Lewis Lapham, the editor of *Harpers Magazine,* blames the sorry state of education on religious fundamentalists who want to take us back to the days when children were taught differently—a period in which they were truly educated. As Lapham said: "across all of the world's time zones, the adherents of one or another of the ancient superstitions wage their furious assaults on what for the last two hundred years has been known as the Spirit of the Enlightenment." He continues in this frame of reference when he said: "it is in that spirit, beginning with autonomous man rejecting God and wisdom that does not come from the mind of man, that has produced more deaths at the hands of governments in this century than any other period in history." As an apostle of enlightenment, Lapham is blinded by his own bias against organized religion and transcendental truth. He fails to recognize the fact brilliantly detailed in R.J. Rummel's seminal study, *Death By Government,* in which he details the many millions of noncombatants killed in the twentieth century by the anti-religious governments in Russia, China, Cambodia, Nazi Germany, Vietnam, and Japan. In *1984,* Orwell wrote of the memory hole in which "all history, all books were to be put down this hole to erase people's memory of their past so totalitarian forces might move in and create a new history." That is what the real enemies of education and of history have done in America. For them, blaming people who believe in a Power higher and greater than themselves is like blaming gravity for killing them when they jump off a tall building.

A third school in this debate is the cyclic school that believes that historical events happen in cycles—what goes around comes around. There are certain stages of growth, maturity, and decadence that recur somewhat predictably and inevitably throughout the ages, but there are usually so many new variables scientific certainty is out of the question. Oswald Spengler gave a powerful voice to this theory with his book, *The Decline of the West.*

Russell Kirk has professed a fourth theory that I fully subscribe to that believes that history is the "record of human existence under God, with meaning only in so far as it reflects, explains and illustrates the order of the soul in society which emanates from divine purpose." It's purpose is to reveal the true nature of being. As Voegelin wrote as his opening sentence in *Israel and Revelation,* "The order of history, emerges from the history of order." History reveals mankind striving for an order of existence within the world while attuning itself with the truth of being beyond the world, and gaining in the process not a substantially better order within the world but an increased understanding of the gulf that lies between immanent existence and the transcendent truth of being. This God-based historical understanding of reality comes closest to my own understanding of all the forces that play upon the study and understanding of history.

The modern education system, especially with regard to our history, has been front-loaded with elitist propaganda that does little to give students a firm foundation of knowledge that will prepare them for the modern world. One recent survey found in many cases that four periods of the school day were consumed by non-academic subjects, such as the environment, sex education, driver's ed, and physical education, and even then much of the core academic subjects has been ruined by submission to the political agenda of the multiculturalists. Some teachers believe that it is more important to study fourteenth century African kings than it is to study the Magna Carta or the American Revolution. As a result, students graduate from high school without the faintest idea of what their own country is all about.

The *National Standards for United States History,* started by Lynne Cheney under the Bush administration, was repudiated in the Senate by a vote of 99-1. While it was originally a voluntary system, it would have had the effect of providing an official knowledge, sort of an official ideology that would have thoroughly repudiated the vaulted origins of the American nation. Cheney later complained that this result was not what she had intended at all. The *Standards* are a 271-page document that attempted to brainwash students with left-wing revisionism that has been flooding the nation's public schools. It was supported by all the left-wing establishment societies, such as the *American Historical Society,* which I belonged to in graduate school. The study sent most prominent American political and military figures down an Orwellian memory hole, replacing them with what Phyllis Schlafly, calls *Oppression Studies.* This discipline featured third-rate feminist and minority writers who attacked Western Civilization as racist, homophobic, sexist, and oppressive.

Its aim was to limit diversity of thought—a sort of one-size-fits-all mode of teaching that would literally dull and dumb down the cognitive faculties of the students of the future. Its history goals would have expurgated American history of all the important figures in traditional history, such as Paul Revere, John Hancock, and the founding fathers in favor of a legion of references to minority figures, such as Harriet Tubman. Disproportionate references were made to the KKK, McCarthyism, and Richard Nixon. This is an ideologically driven program that will produce a generation of students who will not only be ignorant of the prime movers of the country's past, but will have a racially and historically disjointed understanding of the nation's origins and past.

The loss of a firm knowledge of our past is already happening. The *National Assessment of Educational Progress in History* found that 57% of our high school seniors lacked a basic understanding of American history. It starts right from the beginning. The term "BC" has been eliminated to read, instead of Before Christ, as "BCE," Before the Common Era; and "AD" has been reduced to "CE" or Common Era. Instead of learning or reading about history, students are using their imaginations to create fictional conversations among historical figures, role-playing fictional situations, and writing fictional diaries of such historic figures as Christopher Columbus. Columnist Don Feder concluded "it almost seems a conspiracy to create a nation of amnesiac sheep easily herded in the desired direction. How can you understand yourself or the significance of current developments if you know nothing of our society's origins and evolution?" It is ironic that at a time when students need a challenging curriculum to enable them to compete in the world marketplace, our colleges and universities are eliminating requirements and embracing the latest academic fads.

It is apparent that *America 2000/Goals 2000* is moving the nation toward a New World Order. In line with OBE, this educational system focuses on what the student is, not what he knows. It is designed for every student to feel successful although he might not be successful. This behavior methodology is a psychological approach that makes students compliant to business and government, willing adherents to the fascist structure that awaits us in the New World Order. This approach will effectively break the spirit of competition or natural achievement, lessening our abilities to compete in the world marketplace.

The real message is that under the guise of national educational reform, *Goals 2000* aspires to completely restructure society. In light of this plan, I quipped on the radio one day that the goal of *Goals 2000* was to have a 100% illiteracy rate by the year 2000. This is precisely what this kind of anti-literacy and anti-education program is designed to do. You might ask why would teachers want to foster more illiteracy and less education? The point is that socialism thrives on the ignorance, naivete, and misinformation of the middle class. A non-thinking citizen is a person who will not realize, or even care about, what the educated elite are doing to his culture or his society. A non-thinking individual can easily be distracted by the bread and circuses of a calendar filled with ESPN, MTV, and the Jerry Springer Show. They will be easier to govern, easier to fool, and their property will be easier to tax and even confiscate. We are quickly moving toward what Charles Sykes has called the *Dumbing Down of Our Kids*. The country has an "educational system based on the language of the therapeutic culture, the cant of the social workers, psychotherapists, and guidance counselors, which dominates the usual public school statement of philosophy."

The situation is just as serious on the college and university campuses. The *National Association for Scholars* published a report in 1996 that traces the devaluation of higher education. The report shows that requirements in modern language, math and science, composition, and prerequisites had drastically shrunk since World War II. The debasement of higher education has had one advantage. It has enabled college administrators to shorten the school term, meaning less time wasted in classrooms by its faculty. Georgetown University has voted to drop Milton, Chaucer, and Shakespeare as requirements for English majors. In place of these old masters, it is possible for an aspiring English major at Georgetown to substitute courses such as *Gender and Science, History and Theory of Sexuality, Unspeakable Lives: Gay and Lesbian Narratives, Women, Revolution and the Media,* or *How Tasty Were my French Sisters.* According to Georgetown professor John Glavin, this was done because we want students to be aware that there are problems in Shakespeare's plays with the way women are portrayed. It is now possible to go through four years of college at a major school or university and not encounter a single serious subject.

The *Modern Language Association* of America holds its annual convention which displays the sordid and mindless extent to which the politically correct way of thinking has permeated academia. Columnist John Leo attended one such convention in 1993 that attracted 11,000 college teachers of language and literature. On the intellectual menu were such diverse offerings as *Jane Austen and the Masturbating Three-Button Jacket, Between the Body and the Flesh: Performing Lesbian Sadomasochism, The Poetics of Ouija,* and *Transvestite Biography.* The air was thick with incantatory words such as hegemonic, privileged, and dominant. In one room, a professor railed against white supremacist patriarchal capitalism, adding that capitalism must be destroyed in our time. A Yale professor mocked a donation to her school that would have set up a chair for Western Civilization: why not a chair for colonialism, slavery, empire, and poverty? Nowhere could Leo find anyone who talked about the relative merits of literature. This academic *Gong Show* was only concerned with the politics and ideology of teaching within a society whose basic structure they all despised. As Leo put it, these vacationing ideologues "are suffering from a swarm of radical 'isms,' but the central one, totally dead in the real one, is Marxism," a vulgar Marxism adapted by British radicals. Leo described their basic philosophy when he wrote: "whether we acknowledge it or not, everything we do or say works to support our ideological interests." Realizing that all creative writing is already political, the left works to reveal literature as the expression of an elite ruling class.

With this situation in our schools, our nation's future appears bleak unless the schools are recaptured from the secular humanist. In itself, the school could be the most important battleground of the Culture War. People of religious conviction are attempting to enter school board elections and turn the momentum around. The loss of a sense of history, nationhood and civic roots is a most serious problem. Columnist and unsuccessful Republican candidate for the presidential nomination in 1996, Pat Buchanan, has written, "If a country forgets where it came from, how will its people know who they are? Will America one day become like that poor old man with Alzheimer's abandoned in the stadium, who did not know where he came from, or to what family he belonged?" The future is indeed now with regard to American education. Something must be done and done quickly.

15 / Theology In a Wasteland
Movies, Television and Sports

If this is America's team, woe is America!

—William Bennett about the
Dallas Cowboys in *Sports Illustrated,* 1996

Every time I sit in a darkened theater, waiting for the featured film to begin, I am amazed at what a truly remarkable art form the movie is. Larger than life, these cinematic productions can transport us to unimaginable worlds of adventure or romance with a little social commentary often subtlety thrown in. They can do this much more quickly and more vividly than any book or radio could ever do. As anything else, they can be a power for good or a power for evil.

At the conclusion of World War II, our national leaders realized the unmitigated power and influence of the motion picture industry. The Communist influence, real and imagined, seemed to be everywhere. The controversial *Dies Committee,* followed by the *House on Un-American Activities Committee,* conducted several hearings probing the Communist sympathies of many of the directors, producers, and writers in Hollywood. While this issue has been consistently tainted by liberal apologists in the media and on the university campuses, the revelations of the Venona Dispatches and the opening of the KGB files, it is apparent that there was a good deal of truth to many of these accusations. Ronald Reagan, who also was the president of the *Screen Actors Guild,* launched his political career on the basis of his opposition to the Communist activities of many of his cinematic colleagues.

With this brief historical synopsis, it is obvious just how important this industry can be to the culture of a nation. The movies, not only reflect social taste and mores, they also can influence and shape them. I have always liked the movies and have seen hundreds over the course of my life. The advent of the VCR and Blockbuster videos has only increased the volume of time spent studying and involving myself in these cinematic wonders. While Martin Dies and HUAC were looking for Communists and their fellow-travellers, the real importance, and with that its real power, is the mental and social effects its musings have had on impressionable young minds of the nation's children. In the thirties and forties, when censorship and movie production responsibility were more acceptable ideas, Hollywood grudgingly complied with strictures against fostering anything but the strict standards of the country's Judeo-Christian moral code. The *Legion of Decency,* the powerful organ of the Catholic Church and the Hays Committee, listened and watched every action of Mae West and Bette Davis with strict scrutiny. Separate beds, even for married couples, and the often-mocked one-foot-on-the-floor rule persisted on the screen well into the 1950s. The conclusion of World War II unleashed a torrent of social forces that traditional gatekeepers could not totally allay. The movie industry bided its time, unable to thwart Frank Capra from making his *It's A Wonderful Life,* which has touched generations of Americans with its warmth, human interest, and message of hope. Hollywood's moguls complied but deeply resented this kind of artistic censorship. Cultural statements, especially those about sexuality, had to be left until another day. Sex on the screen or in music was implied and never crudely portrayed. Sexually explicit magazines were virtually unattainable for adolescents. What few there were often contained nothing more sinister than black and white photos of happy nudists frolicking on the beach. Priests and nuns sternly moralized on just how far on a girl's body you could tread before entering sinful waters.

As an adolescent, I idolized all the male stars, Reagan, Alan Ladd, John Wayne, and Randall Scott. Their female co-stars were little more than window dressing for their male leads. Women usually had passive roles, as men of action—in war, the open range and the back alley—were the focal point of most of the plots. The violence on the screen was sanitized, much like we would recreate in the backyard. As in our backyard games, there was a lot of verbal shooting, and a great deal of falling down but everybody got up and went home afterward. Hollywood violence was like that. Death was imaginary and certainly not permanent. Heroes and their trusted sidekicks were only winged or suffered flesh wounds. Only the bad guys seemed to die—and that was good. This underscored the belief that God was in His heaven and there was justice in the world. Granted, this is not reality—films, after all, have been and always should be relegated to the realm of fantasy. With today's emphasis on realistic and bloody violence, simulated sexual intercourse, and vulgar language, Hollywood has long stepped over the boundaries of reality into a nether world of surrealism. I would argue that we are now seeing the negative cultural side effects of illegitimacy, divorce, and drug abuse as an indirect result of Hollywood's brazen promotion of libertine life styles.

After I had reached puberty, I noticed how film actresses began to make more of an impression on me. I did not know what decalogue or cleavage meant but I remember how hard it was to look at their faces, so overtly were their breasts thrust in the audience's faces. If I remember anything about the movies of the fifties, it was Anita Eckberg, Gina Lolabrigita, and, of course, Jayne Mansfield. Most of their acting took place on the beach, where women had shed more than half the clothes they had worn only a generation before, or in the Sahara Dessert where belly-dancing and harems opened greater possibilities for voyeurism. These sexual but subtle liberties did lay the basis for the license that would follow in the sixties and the seventies. The popularity of James Bond indicated a new moral code was in place in Hollywood. Bond was a patriotic hero of the Cold War whose unmitigated hedonism never seemed to distract him from saving the world from Spectre. His moral superficiality and sexual promiscuity, couched in a debonair sophistication, made vice seem attractive. The James Bond movies were to sex what *Easy Rider* and its flamboyant message of freedom was to the nascent American drug culture. Peter Fonda, Dennis Hopper, and Jack Nicholson used their formidable acting talents to break down the barriers and boundaries that society had placed on discouraging drug use.

The dike of moral restraint with regard to nudity on the screen showed its first fissure with the critically acclaimed movie, *The Pawnbroker*, which included a black prostitute bearing her naked breasts on the black and white screen. Despite this scene's relevance to the film, its remittent effect was to give Hollywood the opening it needed to turn artistic freedom into a slippery slope of sexual license. Movies such as *Bob, Jane, Ted and Alice, Carnal Knowledge, Joe,* and *Midnight Cowboy,* followed, all of which weakened the limits society would stand for. Promiscuous sex, both male and female full frontal nudity, all kinds of verbal vulgarity, wife-swapping, drug use, and homosexuality became the new standards that drove the Judeo-Christian ethic from the screen. Since then, Hollywood has dug its collective heels in and resisted the religious movement that has attempted to bring motion pictures more in focus with the standards of the past.

Hollywood's cinematic pandering has had a devastating effect on the country's teenage population which frequents the movies more than any other group. The standard school curriculum has not been teaching much critical thinking for the past thirty years, so a teen's attitudes toward life, love, religion, future, careers, the environment, have been molded by the Hollywood image-makers. Susceptible young minds see characters on screen having free and uninhibited sex. Most of this libidinous activity is without risks, without pregnancy, disease, or love. Old standards of mutual respect and chastity were fast being replaced by the motto, *everyone is doing it, so there is something wrong with you if you are not.* The late flamboyant mayor of New York, Jimmy Walker, once quipped, "No girl was ever 'ruined' by a book!" Maybe that was true in 1926 but I would venture an educated guess that several girls have been "ruined" by many of the movies they view today.

There is also a conspicuous absence of religion in movies today. What was the last film you saw that depicted a family that was not either secretly or publicly dysfunctional actually going to church on Sunday morning? When was the last time you saw a movie that portrayed religious figures as anything less than raving, maniacal crazies, intent on violence, rape, incest, unadulterated lust, or bestiality? The religious are portrayed as not only out of touch with reality but real obstacles to the utopian fantasyland promoted by these moviemakers. *Cape Fear* with Robert Mitchum and Polly Bergen was a spine-tingling genre film, depicting themes of rage, vengeance, and a strong hint of pedophilia, as Mitchum stalked not just Bergen but her underage daughter. The modern version of the film by Martin Scorsese revamped the Mitchum character as a born-again, Bible-quoting lunatic whose obvious dementia permeated the entire film. His body was grossly disfigured with tattoos of bible verses and crosses. The obvious message here was that too much of the Bible or religion will turn a person into a demented, mad-dog rapist. There are so many movies like this that they represent more of a cliche than a viable artistic mode. Actor Kiefer Sutherland is quickly establishing himself as the stereotype of the religious right fanatic. In the powerfully dynamic movie, *A Few Good Men,* he plays the only Christian character, a Southern religious fanatic who used force to effect his twisted goals. In *An Eye For An Eye,* Sutherland is identified early in the film as the man who viciously raped and murdered Sally Field's daughter. While en route to stalk his next victim, there is the brief, but noticeable shot of a crucifix dangling from the end of his rearview mirror. In the 1996 film, *A Time To Kill,* he again plays a Southern fanatic, who joins the KKK, spouting his belief in a white supremacist God.

Hollywood has also taken another avenue down the road of undermining the pillars of American society. Not only do many young people get their sense of morality from films, they also learn most of their notion of American history in the darkened theater, from the cinema. In the thirties and forties, Hollywood viewed the world through the lens of its overtly chauvinistic films. American was good and its heart was in the right place. American films glowed with the nation's nascent promise of serving as a beacon of light for the world. Thanks partly to liberal Hollywood producers, screenwriters and actors, this noble attitude has degenerated under a multicultural barrage of angry anti-Americanism that has emanated from the turmoil of the McCarthy days and the debacle in Vietnam. America is now the enemy of the world. Our soldiers are brutes, rapists, and violent misanthropes. Oliver Stone stands at the head of the class in depicting the blatant evil of the Vietnam era. His films, *Platoon* and *Born on the Fourth of July,* take historical facts and mix them with his Marxist mindset to spew out an unappetizing blend of nation-hating self-loathing that the impressionable youth of today think is actual reality. After all, why would Stone lie? Unless of course, it is his obsession with the liberal twist on everything that was once good and decent in this country's past, as if his celluloid sermons will crush and destroy the last vestiges of the country's Judeo-Christian past. Hollywood has also desensitized its audience to violence. The bizarre hit movie *Pulp Fiction* was a pseudo-sophisticated attempt to blend philosophical ruminations with blood and guts, vicious, matter-of-fact brutality and savagery. It lent a comic air to much of the gore, so as to make it more appealing. It is no wonder young people are confused and think nothing of murdering someone who gets in their way. There is little, if any, remorse attached to murder and certainly no need for forgiveness or repentance. Killing is a profession, like being a doctor, a lawyer, or a salesman. The black killer here was also well versed in the Scriptures. Before sending his victims into whatever darkness he might have perceived, he quotes the Bible at length to them. The subtle message is that religion can be a dangerous thing. The only way to normalcy in this country is to purge yourself of any sort of religious training or trappings.

The *New York Times* focused on this movie in a Sunday feature on evil. Even the most liberal publication realizes that something is wrong with our society and maybe there is such a thing as evil. Hollywood has not been able to figure out the nature of its evil but it goes on forcefully selling its perverse message—man is a law to himself. The most pernicious thing that Hollywood has done to our young is having sold them the dark aura of hopelessness. Many of the heroes in today's films are without religious and philosophical moorings. They act on impulse, or internal codes of honor based on the strong sense of existentialism that permeated the writings of Ernest Hemingway. It is man against the evil dictator, capitalists, the elements, his own country, and the demons within. He has nothing to help him but his own physical and mental strength and perhaps a winsome young thing to ease the savage beast within. His soul is empty and his vision is limited to his immediate problems. The *Die Hard* trilogy underscores what movie critic and social commentator Michael Medved has called a "plague of pessimism," in an address given to Hillsdale College. In his experiences as a movie critic and lecturer, Medved noted that the biggest threat movies have for the young are not that they will imitate the behavior they witness on the screen but that "the underlying message of hopelessness conveyed by these ugly, consistently dysfunctional images in our society—a message that encourages both self-pity and fear." This subtle conditioning of the young is responsible for a generation of depressed and hopeless youth who are so bored with their lives that they seem devoid of any real meaning. One need only read the obituaries for teen suicides, which is nearing epidemic proportions, to realize that there is noticeable hollowness in their lives—an abject sense of loneliness, isolation, and alienation from a world that has lost any real value or meaning for them. Meaning and hope are intimately related to the future. The recent rash of school shootings merely adds to this.

What kind of future world does Hollywood predict? I have been taken aback by the plethora of films that depict the future world in surrealistic terms. Life seems much worse. All social norms and decorum that is civilization have broken down. Gangs and tribes rule their turf with an iron fist while social and moral anarchy reigns everywhere. Medved notes the tragic irony in this situation:

> the spread of democracy, free market ideas, and liberating technology has spectacularly brightened the prospects of our children

and grandchildren—those same children and grandchildren who are so powerfully addicted to the media's grim fantasies that they seem paralyzed by pessimism. As if in an unredemptive mode of self-fulfilling prophecy, Hollywood producers have done everything in their power to create the social climate that would inevitably lead to this dystopia.

While abetting the cultural slide into a slough of depravity, Hollywood sanctimoniously warns and frightens young people that the world they will inherit, will be infinitely worse than the situation they live in today. It is no wonder they are depressed.

If the future is not enough to depress young people, Hollywood has employed the use of a new threat—that of the environment as the placid lives of the American population are threatened with natural disasters, emanating from earthquakes, floods, fires, urban violence, and even twisters. With the apparent end of the Cold War, the fear of thermonuclear holocaust has been replaced by a new scare, that of environmental holocaust which fits right in with the apocalyptic environmentalism of the Ted Turners and the other prophets of doom. Hollywood has also attempted to fulfill its liberal agenda with a consistent salvo of R-rated films. Most of these bombs are usually panned by the critics. The public has voted time and time again that it does not like this ever-increasing flood of insipid and sordid films that degrade actors and lessen the inhibitions of its patrons. Two such examples will suffice. The director that gave the movie public a peak at Sharon Stone's pudenda, in *Basic Instinct* also did *Show Girls*, a film so poorly conceived that it had absolutely no redeeming features and *Jade* another sordid film of sexual perversion and herniated plot. Films such as these are nearly comical because their pretentious attempts at artistic expression are so vapid and translucent that the average movie-goer can see through them in an instant. Both films were box office disasters.

There are exceptions to the rule—Mel Gibson's magnificent movie *Braveheart* and *Forrest Gump* pulled on the heartstrings of the American public. Gump was a man who suffered through an unimaginable host of personal problems, tragedies, and disappointments and yet maintained his dignity and integrity with a sense of hope and concern. His travails included being born not only retarded, but crippled and fatherless. In an obvious lapse into moral relativism, his devoted mother even slept with the school principal to keep him out of Special Education. He is laughed at, beaten upon, loses the only girl he ever loved, sees his friends killed and mutilated in Vietnam but never loses his sense of hope and honor. The left-wing critics called the movie "sappy," a sort of feel-good movie that belonged on the shelf with Jimmy Stewart's *Wonderful Life*. Yet it won the Academy Award for Best Picture of 1995, which proves that the general public has not been voided of its capacity for appreciating good movies. But as Medved reminds his readers, does this movie sound like a feel-good movie? If Forrest had been more in tune with the mentality of the 1990s, and our crybaby culture, he would have been entitled to innumerable claims to self-pity and victimhood—as someone who was severely 'mentally challenged,' the son of a single-mother, an abandoned Vietnam vet, the husband of an AIDS patient. The most important message of the movie, according to Medved was the homespun wisdom of his mother, captured in the phrase about life being like a box of chocolates. "You never know what you are going to get." This is reminiscent of Shakespeare's words in *As You Like It:* "Sweet are the uses of diversity." The greatest legacy parents can give their children is the encouragement to make the most of their challenges and adversities. If they act upon that sage advice, then life can be as richly sweet and rewarding as Gump's box of chocolates. An interesting message for a Hollywood that offers nothing but the vinegar of pessimism.

Television is not much better. We, as a people and as a culture, waste too much spare time in front of the boob tube. Medved also made the point that the major problem with the media today is not too much sex or too much violence or too much rude behavior; it is too much TV, period. The quality of television has degenerated to such a dull and boring level that I do not even waste a moment watching any program that does not feature some athlete in a uniform playing some sort of game. The sitcoms are at such an insipidly low level that you would have to be a dim-witted ninny to see any value in them. The only bright spot is an occasional good movie, but again they have sunken to the level of the disease or the female victim of the week. Shows like *Roseanne* border on the maliciously sarcastic. *NYPD Blue* has brought brief nudity and locker room language into the prime time hours so that parents have to spend all of their spare time monitoring programs to see if they are appropriate for children and thereby, creating another fissure in the already-weakened structure of the family. Medved advises parents and teachers to combat the published statistic that the average child watches 26 hours of TV a week. He urges these same parents and teachers to make their children and students keep diaries and logs to monitor the content and extent of their viewing. If these children cut their viewing time by just a half-an-hour a night that would leave an extra three-and-a-half hours a week to read, study, dream or take stock of one's life.

The real cultural wasteland is relegated to the daytime hours. Though the soaps have glorified adulteries, fornication, and sordid activities, it is the talk show that has promoted every perversion, addiction, and malady in the country. With the decline of organized religion and the failure of many people to take advantage of the penitential aspects of religion, the confessional has come to television with the likes of Phil Donahue and Sally Jessy Raphael serving as high priest and priestess. Their shows legitimize these perversions and seem in a heated contest to beat out the competition. The *Jenny Jones Show* proved to be deadly as one of her guests later shot another guest over a homosexual advance made on the air.

The *Jerry Springer Show* makes me feel degraded whenever I have tuned it in. In light of the so-called five sexes, as defined by the Beijing Conference in 1995, Springer's show once revealed what I perceived as a "sixth sex." He was a redneck, dressed in the standard uniform of bib overalls and plaid shirt. The large man sported a thick beard, a baseball cap, and sunglasses. This Southern gentlemen from the hills was upset by a previous show's guest, a transvestite black man, who swished around in a miniskirt and a tight white blouse. If there are straight men and women, gay men and women and bisexuals for the five genders, then this black man in the plaid skirt was indeed a sixth sex. The redneck was also a homosexual but felt the sissy black gay was giving real gay men, like him, a bad reputation. This show was highly reminiscent of the great controversy that raged in Nazi Germany in the early years of the Third Reich between the two factions of the gay netherworld of the Nazi regime, the Ulrichs/Hirschfeld Femmes and the Brand/Friedlander/Roehm Butches. To make the show more exciting, they brought the effeminate black man on stage to confront his antagonist. All of a sudden the screen went dark and when it returned, the white homosexual with the bib overalls was being helped from the floor, his hair askew with his glasses and hat in his hand. The black man was not such a "woman" after all and he had decked the loudmouthed gay redneck. Only in America would people view this as serious entertainment.

Television can also be used to spread the liberal agenda. The NBC production of *Roe vs. Wade* is a good case in point. It was nothing more than pure propaganda. There was no portrayal of the child. All the main opponents of abortion were men, characterized as unfeeling and insensitive plagued by self-doubt. There were no female advocates of pro-life. That McCorvey lied about her rape was made to seem insignificant. Linda Ellerbee did a Maxwell House Coffee commercial. Everyone familiar with the issue recognized her as a leading spokeswomen for Choice. She has done many pro-abortion commentaries seen on cable TV.

Ellen Russell the actress playing McCorvey says erroneously, "I just got no place to go. I can't give up another baby. What could it possibly be like to have a kid out there, getting his butt kicked and you just don't even know?" There were a number of homes for unwed mothers that she could have availed herself of and it is hard to fathom the logic of a mother who would rather see her child dead than take a possible beating in the school of hard knocks. The whole tenure of the movie was to treat adoption with contempt and suspicion. This movie pushed the bromide of abortion as a cure for welfare.

Sports is another segment of this entertainment three-pack that has suffered greatly under the new cultural rules that have permeated American society. The old *Saturday Night Live Show* had Garrett Morris play a Hispanic baseball player whose comic refrain was "baseball bin berry gud to me!" I have always been able to offer a hearty "ditto" to that sentiment until recently. Baseball, as well as all the other major sports I have watched since an adolescent growing up in Queens, has lost much of the magic that so enriched my live for so long. Baseball players, such as Roger Kahn, immortalized in *The Boys of Summer* such as Pee Wee Reese, an octogenarian retired in Florida, and Duke Snider, still handsome and debonair despite his conviction for income tax evasion, served as my early heroes. I set my calendar by their many exploits. Most of my leisure time was devoted to studying the minutiae of their glamorous lives and memorizing all the statistics that gave life to their accomplishments. My life was enriched by the pristine and mathematical beauty of the game they played. Baseball, as well as other sports enhanced my stay on this planet, providing so many warm emotional and exciting experiences they gave joy to my youth. The thrill of the Brooklyn Dodgers winning the pennant almost every year, followed by the draining emotional letdown of their losing the World Series to the hated New York Yankees, seemed to signify an era gone forever. I often feel sad for the young boys of today and in the future who will not experience that glow and that warmth of being a youngster in New York in the fifties. Even the eighties, the thrill of my first World Series game in 1982 between the Milwaukee Brewers and the St. Louis Cardinals and the 1986 World Series with the New York Mets and the Boston Red Sox, meant so much to me at the age of 43. In 1989, my first and only Super Bowl played in Miami between the San Francisco 49ers and the Cincinnati Bengals provided me with a great thrill and an opportunity of bonding with my second son, Matthew. But no sport has meant as much to me or permeated my early existence more than baseball. In many ways, it serves as a metaphor for life itself.

The 1994 baseball strike allowed me time to focus on my long relationship with the game. The more I thought about it, the more I realized what an integral part of my life baseball had been. One of my most pleasant memories was the afternoon I spent watching the Brooklyn Dodgers play at Ebbets Field on television. The grass was real and the fans did not need any escapees from an aviary to cheer for the home team. Roy Campanella, the Brooklyn Dodger Hall of Fame catcher, once said, "to play baseball you have to have a lot of the little boy in you." His axiom equally applied to me as a lifelong fan. I have not only played the game as a youth, I have studied it, written several short books about the game, and met many of the players I saw play as a child. Some of my greatest contributions to society concerned baseball. I am considered by many to be a baseball expert. I define expert as someone who knows 20% about something that most people know just 10% about. I have appeared on dozens of radio and television programs talking about my love of the game, including a three-and-a half minute spot on the *NBC Today Show*, with Gene Shalit in 1974. I even had a local access cable TV show called *The Baseball Professor*, in 1982. Two years later, I founded the *St. Louis Browns Historical Society*, which has as its goal the resurrection and the maintenance of the Browns' historical record. It is a club of 450-500 members that has published books, established a memorabilia wing at the St. Louis Cardinal Hall of Fame across from Busch Stadium, and made the general public aware of the accomplishments of the team that moved to Baltimore after the 1953 season. Whether I like it or not, my name will always be associated with the team's memory. I ran into Joe Garagiola on the field before the second game of the championship series between the San Francisco Giants and the Cardinals in 1987. I had interviewed him for an article in 1974, well before my work on behalf of the Browns. Joe is one of the few men I have ever met who can light up a room just by walking into it—even if that room holds 20,000 people. As I attempted to reintroduce myself to him, he looked at me with his deep Italian eyes and said, "Oh yeah, St. Louis Browns, St. Louis Browns!" Then he walked away. I didn't know what to say.

My dad was forty-six when I was born. I remember playing catch with him just one time. I proudly wore the brand new glove I had gotten for my fifth birthday. After just a few tosses, I fell, skinned my knee and started to cry. My dad responded by abruptly walking me home, thus marking an abbreviated end to an early rite of passage. I learned early that there is "no crying in baseball!" By the time I was forty-six, I had ended a nineteen-year run of painfully blocking balls in the dirt, hitting fungoes, and shouting instructions during hundreds of my sons' games and practices.

My dad took me to my first baseball game when I was ten years old. The Dodgers won that game in the 9th inning on a Pee Wee Reese home run homer to right field in the Polo Grounds. From that moment on, the quiet Kentucky shortstop was my hero. Years later, we sat on the verandah of his modest Louisville home. I sipped twenty-year old Kentucky bourbon while he had cookies and milk. In 1984, like a proud son, I sat in the bright Cooperstown sun as Pee Wee was inducted into the Baseball Hall of Fame. For my eleventh birthday, I begged my dad to take me to the Pittsburgh Pirate/ Brooklyn Dodger double-header, on Labor Day, at Ebbets Field. He refused, saying that a twin bill would take too much time. He offered a night game in exchange. The Dodgers lost to Hoyt Wilhelm and the Giants, 5-3. They also lost both games to the Pirates in the double-header. A tall, lanky first baseman, named Bob Skinner, had a career day with a couple home runs, one a grand slam and several runs batted in. The next year I started taking the F-train from Queens to the games at Ebbets Field with boyhood friend, Eddie Smith. I can still recall the distinctive smell the old ball park emanated. It was a curious mixture of spilled beer, smoke, sweat, and peanuts that made the game even more enjoyable than listening to Red Barber or Vince Scully on the radio.

For my thirty-ninth birthday, I did see the Pirates play a Labor Day double-header, but this time it was in St. Louis and against the Cardinals. I took my six-year old son Matthew with me. We got there early for batting practice. Nine hours later, with two innings still to play, he begged me with his sad, tired eyes to please take him home! My dad had been right, a double-header was too long.

Two years later, on a family trip to Hawaii, Matt and I decided to visit the grave site of Alexander Cartwright, the real founder of baseball. With apologies to Cardinal broadcaster, Mike Shannon, "old Abner Doubleday had not done it again!" Legend has it that the only thing he started was the Civil War, since he was a young Union army officer at Fort Sumter in the Charleston, South Carolina harbor in 1861 when war broke out. We took the #8 bus to Honolulu where Cartwright was buried. I had read that Babe Ruth had visited the site in 1939 and had respectfully placed a flower lei on his grave. The leis from our airport arrival had already wilted so we did the next best thing. Matt had some bubble gum cards with him. Fittingly, we left a cardboard image of Yankee great, Lou Gehrig on Cartwright's grave.

At the 1994 St. Louis Baseball Writers' dinner, I stared shyly at the tall, lanky, worn figure of Bob Skinner as he signed an autograph for a young fan. The child in me wanted to go over to him and berate him for what he had done to my eleventh birthday. The adult said, "have another drink." That Bud was for baseball, my dad, my two sons, and me.

Baseball is indeed a religion for many of us, a game played in "Green Cathedrals." My favorite quote comes from famed announcer, Bob Costas, a personal friend of mine since 1974, who would make an excellent Baseball Commissioner if given the necessary power and leverage. He once said "baseball is the best metaphysical proof of a God. Only God could make a game as perfect as baseball." Saint Thomas Aquinas could not have put it better.

Something is missing from baseball in the nineties. It seems to have lost its poetry, its magic and perhaps its heart and soul. I wish I could be as optimistic as the owners and players are who boast of increasing attendance, a future of inter-league play and a true World Series in Mexico or Japan some day. But I still have my memories of green grass, baggy uniforms and Mickey, Willie, and the Duke roaming the New York outfields, to get me through the bad times.

There will be bad times. Baseball's temples are overrun with money-changers. The game is seriously threatened with a deeper greed than that which seduced Shoeless Joe Jackson and his seven White Sox teammates in the 1919 World Series. I seriously doubt that there is a Kenesaw Mountain Landis or a George Herman Ruth waiting in the wings to resurrect the game. It is arrogant and greedy owners and petulant and greedy players catering to the whims of an ignorant and turgid public that has created the game's current malaise. Add to the self-indulgent musings of cynical sports-writers who have put their petty and inconsequential selves above the purity and essence of the game and you have a sport that is in critical, if not terminal, condition. Something has happened to my enjoyment of the game these past few years. Perhaps it is the exorbitant prices, the callous threat of a lockout, or the hollow enthusiasms of insipid announcers. I almost believe that it was the same kind of relative morality that gave us astroturf, the Houston Astros, multi-colored uniforms, and the Designated Hitter—all to the detriment of the game's transcendent values. Players and owners broke a covenant, or a sacred trust as Costas so cogently put it on *Nightline*, with fans in 1994 when their greed and insouciance caused them to cancel an unbroken string of ninety straight October Classics. Not since proud and feisty John McGraw refused to meet the champions of the upstart American League in 1904, the Philadelphia Athletics, had there not been a World Series in the fall. Two world wars, Korea, Vietnam, a Depression, the Cold War, several recessions, an earthquake, and the first year of the Clinton Presidency all had NOT deterred the games from being played. The strike broke my heart and took away the game that had given so much joy to my youth, a youth that lasted over forty years.

My alienation from the game that gave such joy to my youth can also be generalized to sports in general. Through the magic of cable and the satellite dish, fans today are inundated with innumerable games that seem to go on forever and forever. Sport seasons used to be neatly divided, to nearly parallel nature's quarterly distinctions. Baseball was for spring and summer—long, yes, but well worth it. Football was for late fall and winter. Communications technology, especially television, developed stations just begging for programming. To fill this need, new sports of all kinds were developed to appeal to a mass culture that was literally crying for entertainment—a cotton candy for the mind. At first I welcomed this as a good thing. I had always kept up with the individual teams, players and statistics. As the number of sports and the roster of players continually expanded, it became nearly impossible to keep up with it all. In 1959, there were two leagues and sixteen major league baseball teams, one league and twelve professional football teams, eight basketball teams in one league and just six hockey teams. I could easily keep up with the major players in all these sports.

It was inevitable that greed and an increase in population would demand that there be more teams. Daniel Boorstin, former the director of the Smithsonian, wrote of Boosterism in his book on *The Americans*. He contended that every town in the 19th century yearned to be big league, that is, increase its own self-identity or self-esteem if you would. Nothing does more for a metropolis' self-image today than having big league franchises in all major sports. St. Louis has suffered the indignity of losing several teams throughout the years, including the Browns in baseball to Baltimore in 1954, the Hawks in basketball to Atlanta in 1966, and the Cardinals in football to Arizona in 1987. Some years ago the city nearly lost its hockey team, the Blues, to Saskatoon, Canada. Each of these franchise shifts hurt and embarrassed the city as badly as any divorce ever hurt the respective partners in a marital union gone bad.

This constant sports expansion has resulted in their now being thirty major league franchises in 27 cities with the addition of the Arizona Diamond Backs and the Florida Devil Rays in 1998. With 40 players on a roster, that means that there are approximately 1200 major league baseball players active over the course of a season, compared to roughly 640 in 1959. Football has grown just as fast, with 32 franchises in 31 cities. Basketball now has 29 teams, including two Canadian franchises, added in 1995. Hockey has 26 teams scattered all over the Northern Hemisphere. Add to this the inordinate growth of college basketball and football, where several hundred teams are tracked each and every week. A remote control has become a virtual necessity to surf the air waves for all the games that are broadcast at all hours of the day and night. The 1996 Olympics with its overt commercialism was a sad reminder of just how materialistic the world, led by the United States, has become. My mind and ability to follow all of this has finally reached what my pair of "C's" in Economics taught me in freshman year at Holy Cross, something Samuelson's standard textbook (6th Ed.) called "diminishing marginal returns." The example the professor used was ice cream. If you really liked ice cream and then ate it every day for hours and hours, eventually after a certain point, the more ice cream ingested, the less you would find it rewarding and satisfying. I think the oversaturation of sports, with its expanding rosters and revolving teams and cities, have made me realize how trivial these games, grownups play for millions of semi-literate fans, are and what a gross distraction they are from the eschatological challenges of the United States and the new world order. After fifty years, I think it is time I emerged from the sandbox of sports.

All this is not surprising. It is a fact of life that sports, especially baseball, have always been organized, played, and expanded for many reasons, with money very high on the list. Sports have always been a big business. Granted in the days of the sporting owners, like Tom Yawkey and Phil Wrigley in baseball and Art Rooney and Lamar Hunt in football, money did not seem to be the prime drive behind the owners. Love of the game, winning, and the psychological thrills of owning a big league team dominated most of the sports. Characters like Bill Veeck with their circus-capitalist attitude only added color and illumination to the game. But unknown to much of the public were the coldly capitalistic machinations of many of these owners and the clever manipulations of the players by some of these apostles of the bottom line. With the advent of free agency in 1975, baseball players put aside their duffel bags and carried attache cases into the board rooms to argue for their share of the great American sports dollar pie. Nobody blamed them for attempting to get their rightful share of this huge TV-injected pie but the negotiations, highlighted by the labor strife of the 1990s served to undermine the fan's love of the game. I have always contended that the players should be entitled to get what they can—if the money were there. And until the last baseball contract, the money was there. The predictions are that the TV will be severely curtailed by the next century and that players and owners have to make adjustments. The owners also saw this as an attempt to break up the Players' Association. Their mutual failure to negotiate this situation into an acceptable settlement until a month after the 1996 World Series, has alienated many fans like me. In many ways their collective attitude has chased us away from the games we loved as children. The constant transfer of franchises has also created an animosity and several lawsuits. It is one thing when a team moves because the fans have lost interest or failed to support their team. Art Modell, the owner of the historic Cleveland Browns, played before some of the best and most knowledgeable fans in the league, are now the Baltimore Ravens. He turned his back on their loyal and faithful support because of luxury boxes and the revenue promises of a new and modern stadium. Unadulterated greed has seduced many sports figures. With apologies to Lord Acton, after an indeterminate figure, money corrupts and it corrupts absolutely, no matter where it comes from. In addition to Cleveland, there has been a rash of franchise shifts, especially in football that in 1995-1996 has seen the Rams move from Los Angeles, where they had been since 1946, to St. Louis, the Los Angeles Raiders move back to Oakland, which they had vacated in 1983, and the Houston Oilers apparently headed for an upstart city, like Nashville that finally has its first big league team. The owner of the San Francisco Giants wanted to build a new stadium in San Francisco to house his team. The other owners chided him as foolish since it would upset their grand strategy of getting prestige hungry communities from paying blackmail to maintain their franchises or get new ones.

There is a growing trend among many professional teams in all sports to extract from their supportive communities exorbitant concessions, remunerations, and inducements in the forms of beer sales, luxury boxes, parking revenues, and tax rebates. Local politicians seem mesmerized by the thought of losing their existent franchises, while communities that never have had teams, or had suffered the loss of their teams, seem to want o do anything to regain the privileged status of being big league. St. Louis paid through the nose to get the Rams from Los Angeles in 1995. Nearly 70,000 fans shelled out thousands of dollars to buy Public Seating Licenses, not for any tickets, but merely for the "right" to purchase tickets. I had predicted that the city would not sell 20,000 of these rip-offs. Was I ever wrong on the intense need to have a real football team! After the team had started off on a remarkable note, winning five of its seven games, surpassing the total number of wins I thought they would get, it was discovered that as part of their agreement they could leave St. Louis in ten years if the TWA Dome, as their multi-million dollar stadium was christened, if the facilities were not in the top 25% of all football complexes. With franchise after franchise clamoring for new and improved buildings, more luxury boxes and the like, it is conceivable that the Dome might fail to live up to that stipulation. In Florida, the residents have been hit by an epidemic of greedy owners wanting to better and improve their lot at taxpayer expense. The Tampa Bay Buccaneers threatened to move if they did not get a new stadium. The politicians wanted to add a 5% sales tax to rental cars. The Sunshine State, which does not have a state income tax, taxes virtually everything else, except the air its residents breathe. Their successful hockey team, the Florida

Panthers and the Miami Heat, want a new building, as the existing structure, which holds a mere 14,503 fans and has only a pitiful 16 luxury boxes, is vastly inadequate for the tons of money they hope to bilk from their fans.

The strike exposed an obvious change in players' attitudes toward the game, their fans, and each other. It sickened a growing cynical public. The American paparazzo worsened the situation by poisoning the atmosphere by exploiting petty jealousies among owners and fellow players. Players adopted the blue-collar attitude of many of our unions with its disdain for scabs (marginal players brought in to break the strike). Yes, there was big money here, but how can the ordinary public identify with players making two-three million dollars every year? The demeaning way the regulars treated these replacement players throughout 1995 was a disgrace to all of sports history. Now more than ever, the overt economic interests of both players and fans is too apparent. The financial gap between fans and players has widened over the years so that fans have to nearly mortgage their homes to afford to come to a game. And baseball is cheap when compared to other sports. It costs a family of four nearly one hundred dollars for a game, beer, sodas, hot dogs, a program, and parking, while hockey, basketball, and football cost nearly $200.

Baseball is in jeopardy of losing substantial numbers of its next generation of fans because the game's leadership has failed dismally to attract new fans, who are kept in a constant state of flux due to all the wholesale trades and instability that free agency has caused. Free agency has further alienating fans from players they hardly recognize. The old axiom is more true than ever before, You can't tell the players without a scorecard.

The racial and cultural components of sports have also tended to dampen my enthusiasm for these games. I have had no problem watching and cheering many of the great black athletes throughout the years but the demeanor and attitude of too many black athletes has served as a detriment to the enjoyment of watching these games. The carnavalization of sports began with the high-five, often attributed to Glen Burke, a former member of the Los Angeles Dodgers, and one of the few openly homosexual professional athletes who died of AIDS in 1995. The Houston Oilers' outstanding return man, Billy "White Shoes" Johnson, was known for his pelvic gyrations after scoring a touchdown on kick returns in the seventies. The slam dunk in basketball has its tactical appeal in basketball but it is overdone by overt showmanship and acrobatic swagger that it detracts from the enjoyment of the game. The end zone dancing has taken on the characteristics of a fertility cult that demeans and distracts from the great plays that usually led the athlete to the end zone in the first place. The sophomoric on-the-field antics of "Neon Deon" Sanders approximate a minstrel side-show that degrades his superior athletic performances. The victory struts, the weird and creative prancing after a quarterback sack, are really unprofessional and significant of brutish men/children in the ritualistic throes of puberty. The latest is panning for the camera. After each significant play, the players will unhelmet themselves so the fans at home can see how mean or how pretty they are. Coaches and league officials have attempted to curtail these excesses but it only gets worse with each and every game. Noted psychologists apologetically retort that these mostly African-American athletes are just expressing themselves, searching for their individuality after having been kept in slavery for 400 years. This patented excuse is a derivative of the same type of psychological denial that excused the riots following the first Rodney King jury decision in Los Angeles. Ever since the establishment of the affirmative action mindset, schools and professional sports teams have coddled its athletes, especially its black athletes, for too long with dire consequences to its sports, society, and racial relations.

The Dallas Cowboys are a case in point. Since the demise of coach Tom Landry, long a paragon of virtue, the team has degenerated both on and off the field. Their beefy offensive line often crackbacks opposing linemen, causing serious injury. Players like Michael Irvin appear on national television and utter strings of profanity with a gross disrespect for the viewing public. Later, Irvin was then involved with drugs and a prostitute in an Irving, Texas motel room and was suspended for the first five games of the 1996 season. Erik Williams, who later settled out of court, was charged in 1995 with the sexual assault of a 17-year-old topless dancer. In September of that same year, wide receiver Cory Fleming was arrested for a DWI charge. The following November, both defensive lineman Leon Lett and cornerback Clayton Holmes, were suspended after violating the NFL's substance-abuse policy. In the 4 December 1996, edition of the St. Louis *Post-Dispatch*, former Cowboys' linebacker, Robert Jones exposed the "Boys for what they really were." Jones, who later played for the Rams, said that former Cowboys' coach Jimmy Johnson, reproached him for being too distracted by your wife and child. The article related a story about a little place some of the players bought to house their women for extramarital activities. Instead of naming their love nest, the "greatest little whorehouse," they called it the "white house." I wonder if that had any political implications. The sad truth is that America's Team has degenerated into America's Most Wanted! This negative behavior is not relegated just to the Cowboys. Professional athletes seem much more susceptible to above-the-law behavior. Heavyweight champ Mike Tyson's extramarital activities speak volumes about this trend in anti-social behavior by star athletes. Bill Bennett says about the Irvin incident, "it's one more notch. . . . Civilizations don't collapse all at once, they do it one degree at a time." There is no ironclad law that professional sports and their highly paid mercenaries will be here forever. Baseball does not fit the national character nor the cultural milieu any more. If I were willing to make a prediction, it would be that all major sports will be forced to constrict their operations over the next twenty years as fan apathy, discontent, and alienation grows. Who is to say that would be such a bad thing?

PART V

THE NEW WORLD ORDER

16 / The Great Conspiracy
The Enemy Within

> We shall have world government, whether we like it or not . . . by
> consent or by conquest.
>
> —James Warburg, before a
> Senate Foreign Relations
> Subcommittee in 1950

Conspiracy theories are readily discounted in sophisticated circles. To believe one of the myriad of conspiracy theories proposed today is to be swiftly relegated to the section reserved for the lunatic fringe. Our educated class, perhaps having fallen victim to two hundred years of enlightened and evolutionary ideas, are dangerously prone to believe that events happened by accident more than by the grand design of a hidden power or group. To combat such theories they have created an anti-intellectual milieu which quickly demonizes any theory that presupposes the existence of sinister human forces. It is difficult for them to believe that an individual or an oligarchy of individuals actually have and exert power over their fellow Americans, their fellow human beings. Most people, especially liberals, want to think the best of others, even those with money and power. Life is too accidental—nobody has complete control over events. "We are all children of the enlightenment" to employ Connor Cruise O'Brien's belief. We like to think what evil there is does not reside in the human heart—anybody's human heart. To admit such would be to confess that there may be some evil lurking in our own hearts. But evil does exist in the human heart because there really is such a thing as original sin. Liberalism is intricately mixed up in the idea of a worldwide conspiracy. The French Revolution and all other vain attempts to repeal our original human nature or what Frederic Bastiat called in his short book, *The Law,* that "fatal tendency of mankind," have failed dismally. Over 170 million have died in the twentieth century in pursuit of this ignoble experiment.

People with life and death power over the masses can and do commit evil. It is not irrational to believe that there can be conspiracies since the world has been filled with groups intent on controlling and maintaining a predominant influence in a given community, state, nation, and even region.

The will to power existed centuries before Friedrich Nietzsche. Alexander the Great was a good man, yet he wanted to rule the known world. The Caesars, the tzars, kings, Kaisers, queens, the crusaders, and even presidents have attempted to unite and control the world under one roof—whether in the name of the Lord, the Holy Cross, the emperor, the nation, the flag, or the United Nations. Roman legions, through Hitler's New World Order, based on *Blut und Land,* the Japanese's Sphere of Co-prosperity, the Mafia, the Yukiza, the Black Hand, and other groups that wanted to subvert the freedom and intent of peoples throughout world history. History shows that it is a human impulse to want to control people and events and at the root of this is the need to have the individual's will effected whether the benighted like or not.

As a student in the sixties, I have always been tempted to look in the pages of history for sinister interior combinations of like-minded individuals, bent on controlling future events. My professors held that rational people, especially historians, never fell victim to such wayward and unconventional thinking. Yet I grew up in the fifties, with the Cold War and with parents who supported Senator Joseph McCarthy. Then there was my Catholic faith which ardently preached and warned of the devil and the evils of atheistic Communism. Because of my upbringing, I have had an open susceptibility to such thinking. To believe that the killing of a famous person, especially a president, is accidental smacks too much of the irrational nature of Darwinian evolution and the alleged origins of man. Offering accident as explanation to events, does not satisfy thinking men and women.

When John Kennedy was assassinated in 1963, there was a rush to judgment. Yet the ensuing investigations and revelations about Lee Harvey Oswald and his own convenient assassination at the hands of Jack Ruby just seemed a little too neat for me. Another historical conundrum closer to our own times is the strange and mysterious "suicide" of Vince Foster. There was something about the Clintons' alacrity to bury their long-time friend amid the mysterious circumstances surrounding his death. Lisa Foster, the victim's wife, was too eager in accepting the official verdict as a suicide. Suicide is always a dark reflection on, not only the victim, but also the victim's family. Any other cause of death would have exonerated her husband who had a sterling reputation as a husband, father, and a professional. The suspicious disappearance of files, the actions of the President and First Lady's staff, led by loyal chief of staff Maggie Williams and Bernard Nussbaum, including rifling the dead man's office even before his body was cold, gave rise to fears of plots, subplots, coverups, and hidden meanings. Subsequent news stories about inconsistencies, including a fake suicide note, the position of his body, and the lack of dirt on his shoes awakened in me a hardy sense of skepticism. If Vince Foster had really committed suicide, only the naive or the mentally inert would conclude that he had done it in the manner and fashion promoted by the media. Comprehensive studies done of his death by investigative reporter, Chris Ruddy and author Michael

Kellett have added fuel to the conspiracy fires. Kellett has proposed an extensive theory in his book, *The Murder of Vince Foster*, in which he offered 126 compelling arguments why he believes that President Bill Clinton was involved in a conspiracy to arrange or at least sanction the murder of his childhood friend. Kellett included a chilling photo of Clinton and Foster, taken when they were in pre-school, some forty-three years before Foster's death. Kellett's book and Ruddy's newspaper articles and subsequent book, *The Strange Death of Vince Foster* are not the final word on this subject. There have been too many unanswered questions that would have to be left to chance or accident to dispel all the Foster murder conspiracy questions.

Along similar lines is author Richard Odom's captivating book, *Circle of Death: Clinton's Climb to the Presidency*. Based solely on circumstantial evidence and realistic inference, Odom details all the bodies that have been found over the state of Arkansas that bore any, even if a remote connection, to then Governor Clinton. From drug dealer and later FBI informant Barry Seal of the MENA drug cartel, to Jerry Parks, Clinton's former body guard who had kept a file on the Governor's extensive sexual liaisons, several unsolved mysteries, continue to haunt the Clintons.

No office in the world is surrounded with more power, prestige, and influence than the President of the United States. While our history can not match that of our English forbearers in political and royal intrigue, we have had our share of inexplicable deaths and shadowy circumstances surrounding fatal events. Until film director Oliver Stone and the thousands of conspiracy buffs analyzed every iota of evidence surrounding the assassination of President John F. Kennedy, creating a very lucrative cottage industry in the process, the most notorious conspiracies in this country's history revolved around our entry into World War II and the death of our first assassinated president, Abraham Lincoln, on 14 April 1865. The fact that the United States had broken the Japanese military code revealing their military strategy coupled with the poor and incompetent state of military preparedness in Hawaii, led many to believe that President Roosevelt had deliberately sacrificed over 2000 American lives to get us into a war on the side of God and truth. While this is unlikely, the fact that the British sacrificed hundreds of Canadians at Dieppe and several more hundred at Bristol, does underscore that some leaders have been willing to sacrifice others for the good of the cause.

Abraham Lincoln was assassinated by a cabal of conspirators, led by actor John Wilkes Booth. That same night unsuccessful attempts were made on the lives of Lincoln's Vice-President, Andrew Johnson, and Secretary of State William Seward. Some historians contend that the real culprit behind these attempts was the person with ostensibly the most to gain, namely Lincoln's controversial Secretary of War, Edwin Stanton. While the historiography on the Lincoln murder case, is long and extensive, the first popular explanation of this "mystery" was Theodore Roscoe's *The Web of Conspiracy: The Complete Story of the Men Who Murdered Lincoln*, published in

1959. The only trouble with the Stanton theory is that according to the existent legislation at the time President pro tem of the Senate, Edward Everrett would have ascended to the presidency at the deaths of Lincoln, Johnson and Seward. William Hanchett's survey of all the conspiracy theories on Lincoln's assassination debunks virtually all of them.

Writers Jonathan Vankin & John Whalen have written a valuable and entertaining book, *The 50 Greatest Conspiracies of All Time.* The authors list several reasons why most conspiracy theorists are dismissed without an honest intellectual evaluation. The most salient feature of this kind of dismissal is what they label "the vested interest" or what John McManus the president of the John Birch Society calls "the insiders." Conspiracy theorists generally attack the established authority because that's where the power usually is, and with it, the abuse of power. People in authority, as you would expect, fight to preserve the status quo limited only by the extent of their power and money. A good conspiracy theory requires a herculean effort to fathom and explain. In our inarticulate and anti-intellectual society, it is much easier to accept the standard version of the truth, such as that offered by the Warren Commission, in spite of its contradictions and obvious flaws. Pundits and columnists will often attribute symptoms of varying degrees of mental illness to these theorists, thereby debunking their theories without an honest hearing. The mainstream media has its own vested interest in maintaining its intricate role within the power structure. Conspiracy theories work at their power base, threatening their own vested interest as part of the establishment.

It's A Conspiracy, written and published by the *National Insecurity Council,* is another book with the same theme. In this book the authors have an arrogant vision of the world, laced with a nearly lethal dose of intellectual cynicism that is very difficult to fathom. Their book does document the wide variety of conspiracy theories that abound in American history. Among the sixty different conspiracies this book analyses are the mysterious deaths of Karen Silkwood, Malcolm X, and the possibility that William Randolph Hearst was a paid agent of Adolf Hitler.

With regard to conspiracies, people are left with a choice between an accidental view of history or a conspiratorial view. Facts do not lie. Either they believe that Americans have lost control of their government, their economy, and their future, or they deny everything that has happened as a distortion of reality. Few self-respecting people will admit to the notion of a conspiracy theory because society, the media and college professors tell us nobody would do such a thing. To the contrary, history is filled with one conspiracy after another as men and sometimes women, showed their darker side in a quest for power, money, and celebrity. Wherever there is a concentration of wealth and power, there will always be attempts by rivals to thwart the existing circumstances and to attain those riches and authorities for their own use. Due to man's fallen nature, when ever he has an opportunity to exert power and control over other human beings he will do so, unless restrained by force, edict, or physical threat. Apologists for the establishment play on people's inability to admit that their fellow human beings can be guilty of crime, deception and even evil. They want to believe the best about other people. To think that rich men who have everything and are still not satisfied, would take a quantum leap of faith or what is really, a quantum loss of faith in their fellow man. Most people are unwilling to believe that about our trusted leaders and business professionals. To accept the accidental or Darwinian interpretation is the nonsensical choice. Most events happen for a reason.

Another more concrete and controversial reason for the denigration of conspiracy theorists is the Jewish connection. Conspiracy theories have often been equated with claims about a Jewish plot to control the whole world, mainly through its financial institutions. Anti-Semitic theory has been around for thousands of years and continues to find expression in the ranting of Eastern European politicians and certain African-American orators, such as Louis Farrakhan and Leonard Jefferies. Its existence tends to tarnish legitimate conspiracy concerns.

The code words often denoting the sense of a conspiracy with Jewish overtones, revolves around the term "international bankers." Because some neophytes, such as the apolitical Hall of Fame baseball pitcher, Steve Carlton, once made reference to the twelve Jewish bankers meeting in Switzerland to rule the world, any use of the term international banker is immediately tied to the tin can of anti-semitism. In his book *The New World Order,* evangelist Pat Robertson made allusions to international bankers, such as the Rothschilds, who were Jewish and was immediately hit with the tag of anti-Semitism. In such cases, I believe it is a false argument and an aversion to dealing with the merits of the charge. Destroy the messenger and people will never learn the message. Since all the bankers in Robertson's charge were not Jews, it is clear that he never meant to level his charge solely against the Jewish people.

The right-wing does not have a patent on these theories. Many utopian thinkers in government, social agencies, the press, and the churches believe that all wars result from the conspiracies of munitions makers, right-wing fanatics, or political and military leaders. They believe that peace can only come through a supernational world body with the power to enforce compliance. Disarmament, they contend, will foster universal brotherhood and friendship while space exploration will open new vistas and serve as a distraction from the petty rivalries that keep nations in conflict. The liberal press is convinced the 1995 bombing of the federal building in Oklahoma City was the result of a right-wing conspiracy. The series of devastating fires to black churches throughout the South was erroneously thought to be a white supremacist attack on black people. Just listen to Hillary Clinton.

The "great conspiracy" is one that deserves the most attention. I subscribe to *The National Report,* which is suffused with article after article detailing the One World plot of the United Nations, the Trilateral Commission, and the Council of Foreign Relations to take away our suzerainty, submerging the United States within the confines of a world government. This thinking has been around for a long time. Some very respectable people subscribe to some of these theories, Pat Robertson, Phyllis Schlafly, the head of the Conservative think-tank *The Eagle Forum* in St. Louis, Howard Phillips of the US Taxpayers Party and Republican Pat Buchanan.

Other leaders and thinkers whom I respect very much, such as Rush Limbaugh, will have nothing to do with the great conspiracy. In an atypical fashion, Limbaugh refuses to discuss the great conspiracy, probably for fear of being painted on the radical fringe. Blatant refusals to even discuss things, always raises a question in my mind that maybe there is something there. That's probably why I became a historian—the incessant and unyielding desire to answer the question of "why?" I would like to know why we have come to be the way we are.

James Billington, the current librarian of Congress and a member of the CFR, wrote a seminal work, entitled *The Fire in the Minds of Men: The Origins of the Revolutionary Faith*. Billington documents the impact of occult secret societies—the Bavarian Illuminati in particular—on the French Revolution and subsequent revolutionary upheaval around the world. The book implies that this revolutionary fire is still alive and may be responsible for some of the upheavals and turmoil befalling today's society. This fire could be the inherent weakness in our own social institutions, abetted by groups that would relish to see the country be destroyed from within. Bishop Fulton J. Sheen used to argue that of all the major civilizations in recorded history, all but a few deteriorated and eventually fell due to internal causes. I am starting to hear some of the jeremiads wail that the end is near, at least the end of this country.

According to Thomas Sowell the Culture War is not a result of a conspiracy but the result of simply a whole class of people who hate what this country stands for, who have contempt for its people, and who exploit every opportunity to undermine its institutions and its ideals. Failed Reagan nominee to the Supreme Court, Robert Bork, believes the Culture War is not a conspiracy but a syndrome. No matter what it is called, the end result will predictably be the same.

In the *National Review*, 28 August 1995, Tom Bethel states that conspiracies are wrong. Conspiracy theories do sometimes detect a pattern of events that is real enough but when they assign the term conspiracy to this observed pattern that their adherents often arrive at the wrong conclusion. He believes that to explain an existing pattern as a conspiracy will lead to the charge of paranoia or extremism by the general public. It is this very real fear that has silenced the loquacious Limbaugh on the idea of conspiracy. Bethel believes that the goal of world government is considered ridiculous by some of the very people who dream of it. To reduce this idea of a conspiracy to an absurdity, Bethel cites the World Federalist Movement whose president is comedian and actor Sir Peter Ustinov. This is all well and good but what power or influence does this fringe, unrepresentative group have? How much money and power do they generate? Do they represent all one-world power sources? Bethel's vain attempt to debunk all conspiracies theories by the calculated use of the WFM is preposterous. It is reminiscent of Joseph Stalin's cynical retort about the power of the pope. How many legions does he have?

The key to understanding the idea of a conspiracy, says Bethel, is that it attempts to spring an illegal surprise. To him, illegality is the key— otherwise huddles and surprise parties, would be called conspiracies. To deceive or to falsely condition people to do what they would not have done had they known all the facts is not totally illegal in our society. Let the buyer beware. Say you have a beautiful house built and the construction is not up to standard. Try taking the contractor to court. Unless he's in violation of local ordinances, what he has done is not illegal, just immoral and unethical. Bethel's obsession with the word legal is what invalidates his argument. There can be conspiracies to change or undermine the American system and the American way of life without necessarily running afoul of the law, just like my fictitious contractor. The results may still be devastating—a weakened house or country.

Daniel Pipes in his 1997 book, *Conspiracy: The Power of the Paranoid Style in History*, recognizes a more universal presence of the conspiracy theory. Conspiracism or the irrational belief in conspiracy exists, for him, not just in the Middle East where Arab nationals attribute all their misfortunes to plots orchestrated by malevolent outsiders, but all over the globe. In the United States, he describes a paranoid assembly of militant black leadership and right-wing extremists, from Louis Farrakhan through Pat Buchanan, Ross Perot, and Pat Robertson who think AIDS, black helicopters, the UN, and Manhattan money powers, the *Illuminati*, a secret team, and the Council of Foreign Relations and just waiting for the proper moment to assume control of the US government.

I think the problem is in the *word* conspiracy. Conspiracy theorists must change their vocabulary and come up with a better and a more accurate way of describing the clandestine or secretive planning that goes on behind closed doors, affecting the life, liberty, and happiness of all Americans. Bethel's problem with conspiracy is centered within his understanding of the communist conspiracy during the Cold War. The American public's failure to understand the nature and mission of Communism in the 1940s and 50s was the result of the greatest salesmanship job of the century. In truth, there was a viable international communist conspiracy. Only the very naive or the liberal ideologue would deny this. While the Communist Party of the United States was very clandestine, not everything it did was illegal. If the notion of conspiracy hangs on the idea of illegality than obviously there are few real conspiracies. What we have is a conspiracy of attitude: that is a predisposition to believe and act in a way that supports the liberal credo of big government and sexual license. These goals can be accomplished with public meetings or even private but not secret meetings.

Bethel's conclusions led him to a denunciation of the John Birch Society, more specifically its founder Robert Welch and his inappropriate and unsubstantiated claim about President Dwight D. Eisenhower in 1959. Welsh contended that Ike was a conscious agent of the international communist conspiracy. Much of what Ike did or did not do may have, in effect, unwittingly aided the communist movement but to say he was a card-carrying Communist is a blatant absurdity. Too often Welch confused the so-called fellow-traveler with hardened and conscious agents of the communist conspiracy. The same is true with accusations the right has made against members of the intellectual community, which is riven with thousands of smart, logical people who have adopted the communist philosophy. Too often their predisposition to liberal causes has prompted them to misread the utopian promises of Lenin, Stalin, and Marx. For this they are to be censured. But to say they are part of a conspiracy does great harm to fighting the erroneous messages about this country they promote.

In a muted defense of the Birchers, columnist Joseph Sobran summed up the true nature of the conspiracy in his July '97 newsletter, in a column, entitled *What the Birchers Can Teach Us*. Conspiracies are real, he opined and conspirational behavior is inseparable from politics, since politics is largely the pursuit of power by sneaky people. However, he discounts large conspiracies because they are so hard to hide, Sobran would much rather talk of the tendency of political action. He believes if one were to substitute tendency for conspiracy, these theories would have a certain cogency to them. It is by its very nature that power tends to corrupt, and power itself has that self-fulfilling attraction to grow and consolidate under the seductive guise of empty promises. This has been the history of the United States since its inception. Abraham Lincoln did not intend to centralize government, as part of some worldwide conspiracy. It just worked out that way through the exigencies of historical context. It is the political instinct of any leader to consolidate his power for the good of his agenda. As Sobran continues,

> today's globalists and internationalists, forever pursuing international treaties and alliance, may think they are promoting peace and prosperity, seeing no tyrannical potential in a "new world order." Prompted by the inner drive of the liberal tendency, they may mean well but the consequences of their sinister philosophy has endangered us all.

In his inestimable persuasive logic, Sobran concludes that the very people who are quick to ridicule conspiracy theories are also the people whose conduct invites them.

Bethel also mentions the book, *Proofs of a Conspiracy*, written in 1798, by John Robinson. Robinson describes in detail the *Illuminati*, an invidious group that had been founded by Adam Weishaupt, in 1776. Robinson ratiocinates that the *Illuminati* infiltrated the Free Masons and helped foment the French Revolution. Robinson believed that Free Masonry was an association for the purpose of rooting out all of the religious establishments and overturning all the existing governments of Europe. To most people, Freemasonry is a family-oriented benevolent society. Few are aware of its religious and political underpinnings. Members were recruited by Weishaupt with the promise of wealth, power and influence, and worldly success. Author Malachi Martin drew a similar scenario in his powerful 1996 novel of papal intrigue, "Windswept House."

The *Illuminati* vowed to overthrow the monarchy, the church, civil government, private property and the elevation of a group of enlightened ones—illuminated ones—to world leadership. The *Illuminati* were later suppressed by the Church, but their infiltration by the Free Masons helped to keep the principles of *Illuminism* alive throughout the ages.

Members of the *Illuminati* at the highest levels were satanists and atheists. They believed that Satan was the good god, waiting to liberate mankind from the oppressions of the past. They equated the repression of the Catholic Church with the Judeo-Christian God. They saw their salvation with Lucifer, the new god of light who would allow them to become like gods.

Bethel thinks that the communist conspiracy has been replaced by the Federal Government as the chief mover in the great conspiracy. Alluding to the fact that nature abhors a vacuum, it is creditable that when one enemy seems to be beaten there has to be a new enemy to take its place. Old theories are not discarded, just continually updated. Bethel also believes that in order to keep the conspiracy going, elderly *Illuminati* must have met at some point with fledging Communists, to turn over the keys to the mystery. His arrant attempt at sarcasm betrayed an unschooled naivete that pulled his argument way off its mark. The *Illuminati* were the custodians of an idea that was as old as evil itself. The demise of the *Illuminati* had little or no bearing on the transference of their ideas. I compare this transference to the Coke bottle that was the omphalos in the avant garde movie, *The Gods Must be Angry*. It was a humorous story about how a plane inadvertently dropped a Coke bottle in the Calahari Desert. The strange and exotic soda bottle endured great adventures as it was passed, often accidentally, to many different owners. The bottle seem to have a life of its own as it left chaos, pain and, even happiness in its wake. Another movie, *The Twenty Dollar Bill*, traced the relations and events that were triggered by an issue of US currency. In these movies inanimate objects appeared to influence the many dozens and even hundreds of people who crossed their paths as they went about their daily lives. It does not require a great leap of faith to realize that an idea can remain dormant or inconspicuous for years, maybe even centuries, before it is resuscitated. Some ideas have a nuclear life, in that, they never seem to die. They may fall out of favor or be lost for a long time, but eventually they come back and influence new generations of people. The beliefs of the *Illuminati* and the French Revolution are like that. Free Masonry kept *Illuminism* alive, though in somewhat of a dormant state. The revolutionary idea was eventually passed on to the *League Of Just Men*, which had Karl Marx as a member. This directly led to the Communist League, Progressivism, New Deal Democracy, and Liberalism. Bethel finishes his article with a flourish.

> What many theorists have had in common, from the alleged *Illuminati* to that of the Communists, to today's New World Order, is the belief that, since the time of the French Revolution, secularism and the centralization of power have been consistently pursued. Unquestionably there is a lot of truth to that perception. As trends, they have been real enough. The obvious explanation is that a ruling or political class has long sought these goals, has advocated them openly, and has succeeded in getting enough control over the machinery of government to go a long way toward implementing them. They created the *Zeitgeist*. In order to do this, they did not have to meet secretly at any point.

Bethel is wrong about the *Illuminati* conspiracy being alleged. There is ample documentation to support their existence. Billington's book, *The Fire In the Minds of Men: Origins of Revolutionary Faith*, details the existence of Weishaupt and the *Illuminati* and its expansion. Billington is no ultraconservative dupe since he's the chairman of the left-leaning Woodrow Wilson International Center of Scholars, affiliated with the Smithsonian Institute.

Secrecy has not been totally absent from the conspiracy debate. There have been several secretive or closed door meetings that lend credence to some of these conspiracy theories. The clandestine 1910 meeting at Jekyll Island in Georgia included clearly a quarter of the wealth of the world. While they did conspire in a personal and perhaps, immoral sense, to pass the proper enabling legislation that implanted the Federal Reserve System into place, they broke no laws in meeting. This privately-owned cartel of banks does and has controlled the economic and political destiny of this country for seventy years now. To excuse their concentration of power in the name of that it was not illegal is to miss the magnitude of what these few insiders have accomplished in a short period of time. It matters little how these insiders of the establishment have garnered their power. They have it which they intend to use for their own ends.

Carroll Quigley, President Clinton's mentor at Georgetown and the only teacher he mentioned in his acceptance speech in 1993, wrote the book on how to become one of the insiders. According to Professor Quigley, all of this vision of world unity started in 1870 with the appointment of John Ruskin as a professor of fine arts at Oxford. According to Quigley's *magnum opus*, first published in 1966, Ruskin hit Oxford like an earthquake "because he talked about . . . the empire and England's downtrodden masses." Ruskin told his selected students they "were possessors of a magnificent tradition of education, beauty, rule of law, freedom, decency, and self-discipline but, that this tradition did not deserve to be saved, unless it could be extended to the lower classes in England and to the non-English masses throughout the world."

A wealthy Socialist, Ruskin taught that the state must take control of the means of production and organize the people for the good of the community as a whole. He advocated putting control of the state into the hands of an elite, presumably an enlightened despot. He once wrote: "my continual aim has been to show the eternal superiority of some men to others." Ruskin read Plato every day. He believed in the ideal of a platonic society in which the state would control the means of production and distribution and which in turn is controlled for the benefit of all those who are best suited by aptitude for the task. Plato wanted a ruling class with a powerful army and a society subservient to it.

Ruskin's inaugural address was copied in longhand by one of his most prominent students, Cecil Rhodes, who kept it with him for thirty years. Rhodes would conceive a plan to put Ruskin's ideas into practice. It was the Rothschilds' international banking firm, that financed Cecil Rhodes in Africa. With the cooperation of the Bank of England and the Rothschilds, Rhodes was able to establish a virtual monopoly over the diamond and gold output of South Africa with DeBeers Consolidated Mines and Consolidated Gold Fields, with an estimated annual income of approximately $5 million (one million pounds sterling).

Using his own money, Rhodes developed his elaborate plan for world federation, financed and ruled by the English-speaking nations of the world. The most important feature of this plan was his secret society, founded on the model of St. Ignatius' Society of Jesus. The most important feature of the Jesuits were their requirement of absolute obedience to the Pope, the same idea that Weishaupt had used in founding the Illuminati. Rhodes and his successors were to be the pope and the objects of their members undying loyalty and obedience. Though this dictum was modified after Rhodes' death in 1902, money, power, and dedication to the idea of world peace through a world federation provided the incentives necessary for members to foster lifelong adherence to the organization. Rhodes knew instinctively that only by controlling the wealth of the world could his plan come to fruition. That meant bringing the world's rich into the plan initially to finance it.

The Rhodes Scholarships, as outlined in his will, became the main instrument whereby the most promising young people throughout the English-speaking world were recruited to serve Rhodes' plan. As Quigley wrote in *The Anglo-American Establishment*, "these scholarships are merely a facade to conceal the secret society, or more accurately they were to be one of the instruments by which members of the secret society could carry out this purpose." Like a Ludlum character, Rhodes scholars were to infiltrate major corporations, governments, and educational institutions of the world, subtlety undermining the culture as they went.

Having made all the money a man could hope to spend in two life-times, Rhodes aspired to establish a circle of power that would control a large part of the world's resources, not to mention its history. The secret society of which Rhodes spoke was launched on 5 February 1891. This *Circle of Intimates,* as well as an outer *Association of Helpers,* was comprised of Lord David Balfour, Sir Harry Johnson, Lord Rothschild, Lord Grey, and other members of Britain's aristocratic and financial elite.

Rhodes' paramount design seemed to be mainly political, a policy of painting the world red—the color of British colonies. This irony should not be lost on the reader. Rhodes was primarily an imperialist, though one with higher ideals and a grander design. His goal was world peace under a benign democratic world government, requiring society to promote social equality through social reform. He wanted to draw the United States and England in a league for the purpose of imposing peace or face the possibility of an Armageddon. The scholarship program merely served as a facade to conceal the doings of the secret society, or more accurately, as the instrument by which members of the secret society could carry out its function. Unlike that of Saint Ignatius of Loyola, Rhodes' Round Table was to be secret and decidedly un-Christian. Another of Rhodes' biographers, Sarah Millin wrote, "the government of the world was Rhodes simple desire." Rhodes envisioned this as a great plan that "for the next two centuries for the best energies of the best people in the world." His intellectual descendants would peacefully conquer the world and establish a Republic of the Intellect.

The American counterpart to Rhodes' Round Table is the *Council on Foreign Relations* (CFR). This powerful yet enigmatic organization has numbered among its membership virtually every cabinet member, several presidents, and Supreme Court judges to high offices, but is not widely known. In November 1995, I decided to visit the location of the CFR, at the corner of 68th Street and Park Avenue in midtown Manhattan, in the Pratt Building. After a complicated search, I spent several moments contemplating how much power and money have been concentrated within those four walls since 1921. The CFR boasts among its current membership, President Clinton, Colin Powell, Newt Gingrich, and several other high-placed politicians, and news people, such as Barbara Walters, Dan Rather, and surprisingly, "Conservative Godfather," William F. Buckley. The major public function of the CFR is its journal, *Foreign Affairs* which consistently promotes Rhodes' vision for a world government.

The definitive book on the CFR is *The Shadows of Power,* by James Perloff. He describes it as a front for J. P. Morgan and Company. By 1945, its members had infiltrated the corridors of power, especially in the State Department, giving it virtual control over the country's foreign policy regardless of who was in the White House. Echoing the words of the late

Supreme Court Justice, Felix Frankfurter, Perloff makes an excellent case that "The real rulers in Washington are invisible, and exercise power from behind the scenes." Quigley studied this organization for twenty years and for two years, was allowed in its inner sanctum, studying its papers and its historical documents. Quigley believed the "CFR's role in history is significant enough to be known." His only complaint was that it has remained obscure and even hidden. There is a strong underpinning of Fabian socialism behind Rhodes' notion of a one-world government. The major thinking behind Woodrow Wilson's 14 Points, originated from two Fabian publications, *Labour's War Aims*, written by Fabian founder Sidney Webb and *International Government*, by Leonard Wolf. The Fabian texts were drafted into their 14 Points for Wilson by famed American columnist Walter Lippmann, a Fabian since 1909, and the notorious Edward M. House, who favored socialism as dreamed by Karl Marx. It was the irrepressible Colonel House, who exercised near Svengalian control and influence over President Wilson, in what has been described as the strangest friendships in history. Of House, who was a founding member of the CFR in 1921, it has been written that, "No other American of his time was on such close terms with so many men of international fame." He wanted a one-world economy, a one-world army, government, under a financial oligarchy founded on the Anglo-American model and a world dictator served by a council of twelve faithful men or wise men.

Rhodes scholars have permeated all elitist walks of life from the Presidency of the United States, cabinet positions, heads of influential businesses and industries, to commissions, and Supreme Court Judges, senators, and the president of the Carnegie Foundation. The Association of American Rhodes Scholars has about 1600 alumni who have become part of our new ruling elite. Just some of this elite include economist Lester Thurlow, historian John K. Fairbank, Nicholas Katzenbach, Senator Bill Bradley, Howard K. Smith, the late J. William Fullbright, Carl Albert, the late Dean Rusk, Senator Richard Lugar, David Boren, Michael Kinsley, and Daniel Boorstin. There have been 20 Rhodies in the Clinton administration alone, including Strobe Talbot, Ira Magaziner, and Robert Reich. The Clinton administration marks the high-water mark of the Rhodes' desire for world conquest. He had hoped that by the year 1920 there would be between two and three thousand men in the prime of life scattered all over the world, "each of whom would have been specially gifted—mathematically—selected toward the Founder's purposes." It would appear that he was right on target.

Idealism of the kind demonstrated by Rhodes is not necessarily a bad thing. Oxfordian idealism however invariably was along the lines of humanism/pagan/atheist, collectivism, totalitarianism, gnosticism, globalism, and elitism. These affiliations all may not be apparent but they are certainly implied within the history of the Rhodes scholar. Rhodes scholars believe in government more than anything. It is with and through government that the heirs to Rhodes' lethal legacy expect to effect his quixotic vision.

Given Cecil Rhodes' history and the private activities of his round table and the CFR, it is not difficult to sympathize with the major contentions of some of these conspiracy theorists. The final play in this conspiracy, according to G. Edward Griffin, in his book, *The Creature From Jekyll Island*, a comprehensive study of the Federal Reserve, another private group with vast and inordinate power and control over the everyday economic American life, is the government's use of the Federal Treasury as a piggy bank to bail out Third World investments after they go bankrupt. Anyone studying the Whitewater scandal will immediately recognize this as the same financial pattern employed by the McDougals, and apparently the Clintons, through the Madison Savings and Loan. This financial institution served as their personal piggy bank, financing private deals and political campaigns. The Federal Reserve, in conjunction with international bankers, likewise has been using the Federal Treasury to secure their inadvisable and highly risky loans, like those to Mexico in 1995, which cost the American taxpayers, $50 billion. Forget the fact that this endless stream of red ink weakens every aspect of the nation's economy and trade. The underlying fact of this scenario is that the sapping of the nation's economic vitality will only strengthen their hand as we approach the New World Order. The banks only concern is that their investments are protected.

With his fiery denunciation of President Clinton's role in NAFTA and GATT, as well as on the nation's involvement with the United Nations, the World Trade Organization and the new world order during his ill-fated presidential campaign, Pat Buchanan passionately echoed sentiments of conspiracy theorists. He proposed that big business and big government did not care about the American people, pledging allegiance, not to the flag, but to the dollar of any country where they could get the most return for their investment. Buchanan called the WTO a mere satellite office of the new world order. To Buchanan the NWO is a plot generated by corporate pirates, New York financiers, and supine Establishment politicians to deliver American sovereignty into the hands of world government advocates. According to Buchanan's thinking, "the architects and acolytes of the new world order envision a new world where the UN grows stronger, its military arm is strengthened, and US sovereignty is diminished, and America evolves into the Western hemispheric province of a new world government." To counter Buchanan's argument, Krauthammer offers the lame excuse of a moribund UN that can barely make its own ends meet. While the United Nations may be in severe financial difficulty, its global vision still looms menacingly on the future. The infusion of any substantial financial assistance will quickly raise that vision phoenix like.

While the notion of a One World Government first took the international stage during the administration of Woodrow Wilson, the ideal began to receive its first favorable reviews with the foundation of the United Nations in San Francisco in 1945. With convicted perjurer, and probable Communist spy Alger Hiss as its first Secretary-General, it is not surprising that there is so much animus against the United Nations. In effect, the UN is a Trojan Horse that has carried the enemy into our very midst. It has undermined many of our fundamental institutions and values with an utopian promise of a democratic world—free from war.

The UN has blatantly failed to live up to its utopian promises. The extravagant lifestyle of UN bureaucrats and employees and their tax-free salaries are mostly funded by the American taxpayers. These conniving politicians from tiny Third World countries use the American public trough, much like our own politicians, to bleed the nation's finances dry. Most humanitarian aid never reaches its intended targets, winding up rather in the coffers of the ruling clique of murders who have killed off their opposition in countries, like Somalia and Haiti.

In an excellent two-part series published in the *Reader's Digest* in October and November of 1995, Dale Van Atta describes in great detail the fraudulent and immoral legacy of UN peacekeepers. He charged that UN troops shared Muslim women kidnaped by Serbian forces and that Kenyan peacekeepers sold 25,000 gallons of gas to the Serbs, a gross violation of the UN's alleged neutrality. Prostitution boomed as the UN forces entered Phnom Penh in Cambodia in 1991. These peacekeepers helped contribute to 5,000 new cases of venereal disease. While Somalians starved in Mogadishu, the UN spent $56 million a year dining on such delicacies as Australian beef and South American fruit. UN officials and many employees have a gravy train that makes most United States government perks and inducements look like chicken feed. As of June 1994, the Secretariat had a staff of 33,967 workers in New York, all supposedly engaged in peaceful and humanitarian work. A UN employee earning $72,000 without taxes makes the equivalent to $120,000 a year in real terms. Most employees receive a $1270 allowance for each child up to 18 years of age. The UN also pays $12,675 in tuition to employees for each child attending a private primary school or university. They can retire early at age 55 with pensions that are one-quarter higher than those of comparable US workers.

There is no accountability—just the open trough system of bilking the global public. Mostafa Tolba was executive director of the United Nations Environment Program (UNEP) based in Nairobi, Kenya. At his retirement in 1992, his annual salary approached that of the United states Secretary of Defense. ($143,800)—even though Toriba oversaw a budget of merely $63 million, as opposed to the $282 billion budget of the US Department of Defense. He left with an annual pension of $50,000 and was responsible for the establishment of $200,000 environmental prize. The 1993 recipient? Tolba himself!

As a result of its financial profligacy, it is no surprise the UN has fallen on hard times. Its debts exceed $2.3 billion with its number one patron, the United States, which foots the bill for over 25% of its expenses and a third of its peacekeeping operations, owes it more than a billion dollars. To alleviate this dire financial situation, UN Secretary General Boutrous

Boutrous-Ghalis has a plan to raise taxes on the world to finance his global dream of the so-called, New World Order, a term that dates back to Virgil. The idea of a global tax dates back to James Tobin, a 1981 Nobel Prize winner in Economics, who has called for a tax on spot transactions in foreign exchange. UN officials are ecstatic at Tobin's prediction that the revenue potential is immense, over $1.5 trillion a year. They have attempted to latch onto his prestige by calling it the Tobin Tax. The so-called *Independent Commission on Population and Quality of Life* has issued a report that lists dozens of innovative global devices to tax people, corporations, and international business activities. These include taxes on aviation, traffic and freight, ocean freight and cruises, communication satellites, international postal items, goods and services.

The principle of a global tax was first publicly launched at the UN *World Summit for Social Development,* held in Copenhagen in March 1995. James G. Speth, President Clinton's appointed head of the UN Development Program, called for a global tax on speculative movements of international funds, the consumption of non-renewable energy, environmental permits, and arms transactions. This financial windfall could enable the UN to finance its global operations, independent of the United States, and most likely fund the international police force that many of its proponents are saying is the only solution to world conflicts. Once the basic rule of global taxation to support the UN is firmly established, no matter how remote or limited the idea of global taxation sounds, it will deeply embed itself in the world consciousness and will just become another cost of doing business.

Taxation is a sovereign prerogative. Regardless of how it were implemented, it would establish the United Nations as a superior entity. Once the UN has the power to levy taxes on the world community, even if only on business and travelers, it would, in effect, function as a world government agency. Global taxation would establish an international system of entitlement, like the welfare system that now exists in the United States. While Republican reformers attempt to cut the size of the federal government, President Clinton and his liberal disciples have been attempting to expand the idea of entitlement beyond our national borders. The Oxfam Poverty Report proclaimed that "international aid should be seen as a financial entitlement, and as a part of a compact between citizens in the industrial and developing worlds." The Democratic leadership is suggesting that the United States, which is entrapped by its own entitlement structure, extend its crumpling structure to the entire world. James Burnham was right when he said that liberalism heralded the "suicide of the West."

With this in mind, I agree wholeheartedly with Don Feder's contention that the United States needs the UN like "the US justice system needs another O. J. Simpson trial." It has been just another drain on the US taxpayers—another blatant example of fraudulent bureaucrats bellying up to the bar for another free round. In a 1995 column, John Leo wrote, "an entire industry surrounds the United Nations, including a UN-Speak, a whole language of concealment and pretense."

Much of the liberal philosophy that has permeated our political culture serves as the model for what the UN is attempting to accomplish on the global level. The UN *Convention on the Right of the Child* would authorize a UN bureaucracy to supervise the relationship between parents and children under the guise of protecting the rights of the child. In 1995, President Clinton signed this convention, which the *Children's Defense Fund,* formerly chaired by his wife Hillary Clinton supported. This treaty is a broadside attack on the rights of all Americans and could hasten the eventual breakdown of the family. It effectively elevates children to the level of adults without any concomitant responsibilities.

The UN and the Clinton administration have attempted to engage the United States in a number of different foreign wars, as a means of turning the UN into an international establishment that will someday field its own army. Under the guise of peacekeeping, the United States military, has been turned into a league of armed social workers. The President's secret executive order—Presidential Decision Directive #25—has in effect turned United States military authority over to the UN. This has been a gradual process, dating back to the Korean War that took a quantum leap forward during the 100 hours war of Desert Storm. When Vice President Al Gore made reference to the United States men and women who perished in the skies over Iraq, he told the widows and orphans that these soldiers had died in the service of the United Nations. Gore exposed the president's real aim with the military—to use them as mercenaries all over the world at the whim of the UN bureaucrats.

The American operation in Somalia in 1993 personified future American military involvement in the New World Order. US troops were deployed indefinitely, for unclear reasons, under foreign commanders for the benefit of a globalist socialist order. The UN's operational ineptitude in Somalia is endemic clearly manifested that surrender of military control of our troops to foreign leaders, will seldom have their interests or those of the nation as primary considerations.

The UN's jurisdiction has grown to maintaining internal order within nations and not just as a mediator between nations. With the UN leading the way, the main characteristic of the Post-Cold War period in international relations appears to be the unraveling of national sovereignty through the regulation of domestic and internal affairs in the United States, a direct violation of the UN Charter. The Commission on Global Governance, a private group with government and foundation funding, published a book in 1995 entitled *Our Global Neighborhood.* Their book called for taxes on flight-lanes, sea lanes, and ocean fishing areas. They stated that "they felt it is time for a consensus on global taxation for servicing the needs of the global neighborhood." The report also boasted that the idea of safeguarding and managing the global commons, particularly those related to the physical environment, is now widely accepted. It called for the expansion of the role of the United Nations [as it] is now accepted in relation to military security. The globalist handprints of the CFR are all over this UN study. The late Admiral Chester Ward, who was a member of the CFR for sixteen years, was not exaggerating when he charged that "their agenda was to promote disarmament and submergence of US sovereignty and national independence into an all-powerful one-world government." Its leadership, he wrote, is "comprised of the one-world global-government ideologists—more respectfully referred to as the organized internationalists." Their lust to surrender the sovereignty and independence of the United States "is pervasive throughout most of the membership . . . The majority visualize the utopian submergence of the United States as a subsidiary administrative unit of a global government." It is apparent that the UN would like to see the end to the nation state.

Critics of the United Nations, like Pat Buchanan, rail against the loss of national sovereignty. In a seminal article for *Foreign Affairs*, the intellectual flagship of the CFR, Richard Gardiner advised in 1974 that the house of world order, "will have to be built from the bottom up rather than from the top down by way of an end run around national sovereignty, eroding it piece by piece." Twenty-two years later, William Knoke, the founder and president of the Harvard Capital Group, a global advisory group, opined in his book, *Bold New World: The Essential Road Map to the Twenty-First Century*, that this end-run has nearly been completed. Knoke echoed the sentiments of President Wilson, by urging that businessmen had better learn the discipline of global citizenship. He all but declared the concept of the nation state, dead or obsolete when he wrote, "our passion for the large nation-state, for which our ancestors fought with their blood, will dwindle to the same emotional consequences of a county or province today. A new spirit of global citizenship will evolve in its place, and with the ascendancy of global governance." Treaty agreements, such as NAFTA, GATT, the European Union, and evolving trade blocs in Asia and the Pacific Rim, are preparing the United States to submit to a full-scale global government. What happens in Europe will serve as the model for world consolidation in the next century, not just economically but politically and socially as well. Knoke describes the infamous WTO as "a limited world government with sovereignty over world trade." He added that the "WTO member governments have voluntarily yielded sovereignty over domestic laws governing the environment, food, safety and way of life." Knoke also urges that the UN be granted taxing authority, a standing army, and a world police force with special training and equipment usually not found in regular armies and manned with peacekeepers, who are, "a combination of social worker, policeman, riot police, and Rambo-style SWAT commandos."

A more prominent voice, urging United States participation in the new world order, is former Soviet president, Mikhail Gorbachev. At the State of the World Forum, held in October of 1995, Gorbachev "stressed that we should consider the establishment of a global Brain Trust to focus on the present and the future of our civilization." He was talking about people who are widely respected as world leaders and global citizens. He meant people like Ted Turner, World Watch President, Lester Brown, Senator George Mitchell, chimpanzee expert Jane Goodall, Zbigniew Brezinski, Father Theodore Hesburgh, late of Notre Dame, Alan Cranston, actor Dennis Weaver, singer John Denver, Shirley MacLaine, Timothy Wirth, Carl Sagan, and even Milton Friedman—"selfless billionaires, statesmen, academic double-domes, Nobel laureates, and spiritual mahatmas in the service of humanity and planetary survival." Gorbachev consistently called for an extra-govern-mental body of wise men and "a Council of Elders to solve the world's crucial problems. Gorbachev never addressed how his Brain Trust would solve these problems."

The term "Brain Trust," reeks of socialistic elitism, social engineering, and human manipulation. The term is an epithet to anyone aware of the abuses of liberty perpetrated by the socialist planners of the Roosevelt Brain Trust, of Raymond Moley, Rexford Tugwell, Lindsey Rogers, James W. Angell, Adolf Berle, Hugh Johnson, Charles Taussig, and many others that populated the New Deal. This Brain Trust could be a prescription for global tyranny.

Gorbachev and Ted Turner on the same dais proves conclusively that New World Order politics makes strange bedfellows. Both men are fond of "embracing the task of spiritual renewal, or launching the next phase of human development or developing global consciousness." When this is ac-complished, "civilization will shift and new values and new ways of life will be needed to find real solutions to the problems of our environment, a way out of the ecological crisis." What is required is a change [in] the nature of consumption. I have a vision of bread lines and gas shortages with most human needs going unfulfilled. Gorbachev's only paradigm is what the Soviet state did to its people for seventy-five years. He is the proverbial wolf in sheep's clothing. He said in a 1987 speech, in October 1917, we parted with the old world order, rejecting it once and for all. We are moving toward a new world order, the world of Communism. We shall never turn off that road. Perestroika is a continuation of the October Revolution. "Two years later, this man of peace declared that "I am now, just as I've always been, a convinced Communist." In his Churchill speech at Fulton, Missouri in 1992, Gorbachev called for global government under the United Nations. It echoed his statement, published in the 17 September 1987 issue of the *New York Times,* in which he called for "giving the United Nations expanded authority to regulate military conflicts, economic relations, environmental protection, also for enhancing the power of the afflicted International Court of Justice to decide international disputes."

The thing that strikes me about the former Russian president is the ease with which people have accepted his conversion experience from soviet

Red to Democratic Green. Perhaps the environmental movement is a natural refuge for a 'former" Communist. I queried on my WGNU radio show
in March of 1996 on just what color green and red made.

While the former President of Russia was ruminating about global
belt-tightening, his rapt audience was gorging itself on a sumptuous array of
Epicurean delicacies fit for the royalty they perceived themselves to be:
smoked trout salad, filet of beef in shashik marinade, topped off by a dessert
of panna cotta with autumn fruit, all the gourmet handiwork of celebrity
chef Joyce Goldstein. This hypocritical gentility had paid $5,000 a head to
attend this galaxy of global elite while feigning a selfless pathos and compassion for the world's poor. James Garrison, the co-founder of the Gorbachev
Foundation/USA, let the proverbial cat out of the bag in an interview for
SF Weekly, a liberal publication in San Francisco. After alluding to the
cultural breakdown in many African countries, the violence in Bosnia and
Somalia and the Oklahoma City bombing, he said we have to empower the
United Nations and that we have to govern and regulate human interaction
by whatever means were necessary.

The real threat to American sovereignty is not world government. All
attempts at this utopian structure have met with dismal failure over the last
century. The mindless and rapid disarmament of the United States' nuclear
arsenal is the greatest threat to American freedom and independence since
Lexington and Concord. In most parts of the world, especially in the Middle
East and the former Soviet Union, national independence is on the rise.
Like the boosterism of the American cities in the mid 19th century, most
of these new countries each dying to be considered major league, see arms
and nuclear weapons as the quickest route to world recognition and power.
Because of America's pursuit of the dangerous notion of unilateral disarmament, it has been surrendering the levers of power upon which its capacity
for independent action is based. This is not a call for retreat or circling the
wagons. Any withdrawal from the world will create a power vacuum that
will be filled by those nations that have not compromised their future by
recklessly destroying their means of destruction. The United States should
return to its old policies of balance of power geopolitics. It should never give
up its national identity, even in the smallest ways. Any American investment
in the creation of multilateral organizations through the UN will prove to
be a great blunder. As the last of the super powers, the US should prevent
any power or coalition from rivaling its exhaled status.

17 / Behold A Pale Horse
Pantheism Redux

> The greater majority of men have no right to existence, but are
> a misfortune to higher men.
>
> —Friedrich Nietzsche, *The Will to Power*

Part of the unwritten law of the naked public square has been to disdain
the mingling of religious faith with public policy. Religion was to be relegated to a person's private life, what philosopher, James Wilson called the
hobby principle of religious belief. Bruce Babbitt, President Clinton's Secretary of the Interior, received a great deal of newspaper acclaim for the
rediscovery of his long lost Catholic faith. Babbitt, like all doctrinaire liberals, is pro-choice and has not broken with his Democratic ranks and
joined *Operation Rescue.* He has achieved a new personal spirituality through
a deeper commitment, not to the Catholic Bible, but the *Endangered Species
Act.* In 1995 alone, he added 239 species to the endangered list of animals
and plants. I find it an odd conversion experience of spiritual rebirth that
can extend compassion for green plants but not for unborn children. Babbitt
once said, "outside the Church, I always had a nagging instinct that the vast
landscape was somehow sacred and holy and connected to me in a sense that
my catechism ignored." The media tells us this is Babbitt's "deeper, richer
Catholicism."

How did his rebirth take place? No kindly priest or energetic nun
changed Babbitt's approach. It was a Hopi Indian from northern Arizona
who showed him the way. By the end of that summer, Babbitt has been
quoted as saying "I came to believe, deeply and irrevocably, that the
land . . . and all the plants and animals in the natural world are together a
direct reflection of divinity that creation is a plan of God." Cal Thomas
reasons that Babbitt is an example of liberal politicians and theological
liberals "who need a cause to substitute for their moral obtuseness on such
issues as abortion and homosexual behavior." I would argue that they've
found it in the worship of animals and plants.

Babbitt's new found theology has little in conjunction with Catholic
tradition. In fact, it has helped to spark a new spirit of anticlericalism not
unlike that of the French Revolution. This new world religion wants to

replace organized religion with a more personal, non-denominational creed that adopts the dogma of certain social crusades, such as AIDS research, the environment, the homeless, and the rain forest. At best, Babbitt's thinking is more closely akin to animism or the attribution of conscious life to nature or natural objects. At worst, it is a form of pantheism which excludes the idea of a death with judgment from a personal God. This idea of a new world religion fits in perfectly with the notion of a one-world government because global unity is essential to the god-flow which goes through all natural things. Pantheism originated in the ancient Babylon and then spread to all corners of the globe. According to its doctrine, everything has an equal, intrinsic value. Man has no more value than a tree, rock, water, mouse, mosquito, rattlesnake, or bubonic plague virus. This is the impetus behind the anti-human bias that propels this radical environmentalism.

Since the economic benefits of environmentalism might be negligible, New Age democrats have attempted to argue their case for environmental controls in the rhetorical terms of the religious underpinnings of American history. With organized religion, seemingly in free fall, environmentalism has adjusted the modern value system to give a greater weight to preserving nature from human alteration. Babbitt's injection of overt religious themes into the language of daily policy debate is the logical culmination of a long process. While the environmental movement began with an emphasis on scientific data, Robert Nelson tells us in his incisive article, entitled *Bruce Babbitt, Pipeline to the Almighty,* in the 24 June 1996 issue of *The Weekly Standard* that the movement always had powerful religious overtones. Activists have always resorted to terminology, such as ancient cathedral for native forests and the desecration of nature, warning that an apocalypse would result from human transgressions against Mother Earth. These sentiments harken back to a 1967 article by Lynn White appearing in *Science* magazine that argued that environmentalism would only succeed "when it had a religious foundation." Nelson says that White had fundamentally misread the actual religious origins of environmentalism. He quoted John Muir, the founder of the Sierra Club in 1892, who referred to the sound of wind in the trees as "psalm singing." Muir fought to preserve the wilderness because there it was possible to "find terrestrial manifestations of God, providing a window opening into heaven." Muir obtained his philosophy of nature from New England transcendentalism, which held that nature was the best link between God and humanity. Emerson, Thoreau, and their followers were inspired by their Puritan forbearers in Boston. According to colonial historian, Perry Miller, New England Puritans "were obsessed with the theology of nature." In the Puritan theology of the colonial period, everyday plants and animals of the natural world were like ministers and apostles of God, "the vehicle and the way by which we are carried to God." As John Tierney said in his *Recycling Garbage* article in the 30 June 1996 edition of the *New York Times* magazine, "Americans have embraced recycling as a transcendental experience, an act of moral redemption. We're not just saving the garbage; we're performing a rite of atonement for the sin of excess." This helps to explain why so many people are prone to accept New Age thinking—because it resonates with the Protestant underpinnings of American colonial history. Some might conclude from this that New Age thought is somehow uniquely American and therefore worth preserving. The fallacy with this viewpoint is while New Age ideas make many overtures to religion and the powers of a godhead, that godhead bears no resemblance to the God of the Judeo-Christian roots of American civilization.

The roots New Age environmentalism run very deep. The process of eliminating Christianity from the face of the earth involves more than secularizing Christmas and Easter. This revival of a natural religion opens another front on the war on the middle class and its value structure. Millions of people who fear for their survival and that of the planet will be seduced by this terminology, especially if it clothes itself in the religious terminology of traditional teachings. Before people know it, they will forget the primary purpose of traditional faith—the avoidance of sin and the salvation of one's soul. There is no commandment against littering or wasting tap water. But there is one prohibiting the worship of false gods, the very nexus of what constitutes religious environmentalism.

The radical fringe of the scientific community wants to create a single interconnected civilization, a sort of cosmic government, as advocated by former Czech president Vaclav Havel. He is fond of citing the Gaia Hypothesis or the belief that the Earth's inorganic and organic components form a single system, a mega-organism, a living planet—Gaia. Environmentalism has spawned a revival of pagan earth worship in the form of Gaia, a concept first advanced by atmospheric scientist James Lovelock more than twenty years ago. The basic premise of Gaian theology is that the Earth itself is a superorganism, both living and divine. The movement has also attracted followers among feminists who are drawn to the idea of a Mother Earth or an Earth goddess. All humans are part of this living organism.

Babbitt's thinking echoes that of other New Age Democrats, such as Vice President Al Gore and the director of the National Park Service, Roger Kennedy. Kennedy declared in a 1994 speech to the National Wilderness Conference that "wilderness is a religious concept that should be part of our religious life." In line with the Marxist dictates of Antonio Gramasci, the movement is attempting to forge a new alliance with the churches, especially the Catholic Church through its parochial school system. A great emphasis is placed on the apocalyptic aspect of nature with small children being fearful that the decline of the Latin American rain forests will shorten their life spans by half. Their teachers have gone along with this pedagogy, creating a frightening specter for the future of the species. The erroneous belief that nature is harmonious and filled with good, docile, and peaceful vibration is quickly dispelled after only five minutes of watching the Discovery Channel. The eye of the camera does not lie—real nature is violent and hostile, where beast kills beast for survival. One need only watch a pride of lion cubs with their lioness dine on the torn carcass of a wildebeest too slow for escape, to see how gentle nature is in the wild. New Agers are peddling a view of nature and man that does not reflect the real world we live in.

The case of Barbara Schoener will illustrate their animal bias. She was mauled to death by an 82-pound female cougar in April of 1994. After the animal had crushed her skull, she dragged the hapless jogger 330 yards and devoured her face and most of her internal organs. The Fish and Game officials tracked the beast and killed it much to the chagrin of the State of California's Green lobbyists. One of them wrote the *Sacramento Bee*, complaining that this noble creature may have been venting centuries of mountain-lion anger against the humans who have driven it from its lands, destroyed its home, ruthlessly hunted it down, and debased it to an advertising device to sell cars. This is the same kind of extremist argument that has been given as a defense for the animals who nearly destroyed South LA in the wake of the first Rodney King decision.

While most people tend to favor the environmental movement as a well-intentioned, charitable attempt to protect the planet we all call home from industrial waste and nuclear and chemical production, ideological environmental groups, the media and politicians are creating a climate of hysteria. Zealous groups with a Marxist prejudice against business and industry co-opted the environmental movement in the early seventies and have perverted it in an effort to dismantle and subvert America's capitalist structure. These radicals have played on the public's fear of cancer and other dreaded diseases that may be caused by environmental and chemical forces. Their number might be only ten percent, but their socialist agenda and their disruptive methods have had a strong negative impact on the world population.

As Rush Limbaugh has accurately pointed out, the environmental/New Age movement seems to be the last refuge of the Marxists who have dominated the social justice scene for twenty years. In recent years, they have gotten away from supporting Third World insurgencies in favor of touting the praises of Gaia. The class struggle has been pointedly redefined as a global quest for sustainable development. This has led to what has been termed *Watermelon Environmentalism*—green on the outside and red in the middle.

In his article for the fall 1993 issue of *The Human Life Review*, Robert Whelan wrote, the population controllers have been warning us since the fifties that overpopulation was the cause of all the social evils in the world, plagues, war, famines, crimes. Since then world politicians have fostered a Neo-Malthian approach to population control, based on the distribution of birth control and abortion. Experience, studies, and history have proven that agriculture has kept pace with increased populations. The mass starvations in North Africa, and in Eastern European countries, such as Bosnia, have been the result of political interference and internal warfare, not the inability to grow food due to overcrowding. Gaian beliefs have at their core the repugnant contention that people are the problem because humans are natural polluters. Green literature is filled with misanthropic propaganda, such as an excerpt from a recruiting leaflet produced by Greenpeace: "fascism and environmentalism. Fascists sought to overcome the alienation between humans and nature. Modern civilization with its scientific technology and polluting factories that is the soul of a culture that is tied to the land from which it emerged." Greens view human creativity through a jaundiced eye. Anthropologist W.E.H. Stanner claimed that Australian Aborigines make less impact on the environment than beavers, who build dams, and termites, who build nests. The downgrading of human beings and their enterprises and the elevation of animals is more than an intellectual exercise. All this has profound consequences for the well-being of certain groups of people, including the unborn. The equating of animals with human beings cheapens human life. Since most people freely consume and dispose of lower forms of life, this fundamental equation could lead to more wide scale abortion and the disposal of other unwanted life, like the elderly, the infirm and the mentally incompetent.

We have witnessed throughout the last twenty years a growing movement to establish rights for animals which have been legally guaranteed. Throughout the Western world, a plethora of laws have been passed to protect whales, seals, birds of prey, spotted owls and natterjack toads. There is scarcely any animal or insect species which has not found its constituency of human supporters. At the same time, abortion or "womb cleansing," has become widely accepted as a normal part of Western life styles. Despite the great advances in embryology and fetology, which have established beyond a doubt that the baby in the womb is alive and human from the moment of conception, many Western nations have taken steps to remove legal protection from the unborn. The child in the womb no longer enjoys the most basic of all human rights: the right to life. Abortion has also led to the acceptance of practices, so barbaric that they would have been regarded as unthinkable only thirty years ago. These include the trade in human parts from aborted fetuses, the use of living embryos for experimental purposes, the cannibalizing of aborted babies to patch-up adult patients suffering from Parkinson's Disease, and the infamous partial birth abortions. If human beings are really a form of pollution, a sort of cancer on the face of earth, then it makes sense why the Greens advocate using the abortionist's knife to cut the cancer out. This juxtaposition of basic animal life with human life is just another page torn from the writings of George Orwell.

In his fascinating book, *The Intellectuals and the Masses,* John Carey explored the tendency to dehumanize groups of people by the use of pejorative terms, such as vermin, scum, swarming insects. At the end of the last century, it was commonplace among intellectuals, such as Bernard Shaw, H.G. Wells, Virginia Wolf, E.M. Forster, and others, especially Adolf Hitler, to use such dehumanizing language in describing the Jews. In the same vein, Green literature describes humans as a horde of rats, an uncontrolled virus and an infestation on the planet. *The London Times* in 1989 devoted an issue to *The World Is Dying* with the ominous and threatening subheading, *You Damage the Earth By Living on It.*

The Green Movement has its radical fringe, such as *The Earth First!* These ecoterrorists call for radical reduction of the earth's population. Earth First promotes massive diebacks. Some even have welcomed AIDS as a means of achieving their goals. Some Gaians, such as National Park Service biologist David Graber, even hope for the "right virus to come along, in order to cut down the numbers of homo *sapiens* despoiling the earth." Father Thomas Berry, who *Newsweek* calls one of the "new breed of eco-theologians," believes human beings are the "peril of the planet." It is a common belief among these environmental radicals that modern man has made a rubbish trap of Paradise. Man has multiplied his numbers to plague proportions, caused the extinction of 500 species of animals, ransacked the planet for fuels and now stands like a brutish infant, gloating over his meteoric rise to ascendancy. American population guru Kingsley Davis has said that "if having too many children were considered as great a crime against humanity as murder, rape, and thievery, we would have no qualms about taking freedom away." This sort of rhetoric undermines the Green claims that population reduction can be achieved without coercion. Will there be inducements, penalties, jail terms for those who fail to adhere to this avant-garde solution? What about people's moral and religious principles? What happened to the exalted idea of choice? How will this constitutional right be protected in this population solution? How do we dispose of those 4.5 billion people? By simple attrition? Limit each couple to just one child—a sort of sub-zero population growth rate and eventually the world's population will shrink to that magic number. What if people do not want to limit the size of their families? The writer only has to look to the People's Republic of China to find the paradigm of his *Brave New World.*

To understand the New Age it is necessary to comprehend the writings of Madame Helena Petrovna Blavatsky, who is known as the Mother of the New Age as nineteenth century occultist, a student of theosophy. Theosophy has roots that trace back to hermetic brotherhoods of the 18th century, including the *Illuminati.* Many of her ideas were deeply rooted in the enlightened philosophy of French writers Diderot and Voltaire. Blavatsky was led to Tibet by the masters where she learned the secrets of ancient wisdom. She claimed to be a spiritual tuning fork that vibrated through the same wavelengths as the hidden *Masters of the Occult Universal Brotherhood.* Two years after founding the Theosophical Society, she published her book *Isis Unveiled,* a farrago of mysticism and poorly written pseudo-science that numbered over 1200 pages. Her writings had a deep-seated anti-Christian and anti-Bible bent to them. She said that belief in the Bible was an absurdity and set among her goals, the elimination of its influence from public life. She felt that Jesus Christ was a myth and hoped to destroy the Christian worldview and replace it with a new world spiritual order. Given her beliefs, it is not surprising that historical figures with a power lusts, such as Adolf Hitler, have found her self-actualizing philosophy very attractive of value to their notions of world conquest.

On 15 September 1887, Blavatsky unveiled her monthly publication, *The Lucifer,* which was designed to "bring to light the hidden things of darkness." Under the leadership of Annie Besant, the fabian socialist, who later became the president of the Theosophist Society, its name was wisely changed to *The Theosophist.* The magazine continued its linkage to the *Lucifer Press* whose Lucis Trust sponsored the *Temple of Understanding and Meditation Room* located in the UN building in New York City. Science fiction author, Kurt Vonnegut, a co-endorser of the *Planetary Citizens,* a New Age group with UN affiliation, said of Blavatsky in 1970, that she "brought American wisdom from the East. She was a citizen of the world." This veiled association with the vision of Woodrow Wilson is no odd co-incidence.

New Age thinking has no greater devotee than Vice President Al Gore. In his book, *Earth In the Balance,* Gore insists that Western Civilization is dysfunctional and that those who resist radical environmental prescriptions are in denial. His attempt to label critics of the New Age as mentally infirm, carries with it the supposition that these individuals are not capable or can not be trusted to exercise their rights. In his chapter, *Environmentalism of the Spirit,* Gore follows Blavatsky's template of exalting pagan religious systems, such as Native American spiritualism, Hinduism, Ba'hai, and goddess worship, while at the same time indicting the theology of human dominion over the earth as the root of our environmental crisis. He implies that monotheism is an outdated model for the world of the future. Empowerment must come from "consulting the wisdom distilled by all faiths." Gore believes that the automobile was the greatest threat to the continuation of our civilization. Virtually all of his ecological doomsday talk is a ruse, designed to coerce compliance with the global demands of the establishment. The destruction of a nation's economic strength is a necessary prerequisite to ensnare them in this international web of planned control.

Gore and Babbitt are not the only politicians to have a pantheistic vision of the future. They had a kindred spirit in Henry Wallace, the Marxist Vice President under Roosevelt. He was a doctrinaire theosophist who followed the writings of Blavatsky. It was his friend, a fellow theosophist named Nicholas Roerich, who suggested that the Department of the Treasury adopt the Isiris—the all-seeing eye—on the back of the dollar bill in the 1930s.

The eager acceptance of New Age philosophy has put the country on a course that will eventually lead to a world religion. The final form it will take revolves around the workings of the *World Constitution and Parliament Association* (WCPA), which was founded in Lakewood, Colorado, in 1959. The groups' efforts paid off in Portugal in 1991, at the meeting of the World Constituent Assembly, where plans were made for what this new world order religion would resemble. The WCPA's plan, which includes a ten region world government, has been taken right from the Club of Rome's handbook. It wants a new world monetary system, under the new world economic order. The WCPA is latching its star to the environmental movement to effect its universal changes.

The *Greenhouse Crisis Foundation* and the *Eco-Justice Working Group* branch of the *National Council of Churches* published a booklet, called *101 Ways to Help Save the Earth*. It is more a liturgical guide than a science handbook in that it consists of a 52-weeks of congregational ideas and projects to save the Earth. The program was purged of every remnant of the Christian calendar, making Earth Day its central observance. This signifies a new strain of political theology that links religion, statist politics and apocalyptic environmentalism in one neat package. The *National Religious Partnership of the Environment* spends $5 million a year to distribute thousands of kits to the nation's religious congregations for use on the Earth Day weekend. This group suggests that during the congregations' services that people confess their environmental sins. It is suggested that the minister say we use more than our share of the Earth's resources. "We are responsible for massive pollution of earth, water and sky. We thoughtlessly drop garbage around our homes, schools, churches, places of work, and places of play. We squander resources on technologies of destruction. Bombs come before bread. The congregation is supposed to respond in kind. We are killing the earth. We are killing the waters. We are killing the skies." They even gave some secular holidays, a religious overtone: Mother's Day now became *Gaia Day*. The Fourth of July was to be celebrated as "freedom from pollution day," and Thanksgiving urged people to "give thanks for food from the environment and to those who produce it."

Many people have subscribed to this message and have used environmentalism to fill the spiritual void created by secular humanism. New Agers have tried to superimpose an exalted, ritualistic view of nature that echoes the natural religions of the ancient pagans onto traditional teachings. Matthew Fox, a former Catholic priest and the author of *The Coming of the Cosmic Christ*, describes the Earth as a kind of Christ figure. He deems any theology that views Jesus' personhood as a unique revelation as "Christofascism." He urges Christians to move beyond a theology based on sin and redemption toward a spirituality of creation with nature as its primary revelation. Fox has repudiated Christian tradition and replaced it with a utopian naturalism that totally distorts the Christian message. Another clerical luminary in this new world religion is Father Thomas Berry who has substituted being one with Mother Earth for the traditional biblical relationship with God. His book, *The Dream of the Earth*, has fast become a primary Gaian text. It is laced with sermons that stress the urgency of replacing the old above-the-earth religion with an earth-centered enlightenment.

If this movement were to have a patron saint, it would undoubtedly be French Jesuit, Pierre Teilhard de Chardin. When I was a junior at Holy Cross in 1963, his writings were just coming into vogue. A paleontologist who died in 1955, Father Teilhard made the mistake of mixing religion and philosophy with his science. This mixture has caused him to have been badly misunderstood by a generation of readers. As the author of such books as *The Divine Milieu* and *The Phenomenon of Man,* de Chardin has appealed to many New Agers who have adopted, erroneously assuming that his attempt to reconcile the religious theory of creation with the scientific theory of evolution supported their neopagan view of creation. New Age advocates have interpreted his belief that man was presently evolving mentally and socially toward a final spiritual unity, to mean that we were all one with the earth. While de Chardin emphasized the communion of all men, present, past, and future, his teaching should not be taken to mean that God is a mere impersonal representation of the unity of all things. De Chardin saw the earth as transformed by Christ, arguing that since God took human form humans should also embrace the world rather than reject it. By acting, human beings cooperate in the Almighty's creative powers. But they must act with their faith rooted in the belief that "everything forms a single whole." Philosopher Etienne Gilson has labeled de Chardin's gnostic interpretations of divine revelation as "theology fiction." Like all utopians, de Chardin is apprehensive about human freedom and insisted on reducing it to a strict planned order, recommending eugenic measures to discipline the human race. When the utopian finds that mankind does not fit in or is an obstacle to his order of things, he abandons the idea of political regimentation and directs his plan to medical intervention. As the world saw during the Nazi Utopia total power permitted medical experimentation in view of what is euphemistically called "improving the quality of the race." This idea appealed to both Adolf Hitler and Margaret Sanger. Professor Thomas Molnar argues correctly that it would be an error to separate de Chardin's religious utopianism from the quixotic manifestations of today's totalitarian ideologies and empires. De Chardin's thinking merely sets the problem of man, as the utopian sees it, on a loftier plane although his terminology—a composite of archaeology, sociology, biology, astronomy, and a vulgarized theology—can easily be translated into the language of collectivism and totalitarianism. Like other utopians, de Chardin creates an artificial separation between two imaginary categories of men. He simply calls them "those who believe," and "those who do not." His contributions to utopian philosophy are akin to the sprinkling of some holy water in the form of an undeniable and intangible substance which he calls a "passionate longing to grow and to be consummated human thought." Evolutionary utopians preach, not of freedom, openness, and progress but of a frozen rigidity as to the desirable ideal and the mechanism of adaptations which leads to it.

New Agers agree with many of his theories because they revolve around the abolition of war and the establishment of a world government. This is why liberals can regard the enslavement of millions under communist tyranny as merely a temporary misfortune which will ultimately evolve into something good. However the very idea of global unity assumes the existence of a new and mature mankind, capable of transcending all the evil that used to be mankind. De Chardin's new man is derived, not from religious introspection but from political turmoil. Although this idea of the new man is usually a veiled reference to the French Revolution and its enlightened ideals, it is usually referred to as the revolution of our times whose events extend from 1789 to the present. In this sense, we may speak of a revolutionary spirit sweeping over the globe and feeding the enthusiasm of utopians. Thinkers believe that perfection is an attainable goal on this earth and its religious nature is best reflected in an evolutionary pantheism that will lead them to increase their moral substance among brotherhood that will result in what Father Pierre Teilhard de Chardin called the "divine milieu."

Molnar believes that many atheists, gnostics, anarchists and secular utopians have endorsed de Chardin because the evolutionary outcome he proposed is millions of years away. There is no danger that his Super-Christ will appear anytime soon. In the meantime, they can support his belief in the eventual establishment of the noosphere—that improved world of men, morally and intellectually united who await further centration in omega point the end of the evolutionary phase when superhumanity met the Super-Christ. The religious utopian seeks the invalid baptism of evolutionism when "the ascension of the living toward the ultra-human or of a finally awakened human intelligence at the threshold of a greater consciousness." The problem with de Chardin's thinking is that it resonates with the belief that it is man, not God that is exalted and praised for his accomplishments. His philosophy is reminiscent of the attitude of mind and spirit that preceded the fall of man, an arrogance of intellect that highlights man instead of God. In essence, de Chardin's world view renders the meaning of God meaningless. In Christian revelation, the stress is on the salvation of each individual person. De Chardin's theology stresses the progress of the earth, leading to his Christ-Omega, who bears little resemblance to the Biblical Christ. In his prophetic book, *Trojan Horse in the City of God,* German philosopher, Dietrich von Hildebrand says that de Chardin is a false prophet more dangerous to Catholic teaching than Voltaire, Renan, or Nietzsche because of his apparent devotion to Christian images. In the spirit of communist Antonio Gramasci, von Hildebrand likens de Chardin to one of the "many termites who undermines Christian faith with their claim that they are giving to Christian revelation the interpretation that suits modern man."

Liberals love de Chardin's teachings because they lend the veneer of intellectual and Catholic approval to a system that believes man's destiny should be controlled by other men. At the Democratic National Convention in 1992, presidential nominee Bill Clinton talked about the Biblical covenant and what we can accomplish. God was conspicuous by His absence in the future president's social creed.

Where de Chardin went wrong is that he identified God with the universe—a standard pantheistic procedure that has found a home among New Age philosophers of the new world order. The God of de Chardin's system is tied to the evolution of matter for God could not have created life and later man, unless the material preconditions were ready. According to de Chardin, God is not a static Being but grows along with his creation. He is not an Almighty God, but limited in His powers and His relation to mankind. Sooner or later, the heretic will associate this kind of god with Hegel's Absolute Spirit of history, secularizing the notion of a personalized God. At the *State of the World Forum*, a $250,000 affair underwritten by Archer Daniels Midland, held at the Grand Ballroom of San Francisco Fairmont Hotel in October of 1995, Mikhail Gorbachev addressed the hundreds of people who paid $5,000 each to be there. He talked of his Gorbachev Foundation in San Francisco and Moscow, which he co-founded with James Garrison. Gorbachev is also the president of the International Green Cross. It is not surprising that Gorby has gone from the reigning head of the socialist world to environmentalism. Apocalyptic environmentalism is the new creed that unites the global brain trust. A new civilization would mean, above all, solving the problems that exists between man and the rest of nature, he told *Audubon Magazine* in 1994. This new environmentalism is a quasi-religion, which allows its advocates to talk of values and spirituality and solidarity, maintaining the same fiery revolutionary fervor that has characterized left-wing causes since the French Revolution. Ecological alarmism fills the void left by the fall of the Soviet empire. One of the most revealing talks of this forum, was that of Bill Moyers' protege, and men's movement maven, Sam Keen. His address, *The Global Crisis of the Spirit,* suggested that the solution to the world's environmental crisis lay in a re-enchantment of the world, and the prevention of the colonization of the spirit by commercial interests. Keen spoke for the environmental *Illuminati* when he said there was very strong agreement that religious institutions have to take primary responsibility for the population explosion. This reference to the Catholic Church's opposition to homosexuality, artificial birth control, and abortion only became clearer in the words that followed. We must speak far more clearly about sexuality, about contraception, about abortion, about the values that control the population, because the ecological crisis, in short, is the population crisis. Keen followed these sentiments with his draconian solution for the world's environmental problems by stating that "if we cut the world's population by 90%, there won't be enough people left to do ecological damage." How would he do this? One might argue that Mao, Hitler, and Stalin had made a good start but the United States had obstructed their genocidal policies that, according to Keen, would have been beneficial to the planet's ecology. Is Keen inferring that we need a new holocaust, maybe of Catholics this time? If these radical environmentalists ever get their way, Christians could be facing the lions again and I do not mean those from Detroit.

A frequent writer to the *Post-Dispatch* in St. Louis shares Keen's dire message. He imagines a world where "three-fourths of the world's population are transported to another galaxy, frozen in ice for eons." For the remaining 1.5 billion survivors there would be less crime, unemployment, and criminal behavior. Abortion would be an unnecessary procedure of the past. There also would be no need to pay farmers not to grow crops or let warehouses full of food rot in a world where millions go hungry. There would be more jobs than people to work them, thus eliminating unemployment. What would politicians talk about if there were enough to provide every citizen with a good job, health benefits, pension, or government aid? Individuals like this writer think these problems are caused by overpopulation and not a moral crisis that has identifiable roots in the breakdown of the traditional family.

The most interesting, and perhaps the most powerfully frightening, speaker at this forum was Barbara Marx Hubbard, the author of *The Book of Co-Creation*. In the manner of Cecil Rhodes, Hubbard claims in her curriculum vita to be establishing *Evolutionary Circles of Disciples* worldwide who will emerge as universal humans and founders of a global civilization. Hubbard has impeccable socialist credentials, having been a director of the *Federal Union* founded by Fabian socialist Rhodes Scholar, Clarence Streit. As a psychologist with Task Force Delta, an army think tank of futurists, strategists, and parapsychology researchers, Hubbard is credited with the bizarre notion of bombarding the Soviet Union with psychic love. The credo of these guerrilla gurus is: "I take personal responsibility for generating evolutionary conspiracies as part of my work. I will select and create conspiratorial mechanisms that will create and perform evolutionary breakthrough actions on behalf of people and planet. One people, one planet. Hubbard is worried, says author Texe Marrs, that if the new world order doesn't come into being, then advanced humans like Hubbard may have already provided some of the diabolic details. In her *The Book of Co-creation*, she writes:

> Out of the full spectrum of human personality, one-fourth is elected (by whom) to transcend ... One-fourth is destructive ... they are defective seeds. In the past they were permitted to die a 'natural death.' Now as we approach the quantum shift from the creature-human to the co-creative human— the human who is inheritor of god-like powers—the destructive one-fourth must be eliminated from the social body.

Sounding a little like Al Haig after the attempted assassination of President Reagan in 1981, Hubbard eased the gathering's anxiety by saying, "We are in charge of God's selection process from planet Earth. He selects, we destroy. We are the riders of the pale horse, Death. We come to bring death to those who are unable to know God." According to Hubbard, there are certain of us "who are unevolved and therefore negative and destructive. There can be no world peace until these people, probably me and you, are dealt with. We are going to either have to change or die. That is our choice!" Hubbard's ominous prophecies are a curious mixture of the Book of Revelation and the revolutionary context in which patriot Patrick Henry uttered his famous words, *Give me Liberty or give me Death!* Hubbard warned her audience that there is a revolution with apocalyptic consequences blowing in the wind and she expects to be one of the founding fathers. Hubbard and her followers do have a ready-made solution to the environmental threats of the world's six billion people. Worldwide availability of abortion figures largely in the environmentalists' plans to limit world population. In the late 1960s, *Planned Parenthood* revealed its goal of family limitation to one child. This is not much different then the repressive and violent policies of the People's Republic of China. Stephen Mosher's articles and books on China describe the harrowing tales of truck loads of late-term pregnant mothers on their way to abortion centers. *Planned Parenthood* promised that abortion on demand would result in less child abuse, divorce, and crime. Illegitimacy, and poverty would cease if we just had free, legal, and safe abortion. Since Mosher's first book in 1990, these social pathologies have increased geometrically. While there are approximately 1.6 million annual abortions in the United States, the worldwide figure hovers around 40 million. I often wonder if prophets of doom, such as Hubbard, include themselves in the number of people to be eliminated. The frightening part of their cataclysmic ruminating is that they are deadly serious. If these fanatics actually had control of populations, they would not hesitate to effect their bloody and inhumane formulae on the people of the world.

The NWO elites are prolific in stressing the need for strict population controls as we near the beginning of the Third Millennium. In 1989, the *Washington Post* published an article by foreign policy expert, George Kennan in which he said, "we must prepare instead for an age where the great enemy is not the Soviet Union, but the rapid deterioration of our planet as a supporting structure for civilized life." Lester Brown, director of the *Worldwatch Institute,* wrote in their 1991 annual report, *The State of the World,* that "the battle to save the planet will replace the battle over ideology as the organizing theme of the new world order." The influential Club of Rome, whose membership roster includes CFR members Jimmy Carter, Clairborne Pell, and Sol Linowitz, answers overpopulation with a plan for world government to control birth rates through birth control, abortion, and euthanasia if necessary. In their 1991 book, *The First Global Revolution,* they wrote, "in searching for a new enemy to unite us, we came up with the idea that pollution, the threat of global warming, water shortages, famine, and the like would fit the bill. All these dangers are caused by human intervention. The real enemy, then is humanity itself." Others worried about overpopulation included the late Fabian Socialist, Bertrand Russell. He said that there would be no stability unless there was a world government that could control the world's food supply. If one nation had too many people, the government could withhold their food ration until their population decreased in number. If that failed, he also suggested that a bacterial war could be spread through highly populated areas with each generation. The survivors could procreate freely without fear of filling the earth.

Canadian oil magnate and Secretary-General of the 1992 *Earth Summit* in Rio, Maurice Strong takes a slightly different approach. He paints the United States as an environmental aggressor because its energy prices are too low. Our nation's culture of abundance is an irritation to these one-worlders. The biggest obstacle to their coveted path of world control is a vibrant, materialistic middle class. Strong contends that the world's ecosystems can be preserved only if the affluent nations of the world can be disciplined into lowering their standards of living. For Al Gore, this would mean doing away with the combustion engine. He proposes a world economic crisis that would force nations to apply to the UN for assistance. For environmental terrorism to work, they must eliminate or downgrade middle class aspirations in this country and lower its standard of living.

The late Carl Sagan joined in the fray with a warning for humanity, which he feels faces an "absolutely new, unprecedented series of threats to the global environment that sustains us all." These crises include the depletion of the ozone layer and global warning through the increased greenhouse effect. It was only twenty years ago that these very prophets of environmental doom were predicting a New Ice Age because the earth was getting cooler and there would not be enough sunlight to support life on this planet. Now the earth is getting warmer and we will all burn up in the next generation. It is no wonder young children are scared to death for their future, afraid that there will be nothing left for them. Science takes a long time to prove or disprove something. Theories have to be tested, retested, and then tested again before any conclusion is made. Today's scientists are no longer content with a life of dedicated research. They have been seduced by the fifteen minutes of celebratory fame that comes with predicting, without the proper research methods, some apocalyptic calamity that will surely befall mankind in the next few years. Sagan believed the threat of planetary survival is necessarily a problem for the whole species. This is just another scare tactic designed to limit the freedom of the individual, moving us closer to the planetary governance. Scientists of the Sagan mold are fascist-minded social planners who envision a world where collective security measures under the auspices of the United Nations will be imposed to solve the world's environmental problems.

Techno-savant and consultant to corporate giants and world leaders, John Naisbitt, stressed the need for a new vocabulary, new concepts, and a new world view in order to understand the new paradigm the world has entered. This new model of world order, of course, will require new leadership with a new kind of moral authority. Naisbitt suggested that former Czech president Vaclav Havel, who is also a celebrated socialist playwright, was ideal for the job since he shared: "the commonalty of goals, and shared values of global ethics." Agnostic scientists, and political visionaries are a dangerous combination for the future of the world. Their utopian idealism could possibly make the twenty first century pale in comparison with this one in bloodshed and world conflict.

While the forum touched on every aspect of global unity, it was in the area of spiritual enlightenment that the gathering blossomed. Leading the charge were a host of the reigning Brahmins of new age harmony, including Willis Harman, Matthew Fox, Richard Baker, and, of course, Shirley MacLaine. Harman, new age philosopher and author of books such as the *Global Mind Change* and *The New Metaphysical Foundation of Modern Science,* has been highly influential in new age circles this last decade. He said that "more and more people were perceiving the connectedness of everything to everything and placing emphasis on intuition and the assumption of inner divinity." This New Order, said Harman, is characterized by an emphasis not on goals but on process; the process is "an evolutionary one and the goals are emergent." Where this "process" will take the world is not important to Harman—only that new age converts realize that they know better—those that have been blessed with a special gnosis and with the concomitant responsibility of directing the benighted to achieve their unspecified goals. Harman's essay, *Our Hopeful Future: Creating a Sustainable Society,* grapples with the population problem. In the economy-dominated world, as the outspoken anthropologist Margaret Mead once put it bluntly, "The unadorned truth is that we do not need now, and will not need later, much of the marginal labor—the very young, the very old, the very uneducated, and the very stupid." Harman added that society can't afford "from an environmental standpoint of tearing apart of the social fabric—the economic growth that would be necessary to provide jobs for all in the conventional sense, and the inequities which have come to accompany that growth."

Key to understanding the environment's problems is to explore the relationship between politics and the environment. In his monograph, *The Wealth of Nations and the Environment,* published by the *Institute for Economic Affairs,* Mikhail Bernstam argues conclusively that the issues of pollution and resource consumption are directly linked to the political and economic structure of countries. He further warns that the "future of world environmental conditions depends to a significant extent on the choice of economic system in developing countries." Experience demonstrates that the spread of market economies will lead to a better global environment, while the spread of socialist or centrally planned economies will make it worse. He believes that there is no reason to believe that population growth will make the environment worse or that population shrinkage will make it better. The world can support more people with less pollution as long as countries are prepared to pay for cleaner technologies and as long as they use the intelligence that God has given them to develop the new technologies which will continue to improve the quality of our life on earth.

According to advocates of global warming, the introduction of CO_2 and other greenhouse gases into the atmosphere by fossil fuel power plants and automobiles is causing a warming of the earth's atmosphere. This warming, they contend will undoubtedly melt the polar ice caps, raise sea levels and flood coastal areas. As German Environmental Minister Angela Merkel said at the UN *Climate Conference* held in Berlin in March of 1995, "the green-house effect can threaten the existence of humanity." These conferences, like the *Earth Summit* in Rio de Janeiro, are designed to impress upon the governments of the world the dire necessity of cutting the emission of CO_2 by voluntary regulation or, if that fails, strict government regulation with heavy punitive fines. Lowering these emissions to 1990 levels by the year 2000 would have a profound negative effect on the American economy. In 1992, *CONSAD Research Corporation* estimated that a carbon tax designed to achieve this goal would cost the economy over 600,000 jobs and produce annual losses of 1.7% through the year 2020. Jay H. Lehr, a senior scientist at the *Environmental Education Enterprises Inc.,* warns that pesticide residues in parts per quadrillion pose a great risk to society. Lehr asserts that the three groups that energize environmental hysteria are: first, groups driven by a small number of people with strong socialist ideologies; secondly, the mass media, which makes huge profits when a negative, frightening menace to the public's health, with or without scientific confirmation, is their feature story; and finally, there are the politicians who have used environmental reform as a ready platform to enhance their standing within the body politic.

The Green agenda is to effectively reduce the middle class and its control over American culture. As Strong, who chaired the *Earth Summit* in Rio said, "it is clear that current lifestyles and consumption patterns of the affluent middle class—involving high meat intake, consumption of large amounts of frozen and convenience food, use of fossil fuels, ownership of motor vehicles and small electrical appliances, home and workplace air-conditioning, and suburban housing—are not sustainable."

A term that crops up in much of the literature from the UN on the environmental issue revolves around the term of "sustainable development"—a euphemism for global socialism and population control. Coined by the *Commission on Our Common Future* under the direction of Norwegian Prime Minister Gro Harlem Bruntland, this term refers to "a political and eco-nomic system managed by a global elite in the supposed interest of preserv-ing the environment for future generations." To support this agenda of sacrifice among the middle class, doomsayers such as Strong use highly questionable scientific data. The *Intergovernmental Panel on Climate Change* published its 1990 report *Scientific Assessment of Climate Change*. Its steering committee erroneously reported that there was a consensus among these 170 scientists on the subject of the earth's warming. Not enough is known about this scientific phenomena to reach any solid scientific conclusions. Reduced population advocate Tim Wirth is untroubled by the lack of scientific certitude. The February *Reader's Digest* quoted him as saying in 1990: "we've got to ride the global-warming issue . . . Even if the theory is wrong, we will be doing the right thing in terms of economic and environmental policy."

While the Climate Conference was being held in Berlin, the *George C, Marshall Institute* released a new study refuting global warming fears. The *Marshall Institute*, which conducts technical assessments of scientific issues that impact public policy, issued the statement that "real world temperature measurements show that computer studies of the greenhouse effect have exaggerated global warming." In actuality, the earth has gotten a little cooler. Harvard astrophysicist and chair of the *Marshall Science Advisory Board*, Dr. Sallie Balinunas said "the overwhelming evidence is that the computer models are not able to predict changes in global temperatures based on CO_2 levels." In November of 1994, Dr. Robert C. Balling Jr., director of the Office of Climatology at Arizona State University stated, "present day climatologic predictive models that serve as the basis for global warming catastrophe scenario fail to accurately stimulate climate responses to greenhouse gas build-up." Balling noted that nearly 70% of the earth's warming that has taken place since 1881 occurred prior to 1937, before the large build-up in CO_2 gases even took place. Since then, we have seen only an increase of one-half degree Celsius. Balling states that the "scientific evidence argues against the notion that realistic policies could achieve any meaningful impact, and against the claim that urgent action is necessary to reduce the greenhouse threat." To people intent on absorbing as much power and money as they can, a global crisis, in which the survival of the planet and of all life was at stake would greatly work to catch people off guard. Drastic solutions would be demanded and this power elite would be more than willing to step in and save the planet.

Many liberals would agree with the belief that the new world religion is more an absolute faith in mankind. Machiavelli was responsible for transferring religious fervor from eternal spiritual goals to socio-political ends. He held that religion is good only when it serves the State by encouraging civil virtues. While Machiavelli would be right at home with regard to the politization of environmental problems, it is difficult to believe that he would approve of our civil virtues of aberrant homosexual behavior and unrestricted abortion rights. According to Thomas Molnar, "religion in the eyes of Machiavelli and Saint-Simon is merely a phase in man's gradual understanding of himself and his environment." This places him in basic agreement with Julian Huxley, whose religious cynicism prompted him to write "religiousness is to be equated with cynicism, stupidity, dishonesty, and ignorance." This is the same Huxley who wrote that "gods are peripheral phenomena produced by evolution, leaving us to conclude that stupidity, dishonesty, and ignorance—all shelters for religious belief—are only the peripheral manifestations of an inferior phase in evolution, all of which, except for a few fossilized specimens, will vanish why higher phases have vanished." Once this higher plateau is reached, men will no longer have any use for the god hypothesis because they will be intelligent and educated. This sentiment adapts perfectly to the neo-gnostic sense of elitism that propels much of the environmental movement in the world.

In the final analysis, it is important that the New Age movement be scrutinized for what it has in mind for the unenlightened within the world community. Conspiracy theorists have presented a creditable and well-documented case that demonstrates that there is a slender thread running through the *Council of Foreign Relations,* the *Trilateralists, Bilderburgers,* and the New Age Religion. There's an indelible link between *Illuminati,* communists, and the privileged elite that dominate our politics, our industries, and the new age agenda. We should be eternally vigilant as these proponents of this new spirituality be exposed of just modern day shamans with the tired and worn-out pantheistic nonsense.

With regard to the social problems that lend credence to the New Age movement, the conventional wisdom in this country has been an abject failure because all population control offers is death and dying to solve the social ills of the times. Crimes aren't ordinarily committed out of need but out of a desire for power and control. You would still have the few who wish to control the many. What the world needs is not fewer people but better people. People have to learn to treat others with more kindness and dignity instead of finding ways to eliminate them.

And what does the future hold?

Conservative philosopher Russell Kirk believes that the United States needs a Don Quixote figure to get the country out of its moral malaise. In his book, Prospects for Conservatives, he writes,

> in Don Quixote, we see the spirit of a gentleman, and the age
> of chivalry, and the idea of honor, and the unbought grace of
> life. . . . the great soul of the last knight-errant rises superior to
> his madness and his misfortunes . . . We are perishing for a lack
> of Don Quixotes to attack the windmills of our modern servility
> and our modern boredom.

No matter what the future may hold, now is the time for all good cultural warriors to pick up their lances and charge the cultural windmills before American civilization is blown off the pages of history. We must do it in the trusting spirit of John Quincy Adams who avouched, "The duty is mine and the outcome belongs to God."